The Impact of the European Convention on Human Rights on Private International Law

Louwrens R. Kiestra

The Impact of the European Convention on Human Rights on Private International Law

ASSER PRESS

Springer

Louwrens R. Kiestra
Maastricht
The Netherlands

ISBN 978-94-6265-031-2 ISBN 978-94-6265-032-9 (eBook)
DOI 10.1007/978-94-6265-032-9

Library of Congress Control Number: 2014945345

Published by T.M.C. ASSER PRESS, The Hague, The Netherlands www.asserpress.nl
Produced and distributed for T.M.C. ASSER PRESS by Springer-Verlag Berlin Heidelberg

Printed on acid-free paper

Springer is part of Springer Science+Business Media (www.springer.com)

Preface

In this book interaction between the rights guaranteed in the European Convention on Human Rights (ECHR) and private international law has been analysed by examining the case law of the European Court of Human Rights (the Court) in Strasbourg and selected national courts. In doing so the book has focused on the impact of the ECHR on all three of the main questions of private international law: jurisdiction, the applicable law and the recognition and enforcement of foreign judgments. First, a concise introduction to both private international law and the ECHR has been provided. Next, an important preliminary question has been answered: what is the meaning of Article 1 ECHR for private international law? Thereafter, the impact of the ECHR on the three main issues of private international law has been examined in depth. It has been demonstrated in this book that the impact of the ECHR on private international law is indeed considerable, and that its impact in some areas of private international law is still somewhat underestimated.

This book is based on the research which I mostly carried out at Amsterdam University's Amsterdam Center for International Law (ACIL) during the period 2008–2013. A small part of the research was carried out at the Swiss Institute for Comparative Law. I would like to thank the staff of the Institute for their hospitality.

This research was made possible by the Netherlands Organization for Scientific Research (NWO). It was part of the VICI project on 'The emerging international constitutional order—the implications of hierarchy in international law for coherence and legitimacy of international decision making.' I am grateful to Erika de Wet for giving me the opportunity to be a part of this research project, which allowed me to combine two of my favourite subjects of law.

An older—and abbreviated—version of chapter 4 of this book is based on a presentation delivered at the Colloquium 'The Impact of the European Convention on Human Rights on Private International Law', organized by the University of Amsterdam on 12 November 2010. This presentation was first published in the journal *Nederlands Internationaal Privaatrecht (NIPR)*. My thanks are extended to all the participants at the conference, who provided me with useful commentary.

Many other people have contributed—either directly or indirectly—to this book. I would like to thank, first of all, Jannet Pontier, and Marieke Oderkerk, who helped to guide my research together with Erika de Wet. I would also like to thank Prof. Gerards, Prof. Van Hoek, Prof. Kinsch, Dr. Mak, and Prof. Nollkaemper for their comments on an earlier version of the manuscript.

This book has certainly also benefited from my many discussions on international law—and other miscellaneous subjects—with my former colleagues at the University of Amsterdam, and particularly my colleagues at the Amsterdam Center for International Law. My thanks go out to all of them. I would like to single out my long-time room-mates Lisa Clarke and Stephan Hollenberg, as well as the next-door neighbours Christina Eckes and Jure Vidmar. In no small part thanks to you, it was always a pleasure to work in Amsterdam. Special thanks are also extended to José Visser and Eric Breuker, who were always there for our VICI group.

I would also like to thank my family and friends who have demonstrated so much patience. I would like to specifically thank David van Bemmel and Peep Schaepman for being there during my hour of need. And, of course, special thanks to my parents, who have always supported all my endeavours. Lastly, my thanks go out to the one whose patience and understanding I have tested to the full during the past few years: my loved one, Eeke. The book is finally complete, my dear.

The research in this book was largely completed in the spring of 2013. However, since then new literature has been added and the case law of the Court in Strasbourg has been updated until the end of 2013.

Maastricht, June 2014 Louwrens R. Kiestra

Contents

Chapter 1
Introduction

Contents

1.1 Background and Purpose

This book analyzes the impact of the rights guaranteed in the European Convention of Human Rights and Fundamental Freedoms (hereafter ECHR) on private international law by examining the case law of the European Court of Human Rights (hereafter the Court) in Strasbourg and selected national courts. Private international law is traditionally concerned with the fair and efficient regulation of issues of private law stemming from the concurrence of legal systems of different countries.[1] The diversity of the world's legal systems concerning private law is the *raison d'être* of private international law. This area of the law is thus only concerned with cases that contain a foreign element. In handling this diversity of legal systems, private international law deals primarily with three main issues.[2] The first of these is the issue of jurisdiction—in an international case, the court of which country is competent to hear a case? The second issue is that of the applicable law—the law of which country shall be applied to this international case? The third and last main issue is that of the recognition and enforcement of foreign judgments—under what circumstances may a foreign judgment either be recognized and/or enforced in the forum? Clearly, private international law requires a willingness to accept foreign solutions to legal

[1] See, e.g., Cheshire et al. 2010, pp. 3–5; Dicey et al. 2012, pp. 3–5; Strikwerda 2012, p. 2.
[2] See for a further elaboration of the notion of private international law infra Chap. 2.

L.R. Kiestra, *The Impact of the European Convention on Human Rights on Private International Law*, DOI 10.1007/978-94-6265-032-9_1

issues with foreign elements in order to facilitate cross-border legal relationships of a private law nature.[3]

Private international law is also an area of law which is currently undergoing a transformation, as its role and traditional foundations may be changing.[4] Several factors lie at the root of this. The continuing increase in interaction between people from different countries, because of advances in transportation and telecommunication—a phenomenon commonly referred to as globalization—has, for example, emphasized the importance of private international law, while it has, simultaneously, increased the demands on this area of law.[5] Moreover, while private international law and public international law appeared to have grown apart and were consequently treated as separate areas of law, there are indications suggesting a reversal of this trend.[6] It has, for example, also been contended that private international law could play a more prominent role in the 'global governance debate'.[7]

Another important development concerning private international law is that the European Union has gradually discovered this area of law. This has made its role more important, and has also had an impact on national rules of private international law, as more and more areas covered by national private international law have been and are being replaced by European private international law.[8] This may be a common refrain: these developments in public international law and European law have brought changes to the traditional paradigm of private international law, as concepts of these systems of law have put pressure on private international law.[9] Private international law can no longer claim an isolated role, as it is being influenced by other areas of law. The rights guaranteed in the ECHR may similarly have an impact on private international law. This necessitates an analysis of that impact.

The ECHR is an international treaty containing a catalogue of rights that the States which are parties to this instrument undertake to respect and guarantee to everyone within their jurisdiction. These rights may—if this is at all possible—only be limited insofar as the possibility thereto is contained within the instrument itself.[10] The ECHR thus establishes certain minimum requirements concerning the rights contained in the Convention which the Contracting Parties are bound to guarantee. These minimum requirements also apply to private international law cases. It is not difficult to see how private international law and the rights guaranteed in the ECHR could clash, as, for example, the application of a foreign law

---

[3] See, e.g., Struycken 2009, p. 55ff.

[4] See, e.g., Mills 2012, pp. 371–375.

[5] See with regard to the impact of globalization on private international law, e.g., Basedow 2000, pp. 1–10; Wai 2002, pp. 209–274.

[6] See on this subject, e.g., Mills 2009. See for a more critical approach to this trend, e.g., de Boer 2010, pp. 183–207. See also Reed 2005, pp. 177–410.

[7] Muir Watt 2011, pp. 347–428.

[8] See with regard to the Europeanization of private international law further Infra Sect. 2.4.1.

[9] See, e.g., Kuipers 2012, p. 2ff.

[10] See with regard to the ECHR further infra Chap. 3.

or the recognition and enforcement of foreign judgments may result in a violation of one of the rights guaranteed in the ECHR, particularly where the foreign law or the foreign judgments originate from non-Contracting Parties.

Although private international law is certainly not deaf to the rights and obligations of individuals, the most important function of private international law is to coordinate the differences between legal systems. The ECHR, however, as a human rights instrument, offers a number of fundamental rights to individuals which the Contracting Parties are obligated to respect and guarantee. It is clear that the creation of an efficient regulatory system can collide with the rights of an individual. If too much emphasis is put on the rights of the individual within such a system, the system will ultimately suffer. However, too much emphasis on the functioning of the system of private international law at the expense of the rights of individuals, which can be derived from the ECHR, could trigger state responsibility for the Contracting Parties under this instrument. For example, it may, from the point of view of co-operation between different States, be worthwhile to recognize and enforce each other's (foreign) judgments readily without too many formalities. However, if omitting such formalities were to mean that a judge could no longer check whether a fair trial has preceded the foreign judgment to be enforced, the individual may be wronged.[11]

The relationship between private international law and human rights has, incidentally, also come up in a slightly different context. It has recently been attempted to hold multi-national corporations accountable for human rights violations allegedly committed in distant parts of the world. An example is a case before the United States Supreme Court, *Kiobel,* et al.*, v. Royal Dutch Petroleum,* et al.,[12] in which 12 individuals are seeking to hold major oil corporations accountable in the United States for alleged human rights violations perpetrated in Nigeria. Rules of private international law will in such cases determine if a court has jurisdiction, and which law should be applied. However, this aspect of the relationship between private international law and human rights will not be further considered here, as this book will be confined to the question of what the impact of the ECHR is on the three main issues of private international law. Whether private international law can be used with regard to human rights violations, and if so, how that may be achieved, are related, but separate, questions.[13]

---

[11] See further infra Chaps. 7–8.

[12] *Kiobel,* et al.*, v. Royal Dutch Petroleum,* et al., 132 S.Ct. 472 (US 2011). See with regard to this case, e.g., Enneking 2012a, pp. 396–400. See generally on the related discussion of liability of multinational corporations under international law, e.g., Kamminga and Zia-Zarifi 2000. See also Enneking 2012b.

[13] See with regard to the question of whether private international law may function in such a way within the EU, e.g., van den Eeckhout 2008, pp. 105–127. Another discussion concerned with whether private international law can play a role with regard to human rights violations is the discussion on universal civil jurisdiction. See in this regard, e.g., Donovan and Roberts 2006, pp. 142–163; Mora 2010, pp. 367–403. See also the contributions in 99 *Annual Proceedings of the American Society of International Law* (2005), pp. 120–128.

The impact of human rights, or fundamental rights, on private international law is, of course, not an entirely new phenomenon. The German *Bundesverfassungsgericht* held for the first time back in 1971[14] that the German rules of private international law had to comply with the fundamental rights enshrined in the German *Grundgesetz*.[15] This decision resulted in a discussion of whether the connecting factors used in choice-of-law rules were discriminatory in using the national law of the man as the connecting factor, which eventually led to a legislative reform of German private international law in the area of family law.[16] Similar developments have taken place in other Western European countries.[17]

Yet besides this impact on the connecting factor in choice-of-law rules, the impact on private international law of fundamental rights, and particularly those rights guaranteed in the ECHR, has been rather limited for a long time. The subject was seldom broached by courts and similarly was not frequently discussed in the literature.[18] That has, however, gradually changed. The number of publications on the subject, for example, has steadily increased since the turn of this century. The most interesting development has been, however, the increase in the number of court decisions dealing with the impact of the ECHR. In particular, the fact that the European Court of Human Rights (the Court) has since decided a number of cases specifically dealing with issues of private international law is of great interest, and the issue also appears to have been taken up more by national courts of the Contracting Parties.

In light of this increased attention by the Court, a new book on the impact of the rights guaranteed in the ECHR on issues of private international law is necessary in order to further assess what the ECHR's impact on private international law is, and how the Contracting Parties (or their courts) can fulfill their obligations under the Convention in issues of private international law. While a fair number of interesting studies on the impact of the ECHR in cases dealing with issues of private international law have appeared, not many of them deal with all three main questions of private international law, but instead restrict themselves to one or two of them. There are two important studies that are exceptions to this.[19] However since the publication of these studies there have been significant further

[14] *Bundesverfassungsgericht* 31 May 1971, 31 BVerfGE 58; *NJW* 1971, p. 1508.

[15] This case has been much discussed. See further infra Sect. 6.3.

[16] See, e.g., Hofmann 1994, p. 148ff.

[17] A judgment of the Italian Constitutional Court on 26 February 1987 started a similar discussion in Italy. See *Rev.crit.dr.int* 1987, p. 563 (note Ancel). See also van Loon 1993, pp. 141–142 with regard to the developments in the Netherlands.

[18] See, e.g., Docquir 1999, p. 473, who noted—in 1999—that the impact of the ECHR on private international law has (still) not received a lot of attention, notably not by the courts, although he did point out that there are a number of interesting studies on the subject. See for some interesting earlier studies on the subject, e.g., Cohen 1989, pp. 451–483; Engel 1989, pp. 3–51; Goldman 1969, pp. 449–466; Matscher 1985, pp. 459–478; Mayer 1991, pp. 651–665. See also generally on the impact of human rights Lerebours-Pigeonnière 1950, pp. 255–270.

[19] See Kinsch 2007, pp. 9–332 and Marchadier 2007.

developments with regard to private international law in the Court's case law. Moreover, this book will add a further focus on the meaning of Article 1 of the ECHR for private international law. Finally, what this book will add to the debate on the impact of the ECHR on private international is a further examination of case law originating from three legal orders: England, the Netherlands, and Switzerland, where the issue of the impact of the ECHR on private international law has not been very frequently discussed.[20]

1.2 Structure of the Book and Further Delineation of the Subject

As stated above, this book analyzes the impact of the rights guaranteed in the ECHR on private international law by examining the Court's case law as well as national case law. The over-arching question is: what is the impact of the ECHR on private international law? This book departs from the assertion that the case law of the Strasbourg Institutions (the Court and the Commission)[21] best illustrates the manner in which the ECHR may have an impact on private international law and how possible violations of the ECHR in issues of private international law may be prevented. The Court is particularly well positioned to offer binding guidance, as it has final jurisdiction over the interpretation of the rights guaranteed in the ECHR and the compliance of the Contracting Parties with the ECHR.[22]

To answer this broad question, it must be divided into three sub questions which correspond with the three main issues of private international law. In other words: the impact of the ECHR on private international law will be studied separately with regard to jurisdiction, applicable law, and the recognition and enforcement of foreign judgments. Prior to this, though, it is necessary to examine how the basic obligation undertaken by the Contracting Parties in Article 1 ECHR relates to their responsibilities in issues of private international law.

At an early stage the choice was made to include all three main questions of private international law, as this would provide a full overview of the issues. However, the subject became rather broad as a result. In order to ensure that the book could be completed within a reasonable time some difficult choices had to be made. Private international law has therefore been limited in this research to the afore-mentioned three main issues. As a result, other topics, some of which are considered to be part of private international law in at least some legal orders and which may also raise interesting questions with regard to the impact of the rights guaranteed in the ECHR, are not included in this book.[23] Examples of such topics

[20] See with regard to the selection of the legal orders further infra Sect. 1.2.

[21] See further infra Sect. 3.2.

[22] Stone Sweet and Keller 2008, p. 4.

[23] See further with regard to the notion of private international law infra Chap. 2.

falling outside the scope of this study would be international arbitration,[24] taking evidence abroad, and the service of documents in international cases, which will be treated only marginally as a topic relevant to the recognition and enforcement of foreign judgments.[25]

Some topics that do arguably fall within the three main issues of private international law, which have been examined by the Court, also had to be left out of this study because they are largely not truly concerned with a topic of private international law. In some legal orders immunities, for example, are considered to be part of the issue of jurisdiction in private international law and as such are discussed in treatises on private international law.[26] The Court has also developed important case law on the relationship between the right of access to a court *ex* Article 6(1) ECHR and immunities.[27] However, as immunities are more of a restriction derived from public international law, this topic has not been included in this study.[28]

International child abduction is another topic that is considered to be part of private international law, but which does not fit perfectly in this book. Although the Court has discussed this issue extensively in its case law and the reasoning used may be interesting for topics which are part of this book, it has been decided not to include international child abduction as this would result in so much more material that deserves and requires a separate study.[29] Moreover, even though international child abduction is considered to be an issue of private international law, one should realize that the return orders in such cases are actually national decisions, albeit in an international context, which distinguishes them from the decisions discussed in Chaps. 7 and 8, in which the recognition and enforcement of foreign judgments are discussed.

As stated above, the starting point in the search for the impact of the ECHR is mainly confined to case law, particularly that of the Court. This means, for example, that the impact of the ECHR on choice-of-law rules, and particularly on connecting factors, is a topic that is only treated marginally, as the Court usually limits its assessment of a case to whether the actual application of such rules (e.g., the applicable law in question) is in conformity with the ECHR. The Court, in principle, does not review legislation *in abstracto*.[30] The principle of

---

[24] See in this regard, e.g., De Ly 2011, pp. 181–205.

[25] See infra Chap. 7.

[26] See, e.g., Cheshire et al. 2010, p. 491ff; Dicey et al. 2012, p. 273ff.

[27] See with regard to immunities and the right of access to a court *ex* Article 6(1) ECHR, e.g., Kloth 2010; Voyiakis 2002, pp. 297–332.

[28] See in this regard the fairly recent decision of the International Court of Justice in *Jurisdictional Immunities of the State (Germany v. Italy: Greece intervening)*, judgment of 3 February 2012. See generally with regard to immunities in (public) international law, e.g., van Alebeek 2008; Pavoni 2012, pp. 133–207. See also van Hoek et al. 2011.

[29] There have, incidentally, already been studies into the impact of the Court's case law on international child abduction. See, e.g., Beaumont 2009, pp. 9–103.

[30] See, e.g., *Klass and Others v. Germany*, 6 September 1978, para 33, Series A no. 28; *Marckx v. Belgium*, 13 June 1979, para 27, Series A no. 31.

discrimination in relation to the connecting factors used in choice-of-law rules will therefore not be fully examined.[31] The book will thus assess the impact of the ECHR by examining the relevant case law of the Strasbourg Institutions as well as case law from selected national legal orders in Europe, but, where relevant to the discussion, the doctrine in issues of private international law will also be included.

The book is concerned with the impact of the ECHR on private international law, and while many rules of private international law are of international origin,[32] every country does have its own rules of private international law. Therefore the number of legal systems which could, theoretically, be drawn upon for case law is, of course, the same number of Member States of the Council of Europe: forty-seven.[33] However, including all systems is neither desirable nor necessary. It is not necessary, as the case law and practice of the national courts of the Contracting Parties are primarily used as illustrations of the handling of the ECHR in issues of private international law. It is not desirable, since including all systems would mean a sacrifice of thoroughness. Consequently, this book will focus in its assessment on the case law of the national courts and practice of England,[34] the Netherlands, and Switzerland.[35] Occasionally, reference will also be made to developments in other Contracting Parties—particularly Germany and France—that illustrate important findings. In addition to case law, the doctrine and legislation, in the broadest sense of the word,[36] will be touched upon in this research.

Why the focus on England, the Netherlands, and Switzerland? As the national case law is used in this research to unearth the solutions found in national legal orders to possible conflicts between the rights guaranteed in the ECHR and private international law, it is necessary and most interesting to choose legal systems which are not only influential, but also diverse. Furthermore, it is in this context most interesting to choose legal orders where the impact has been examined, but where this issue has not yet fully been assessed. All these factors have been accounted for in the choice of these three jurisdictions.[37]

Above, it was indicated that Germany is, in a way, the birthplace of the discussion of the impact of fundamental rights on private international law. It is not

---

[31] See with regard to discrimination and choice-of-law rules Kinsch 2011, pp. 19–24.

[32] See further infra Sect. 2.4.

[33] See for a little background regarding the origins of the ECHR infra Chap. 3.

[34] In this research I will focus on English cases of private international law and practice. One should note in this regard, though, that England, Scotland, and Northern Ireland share the Supreme Court. Moreover, many statutes, particularly those based on international treaties, apply to all three parts of the United Kingdom. Finally, one should note that in relation to the case law of the Court in Strasbourg, the United Kingdom is the respondent Contracting Party.

[35] See with regard to these legal systems also infra Sects. 2.4.3 and 3.3.

[36] This would include, in addition to national legislation, internationalized sources, such as EU law and international treaties. See with regard to the sources of private international law infra Sect. 2.4.

[37] See generally with regard to the selection of legal systems in comparative legal research Oderkerk 2001, pp. 293–318.

surprising to find that this subject has been discussed often in the German literature.[38] There is also a lively debate on the subject in France.[39] However, in the selected legal systems—England, the Netherlands, and Switzerland—the issue of the impact of the ECHR on private international law has been less frequently and not so elaborately discussed,[40] and it is therefore of interest to examine the case law from these jurisdictions. Moreover, for a researcher trained in Dutch law and based at a Dutch university, the Netherlands is an obvious choice as one of the three jurisdictions.

While the Netherlands is a civil law country, England has a common law tradition and consequently takes quite a different approach to issues of private international law. Furthermore, the position of the ECHR in the English legal order is quite different from its position in the Dutch legal system. While the Netherlands—and Switzerland—have a 'monist' tradition with regard to the relationship between national and international law, the United Kingdom follows the dualist approach.[41] In monist countries the ECHR is automatically part of the national law. In dualist countries, however, further legislative action is required following the ratification of an instrument in order for the ECHR to be enforceable in national courts. The precise way in which it is enforceable depends on the terms of the national legislation. In the United Kingdom the Human Rights Act 1998 has indirectly incorporated the rights flowing from the ECHR into national law.

The choice of Switzerland adds another dimension to the discussion. While both the Netherlands and the United Kingdom are members of both the Council of Europe and the European Union, Switzerland is only a member of the Council of Europe. In the interest of completeness it should be noted that Switzerland—like the Netherlands—follows a monist approach and the ECHR provisions are applied as self-executing in the national courts.[42]

1.3 Overview

After having set out the scope of this book in the introduction, the study will continue in Chaps. 2 and 3 with a concise introduction to both private international law and the ECHR. These two introductory chapters are included for readers, who

---

38 See, e.g., Thoma 2007; Voltz 2002.

39 See, e.g., supra n. 19. See also the contributions in the *European Journal of Human Rights* 2013/3.

40 There are, of course, exceptions to this general statement. See in addition to works cited above, e.g., Fawcett 2007, pp. 1–47; Juratowitch 2007, pp. 173–199 (England); Bitter 1979, pp. 440–447; Rutten 1998, pp. 797–811; Vonken 1993, pp. 153–185 (The Netherlands); and Bucher 2011; Othenin-Girard 1999 (Switzerland).

41 See with regard to the differences between the monist and dualist approaches, e.g., Brownlie 2008, p. 31ff.

42 See generally on the position of the ECHR in the domestic law of the respective Contracting Parties, e.g., Blackburn and Polakiewicz 2001; Keller and Stone Sweet 2008.

are less familiar with either of these two areas of the law. In Chap. 2 the particularities of private international law will be dealt with, including the importance of the different sources of this area of law. This chapter will also provide a first foray into an important part of this research by examining the public policy exception, which is the traditional instrument used in private international law to deal with fundamental rights. Chapter 3 provides a general introduction to the rights guaranteed in the ECHR. Here, one will find a review of the structure of the Convention as well as its most important characteristics. In Chap. 4 an important preliminary question to the research in this book will be answered: is the ECHR at all applicable to issues of private international law? In this chapter the relationship between Article 1 of the ECHR, which defines the scope of the Convention, and private international law will be further discussed. Hereafter, the impact of the ECHR on the three main issues of private international law will be elaborated upon. In Chap. 5 the issue of jurisdiction in private international law will be dealt with. The issue of applicable law is the subject of Chap. 6. The discussion of the issue of the recognition and enforcement of foreign judgments will be divided into two parts, as the Court has delivered far more case law on this subject compared to jurisdiction and applicable law. In Chap. 7 the obligation to recognize and enforce foreign judgments, which may follow from the ECHR, will be examined. Chapter 8 will discuss the possibility to invoke one of the rights guaranteed in the ECHR against the recognition and enforcement of foreign judgments. Chapter 9 sets out the conclusions of the book.

References

Basedow J (2000) The effects of globalization on private international law. In: Basedow J, Kono T (eds) Legal aspects of globalization: conflict of laws, internet, capital markets and insolvency in a global economy. Kluwer International, The Hague, pp 1–10

Beaumont P (2009) The jurisprudence of the European Court of Human Rights and the European Court of Justice on the Hague convention on international child abduction. Recueil des Cours 335:9–103

Bitter JW (1979) De Nederlandse Grondwet en de bescherming van grondrechten in het Nederlands internationaal privaatrecht [The Dutch Constitution and the protection of fundamental rights in Dutch private international law]. Ars Aequi 23:440–447

Blackburn R, Polakiewicz J (2001) Fundamental rights in Europe: the European convention on human rights and its member states, 1950–2000. Oxford University Press, Oxford

Brownlie I (2008) Principles of public international law. Oxford University Press, Oxford

Bucher A (ed) (2011) Loi sur le droit international privé. Convention de Lugano. Helbing Lichtenhahn, Bâle

Cheshire GC, North P, Fawcett JJ et al (2010) Private international law. Oxford University Press, Oxford

Cohen D (1989) La Convention européenne des droits de l'homme et le droit international privé. Rev crit dr int priv 78:451–483

de Boer Th M (2010) Living apart together: the relationship between public and private international law. NILR 57:183–207

De Ly F (2011) Arbitration and the European convention on human rights. In: Lévy L, Derains Y (eds) Liber Amicorum En L'honneur de Serge Lazareff. Pedone, Paris, pp 181–205

Dicey AV, Morris JHC, Collins LA (2012) The conflict of laws. Sweet & Maxwell, London
Docquir B (1999) Le droit international privé à l'épreuve de la Convention européenne des droits de l'homme. Annales de Droit de Louvain 59:473–522
Donovan SF, Roberts A (2006) The emerging recognition of international civil jurisdiction. AJIL 100:142–163
Engel C (1989) Ausstrahlungen der Europäischen Menschenrechtskonvention auf das Kollisionsrecht [Emanations of the European Convention on Human Rights on conflict of laws]. RabelsZ 53:3–51
Enneking LFH (2012a) Multinational corporations, human rights violations and a 1789 US Statute: a brief exploration of the case of Kiobel vs. Shell. NIPR 30:396–400
Enneking LFH (2012b) Foreign direct liability and beyond. Exploring the role of tort law in promoting international corporate social responsibility and accountability. Eleven International Publishing, The Hague
Fawcett JJ (2007) The impact of article 6 (1) ECHR on private international law. ILCQ 56:1–48
Goldman B (1969) La protection internationale des droits de l'homme et l'ordre public international dans le fonctionnement de la règle de conflict de lois. Cassin R, Amicorum Discipulorumque Liber I: Problèmes de Protection Internationale Des Droits de L'homme. Pédone, Paris, pp 449–466
Hofmann R (1994) Human rights and the ordre public clause of German private international law. Tel Aviv Univ Stud Law 12:145–155
Juratowitch B (2007) The European Convention on Human Rights and English private international law. J Private Int Law 3:173–199
Kamminga MT, Zia-Zarifi S (eds) (2000) Liability of multinational corporations under international law. Kluwer Law International, The Hague
Keller H, Stone Sweet A (eds) (2008) A Europe of rights: the impact of the ECHR on national legal systems. Oxford University Press, Oxford
Kinsch P (2007) Droits de l'homme, droits fondamentaux et droit international privé. Recueil des Cours 318:9–332
Kinsch P (2011) Choice-of-law rules and the prohibition of discrimination under the ECHR. NIPR 29:19–24
Kloth M (2010) Immunities and the right of access to court under Article 6 of the European convention on human rights. Martinus Nijhoff Publishers, Leiden
Kuipers JJ (2012) EU law and private international law: the interrelationship in contractual obligations. Martinus Nijhoff Publishers, Leiden
Lerebours-Pigeonnière P (1950) La Déclaration universelle des droits de l'homme et le droit international privé français. Le droit privé français au milieu du XXe siècle, Études offertes à Georges Ripert. Pichon et Durand-Auzias, Paris, pp 255–270
Marchadier F (2007) Les objectifs généraux du droit international privé A L'épreuve de la Convention européenne des droits de l'homme. Bruylant, Bruxelles
Matscher F (1985) IPR und IZVR vor den Organen der EMRK: Eine Skizze–. In: Barfuss W (ed), Festschrift für Karl H. Neumayer zum 65. Geburtstag, Nomos, Baden-Baden, pp 459–478
Mayer P (1991) La Convention européenne des droits de l'homme et l'application des normes étrangères. Rev crit dr int priv 98:651–665
Mills A (2009) The confluence of public and private international law: justice pluralism in the international constitutional ordering of private law. Cambridge University Press, Cambridge
Mills A (2012) Rediscovering the public dimension of private international law. NIPR 30:371–375
Mora PD (2010) The legality of civil jurisdiction over torture under the universal principle. Ger Yearb Int Law 52:367–403
Muir Watt H (2011) Private international law beyond the schism. Transnational Legal Theory 2:347–428
Oderkerk AE (2001) The importance of context: selecting legal systems in comparative legal research. NILR 48:293–318

Othenin-Girard S (1999) La reserve d'ordre public en droit international privé suisse. Schulthess, Zurich
Pavoni R (2012) Human rights and the immunities of states and international organisations. In: Vidmar J, De Wet E (eds) Hierarchy in international law: the place of human rights. Oxford University Press, Oxford, pp 133–207
Reed L (2005) Mixed private and public international law solutions to international crises. Recueil des Cours 306:177–410
Rutten SWE (1998) Mensenrechten en het ipr: scheiden of trouwen? [Human rights and private international law: to divorce or to marry?]. NJCM-Bulletin 23:797–811
Stone Sweet A, Keller H (2008) The reception of the ECHR in national legal orders. In: Keller H, Stone Sweet A (eds), A Europe of rights: the impact of the ECHR on national legal systems. Oxford University Press, Oxford
Strikwerda L (2012) Inleiding tot het Nederlandse internationaal privaatrecht [Introduction to Dutch private international law]. Kluwer, Deventer
Struycken AVM (2009) Co-ordination and co-operation in respectful disagreement: general course on private international law. Recueil des Cours 311, Martinus Nijhoff Publishers, Leiden
Thoma I (2007) Die Europäisierung und die Vergemeinschaftung des nationalen Ordre Public [The Europeanization and Communitarization of domestic public policy]. Mohr Siebeck, Tübingen
van Alebeek R (2008) The immunity of states and their officials in international criminal law and international human rights law. Oxford University Press, Oxford
van den Eeckhout V (2008) Promoting human rights within the Union: the role of European private international law. Eur Law J 14:105–127
van Hoek AAH et al (2011) Making choices in public and private international immunity law: Preadviezen. T.M.C. Asser Press, Den Haag
van Loon JHA (1993) De wisselwerking tussen internationaal privaatrecht en rechten van de mens [The interaction between private international law and human rights]. In: van Dijk D et al (eds) Grensoverschrijdend privaatrecht: een bundel opstellen over privaatrecht in internationaal verband [Cross-border private law: a collection of essays on private law in an international context]. Kluwer, Deventer, pp 135–148
Voltz M (2002) Menschenrechte und Ordre Public im internationalen Privatrecht [Human rights and public policy in private international law]. Lang, Frankfurt am Main
Vonken APMJ (1993) De reflexwerking van de mensenrechten op het ipr [The reflex of human rights on private international law]. In: Cliteur PB, Vonken APMJ (eds) Doorwerking van mensenrechten [The Impact of Human Rights]. Wolters-Noordhoff, Groningen, pp 153–185
Voyiakis E (2002) Access to court v state immunity. ICLQ 52:297–332
Wai R (2002) Transnational liftoff and judicial touchdown: the regulatory function of private international law in an era of globalization. Columbia J Transnational Law 40:209–274

Chapter 2
Introduction to Private International Law

Contents

2.1 Introduction

This research has as its subject the impact of the rights guaranteed in the ECHR on private international law. A necessary first step in such a discussion is an introduction to private international law. It should be understood from the outset that every country has its own system of private international law. This also applies to the Contracting Parties to the ECHR. Moreover, what is exactly understood as private international law even differs from country to country. While every State has its own national rules on private international law, many States are also party to international or bilateral treaties regarding issues of private international law. Furthermore, the EU Member States, which are all also Contracting Parties to the ECHR, are bound by EU rules on private international law.

L.R. Kiestra, *The Impact of the European Convention on Human Rights on Private International Law*, DOI 10.1007/978-94-6265-032-9_2

It is, of course, impossible to discuss all the different rules of private international law in this chapter, or to do justice fully to all the intricacies of private international law.[1] The aim of this chapter is merely to introduce the general notion of private international law and some of its particularities to the reader who may be less familiar with issues of private international law. Additionally, a first foray into the discussion of the impact of the ECHR on private international law will be offered, by discussing how private international law has traditionally dealt with fundamental rights.

In order to do so, first the notion of private international law will be further introduced (in Sect. 2.2). Next, some of the goals of private international law will be examined (Sect. 2.3). Thereafter, the sources of private international law will be discussed (Sect. 2.4). Finally, a first foray into the subject of this research will be made by an examination of the role of the public policy exception in private international law, particularly with regard to fundamental rights. The notion of mandatory rules will also come up here (Sect. 2.5).

2.2 The Notion of Private International Law

As stated above, every legal order in the world has its own rules relating to matters of private law. Private law is concerned with all legal relationships between private entities and thus includes, for example, family law and the law of contracts and obligations. These laws differ from country to country. However this does not stop interaction between people in different countries. People may, for example, marry someone from another country or find a job in a different country. As has been remarked in Chap. 1, it is this simple fact that is the *raison d'être* of private international law. Private international law is the area of law that comes into play whenever a court is faced with a question that contains a foreign element, or a foreign connection. The mere presence of such a foreign element in a legal matter raises a number of questions and it is the function of private international law to provide an answer to these questions and to ensure just solutions.

It has been established in Chap. 1 that private international law is concerned with three main issues. The first issue with which one may be faced in a case with a foreign element is the issue of jurisdiction: which court is competent to hear such an international case? If, for example, a conflict arises concerning a contract between an English company and a Dutch company, should this issue be brought before a court in England or the Netherlands? The second issue that could arise after a decision on the competent court has been made is whether, for example, English or Dutch law would be applied to this case. Or, perhaps, the parties have

[1] See for a general overview with regard to private international law, e.g., Bucher 2011; Cheshire et al. 2010; Clarkson and Hill 2011; Dicey et al. 2012; Dutoit 2005; Niboyet and De Geouffre de la Pradelle 2011; Siehr 2002; Strikwerda 2012.

chosen the law of a third country, or a uniform international law may even apply to their dispute. Finally, after the case has been decided, it is necessary to determine if, and under what circumstances, this decision can be recognized and enforced in another country.

These three issues could be considered to be the nucleus of private international law, as it is generally accepted in most countries that these issues are part of private international law.[2] As noted above, the rules of private international law are not understood to include exactly the same topics in every country. For example, in France and Belgium the rules on nationality are considered part of private international law.[3] In Switzerland one may, for example, find rules on (international) arbitration in the private international law statute.[4] However these topics will not be included in this book.[5]

One of the particularities of private international law rules is that they merely refer to either a competent court, the applicable law, or whether recognition and enforcement are possible. One could therefore think of private international law rules as procedural rules, or perhaps rather as technical or formal rules, which are not concerned with the substance of a dispute.[6] One should, incidentally, also note that the nature of private international law rules relating to the applicable law (conflict rules) is generally considered to be different from the rules relating to jurisdiction and recognition and enforcement, if solely because only conflict rules may lead to the application of foreign law.[7] The latter rules are thus considered to be of a more substantive nature, while rules regarding jurisdiction and the recognition and enforcement have a procedural character.

It is important to note that in this book, the impact of the Court's case law on issues of private international law will be examined in the first place.[8] As has been noted in Chap. 1, the Court, in principle, does not review measures taken by the Contracting Parties *in abstracto* and will consequently only assess the result of the application of private international law rules. Therefore, the impact of the ECHR on the three main issues of private international law should be understood as the impact of this instrument on the result of the application of private international law rules. The peculiar nature of private international law rules is thus of little consequence for this book.

---

[2] Cf. Kegel 1994, Chap. 1, pp. 1–2.

[3] See with regard to France, e.g., Audit 2008, p. 767ff; see with regard to Belgium, e.g., Erauw 2006, pp. 7–8.

[4] See infra n. 38.

[5] See also supra Chap. 1.

[6] See, e.g., Bogdan 2011, p. 71ff.

[7] See, e.g., Bogdan 2011, p. 85.

[8] See supra Sect. 1.1.

2.3 Objectives of Private International Law

One of the main reasons for States to have a system of private international law—which will occasionally lead to the assertion of jurisdiction in a case with international connections, the application of a foreign law, or the recognition and enforcement of foreign judgments—is the reasonable and legitimate expectations of the parties.[9] Completely disregarding foreign laws and decisions, or even the willingness to entertain international cases, would lead to injustices for the parties involved in such international proceedings.[10]

Another important objective of private international law is the international harmony of decisions.[11] This classic goal of private international law was first introduced by von Savigny.[12] It entails that countries should strive to reach the same decisions in problems of private international law. This latter objective, however, is difficult to achieve, as every country is, in principle, free to decide how to deal with issues of private international law. This does not take anything away from the importance of this notion. The international harmony of decisions is not an empty vessel. The taking into account of foreign laws and decisions by States helps avoid 'limping' legal relationships, i.e., legal relationships that are recognized in one country but not in another. One should not lose sight of the fact that rules of private international law are also in the interest of the (forum) State, as it benefits from stability with regard to cross-border legal relationships.[13]

2.4 Sources of Private International Law

Another particularity of private international law is the variety of its sources. Rules of private international law can be found not only in the national legislation of States, but also in international treaties and European law. The internationalization (and Europeanization) of rules of private international law is becoming increasingly more important for this area of law.[14] For Member States of the EU, for example, the European legislator is by now the most important legislator in the area of private international law. This is due to what has been called the 'Europeanization' of private international law (Sect. 2.4.1). Many rules of private international law have traditionally also been concluded between different States and laid down in international or bilateral treaties (Sect. 2.4.2). Finally, every State also has national legislation on private international law (Sect. 2.4.3).

---

[9] See, e.g., Dicey et al. 2012, pp. 4–5; Clarkson and Hill 2011, pp. 9–12.

[10] See, e.g., Dicey et al. 2012, p. 5.

[11] See, e.g., Clarkson and Hill 2011, pp. 18–19.

[12] Von Savigny 1880, p. 64ff.

[13] Bogdan 2011, pp. 49–70.

[14] See, e.g., Gaudemet-Tallon 2005, p. 47.

2.4.1 The Europeanization of Private International Law

The most important recent development for private international law in Europe is the so-called Europeanization or—at the time—'Communitarization' of private international law,[15] which essentially entails the continued involvement of the European Union legislator in the field of private international law. It was not truly possible for the European Community (now Union) legislator to introduce legislation in the area of private international law until the Treaty of Amsterdam.[16] It should not be forgotten that before this development there were also private international law instruments created in a European context, but these had the form of international conventions, which had to be signed and ratified by all participating countries. Examples of such initiatives are the Brussels Convention concerning jurisdiction and the recognition and enforcement of foreign judgments[17] and the Rome Convention concerning applicable law.[18] The Brussels Convention has, incidentally, been copied by the Lugano Convention,[19] thus enlarging the number of States party to the Convention with some non EU-Member States.[20] The disadvantage of merely cooperating by way of international conventions in the field of private international law is evident. Upon every accession of a new member State, the convention had to be updated and ratified again by all the members. This has happened several times with regard to both the Brussels and the Rome Convention, but this ultimately proved to be too slow and difficult a process and it became more burdensome with the increasing number of Member States.[21]

With the entry into force of the aforementioned Treaty of Amsterdam on 1 May 1999, the Community legislator entered the field of private international law, and one could say that it has not held back. Numerous new initiatives have been taken on the European level. The Brussels and Rome Conventions have, for example,

---

[15] See, e.g., Basedow 2000, pp. 687–708; Kuipers 2012, pp. 6–27; Stone 2010. The (increasing) importance of European law has also been the subject of study at the Hague Academy a number of the times during the past years: see, e.g., Borrás 2005, pp. 313–536; Fallon 1995, pp. 8–282; Struycken 1992, pp. 256–383.

[16] *Treaty of Amsterdam*, *OJ* 1997, C 310. With this Treaty the responsibility for creating legislation with regard to international judicial co-operation in civil matters was shifted from the third pillar to the first pillar, i.e. the Community legislator.

[17] The Brussels Convention on jurisdiction and the enforcement of foreign judgments in civil and commercial matters, 27 September 1968, *OJ* 1998, C 27/1 (consolidated version following the accession of Austria, Finland, and Sweden).

[18] The Rome Convention on the law applicable to contractual obligations, *OJ* 1998, C27/34 (consolidated version following the accession of Austria, Finland, and Sweden).

[19] Lugano Convention, 24 October 1988, *OJ* 1988, L 319/9. The Lugano Convention has since been replaced by a new Lugano Convention. See *OJ* 2007, L 399/1.

[20] These States are the Member States to the European Free Trade Association: Iceland, Norway, and Switzerland.

[21] The Commission became so concerned that it even openly discussed sanctions for states that did not approve amendments. See the answer by Commissioner Monti to the European Parliament, *OJ* 1997, C83/85.

both been transformed into EU instruments, and are now known respectively as the Brussels I Regulation[22] and the Rome I Regulation.[23] A number of complementary instruments to the Brussels I Regulation have been introduced, which basically deal with smaller, simple claims.[24] The so-called Rome II Regulation has been introduced with regard to the law applicable to non-contractual obligations. [25] The EU legislator has also delved into the area of family law with the Brussels II *bis* Regulation[26] and the Rome III Regulation.[27]

It is clear that the ongoing harmonization of the rules of private international law of the EU Member States is here to stay and that the further Europeanization of the rules of private international law will undeniably have major consequences for the respective systems of private international law of the Member States. An important factor therein is the fact that the Europeanization of private international law not only brings further harmonization, but concomitantly adds objectives following from European law which are unfamiliar to private international law, to the conflict of laws methodology in Europe. Important elements of European law thus suddenly enter the realm of private international law and in this way an 'instrumentalisation' of private international law in Europe has been introduced.[28] Rules of private international law are thus permeated by the four fundamental freedoms of the EU Treaty, by a focus of the principle of non-discrimination, the impact of fundamental rights, and the rule of mutual recognition.[29] Since the entry into force of the Lisbon Treaty the harmonization of the rules of private international law is now governed by Title V, which will bring further changes to private international law within the EU.[30]

---

[22] Council Regulation (EC) No. 44/2001 on jurisdiction and the recognition and enforcement of judgments in civil and commercial matters (Brussels I). This instrument has already a successor: Regulation (EU) No. 1215/2012 of the European Parliament and of the Council of 12 December 2012 on Jurisdiction and the Recognition and Enforcement of Judgments in Civil and Commercial Matters (Recast), *OJ* 2012, L 351/1. The Recast will apply from 10 January 2015 (see Article 81 of the Recast).

[23] Regulation (EC) No. 593/2008 on the law applicable to contractual obligations (Rome I).

[24] See, e.g., Regulation (EC) No. 805/2004 creating European Enforcement Order for Uncontested Claims, *OJ* 2004, L 143 (Amending Act Regulation (EC) 1869/2005, *OJ* 2005, L 300) and the Regulation EC 861/2007 establishing a European Small Claims Procedure, *OJ* 2007, L 199.

[25] Regulation (EC) 864/2007 on the law applicable to non-contractual obligations, *OJ* 2007, L199/40 (Rome II Regulation).

[26] Council Regulation (EC) No. 2201/2003 concerning jurisdiction and the recognition and enforcement in matrimonial matters and the matters of parental responsibility, *OJ* 2003, L 338/1 (Brussels II*bis* Regulation).

[27] Council Regulation (EU) No. 1259/2010 implementing enhanced cooperation in the area of the law applicable to divorce and legal separation, *OJ* 2010, L 343/10 (Rome III Regulation).

[28] Meeusen 2007, pp. 287–305.

[29] von Hein 2008, p. 1676ff; Meeusen 2007, p. 291ff.

[30] See further, e.g., de Groot and Kuipers 2008, pp. 109–114.

2.4.2 International Treaties

The Hague Conference of Private International Law, an international organization established in 1893, is the most prominent organization the field of private international law and as such is responsible for many conventions concerning issues of private international law. Over the years the Hague Conference has developed conventions in the areas of international family law, international legal cooperation and litigation, and international commercial law.[31] It should be noted that the European Community decided to accede to the Hague Conference of Private International Law in 2006.[32] In the field of international trade law and arbitration the United Nations (UN) is an important player.[33]

In addition to multilateral treaties, there are also many bilateral treaties between countries in the area of private international law. Such bilateral treaties only operate between two countries and the precise content of such agreements varies. One could say with regard to European countries that such bilateral treaties are generally being replaced by multilateral conventions, but the varying contents of bilateral agreements preclude them from becoming totally meaningless, as some aspects of private international law issues between the two countries may fall outside the scope of the multilateral conventions.[34]

2.4.3 National Legislation

The importance of national legislation on private international law has declined within Europe. Many of the relevant rules of private international law have an international origin,[35] while for the EU Member States, EU legislation is of particular importance. Nevertheless, this has not stopped European countries from

---

[31] See for an overview of the conventions the website of the Hague Conference [www.hcch.net].

[32] See Council Decision (EC) 2006/719 of 5 October 2006 on the accession of the Community to the Hague Conference on Private International Law, *OJ* 2006 L 297/1.

[33] Particularly, the United Nations Commission on International Trade Law (UNCITRAL) has drafted some important conventions. The number of conventions concerning private international law concluded by the UN pales in comparison to the number concluded by Hague Conference. Nevertheless, some of them are very important. Examples are the Vienna Convention on the Law Applicable to the International Sale of Goods and the New York Convention on the Recognition and Enforcement of Arbitral Awards.

[34] See, e.g., Articles 69–72 of the Brussels I Regulation (supra n. 22). See with regard to the concurrence of international and bilateral treaties on private international law, e.g., de Boer 2010, pp. 308–315.

[35] See with regard to the impact of such treaties on national legislation Siehr 1996, pp. 405–413.

developing new codifications of private international law. This development started in Switzerland and many European countries have since followed suit.[36]

In Switzerland, for example, private international law is governed by the Federal Law on Private International Law of 18 December 1987.[37] This law regulates virtually all aspects of private international law in Switzerland.[38] The Netherlands has recently finally codified a number of rules of private international law (mostly choice of law rules) in Book 10 of the Dutch Civil Code.[39] In England, private international law rules consist of both statutes and case law. Historically, case law was the most important source of private international law, England being a common law country, but legislation now also has an important role.[40]

2.5 The Impact of Fundamental Rights on Private International Law

In the next chapter the rights guaranteed in the ECHR will be discussed, and thereafter the examination of the impact of this instrument on the three main issues of private international law will begin in earnest.[41] However, this would appear to be the proper place to further reflect on the fact that private international law has previously dealt with the impact of fundamental rights. The public policy exception has historically been the instrument of private international law used to deal with the impact of fundamental rights.[42] Therefore, it deserves separate discussion

---

[36] Switzerland's codification came into force in 1987. See on the development of this law, e.g., Vischer 1977, pp. 131–145; Belgium has, for example, introduced a codification of private international law rules in 2004. See with regard to the realization of this law, e.g., Erauw 2006, pp. 19–21. The Netherlands has recently also codified a number of rules of private international law. See infra n. 39. See generally on the codification of private international law Siehr 2005, pp. 17–61.

[37] Loi féderale du 18 décembre 1987 sur le droit international privé (LDIP), *RS* 291, *RO* 1988 1776.

[38] The Swiss Private International Law Act has 12 chapters and roughly 200 articles. In the first chapter of the Law general issues of jurisdiction, applicable law, and the recognition and enforcement of foreign judgments are dealt with, in addition to a definition of domicile and nationality. This general chapter is followed by chapters on natural persons (Chap. 2), marriage (Chap. 3), children and adoption (Chap. 4), guardianship (Chap. 5), succession (Chap. 6), property (Chap. 7), intellectual property (Chap. 8), obligations (Chap. 9), corporations (Chap. 10), international bankruptcy (Chap. 11), and international arbitration (Chap. 12).

[39] *Vaststellings- en Invoeringswet Boek 10 Burgerlijk Wetboek* [Determination and Implementation Book 10 of the Dutch Civil Code], 19 May 2011, *Stb.* 2011, 272. See on the realization of this codification, e.g., Vlas 2010, pp. 167–182.

[40] See, e.g., Dicey et al. 2012, pp. 10–11.

[41] See infra Chaps. 5–8.

[42] See Kinsch 2007, pp. 171–192 for an overview of the historical use of the public policy exception in this regard. See also Kinsch 2004, pp. 419–435.

here in this introduction to private international law. In the subsequent chapters the precise role of this instrument with regard to the impact of the rights guaranteed in the ECHR will also be further discussed.[43]

When the application of a foreign law or the recognition or enforcement of a foreign judgment would result in a violation of the fundamental values of the forum, the public policy exception or *ordre public* will be invoked in order to set aside such a repugnant result.[44] The public policy exception is present in virtually all systems of private international law and can be found in statutes, codes, and international conventions. It has even been referred to as a general principle of international law by Judge Lauterpacht in his separate opinion in the *Boll* case.[45] He opined that:

> [I]n the sphere of private international law the exception of *ordre public*, of public policy, as a reason for the exclusion of foreign law in a particular case is generally – or, rather, universally – recognized. (…) On the whole, the result is the same in most countries – so much that the recognition of the part of *ordre public* must be regarded as a general principle of law in the field of private international law.[46]

This would indicate that the public policy exception may even be invoked in cases in which an international treaty is silent on the matter.[47] However, this is not to say that the public policy exception cannot be consciously left out of a treaty. If a public policy exception has been deliberately omitted in an international treaty, it cannot be invoked.[48] This, incidentally, leaves unanswered the question of whether it is possible to invoke one of the rights guaranteed in the ECHR in such a situation. This is essentially a question of the hierarchy between international instruments and will be discussed in relation to the ECHR in the next chapter.[49]

The public policy exception is clearly the safety valve, or the escape hatch, of private international law. As was discussed above, private international law by its nature leaves room for judicial solutions that are alien to the forum. Such flexibility is necessary in order to regulate cross-border affairs efficiently and reasonably. However, this flexibility finds it limits in the public policy exception.

---

[43] See particularly infra Sects. 4.4; 4.4.3.2; 6.3; 8.2.3.

[44] See for an extended discussion of the public policy exception, e.g., Lagarde 1994, Chap. 11; Mills 2008, pp. 201–236.

[45] International Court of Justice, *Netherlands v. Sweden (Case concerning the Application of the Convention of 1902 governing the Guardianship of Infants*, Judgment of 28 November 1958), ICJ Rep. 55.

[46] Separate Opinion of Judge Sir Hersch Lauterpacht in the *Boll* case, p. 92 (41) (supra n. 45).

[47] Cf. Mills 2008, p. 201. See also HR 10 September 1999, *NJ* 2001, 41.

[48] An (in)famous historical example of an international convention without a public policy exception is the 1902 Hague Convention relating to the settlement of the conflict of the laws concerning marriage. Instead of a general public policy exception, this convention contained a list of outlawed marriage impediments. However, racial impediments were not on the list, which became a problem in many countries party to this convention during the years leading up to World War II. Cf. Strikwerda 2012. See also Bogdan 2011, pp. 169–170.

[49] See infra Sect. 3.3.

The exact composition of the public policy exception—its content—is necessarily vague, as it comprises the fundamental values of the forum. This inevitable vagueness is exactly what some regard as a fundamental problem of public policy.[50]

It should also be understood that public policy differs from country to country, as values differ from country to country. At the start of the twentieth century public policy was already being referred to as 'the most evident principle of our science and at the same time the one which is the most difficult to define and to analyse.'[51] In addition to national fundamental values, it has generally been accepted in most countries that human rights are part of the public policy exception. This means that in the Member States of the Council of Europe, the ECHR may be considered part of public policy, as will be further discussed in the subsequent chapters of this research.[52]

Compared to the inherent vagueness of the content of public policy, the invocation and working of the exception is relatively clear. The public policy exception will be invoked if the result of the application of a foreign law or the recognition or enforcement of a foreign judgment would lead to an untenable result. It should be noted that the exception is thus invoked against the actual result of the application of the foreign law; it is not the foreign law in general that is tested, but rather the result of the application of that law. Public policy should be used only under exceptional circumstances, hence the frequent use of the expression of the public policy *exception*.[53] It has generally been accepted that it should not be used every time the application of a foreign law would lead to an undesirable result, but only in cases in which such application would lead to a truly unacceptable result. This cautious use of the public policy exception is, in international conventions, often emphasised by the insertion of the expression 'manifestly incompatible'.[54]

An important characteristic of the public policy exception is its relative character.[55] This naturally stems from the goals of private international law, which include the respect for other legal cultures. This relative character is manifested by the fact that it is generally observed that the operation of the public policy exception is related to the proximity between the issue and the forum. If a case has little or no connection to the forum, the public policy exception cannot be invoked—with the exception of certain extreme cases, in which the applicable law is so fundamentally against the values of the forum that the application of that law

---

50 See, e.g., Mills 2008, p. 202.

51 Pillet 1903, p. 367. Translation provided by Dolinger 2000, p. 275.

52 See further infra Sect. 6.3.3.3.

53 Although some debate over this issue remains. See Dolinger 2000, p. 289ff.

54 See, e.g., Article 16 of the 1980 Rome Convention on the Law Applicable to Contractual Obligations, *OJ* 1998, C27/34. This is also a condition for the application of the public policy exceptions found in national legislation. See, e.g. Articles 15 and 27 of the Swiss Private International Law Act.

55 See, e.g., Lagarde 1994, p. 21ff.

would never be permitted in the forum. If a case has more connections or links with the forum, the threshold for the application of the public policy exception is lower. This thus entails that if a case has a closer connection to the forum, because, for example, the parties reside in the forum, then the public policy exception is more likely to be successfully invoked than in the event of the parties residing abroad. There are some differences of opinion as to the exact functioning of this relative character of the public policy exception—compare, for example, the German theory of *Binnenbeziehung* or *Inlandsbeziehung* and the French theory of the *effet attenué* of *ordre public*—but the general principle is widely accepted and its operation is not that different in practice.[56]

The aforementioned fundamental values of the forum, which would ensure that the public policy exception could be invoked regardless of the proximity of the case to the forum, are part of what has been dubbed the 'iron core' of public policy.[57] This idea has also found acceptance in other countries.[58] What this iron core exactly entails, though, is a matter for discussion. It has been argued that international, universal norms are being protected in this manner; this public policy has therefore also been referred to as 'truly international public policy'.[59] This raises the question of whether human rights, and particularly the rights guaranteed in the ECHR, are also protected in this way, or perhaps, whether only a number of rights guaranteed in the ECHR may be so protected.[60] Another important question, specifically with regard to how the relative character of the public policy exception relates to the protection of human rights and particularly the basic obligation of the Contracting Parties under Article 1 ECHR, will be discussed in Chap. 4. Other aspects of the role of the public policy exception and the role of the rights guaranteed in the ECHR in this regard will naturally also be further discussed in this book.[61]

Finally, the public policy exception should be distinguished from another concept of private international law, the mandatory rule (also referred to as internationally mandatory rules, *lois de police*, *lois d'application immédiate*, or *Eingriffsnormen*). As noted above, the public policy exception is a corrective device, as it is invoked to alter the outcome of the application of the choice of law rules of the forum, if the application of these rules would result in the application foreign law, which in turn would lead to an unacceptable result. The public policy

[56] See, e.g., Bogdan 2011, pp. 174–179; Bucher 1993, pp. 47–56; Lagarde 1994, pp. 21–43 (11-24–11-51). Cf. de Boer 2008, pp. 298–300. See on the functioning of the public policy exception also the handbooks cited supra n. 1.

[57] See Jessurun d'Oliveira 1975, pp. 239–261.

[58] Bucher 2004, p. 18. See further also infra Sect. 6.3.3.3.

[59] See, e.g., van Houtte 2002, p. 846; cf. Mills 2008, p. 213ff. See also more recently Chong 2012, pp. 88–113. However, whether such a universal public policy exception truly exists has been questioned. See, e.g. Bogdan 2011, p. 178.

[60] See on the idea that not all the rights guaranteed in the ECHR may belong to a core that always needs protection also further infra Sect. 4.4.2.

[61] See further Sect. 6.3.3.3.

exception is thus a defensive mechanism. Mandatory rules are rules, which are deemed so important that they should be applied to a (cross-border) case by a court, even if the issue is, in principle, governed by another law according to the choice of law rules of the forum.[62] These mandatory rules may, incidentally, either be rules of the forum or foreign rules.[63] Mandatory rules thus also set aside a foreign law if a fundamental interest is at stake, and in this regard their purpose is somewhat similar to that of the public policy exception. However, mandatory rules have a positive character—they apply irrespective of the normally applicable (foreign) law—and this is what sets them apart from the public policy exception, which intervenes after the fact.[64] Mandatory rules do not—as of yet—play an important role in the discussion concerning the impact of the ECHR on private international law. As will be discussed in this book, though, it could be argued that the rights guaranteed in the ECHR in some ways function as mandatory rules.[65]

References

Audit B (2008) Droit international privé. Economica, Paris

Basedow J (2000) The communitarization of the conflict of laws under the Treaty of Amsterdam. CML Rev 37:687–708

Bogdan M (2011) Private international law as component of the law of the forum: general course on private international law. Recueil des Cours 348

Bonomi A (1999) Mandatory rules in private international law: the quest for uniformity of decisions in a global environment. Yearb Private Int Law 1:215–247

Borrás A (2005) Le droit international privé communautaire: realités, problèmes et perspectives d'avenir. Recueil des Cours 317:313–536

Bucher A (1993) L'ordre public et le but social des lois en droit international privé. Recueil des Cours 239:9–116

Bucher A (2004) Le couple en droit international prive. Helbing & Lichtenhahn, Basel

Bucher A (ed) (2011) Loi sur le droit international privé. Convention de Lugano. Helbing Lichtenhahn, Basel

Cheshire GC et al (2010) Private international law. Oxford University Press, Oxford

Chong A (2012) Transnational public policy in civil and commercial matters. LQR 128:88–113

Clarkson CMV, Hill J (2011) The conflict of laws. Oxford University Press, Oxford

de Boer Th M (2008) Unwelcome foreign law: public policy and other means to protect the fundamental values and public interests of the European Community. In: Malatesta A et al (eds) The external dimension of EC private international law in family and succession matters. CEDAM, Padova, pp 295–330

---

[62] See with regard to mandatory rules, e.g., Bonomi 1999, pp. 215–247; Cheshire et al. 2010, pp. 150–151; Strikwerda 2012, p. 54, 63–70.

[63] See, e.g. Article 7(1) of the Rome Convention {look up} and Articles 17 and 18 of the Swiss Private International Law Act.

[64] See Bonomi 1999, pp. 229–230, who argues that the difference between the two mechanisms is very subtle.

[65] See further Sects. 4.4 and 6.3.3.3.

de Boer Th M (2010) Samenloop van verdragen en verordeningen op het terrein van het internationaal familierecht [Concurrence of treaties and regulations in the area of international family law]. Familie en Jeugdrecht 32:308–315
de Groot G-R, Kuipers JJ (2008) The new provisions on private international law in the Lisbon Treaty. Maastricht J Eur Comp Law 15:109–114
Dicey AV, Morris JHC, Collins LA (2012) The conflict of laws. Sweet & Maxwell, London
Dolinger J (2000) Evolution of principles for resolving conflicts in the field of contracts and torts. Recueil des Cours 283:187–512
Dutoit B (2005) Droit international privé Suisse. Helbing & Lichtenhahn Verlag, Basel
Erauw J (2006) Handboek Belgisch international privaatrecht [Handbook Belgian private international law]. Kluwer, Mechelen
Fallon M (1995) Les conflits de lois et de juridictions dans une espace économique integré. Recueil des Cours 253:8–282
Gaudemet-Tallon H (2005) Le pluralisme en droit international privé: richesses et faiblesses. Recueil des Cours 312:9–488
Jessurun d'Oliveira HU (1975) Openbare orde en rechtsvergelijking [Public policy and comparative law]. In: Jessurun d'Oliveira HU et al (eds) 't Exempel dwinght. Opstellen aangeboden door vrienden en vereerders and prof. mr. I. Kisch ter gelegenheid van zijn 70ste verjaardag, Tjeenk Willink, Zwolle, pp 239–261
Kegel G (1994) Introduction, international encyclopedia of comparative law, vol III. Mohr, Tübingen
Kinsch P (2004) Sklavenbesitz, religiöse Ehehindernisse und entschädigungslose Enteignungen: zur Vorgeschichte der Frage nach der Einwerkung der Grund- und Mensenrechte auf die Anwendung ausländischen Rechts [Ownership of slaves, religious impediments to marriage, and uncompensated expropiation: the history of the question of the impact of fundamental- and human rights on the application of foreign law]. In: Mansel H-P et al (eds) Festschrif für Erik Jayme Band I. Sellier, Munich, pp 419–435
Kinsch P (2007) Droits de l'homme, droits fondamentaux et droit international privé. Recueil des Cours 318:9–332
Kuipers JJ (2012) EU law and private international law: the interrelationship in contractual obligations. Martinus Nijhoff Publishers, Leiden
Lagarde P (1994) Public policy, international encyclopedia of comparative law, vol III. Mohr, Tübingen
Meeusen J (2007) Instrumentalisation of private international law in the European Union: towards a European conflicts revolution? Eur J Mig Law 9:287–305
Mills A (2008) The dimensions of public policy in private international law. J Private Int Law 4:201–236
Niboyet M-L, De Geouffre de la Pradelle G (2011) Droit international privé. L.G.D.J., Paris
Pillet A (1903) Principes de droit international privé, Paris
Siehr K (1996) The impact of international conventions on national codifications of private international law. In: Borras Rodriguez A et al (eds) E pluribus unum: liber amicorum Georges A.L. Droz. Martinus Nijhoff Publishers, The Hague, pp 405–413
Siehr K (2002) Das Internationale Privatrecht der Schweiz [The private international law of Switzerland]. Schulthess, Zürich
Siehr K (2005) General problems of private international law in modern codifications—de lege lata and—de lege europea ferenda. Yearb Private Int Law 7:17–61
Stone P (2010) EU private international law. Elgar European Law, Cheltenham
Strikwerda L (2012) Inleiding tot het Nederlandse internationaal privaatrecht [Introduction to Dutch private international law]. Kluwer, Deventer
Struycken AVM (1992) Les conséquences de l'intégration européenne sur le développement du droit international privé. Recueil des Cours 232:256–383
van Houtte H (2002) From a national to a European public policy. In: Nafziger JAR, Symeonides SC (eds) Law and justice in a multistate world: essays in honor of Arthur T. von Mehren. Transnational Publishers, Ardsley, pp 841 et seq

Vischer F (1977) Drafting national legislation on the conflict of laws: the Swiss experience. Law Contemp Probl 41:131–145
Vlas P (2010) On the development of private international law in the Netherlands: from Asser's days to the codification of Dutch private international law (1910–2010). NILR 57:167–182
von Hein J (2008) Something old and something borrowed, but nothing new? Rome II and the European choice-of-law. Tulane Law Rev 82:1663–1707
von Savigny FC (1880) A treatise on the conflict of laws, and the limits of their operation in respect of place and time (trans: Guthrie W). Clark, Edinburgh

Chapter 3
Introduction to the European Convention on Human Rights

Contents

3.1 Introduction

As this research has as its subject the impact of the European Convention on Human Rights on private international law, it is prudent to provide the reader with an introduction to the ECHR. However, this should be read in light of the subject of this research. This discussion will focus on the most important aspects of the ECHR with regard to issues of private international law. For a more detailed overview one should turn to one of the many excellent handbooks on the ECHR.[1]

The ECHR has been one of the most important accomplishments of the Council of Europe, an international organization established after the Second World War to foster co-operation in Europe. It is an international treaty, which was adopted in

[1] To name just a few in the English language: van Dijk et al. 2006; Harris et al. 2009; White and Ovey 2010; Janis et al. 2008; Lawson and Schermers 1999; Mowbray 2012.

L.R. Kiestra, *The Impact of the European Convention on Human Rights on Private International Law*, DOI 10.1007/978-94-6265-032-9_3

Rome on 4 November 1950 and entered into force on 3 September 1953 after ratification by ten States.[2] The ECHR was the culmination of increased attention towards the international protection of human rights following the Second World War and represented 'the first steps for the collective enforcement of certain of the rights stated in the Universal Declaration [of Human Rights].'[3] It was the first international legally binding treaty translating some of the rights derived from the 1948 Universal Declaration of Human Rights (Universal Declaration) into a regional vocation thereof.

One should note, though, that the ECHR is certainly not a carbon copy of the Universal Declaration, as not all of the rights contained in the latter can be found in the former. In fact, one could say that it is mainly those rights that are covered by the later-created category of 'civil and political rights' of the Universal Declaration that are contained in the ECHR, which was mostly a matter of tactics and priorities.[4] However, some of the rights initially not included have subsequently been added in additional Protocols to the ECHR and in other conventions, particularly the European Social Charter of 1961. In 2012, the ECHR had forty-seven Contracting Parties, comprising all the countries on the European continent with the exception of Belarus.[5]

This overview of the characteristics of the ECHR which are particularly relevant to the discussion of the impact of this instrument on issues of private international law will start with a discussion of the enforcement machinery of the ECHR. Here, attention will also be paid to the admissibility criteria of the ECHR (in Sect. 3.2). Thereafter, one will find an examination of the status of the ECHR in the national and international legal orders. This section will include a discussion of conflicts between international treaties, as this issue could arise with regard to the impact of the ECHR on private international law (Sect. 3.3). Next, a brief overview of the most relevant Articles of the ECHR with regard to private international law will be given (Sect. 3.4). This will be followed by a discussion of the nature of the Contracting Parties' obligations following from the rights guaranteed by the ECHR, where it will be observed that these entail not only negative obligations, but also positive obligations. Thereafter, the nature of the rights guaranteed will be further examined, and particularly the manner in which these rights may be limited under specific circumstances (Sect. 3.5). In

---

[2] See for an elaborate overview of the historical development of the ECHR the *Collected Edition of the 'Travaux préparatoires' of the European Convention on Human Rights*. See for a more concise, yet more extensive overview than one may find in the modern handbooks cited directly above, e.g., Robertson 1977, pp. 1–25.

[3] The Preamble of the Convention.

[4] Harris et al. 2009, p. 3.

[5] The 47 Contracting Parties are in alphabetical order: Albania, Andorra, Armenia, Austria, Azerbaijan, Belgium, Bosnia and Herzegovina, Bulgaria, Croatia, Cyprus, Czech Republic, Denmark, Estonia, Finland, France, Georgia, Germany, Greece, Hungary, Iceland, Ireland, Italy, Latvia, Liechtenstein, Lithuania, Luxembourg, "The former Yugoslav Republic of Macedonia", Malta, Moldova, Monaco, Montenegro, the Netherlands, Norway, Poland, Portugal, Romania, Russian Federation, San Marino, Serbia, Slovakia, Slovenia, Spain, Sweden, Switzerland, Turkey, Ukraine, and the United Kingdom.

conclusion, recent developments concerning the system of protection offered by the ECHR and the future of the Court will be discussed (Sect. 3.6).

3.2 The Enforcement Machinery

One of the aspects that makes the ECHR stand out among other international human rights treaties is its enforcement machinery. It should be noted that the primary responsibility for guaranteeing the rights and freedoms contained in the ECHR principally rests upon the Contracting Parties, as the Strasbourg enforcement machinery is subsidiary to the national systems safeguarding human rights.[6] It is for the Contracting Parties themselves as to how to ensure these rights, as the Court held in the *Handyside* case, where it with an eye hereto introduced the so-called 'margin of appreciation'.[7] The subsidiary nature of the ECHR is also reflected in the fact that before bringing a case before the Court in Strasbourg, an applicant must first have exhausted all of his or her legal remedies in the Contracting Party against which the complaint is directed.[8]

What makes the enforcement machinery particularly unique and effective is that it provides for individual applications. Previously this required separate declarations by the Contracting Parties recognizing this right.[9] It took quite some time for all the Contracting Parties to recognize the jurisdiction of the Court. However, with the entry into force of Protocol 11 in 1998, the Court now automatically has jurisdiction over individual as well as intra-State applications.[10] Protocol 11 also marked the end of the Commission. A new permanent Court was introduced, which replaced the European Commission of Human Rights (Commission) and the old European Court of Human Rights.[11] Originally, the Strasbourg machinery consisted of three entities: the Commission, established in 1954; the European Court of Human Rights (the old Court), established in 1959; and the Committee of

---

6 See generally with regard to the principle of subsidiarity and the ECHR, e.g., Petzold 1993, pp. 41–62.

7 *Handyside v. the United Kingdom*, judgment of 12 December 1976, paras 49–50, ECHR Series A-24. See also infra Sect. 3.5.2.

8 See further infra the text following n. 12.

9 Declarations under Article 25 ECHR were required for the jurisdiction of the Commission, while the jurisdiction of the Court had to be recognized under Article 48 ECHR.

10 Protocol 11 was adopted in 1994 and entered into force in 1998.

11 See Article 32 ECHR.

12 The Committee of Ministers did retain its supervisory role with regard to the execution of the Court's judgments See with regard to the supervisory task of the Committee of Ministers e.g. van Dijk et al. 2006, pp. 291–321.

13 See, e.g., *Matthews v. the United Kingdom* [GC], no. 24833/94, paras 39, 40 and 59, ECHR 1999-I, in which the Grand Chamber of the new Court referred to the old Court's and Commission's case law as its own.

Ministers of the Council of Europe.[12] The new Court emphasized in its first cases after the entry into force of Protocol 11 that it considered the existing case law of both the Commission and the old Court as its own.[13]

An important issue related to the Strasbourg enforcement machinery is who can bring an individual application, and under what conditions? It follows from Article 34 ECHR that an application can be received 'from any person, non-governmental organization or group of individuals', provided that such an applicant is a victim of the alleged violation. In this Article the Contracting Parties have also undertaken to refrain from any hindrance in the effective exercise of this right to bring an application. Yet it should be noted that in order for such an application to be admissible, a few criteria have to be met. The various conditions of admissibility can be found not only in Article 34 ECHR, but also in Article 35 ECHR.[14] The Court has held frequently with regard to these criteria that they should be interpreted with some degree of flexibility and without excessive formalism.[15]

Article 35(1) ECHR contains two of the most important criteria in this respect, as it provides that all domestic remedies must first have been exhausted and that the application must be brought within six months after the final decision has been taken. These are the procedural grounds for inadmissibility.[16] Other important admissibility criteria of Articles 34 and 35 ECHR concern the competence of the Court and may be summarized as follows: who is competent to bring a case and against whom (compatibility *ratione personae*); what is the subject matter of the application (compatibility *ratione materiae*); where did the alleged violation take place (compatibility *ratione loci*); and when did it allegedly take place (compatibility *ratione temporis*)?[17] A newly added criterion is that of the "significant disadvantage," which has been added in light of the Court's ever increasing workload, and entails that the Court may reject cases, where the applicant has not suffered any significant disadvantage. The new provision does contain two safeguard clauses: the Court may only reject an application on the basis of this criterion, if the application has been duly considered at the national level. Moreover, respect for the rights guaranteed in the ECHR may require the Court to examine the merits of the case after all. The precise interpretation of the new admissibility criterion and its two safeguard clauses will have to be further clarified by the Court.

---

[14] See generally with regard to the admissibility criteria of the Court, e.g., Harris et al. 2009, pp. 757–810; van Dijk et al. 2006, pp. 98–203. The Research Division of the Court has published the *Practical Guide on Admissibility Criteria*, which is available at www.echr.coe.int (last updated version March 2011).

[15] See, e.g., *Cardot v. France,* 19 March 1991, Series A no. 200; *İlhan v. Turkey* [GC], no. 22277/93, ECHR 2000-VII.

[16] The rationale behind the exhaustion rule is that the national authorities of the Contracting Parties should have had the opportunity to deal with the alleged violation of the ECHR. The assumption that there are remedies available within the national legal orders is also reflected in Article 13 ECHR, which guarantees an effective remedy before a national authority.

[17] See, e.g., White and Ovey 2010, pp. 33–34.

[18] Article 35(3) ECHR.

Even if an application is completely compatible with the ECHR and fulfills all the (formal) admissibility criteria mentioned above, an application may still be found inadmissible on the merits. The most frequent reason for this is that an application is held to be 'manifestly ill-founded'.[18] The use of the term 'manifestly' is, in this context, somewhat misleading, as it has been abundantly established in the Strasbourg case law that this term is always used when it is decided that an application does not warrant a formal examination of the merits (and a likely resulting judgment on the merits) after a preliminary examination of the case has demonstrated no apparent violation of any of the rights guaranteed in the ECHR.[19] The term does not refer to a threshold and nor does it necessarily suggest a cursory review of the application.[20] In fact, as will be demonstrated in subsequent chapters, applications which are held to be 'manifestly ill-founded' may be rather extensively reasoned and may, for example, provide valuable insights into issues of private international law. A newly added criterion for admissibility in Article 35(3) under -b ECHR is that the applicant must have suffered a significant disadvantage. This criterion allows the Court to reject minor cases. The exact scope of this latter criterion will have to be further developed by the Court in its case law.

It is important to understand that most of the applications brought to Strasbourg actually end up being found inadmissible. In 2011, for example, 52,188 applications were handled by the Court. Of these, 50,677 applications resulted in a decision by the Court in which they were either found to be inadmissible or were struck out.[21] The Court only delivered a judgment in 1,157 cases concerning 1,511 applications.

3.3 The Status of the ECHR in the Domestic and International Legal Orders

An important aspect of the relationship between the Court in Strasbourg and the Contracting Parties is how the ECHR is generally applied by the national courts of the respective Contracting Parties and the position of the ECHR in the respective national legal orders. This varies from Contracting Party to Contracting Party, but

---

[19] See, e.g., Leach 2011, p. 157.

[20] See, e.g., *Mentzen alias Mencena v. Latvia* (dec.), no. 71074/01, 7 December 2004, for an example of a lengthy exposition in a case which was ultimately found to be inadmissible on the merits. See generally, on the notion of manifestly ill-founded, e.g., the Court's *Practical Guide on Admissibility Criteria* supra n. 14, at pp. 68–74.

[21] See for the numbers the Analysis of the Statistics 2011, which can be found at: [www.echr.coe.int/NR/rdonlyres/11CE0BB3-9386-48DC-B012-AB2C046FEC7C/0/STATS_EN_2011.PDF], visited August 2012.

[22] See *Swedish Engine Drivers' Union*, 6 February 1976, Series A no. 20. See also *Ireland v. the United Kingdom*, 18 January 1978, para 239, Series A no. 25, in which the Court appears to display a preference for the incorporation of the ECHR into domestic law, though.

may be an important factor for the impact of the ECHR on any given area of law, including private international law.

From the point of view of the Court, Contracting Parties are not obligated to incorporate the ECHR into their respective laws and may satisfy their commitments as to Article 1 ECHR in any way they choose.[22] Nevertheless, all Contracting Parties have now incorporated the ECHR into their domestic laws in one way or another, taking into account that in some Contracting Parties incorporation was not necessary.[23] This does not mean that the position of the ECHR is identical in every Contracting Party; quite the contrary—the position of the ECHR may differ considerably. The situation varies, for example, in the three jurisdictions—England (United Kingdom), The Netherlands, and Switzerland—whose case law will most often be referred to in this study.

England, or rather the United Kingdom (UK), was late in integrating the ECHR into its national legal order. The UK follows the dualist tradition with regard to the relationship between international law and national law,[24] meaning that additional legislative action was needed in order to make the ECHR enforceable before English courts. Not until the entry into force of the 1998 UK Human Rights Act (HRA) in 2000 did the ECHR and the Court's case law become part of domestic law in the UK. With the HRA, the ECHR's rank in the UK's domestic law has become somewhat unclear: while the HRA does not render any constitutional priority of ECHR rights over earlier or subsequent legislation, only Parliament's clear and express intention can lead to non-ECHR compliant legislation, and even then courts may issue a declaration of incompatibility.[25] Such a declaration does not directly affect the validity of legislation, but does put pressure on the government to amend a law.[26]

The Netherlands has a monist tradition regarding the relationship between international and domestic law, and the Dutch Constitution, furthermore, guarantees a paramount position to international treaty law.[27] Consequently Dutch courts can directly apply the ECHR, as this treaty is intended to create directly enforceable rights for individuals and the rights contained in the ECHR are capable of being enforced directly.[28] It also follows from the Dutch Constitution and the case law of the Dutch *Hoge Raad* (Supreme Court) that in the case of a conflict between the application of domestic law and the ECHR, the ECHR will prevail and the national court is obliged to set aside that law.[29] It should also be

---

[23] See, e.g., Blackburn and Polakiewicz 2001; Keller and Stone Sweet 2008.

[24] See on the monist and dualist approach to international law, e.g., Brownlie 2008, pp. 31–33.

[25] Besson 2008, p. 10.

[26] Harris et al. 2009, p. 24.

[27] See Articles 93 and 94 of the *Grondwet* (Dutch Constitution).

[28] See, e.g., De Wet 2008, pp. 235–236; Hins and Nieuwenhuis 2010, p. 61ff.

[29] Hins and Nieuwenhuis 2010, p. 61ff.

[30] De Wet 2008, p. 237.

[31] Aemisegger 2005, p. 309; Thurnherr 2008, p. 329.

noted that Dutch courts, in principle, should have regard to all relevant judgments of the Court in Strasbourg for the interpretation of the relevant provisions of the ECHR; they should not limit themselves to judgments against the Netherlands.[30]

Switzerland, like the Netherlands, also adheres to a monist approach with regard to the relationship between international and national law, rendering all self-executing provisions of international law binding for Switzerland.[31] In 1977 the Swiss *Tribunal fédéral* (Federal Supreme Court) found that the substantial guarantees in the ECHR—with the exception of Article 13 ECHR—were directly applicable in Switzerland from the moment of the entry into force of the ECHR.[32] Despite this monistic approach, the hierarchical relationship between domestic and international law is, however, not entirely clear, except in the case of norms of *jus cogens*,[33] although in its more recent case law the *Tribunal fédéral* stresses the prevalence of international law.[34]

3.3.1 The ECHR and Other Private International Law Treaties[35]

In the previous chapter it has been established that rules of private international law of the Contracting Parties, regardless of whether they pertain to issues of jurisdiction, applicable law, or the recognition and enforcement of foreign judgments, may emanate from international sources.[36] Contracting Parties may thus have entered into multilateral conventions on issues of private international law, such as one of the various treaties of the Hague Conference of Private International Law,[37] but also bilateral treaties,[38] while Contracting Parties doubling as EU Member States are also bound by many EU private international law instruments.[39] The international origin of these rules may lead to a particular issue if (the result of) the application of such private international law rules would result in a violation of one of the rights

---

[32] ATF 103 V 190, 192. See particularly 2 a).

[33] See Article 193 and 194 of the Swiss Constitution with regard to *jus cogens*.

[34] See Aemisegger 2005, pp. 309–310; Thurnherr 2008, pp. 329–331 and the case law cited in both contributions.

[35] See generally with regard to the relationship between the ECHR and international law, e.g., Wildhaber 2007, pp. 217–232.

[36] See supra Sect. 2.4.

[37] See www.hcch.net.

[38] See, e.g., infra n. 49.

[39] See supra Sect. 2.4.1.

[40] One should, incidentally, note that the increase of international treaties concerning private international law not only may result in a possible conflict with the ECHR, but could also lead to conflicts between two treaties concerned with similar issues of private international law. This is, particularly in the area of international family law, a growing concern for national courts. See on this issue, e.g., de Boer 2010, pp. 308–315.

guaranteed in the ECHR. In that case a Contracting Party would essentially be faced with two conflicting norms originating from international treaties.[40]

Before further examining the guidelines concerning the concurrence of two international treaties, it should, first of all, be noted that a conflict between private international law rules from an international source and the obligations following from the ECHR is quite rare. This is largely due to the fact that there can only be a true conflict of norms if a Contracting Party is actually unable to 'simultaneously comply with its obligations under both treaties.'[41] This will only exceptionally be the case with regard to international treaties concerning issues of private international law, as most such treaties will include a public policy exception.[42] If it is, for example, possible to set aside a foreign applicable law or judgment violating one of the rights guaranteed in the ECHR by invoking the public policy exception, there is no true conflict. Similarly, with regard to rules originating from EU private international law instruments, the argument could be put forward that, even if a public policy exception may be missing, the rights guaranteed in the ECHR are still deemed part of the fundamental principles of EU law, which may ultimately bring relief in such a situation.[43]

In the event, though, that the obligations flowing from an international treaty on private international law and the ECHR could not possibly be complied with simultaneously, one could turn to the classic conflict rules regarding obligations arising out of international treaties: the rules of *lex specialis derogat legi generali* and *lex posterior derogat legi priori*.[44] These rules, unfortunately, are not a great help for conflicts between international treaties on private international law and the ECHR from the viewpoint of the protection of human rights. The *lex specialis* in an issue of private international law would undoubtedly be the rule of private international law which could lead to a violation of the ECHR, although one could also argue that in such a case there are actually two different *lex speciali*. This would not lead to a solution. The other rule, *lex posterior*, would only offer a solution if the international treaty on private international law was older than the ECHR, as in that case the ECHR would apply. Another possible solution would be to regard human rights norms as the hierarchically superior norm. One could, for example, infer that human rights norms are norms of *jus cogens*,[45] which arguably

---

41 Jenks 1953, p. 426.

42 But see supra Sect. 2.5.

43 See further infra Sect. 8.2.4.

44 See for an overview of all the rules for resolving conflicts between treaties which have been used by national courts, e.g., Sadat-Akhavi 2003, p. 99ff.

45 See Article 53 of the Vienna Convention on the Law of Treaties. See generally Shelton 2006, pp. 291–323.

46 Even though this may not necessarily be a given. See, e.g., Vidmar and De Wet 2012, pp. 3–4.

47 There is much discussion on which could be regarded as norms of *jus cogens*. See for a list of the most commonly accepted norms of *jus cogens* the ILC Articles on State Responsibility, Commentary to Article 40, paras 4–5.

48 See, e.g. Vidmar and De Wet 2012.

could be regarded as the hierarchically superior norm.[46] However, the majority of the rights guaranteed in the ECHR are not considered to be norms of *jus cogens*.[47] Whether it is possible to regard human rights norms as hierarchically superior is a discussion fraught with difficulties.[48]

Again, the issue of conflicting norms between international treaties concerning issues of private international law and the ECHR is a rare phenomenon. However, in French case law it has arisen in the past in connection with the recognition of Moroccan repudiations. On the basis of a bilateral treaty between France and Morocco of 10 October 1981,[49] French courts had to recognize these repudiations with regard to Moroccan nationals living in France, even though at the time it was only possible for a man to repudiate his wife, and not vice versa. This is a violation of Article 5 of Protocol No. 7 ECHR, which guarantees equality between spouses.[50] It was not possible to rely on a public policy exception, turning this into an example of two conflicting treaty obligations.

This example, incidentally, offers an additional complicating factor in that Morocco is not a Contracting Party to the ECHR. Therefore, the afore-mentioned rule of *lex posterior derogat legi priori* is rendered somewhat meaningless, as one of the two international treaties does not apply between both parties.[51] A possible solution to this situation could have been to regard equality between spouses as a norm of *jus cogens*.[52] However, it has been pointed out that this right is not a universal norm.[53] In the end, the French *Cour de Cassation* came up with a different solution and avoided the conflict between the treaties altogether. Instead of referring to the bilateral treaty of 1981, the French court referred to an older treaty between the two countries that did include a public policy exception.[54] It could consequently rely on a public policy exception to stave off the recognition and there was no longer a conflict. However, this was not an elegant solution from the point of view of the *lex posterior* rule.

In conclusion, one should reiterate that the issue of conflicting obligations between private international law treaties and the ECHR is uncommon. It appears to be an issue that courts would prefer to avoid dealing with, which, given the uncertainties regarding this issue, is quite understandable.

---

[49] Convention entre la République Française et le Royaume du Maroc relative au status des personnes et de la famille et à la cooperation judiciaire, 10 August 1981. See for the text *JDI* 1983, pp. 922–928.

[50] See also *D.D. v. France* (dec.), no. 3/02, 8 November 2005, which is discussed infra Sect. 7.6.

[51] See, e.g., Sadat-Akhavi 2003, p. 64.

[52] Lequette 2004, p. 113.

[53] Gannagé 2001, pp. 258–260. See also supra n. 47.

[54] See Cass.civ. 1 June 1994, *Rev.crit.dr.int.* 1995, p. 103 (note Déprez); Cass.civ. 11 March 1997. Cf. Lequette 2004, p. 113. Incidentally, one could wonder how the principle of *lex posterior derogat legi priori* relates to this solution.

3.4 The Most Relevant Articles of the ECHR with Regard to Private International Law

It is not necessary to discuss all the rights and freedoms contained in the ECHR and its additional Protocols, as only a limited number of rights may impact upon issues of private international law. It will be demonstrated in the subsequent chapters that Article 6(1) ECHR, which guarantees the right to a fair trial, and Article 8 ECHR, which, inter alia, guarantees the right to private and family life, are the most relevant rights with regard to issues of private international law. Yet the impact of the ECHR on issues of private international law is not limited to these two Articles. In principle, all rights guaranteed in the ECHR that are capable of having an impact on issues of private law could have an impact on private international law. Family life, for example, is not only protected in Article 8 ECHR, but aspects of it are also protected in Article 12 ECHR and Article 5 of Protocol No. 7 ECHR. Moreover, the prohibition on discrimination, which can be found in Article 14 ECHR as well as Protocol No. 12 ECHR, could have an impact on issues of private international law.[55] Article 10 ECHR, guaranteeing the right to freedom of expression, has also occasionally played a role in issues of private international law. Finally, the right to property, which is guaranteed in Article 1 of Protocol No. 1 ECHR, has a considerable role, particularly with regard to the obligation to recognize and enforce certain foreign judgments. It could therefore be observed that most of the formal and material subjects with which private international law is concerned are, at least to some extent, covered by the rights guaranteed in the ECHR.

3.5 The Nature of the Contracting Parties' Obligations and of the Rights in the ECHR

Article 1 ECHR obliges the Contracting Parties to 'secure' the rights and freedoms contained in the Convention. This obligation, taken together with the text of the several following Articles, has been interpreted as imposing both negative and positive obligations. Classic civil and political rights guarantees traditionally entailed negative obligations for the State, such as the requirement to abstain from torture, which can, for example, be found in Article 3 ECHR. In addition to the various negative obligations, there are also some positive obligations expressly stated in the ECHR, or they necessarily follow from the ECHR. An example is the obligation to protect the right to life by law, which can be found in Article 2(1) ECHR.[56]

---

[55] The impact of the principle of discrimination is not part of this research, though. See supra Chap. 1.

[56] See, e.g., Harris et al. 2009, pp. 18–19.

[57] See, e.g., Mowbray 2004; Xenos 2012.

[58] *Marckx v. Belgium*, 13 June 1979, ECHR Series A-31.

[59] *Marckx v. Belgium*, 13 June 1979, para 31, ECHR Series A-31.

There is, however, also a category of positive obligations which have been read into the ECHR by the Court.[57] This practice started in the famous *Marckx* case.[58] In this case the Court held that with regard to 'family life' in Article 8 ECHR, 'it does not merely compel the State to abstain from such interference: in addition to this primarily negative undertaking, there may be positive obligations inherent in an effective "respect" for family life.'[59] Since this case the Court has, on numerous occasions, and especially often with regard to Article 8 ECHR, found that positive obligations had been infringed, usually justifying such a stance by stating that the finding of positive obligations is necessary in order to make ECHR rights effective.[60] It has now generally been accepted that all the rights guaranteed in the ECHR entail both negative and positive obligations for the State.[61]

There is, finally, another category of positive obligations that may be distinguished. The Court has also found that Contracting Parties have the positive obligation to protect rights guaranteed in the ECHR by protecting such rights of persons against the acts of others. The first signs of such a practice were visible in the case of *X and Y v. the Netherlands*.[62] The Court held that the obligation derived from Article 8 ECHR to respect an individual's privacy imposed positive obligations that 'may involve the adoption of measures designed to secure respect for private life even in the sphere of the relations of individuals themselves.'[63]

Later, in entirely different settings, this line of reasoning was used again. In *Platform 'Ärtze für das Leben' v. Austria*, the Court held that the State must take reasonable and appropriate measures to ensure that a demonstration can take place and that Article 11 ECHR thus contains a positive obligation to protect demonstrators from interference by others.[64] Another example of such a positive obligation can be found in *Von Hannover v. Germany*, in which the Court held that Article 8 ECHR contains the positive obligation to protect one's privacy.[65]

For the question concerning the third-party applicability of human rights—the protection under the ECHR of individuals against other private persons—the term *Drittwirkung* is used in the German literature.[66] This term is consequently often also used to describe the last-mentioned category of positive obligations under the ECHR. However, this is somewhat misleading, as this notion in the German literature is concerned with the possibility of a private person relying on a national bill of rights to bring a claim against another individual.[67] Human rights have to be

---

[60] Harris et al. 2009, p. 7.

[61] Mowbray 2004, p. 224.

[62] *X and Y v. the Netherlands*, 26 March 1985, ECHR Series A no. 91. See also Alkema 1988, p. 37; Clapham 1993a, pp. 163–164.

[63] *X and Y v. the Netherlands*, 26 March 1985, para 23, ECHR Series A no. 91.

[64] *Platform Ärtze für das Leben v. Austria*, 21 June 1988, ECHR Series A no. 139.

[65] *Von Hannover v. Germany*, no. 59320/00, ECHR 2004-VI.

[66] See for an elaboration of the principle of *Drittwirkung*: Alkema 1988, pp. 33–45; Clapham 1993b, pp. 63–82; see also Clapham 1993a.

[67] See Lewan 1968, p. 571ff.

respected by the State and consequently by all of its institutions. However, can other parties also be bound by the ECHR? It is clear that even if the ECHR is valid between private parties, only States can be held accountable before the Court in Strasbourg. Thus one could say that with regard to the ECHR, there is only place for indirect third party applicability, or *mittelbare Drittwirkung*, which is reminiscent of the positive obligation construction of Contracting Parties being responsible for the protection of ECHR rights of people against third parties, discussed above.

Thus one could state that the ECHR has a certain 'horizontal effect' in the sense that one can bring up the ECHR against other individuals, but one can do this only indirectly, as such a complaint must be phrased as a complaint against one of the Contracting Parties. One can only succeed in this endeavor by phrasing such a complaint as a situation in which the Contracting Party failed to live up to its positive obligations under a certain right guaranteed in the ECHR.

This horizontal effect of the ECHR could naturally be important with regard to issues of private international law, as private parties are the subjects of private international law. An example of such use of the ECHR in an issue of private international law can, for example, be found in certain cases concerning international child abduction. These cases commence with a complaint by one parent against the abducting parent, but if such a case ends up before the Court in Strasbourg the complaint is no longer directed against the abducting parent (which would be fruitless), but instead against the Contracting Party which has allegedly failed its positive obligation following from Article 8 ECHR in re-uniting the child and the parent left behind.[68]

3.5.1 The Nature of the Rights Guaranteed in the ECHR

It is possible to categorize the rights guaranteed in Section I of the ECHR in several distinctive ways. For example, the rights guaranteed in the ECHR can be categorized as either absolute rights, qualified rights, or limited rights.[69] One should note that this latter category of limited rights is not often distinguished. However this distinction is useful for our discussion because it corresponds with whether it is possible for the Contracting Parties to restrict these rights in their operation and, if so, under which conditions. An important issue of this research will be the extent to which Contracting Parties may restrict the rights guaranteed in the ECHR in issues of private international law. The theoretical framework provided by the categorization of rights as absolute, qualified, and limited is thus valuable for this research. Moreover, this categorization will offer the opportunity

68 See, e.g., *P.P. v. Poland*, no. 8677/03, para 81, 8 January 2008; *Ignaccolo-Zenide v. Romania*, no. 31679/96, para 94, ECHR 2000-I.

69 See, e.g., Lambert 2006, p. 27ff; Cf. White and Ovey 2010, p. 9, who merely distinguish between unqualified and qualified rights.

70 See, e.g., White and Ovey 2010, pp. 8–10.

to further discuss the restrictions or limitations that are possible under the respective rights guaranteed in the ECHR. I should emphasize that regardless of this categorization, there is no formal hierarchy between the rights and freedoms that are guaranteed in the ECHR.[70] This means that in the case of a conflict between individual freedom rights, the Court (or, in an earlier stage, national courts) will have to strike a balance between the competing rights of individuals.

3.5.1.1 Absolute Rights

Absolute rights under the ECHR are the rights which are non-derogable under Article 15 ECHR. Article 15 ECHR, in the first paragraph, allows the Contracting States to derogate from a number of provisions during times of war or other public emergencies threatening the nation, but the second paragraph sets out a number of rights which cannot be derogated from under any circumstances. These are, respectively, the right to life in Article 2 ECHR (even though some exceptions are listed in this Article); the prohibition of torture, inhuman or degrading treatment in Article 3; freedom from slavery and forced or compulsory labor in Article 4; and freedom from the retrospective effect of penal legislation in Article 7 ECHR. It should be noted, however, that the absolute rights are not particularly relevant with regard to the impact of the ECHR on private international law, as issues of private international law are usually not concerned with the above-mentioned rights.

3.5.1.2 Qualified Rights

Qualified rights are rights which are subject to interference by the Contracting Party in order to secure certain interests, which are expressly stated in the Article itself. These interests are either the operation of the rights of others, or the needs of society. These rights thus require a balancing act by the Contracting Party, whereby a possible limitation of the rights should be weighed against the rights of others or the well-being of society. The Court's assessment of a Contracting Party's weighing of interests follows a set pattern, which will be discussed in the next paragraph. Qualified rights include, inter alia, the right to respect for private and family life, home, and correspondence in Article 8 ECHR; freedom of thought, conscience, and religion in Article 9 ECHR; freedom of expression in Article 10 ECHR; and freedom of assembly and associations in Article 11 ECHR, and also Article 1 of Protocol No. 1 ECHR. As noted above, Article 8 ECHR and Article 1 of Protocol No. 1 ECHR are particularly relevant rights with regard to the impact of the ECHR on private international law.

The Court has developed a set pattern with regard to its assessment of restrictions to qualified rights. The qualified rights of Articles 8 to 11 of the ECHR have, for example, a similar limitation clause. If an interference of one of the rights contained in these Articles is found, one has to determine whether such interference can be justified on the basis of the three standards that are laid down in the second paragraph of the respective Articles. When the Court identifies an interference of one of these Articles, it has to determine whether such interference was 'in accordance with law' or 'prescribed by law', whether it pursued a legitimate aim—whether the restriction matches one of the aims which are exhaustively provided in the second paragraph of Articles 8 to 11 ECHR and which vary slightly—and whether the interference was 'necessary in a democratic society'. These requirements are cumulative. The Court has expanded on these points in its case law.

It follows from the case law that the Court usually works through these points in order, but it will occasionally skip a point, if it can easily establish that one of the other points will lead to an unlawful interference. It also follows from the case law that the second condition, the legitimate aim, is not a difficult hurdle to overcome for the Contracting Parties, as the Court will usually accept the aims put forward by the Contracting Parties.[71] However, the first restriction concerning the prescription by law is examined quite strictly by the Court, and the third condition concerning necessity in a democratic society in particular will be scrutinized meticulously.[72]

The required legal basis for an interference means that the restriction must have some basis in the national law of the Contracting Party, and this law must also be foreseeable and accessible.[73] The Court will, in principle, accept the interpretation of the national law given by the national courts, unless there are very compelling reasons not to do so.[74] The law does not need to be a (national) statute: common law rules are accepted,[75] as well as rules following from an international treaty,[76] a (formerly) EC Regulation,[77] and under certain circumstances, even an order by the authorities.[78]

---

71 See for a rare exception, e.g., *Darby v. Sweden*, 23 October 1990, Series A-187. See also *Sidiropoulos and Others v. Greece*, 10 July 1998, Reports of Judgments and Decisions 1998-IV.

72 Cf. van Dijk et al. 2006, p. 335.

73 See, e.g., *Sunday Times v. the United Kingdom*, 26 April 1979, paras 46–53, ECHR Series A no. 30.

74 See for such a rare exception *Roche v. the United Kingdom*, para 120.

75 *Sunday Times v. the United Kingdom*, 26 April 1979, ECHR Series A no. 30.

76 *Slivenko v. Latvia* [GC], no. 48321/99, ECHR 2003-X.

77 *Bosphorus Hava Yolları Turizm ve Ticaret Anonim Şirketi v. Ireland* [GC], no. 45036/98, ECHR 2005-VI.

78 *Oliveira v. the Netherlands*, no. 33129/96, ECHR 2002-IV.

79 One could with regard to this requirement in relation to the subject of this research wonder whether rules of private international law are at all necessary in a democratic society. However, the Court has clearly not approached this requirement in such a manner, as follows from its case law concerning issues of private international law.

80 See, e.g., *Sunday Times v. the United Kingdom*, 26 April 1979, ECHR Series A no. 30.

81 See with regard to the notion of the margin of appreciation infra Sect. 3.5.2.

82 See, e.g. *Groppera Radio AG and Others v. Switzerland*, 28 March 1990, para 72, ECHR Series A no. 173. See for the classic formulation of whether a restriction is necessary in a democratic society *Silver and Others v. the United Kingdom*, 25 March 1983, para 97, Series A no. 61.

What the requirement of 'necessary in a democratic society' entails has been established by the Court in its case law.[79] For an interference to be necessary in a democratic society, there must be 'a pressing social need'.[80] It is, in principle, for the Contracting Party to assess whether there is such a pressing social need and the Contracting Party does enjoy a margin of appreciation.[81] However, in reviewing the Contracting Party's assessment in this regard, the Court will evaluate whether the restriction was proportionate to the legitimate aim pursued and whether perhaps another less invasive measure could have been taken by the authorities.[82] The Court thus introduces here a fair balance test, having regard to the principles of proportionality (whether the measure was proportionate to the legitimate aim pursued) and subsidiarity (whether a less invasive measure could have been taken by the authorities).[83]

3.5.1.3 Limited Rights

Limited rights are rights which may only be limited under particular circumstances. Unlike qualified rights, these circumstances are not prescribed in the Article itself, but it is generally accepted that the Contracting Parties have less discretion in restricting these rights.[84] These limitations have also been referred to as 'inherent limitations'.[85] An example of a limited right is Article 6(1) ECHR, which guarantees the right to a fair trial. Under particular circumstances this right may be limited. These implied limitations are particularly relevant with regard to issues of private international law, as the following examples will further demonstrate.

In *Soering v. the United Kingdom*[86] the Court found that Article 6(1) ECHR has an extra-territorial effect in cases concerning extradition, and that it would be possible under that Article to raise the argument that Article 6 ECHR would have been violated 'where the fugitive has suffered or risks suffering a flagrant denial of a fair trial in the requesting country.'[87] This approach was confirmed in *Drozd and Janousek v. France and Spain.*[88] This standard has since also been discussed among specialists of private international law with regard to both the application of a foreign law and the recognition and enforcement of foreign judgments.[89]

In these cases concerning Article 6 ECHR and international co-operation, the Court has thus introduced the standard of 'a flagrant denial of justice', which could

---

[83] See with regard to these principles generally, e.g., Christoffersen 2009; Eissen 1993, pp. 125–146. See also Arai-Takahashi 2002.

[84] Cf. Lambert 2006, p. 47.

[85] van Dijk et al. 2006, p. 343ff.

[86] *Soering v. the United Kingdom*, 7 July 1989, Series A no. 161.

[87] *Soering v. the United Kingdom*, para 115, 7 July 1989, Series A no. 161.

[88] *Drozd and Janousek v. France and Spain*, 26 June 1992, Series A no. 240.

[89] See infra Sects. 6.3.2 and 7.5–6.

[90] Cf. Lambert 2006, pp. 47–48.

be viewed as an inherent limitation to the right to a fair trial under particular circumstances in the sense that the threshold for finding a violation of Article 6(1) ECHR under such circumstances is high.[90] In such cases, which are concerned with the applicability of the ECHR to situations taking place in another country, particularly in third countries, the Court thus does find that Article 6(1) ECHR may be violated, but only in the event of a 'flagrant denial of justice'. The Court, taking account of the cross-border dimension of these cases, thus introduces an attenuated standard of control of the ECHR in such cases. It is clear that such a standard of control in cross-border cases is highly relevant for cases concerning private international law (refer footnote 89).

Another example of a right which is susceptible to being inherently limited is the right of access to a court, which is a right derived from Article 6 ECHR.[91] When the Court first derived this right from the right to a fair trial in *Golder v. the United Kingdom*,[92] it had actually already held that this right was inherently limited.[93] It will be demonstrated that this right of access to a court plays an important role with regard to the impact of the ECHR on the issue of jurisdiction in private international law.[94]

3.5.2 The Margin of Appreciation

The margin of appreciation doctrine plays an important part in the interpretation of the rights guaranteed in the ECHR.[95] The doctrine of the margin of appreciation is an expression of the Court's 'delicate task of balancing the sovereignty of Contracting Parties with their obligations under the Convention.'[96] It has been argued that the doctrine is founded upon subsidiarity.[97] The Court merely reviews the measures taken at a national level and in that regard it has held that national authorities are often better equipped to evaluate local issues. However, the Court, naturally, has the final word in these matters and decides whether Contracting

[91] One should note that is also possible to distinguish inherently limited rights as a separate category of rights, which may be limited, but where the grounds for such limitation are not included in the Article. See, e.g., Gerards 2011, p. 108ff.

[92] *Golder v. the United Kingdom,* 21 February 1975, Series A no. 18.

[93] See *Golder v. the United Kingdom,* 21 February 1975, paras 21, 37–41, Series A no. 18; cf. *Osman v. the United Kingdom*, 28 October 1998, para 147, Reports of Judgments and Decisions 1998-VIII; see also, e.g., van Dijk et al. 2006, p. 343ff.

[94] See infra Chap. 5.

[95] The doctrine is one of one of the most frequently discussed aspects of the ECHR. See, e.g., Arai-Takahashi 2002; Greer 2000; Kratochvíl 2011, pp. 324–357 as well as the handbooks cited supra n. 1.

[96] MacDonald 1992, p. 103.

[97] See, e.g., Gerards 2005, p. 166.

[98] See supra Sect. 3.5.1.2.

Parties are left a margin of appreciation and consequently what its scope will be. In *Handyside* the Court found that Contracting Parties have a margin of appreciation with regard to the standard of 'necessary in a democratic society', as, for example, found in the second paragraph of Articles 8 to 11 ECHR, and generally with regard to qualified rights.[98]

However, the Strasbourg Institutions have extended the use of this doctrine by finding that national authorities have a margin of appreciation when they have to strike a balance between the right of an individual and the interests of society as a whole.[99] The Court has also used the doctrine for evaluating emergency measures *ex* Article 15 ECHR.[100]

The margin of appreciation differs from right to right and from case to case; it is impossible to establish a State's margin of appreciation *in abstracto*.[101] The Court often finds that the Contracting Parties have 'a certain margin of appreciation' without further detailing the extent of the margin.[102] Generally speaking, the Court adheres to strict(er) scrutiny of the margin of appreciation (a narrow margin) where there is a common European standard, while it uses a wide margin in the absence of such a European standard.[103] It is, for example, possible to speak of a common European standard with regard to Article 6 ECHR, the right to a fair trial.[104] Here, a Contracting Party's margin of appreciation would be more limited than compared, for example, to an issue concerning 'good morals', in relation to which the Court has frequently held that the Contracting Parties would have a more considerable margin.

---

99 Arai-Takahashi 2002, p. 8.

100 See *Lawless v. Ireland*, no. 332/57, 2 Yearbook of European Commission on Human Rights (1960), p. 318. See also O'Boyle 1998, pp. 23–29.

101 See, e.g., the dissenting opinion of Judge Malinverni, joined by Judge Kaladjieva, in *Lautsi v. Italy* [GC], no. 30814/06, 18 March 2011. Judge Malinverni held that '[w]hilst the doctrine of the margin of appreciation may be useful, or indeed convenient, it is a tool that needs to be handled with care because the scope of that margin will depend on a great many factors: the right in issue, the seriousness of the infringement, the existence of a European consensus, etc.'

102 This practice started in *Sunday Times v. the United Kingdom*, 26 April 1979, para 62, Series A No. 30.

103 See further on the scope of the margin of appreciation, e.g., Lawson and Schermers 1999, pp. 38–39.

104 See, e.g., Arai-Takahashi 2002, p. 15; White and Ovey 2010, p. 329.

105 Greer 2000, p. 5. It is, incidentally, interesting to observe the similarities between the manner in which the margin of appreciation and the public policy exception in private international law are described. See supra Sect. 2.5.

106 See, e.g., Arai-Takahashi 2002, p. 8; Greer 2000, p. 5. It is also interesting to discuss and compare this notion with the functioning of the public policy exception in private international law. See supra Sect. 2.5.

107 See particularly Chaps. 5–8.

However, it should be stressed again that the interpretation of the margin of appreciation is notoriously difficult: it has a 'casuistic, uneven, and largely unpredictable nature.'[105] What the margin has to offer, though, is a certain latitude or room for maneuver for Contracting Parties as to how they fulfill their obligations following from the ECHR.[106] It is this room that may be crucial for the application of the rights guaranteed in the ECHR to private international law disputes. As will be discussed in this research, it has been argued that as private international law is inherently concerned with a foreign element, there may be a need for the attenuation of the standards provided by the ECHR.[107] The margin of appreciation is a prime candidate for providing such flexibility.[108] It should also be noted that the Court is of the opinion that the margin of appreciation solely concerns the relationship between the domestic authorities and the Court. It should not be used in the same manner by national courts.[109]

3.6 The Future of the System of Protection Offered by the ECHR

A look at the future of the system of protection offered by the ECHR should not be excluded from this chapter, as future developments may have an impact on the direction of the Court's case law,[110] which in turn will also impact upon the findings of this research. There are two developments that can be distinguished which may alter the way the Court will work in the future. One is related to a problem that has plagued the Court for quite some time, but which the Court and the Contracting Parties have not yet been able to get under control, and that is the Court's case-load.

---

[108] See further particularly the discussion on the attenuation of the standards of the ECHR in Sect. 6.3.2.

[109] *A. and Others v. the United Kingdom* [GC], no. 3455/05, para 184, ECHR 2009.

[110] There is much discussion on the future direction of the Court. See, e.g., Gerards and Terlouw 2011.

[111] See 'The ECHR in facts & Figs. 2011' The various reports on statistical information regarding the ECHR may be found at: http://www.echr.coe.int/Pages/home.aspx?p=reports&c=. Accessed March 2014.

[112] Supra n. 111.

[113] The number of applications allocated to a judicial formation in the past five years shows a steady influx of new applications: 2007: 41,650 applications; 2008: 49,850 applications; 2009: 57,100 applications; 2010: 61,300 applications; 2011: 64,500 applications. See further supra n. 111.

[114] van Dijk et al. 2006, p. 36.

On 1 January 2012 approximately 151,600 applications were pending.[111] Considering that in 2011 the Court handled 52,188 applications,[112] and that a steady influx of new applications is to be expected,[113] it should be clear that this is an enormous problem for the Court. This problem, of course, did not materialize overnight. In fact, in the past a number of actions have been taken to reverse this trend. The reform of the supervisory system brought about by Protocol 11 was largely motivated by the increasing workload of the then existing institutions.[114] This reform proved to be inefficient in dealing with the ever-increasing workload, and subsequently Protocol 14 was introduced to further streamline the process, mainly by allowing the Court to devote less time to clearly inadmissible cases.[115] However, as acknowledged in the Brighton Declaration, even these changes did not prove to be enough and a further revision of the system will be pursued.[116]

Another development that should be mentioned is the discussion on whether the Court should focus more on the most serious cases and whether it should be more deferential in other cases. The latter part of the discussion was rekindled in the run-up to the Brighton Conference because public officials in the United Kingdom (UK) openly questioned whether the UK should defy the Court's judgment in *Hirst No. 2 v. the United Kingdom*,[117] in which the Court rejected the blanket ban on a prisoner's right to vote.[118] The Brighton Declaration could be read as an attempt to rein in the power of the Court in Strasbourg, as the role of both the principle of subsidiarity and the margin of appreciation is emphasized by the Contracting Parties in this document.[119] However it should also be noted that the Contracting Parties open the Brighton Declaration with a reaffirmation of their 'deep and abiding commitment' to the ECHR.[120]

The related discussion on whether the Court should not focus more on the most serious violations is not new. Back in 1986 the President of the Court noted that

---

[115] Protocol 14 finally entered into force on 1 June 2010, three months after the ratification by the last State to do so, which was Russia. Protocol No. 14 was originally adopted by the Council of Europe Committee of Ministers in May 2004. It took Russia a long time to ratify the Protocol. In fact, it took so long—while the Court's case load continued to grow—that the Committee of Ministers adopted Protocol 14 *bis* in the meantime, in order to provisionally apply certain measures provided by Protocol 14. Protocol 14 *bis* ceased to be in force from the moment Protocol 14 entered into force. See with regard to Protocol No. 14, e.g., Reiss 2009, pp. 293–318; see also the 'Explanatory Report' to Protocol No. 14, which is available at: conventions.coe.int/Treaty/EN/Reports/Html/194.htm. Accessed March 2014.

[116] See no. 6 of the 'Brighton Declaration', which is available at: http://hub.coe.int/en/20120419-brighton-declaration/. Accessed March 2014.

[117] *Hirst v. the United Kingdom (no. 2)* [GC], no. 74025/01, ECHR 2005-IX.

[118] See, e.g., Davis and Straw 2012.

[119] See particularly no. 12 (a) and (b) of the Brighton Declaration supra n. 117. See also no. 11 and no. 15 (d).

[120] See no. 1 of the Brighton Declaration supra n. 117.

[121] Ryssdal 1996, pp. 22–23.

[122] Cf. Mahoney 1999, pp. 2–4. See with regard to the possible limitations under the ECHR supra Sect. 3.5.1.

the ECHR was being applied to relatively minor and technical matters, which were far removed from the issues which the drafters had in mind back in the day.[121] One could say in this regard that there are two categories of violations: the ECHR after all not only protects against the abuse of power by the State, but also against limitations on the rights and freedoms guaranteed in the ECHR where such limitations go beyond what is necessary.[122] From the beginning—when only Western European countries were Contracting Parties—the Court focused more on the latter violations over the course of time. This changed with the expansion of the Council of Europe into Eastern Europe after the fall of the Berlin Wall. Suddenly the first category of abuse of power by the State returned to the forefront. The Court has had to deal with both categories of violations simultaneously ever since. It should be clear that if the Court was to focus on the more serious violations of the ECHR to a greater extent in the future, this would lead to fewer cases concerning issues of private international law.

References

Aemisegger H (2005) The Federal Judge vis-à-vis the Jurisdiction of the ECHR. In: Pernice I, Stöbener P (eds) The future of the European judicial system in a comparative perspective. Nomos, Baden-Baden, pp 309–314

Alkema EA (1988) The third-party applicability or 'Drittwirkung' of the European convention on human rights. In Matscher F, Petzold H (eds), Protecting human rights: the European dimension. Studies in honour of Gérard J. Wiarda. Carl Heymanns Verlag KG, Köln, pp 33–45

Arai-Takahashi Y (2002) The margin of appreciation doctrine and the principle of proportionality in the jurisprudence of the ECHR. Intersentia, Antwerp

Besson S (2008) The reception process in Ireland and the United Kingdom. In: Keller H, Stone Sweet A (eds) A Europe of rights: the impact of the ECHR on national legal systems. Oxford University Press, Oxford, pp 31–106

Blackburn R, Polakiewicz J (2001) Fundamental rights in Europe: the European convention on human rights and its member states, 1950–2000. Oxford University Press, Oxford

Brownlie I (2008) Principles of public international law. Oxford University Press, Oxford

Christoffersen J (2009) Fair balance: proportionality, subsidiarity and primarity in the European convention on human rights. Nijhoff, Leiden

Clapham A (1993a) Human rights in the private sphere. Clarendon Press, Oxford

Clapham A (1993b) The 'Drittwirkung' of the convention. In: MacDonald R St J, Matscher F et al (eds) The European system for the protection of human rights. Martinus Nijhoff, Dordrecht, pp 63–82

Davis D, Straw J (2012) We must defy Strasbourg on prisoner votes. The Telegraph, 24 May. www.telegraph.co.uk/news/uknews/law-and-order/9287633/We-must-defy-Strasbourg-on-prisoner-votes.html. Accessed Mar 2014

de Boer Th M (2010) Samenloop van verdragen en verordeningen op het terrein van het internationaal familierecht [Concurrence of treaties and regulations in the area of international family law]. Familie en jeugdrecht 32:308–315

De Wet E (2008) The reception process in the Netherlands and Belgium. In: Keller H, Stone Sweet A (eds) A Europe of rights: the impact of the ECHR on national legal systems. Oxford University Press, Oxford, pp 229–309

Eissen MA (1993) The principle of proportionality in the case-law of the European Court of Human Rights. In: MacDonald R St J, Matscher F et al (eds) The European system for the protection of human rights. Martinus Nijhoff, Dordrecht, pp 125–146
Gannagé L (2001) La hiérarchie des normes et les méthodes du droit international privé: etude de droit international privé de la famille. L.G.D.J, Paris
Gerards JH (2005) Judicial review in equal treatment cases. Nijhoff, Leiden
Gerards JH (2011) EVRM. Algemene beginselen [ECHR. General principles]. Sdu Uitgevers, Den Haag
Gerards JH, Terlouw A (eds) (2011) Amici Curiae. Adviezen aan het Europees Hof voor de Rechten van de Mens [Amici Curiae. Advice to the European Court of Human Rights]. Wolf Legal Publishers, Nijmegen
Greer SC (2000) The margin of appreciation: interpretation and discretion under the European convention on human right. Council of Europe, Strasbourg
Harris DJ et al (eds) (2009) Law of the European convention on human rights. Oxford University Press, Oxford
Hins AW, Nieuwenhuis AJ (2010) Hoofdstukken grondrechten [Chapters fundamental rights]. Ars Aequi Libri, Nijmegen
Janis MW et al (2008) European human rights law: text and materials. Oxford University Press, Oxford
Jenks CW (1953) The conflict of law-making treaties. BYIL 30:401–453
Keller H, Stone Sweet A (eds) (2008) A Europe of rights: the impact of the ECHR on national legal systems. Oxford University Press, Oxford
Kratochvíl J (2011) The inflation of the margin of appreciation by the European Court of Human Rights. Neth Q Hum Rights 29:324–357
Lambert H (2006) The position of aliens in relation to the European convention on human rights. Council of Europe Publishing, Strasbourg
Lawson RA, Schermers HG (1999) Leading cases of the European Court of Human Rights. Ars Aequi Libri, Nijmegen
Leach P (2011) Taking a case to the European Court of Human Rights. Oxford University Press, Oxford
Lequette Y (2004) Le droit international privé et les droits fondamentaux. In: Cabrillac R et al (eds) Libertés et droit fondamentaux. Dalloz, Paris, pp 97–118
Lewan KM (1968) The significance of constitutional rights for private law: theory and practice in West Germany. ICLQ 17
MacDonald R St J (1992) The margin of appreciation in the jurisprudence of the European Court of Human Rights. Collected courses of the Academy of European Law 1 book, vol 2. Kluwer Academic Publishers, Dordrecht, pp 95–161
Mahoney P (1999) Speculating on the future of the reformed European Court of Human Rights. Hum Rights Law J 20:1–4
Mowbray AR (2004) The development of positive obligations under the European Convention on Human Rights by the European Court of Human Rights. Hart Publishing, Portland
Mowbray AR (2012) Cases, materials, and commentary on the European Convention on Human Rights. Oxford University Press, Oxford
O'Boyle M (1998) The margin of appreciation and derogation under article 15: ritual incantation or principle? Hum Rights Law J 19:23–29
Petzold H (1993) The convention and the principle of subsidiarity. In: MacDonald R St J, Matscher F et al (eds) The European system for the protection of human rights. Martinus Nijhoff, Dordrecht, pp 41–62
Reiss JW (2009) Protocol No. 14 ECHR and Russian non-ratification: the current state of affairs. Harv Hum Rights J 2:293–318

Robertson AH (1977) Human rights in Europe. Manchester University Press, Manchester
Ryssdal R (1996) The coming of age of the European convention on human rights. Eur Hum Rights Law Rev 1:18–29
Sadat-Akhavi SA (2003) Methods of resolving conflicts between treaties. Martinus Nijhoff Publishers, Leiden
Shelton D (2006) Normative hierarchy in international law. AJIL 100:291–323
Thurnherr D (2008) The reception process in Austria and Switzerland. In: Keller H, Stone Sweet A (eds) A Europe of rights: the impact of the ECHR on national legal systems. Oxford University Press, Oxford, pp 311–391
van Dijk P et al (eds) (2006) Theory and practice of the European convention on human rights. Intersentia, Antwerp
Vidmar J, De Wet E (eds) Hierarchy in international law: the place of human rights. Oxford University Press, Oxford
White RCA, Ovey C (2010) The European convention on human rights. Oxford University Press, Oxford
Wildhaber L (2007) The European convention on human rights and international law. ICLQ 56:217–232
Xenos D (2012) The positive obligations of the state under the European convention of human rights. Routledge, London

Chapter 4
Article 1 ECHR and Private International Law

Contents

4.1 Introduction

In discussions concerning the impact of the European Convention on Human Rights on private international law, the relationship between its Article 1 ECHR, which defines the scope of the ECHR, and private international law does not generally receive a great deal of attention.[1] Occasionally the relationship is

[1] An early—and much shorter—version of this chapter was presented at the Colloquium 'The Impact of the European Convention on Human Rights (ECHR) on Private International Law', organized by the University of Amsterdam on 12 November 2010, as a part of the VICI Project of the Netherlands Organisation for Scientific Research entitled: The Emerging International Constitutional Order: the Implications of Hierarchy in International Law for the Coherence and Legitimacy of International Decision-making. This presentation was subsequently published in the journal *Nederlands Internationaal Privaatrecht (NIPR)*, which devoted a special edition to the subject of human rights and private international law. See Kiestra 2011, pp. 2–7. See also Stürner 2011, pp. 8–12.

L.R. Kiestra, *The Impact of the European Convention on Human Rights on Private International Law*, DOI 10.1007/978-94-6265-032-9_4

discussed in the literature,[2] but national courts, in particular, appear to pay relatively little attention to the issue of the applicability of the ECHR to private international law cases. This is, however, exactly what is at stake: is the ECHR at all applicable to private international law cases? This is an important preliminary question to the issue of what the impact of the ECHR may be on private international law.

Private international law by its very nature introduces foreign elements to legal orders. Intermittently, private international law will introduce foreign elements originating from third countries, i.e. countries that are not Contracting Parties to the ECHR. In the case of, for example, a foreign applicable law or a foreign judgment from a third country, it is interesting to see what the role of Article 1 ECHR is. One could argue that by virtue of extending the control of the ECHR over the foreign law originating from a third country, a notion of extra-territoriality is introduced in the sense that the ECHR would then apply to a law originating from a country that has never signed this instrument. A similar reasoning applies to foreign judgments emanating from third countries.

In order to examine this issue, a closer examination of the meaning and background of Article 1 ECHR is required (in Sect. 4.2), whereby the notion of 'jurisdiction' contained in this Article will be scrutinized (Sect. 4.2.1). This is important because the term jurisdiction has several distinct meanings in (private) international law and without further clarification the use of this term may lead to confusion. The afore-mentioned notion of extra-territoriality will also receive due attention (Sect. 4.2.2), as well as the case law of the European Court of Human Rights on this subject (Sects. 4.2.3 and 4.2.4). Next, the relationship between Article 1 ECHR and private international law will be further examined (Sect. 4.3). Thereafter some consequences of the findings will be discussed, accompanied by a brief survey of national case law dealing with Article 1 ECHR and private international law (Sect. 4.4), before a brief conclusion is offered (Sect. 4.5).

Before moving on to this discussion I would like to quickly turn to a Dutch case that further illustrates exactly what the issue is here.

In a case before the Dutch Supreme Court (*Hoge Raad*) of 12 December 2008,[3] the mother of a child wanted to judicially establish the paternity of a man of her child. The mother and child both had Surinamese nationality and that is where they also had their habitual residence. The prospective father had Dutch nationality and lived in the Netherlands. The man had acknowledged being the biological father of the child. According to the relevant Dutch choice-of-law rules in force at the time,[4]

---

[2] See, e.g., Bucher 2000, pp. 82–86; Docquir 1999, pp. 476–481, 507; Flauss 2002, pp. 69–71; Kinsch 2007, p. 226ff; Thoma 2007, p. 91ff.

[3] *HR* 12 December 2008, *RvdW* 2009, 41; *NIPR* 2009, 1.

[4] Article 6 *Wet conflictenrecht afstamming* [Parentage (Conflict of Laws) Act], 14 March 2002, *Stb.* 2002, 153. This law has since been replaced by Boek 10 *Burgerlijk Wetboek*. See with regard to parentage particularly Title 5, Article 10:92 BW onwards. *Vaststellings- en Invoeringswet Boek 10 Burgerlijk Wetboek* [Determination and Implementation Book 10 of the Dutch Civil Code], 19 May 2011, *Stb.* 2011, 272.

the law of Surinam was applicable in this case. However under Surinamese law it is not possible to judicially establish the paternity of a child. At issue was whether the application of Surinamese law, which would lead to a denial of the mother's request, would violate the Dutch *ordre public* and/or Articles 8 and 14 ECHR and that thus Dutch law would consequently have to be applied to this case. The two lower courts rejected the mother's request. The *Gerechtshof* (the Court of Appeal) held that the child could also be recognized by the man abroad. The mere fact that the applicable foreign law in question does not include the possibility to judicially establish paternity, while Dutch law does, cannot lead to the setting aside of the normally applicable foreign law. Only exceptional circumstances, which would lead to an untenable situation for the child, could suffice for such a solution. There were no such circumstances in this case, according to the appeal court.[5] Before the *Hoge Raad* the appeal by the mother was dismissed, because her complaints could not lead to cassation (appeal).

The most pressing issue in this case for our purposes in this chapter concerns a point raised by the Advocate General Strikwerda in his Conclusion. He asked—in passing, I should add—whether the minor in this case came within the jurisdiction of the Netherlands, as understood in Article 1 ECHR. He immediately made clear that due to the circumstances of the case, this question did not need an answer, but he did briefly point to four cases which could be of guidance.[6] The first is the rather famous *Banković and Others v. Belgium and Others* case,[7] which will be discussed below. The other three cases the Advocate General mentioned are cases which came before the *Hoge Raad*.[8] These cases cover miscellaneous subjects, ranging from a family law case concerning a claim against a mother to surrender her child, to the extradition of an American soldier suspected of murder, to a case similar to the afore-mentioned *Banković* case. The common feature of these cases is that they concern the application of Article 1 ECHR.

The Advocate General ultimately only gave these hints in the Surinam case and did not answer the question he posed. Other interesting issues were also raised in this case, but unfortunately no substantive decision was taken by the *Hoge Raad*.[9] In my opinion, this case neatly illustrates the issue with which this chapter is concerned. What is the role of Article 1 ECHR in private international law cases? What are the limits of the application of the ECHR in this regard? When the applicants who invoke the ECHR come from a non-Contracting Party and either

---

[5] See Hof 's-Gravenhage 3 October 2007, *NIPR* 2008, 7. See, particularly no. 8.

[6] Para 13 of the Conclusion supra n. 3.

[7] *Banković and Others v. Belgium and 16 Other Contracting States* (dec.) [GC], no. 52207/99, ECHR 2001-XI.

[8] He mentioned respectively HR 30 March 1990, *NJ* 1991, 249; HR 15 April 1994, *NJ* 1994, 576, *NIPR* 1994, 210; and HR 29 November 2002, *NJ* 2003, 35.

[9] See for a more detailed discussion of this case and two other Dutch cases concerning the judicial establishment of paternity: Kiestra 2010, pp. 27–30. Incidentally, in the other two cases two—lower—courts held under similar circumstances that the normally applicable foreign law had to be set aside. See for a discussion of these cases infra Chap. 6.

the law which is applicable to the case or the foreign judgment at issue also originates from a non-Contracting Party, can the ECHR still be invoked? Are *Banković* and related cases indeed the best model to explain the applicability of Article 1 ECHR in private international law cases? These are the questions that will be discussed in this chapter.

4.2 The Meaning of Article 1 ECHR and the Notion of Jurisdiction

Article 1 ECHR states as follows:

> The High Contracting parties shall secure to everyone within their jurisdiction the rights and freedoms defined in Section I of this Convention.[10]

Article 1 ECHR does not contain a specific right, but it does transform the ECHR into more than a mere declaration, as it clearly places an obligation on the Contracting Parties to secure the rights guaranteed in the ECHR. Further, it also delineates the scope of the ECHR.[11] The Article noticeably contains a scope requirement enclosed in the clause 'everyone within their jurisdiction'. The meaning of this phrase and the ensuing scope of the ECHR in general have been much discussed. A principal question in the Court's case law in this regard has been whether the ECHR can be said to be applicable extra-territorially, i.e. outside the territories of the Contracting Parties. I will return to this notion of extra-territoriality,[12] but before we further delve into that, it is prudent to first discuss the word 'jurisdiction' which is included in Article 1 ECHR, as this notion is used in several settings and may therefore easily be misunderstood. It will be demonstrated that the term 'jurisdiction' as used in Article 1 ECHR has little to do with how this term is normally used in private international law, while the relationship with how the term is used in public international law is unclear.

4.2.1 The Notion of Jurisdiction

The word jurisdiction has different meanings. It has even—rightfully, it appears—been remarked that the usage of the term jurisdiction is so varied that it is only possible to determine its exact meaning from context.[13] For specialists in the field of private international law, the term usually refers to the competence of a

[10] For good measure, its French counterpart reads: 'Les Hautes Parties contractantes reconnaissent à toute personne relevant de leur juridiction les droits et libertés définis au titre I de la présente Convention.'

[11] See, e.g., White and Ovey 2010, p. 84ff.

[12] See infra Sect. 4.2.4.

[13] Smit 1961, p. 164.

particular judge or, rather, the court(s) of a national State to hear an international case. As was discussed in Chaps. 1 and 2, this notion of jurisdiction is considered to be one of the three main issues of private international law, the other two being the issue of the applicable law and the recognition and enforcement of foreign judgments, respectively.[14]

Jurisdiction in this private international law sense has also been referred to as judicial or adjudicatory jurisdiction (the power of a State's court to hear cases), if put in terms of the jurisdiction of a State in public international law.[15] This type of jurisdiction should then be distinguished from the other two types of jurisdiction which are generally differentiated in (public) international law: legislative (or prescriptive) jurisdiction (the power of a State to legislate), and enforcement jurisdiction (the power of physical intervention by the executive, such as, for example, by seizing property or arresting a person).[16] It should also be understood that jurisdiction in private international law refers to (international) civil jurisdiction (as opposed to, for example, criminal jurisdiction). The afore-mentioned types of jurisdiction in public international law—the jurisdiction to legislate, to adjudicate, and to enforce—naturally do not exclusively deal with private (international) law.

The notion of adjudicatory jurisdiction, and more specifically international civil jurisdiction, will be examined more closely in the next chapter, which deals with jurisdiction in private international law and the impact of the ECHR.[17] However, it appears to be prudent to briefly dwell on the more general notion of jurisdiction in (public) international law here, if only because the Court in Strasbourg has often referred to this concept in its case law concerning the interpretation of the phrase 'everyone within their jurisdiction', albeit without always succeeding in offering much clarity on the subject.

4.2.2 The Notion of Jurisdiction in Public International Law

Jurisdiction in public international law is concerned with the authority of a State to regulate the conduct of all of its subjects and usually refers to the power exercised by a State over people, property, and events.[18] Jurisdiction is thus closely linked with the concept of state sovereignty.[19] It is possible to divide the concept of jurisdiction into three different types of jurisdiction, which are linked with

---

[14] See for a discussion of the impact of the ECHR on these three issues infra Chaps. 5–8.

[15] See further infra Sect. 4.2.2.

[16] See on the notion of jurisdiction Akehurst 1972–1973, pp. 145–257; Lowenfeld 1996; Mann 1964, pp. 1–162; Mann 1984, pp. 9–116; McLachlan 1993, pp. 125–144.

[17] See infra Sect. 5.2.

[18] Cf. Akehurst 1972–1973, p. 145; Mann 1964, pp. 9–10; Shaw 2008, pp. 645–649.

[19] See, e.g., Mann 1964, p. 20 Cf. Brownlie 2008, pp. 105–106; Cassese 2005, pp. 49–50.

different competences of a State.[20] These three were mentioned above.[21] It has been argued with regard to this subdivision that adjudicatory jurisdiction is 'not a separate type of jurisdiction, but merely an emanation of the international jurisdiction to legislate: a State's right of regulation is exercised by legislative jurisdiction which includes adjudication.'[22] However, this approach underestimates the distinctive features of a court's function in settling a dispute between two private parties and the State's power to draft legislation.[23]

It should be noted that the general principles guiding the assertion of jurisdiction may differ depending on which type of jurisdiction is at hand. However, it can safely be stated that the leading principle of jurisdiction is the territorial principle.[24] This naturally follows from the afore-mentioned link with sovereignty. All types of jurisdiction may be asserted by the State on its own territory. On its own territory the State's courts can unquestionably hear cases, regulate behavior by legislation, and enforce any decisions. The extent to which States are allowed to assert jurisdiction outside their territory, however, differs depending on the type of jurisdiction concerned.

The jurisdiction to enforce, for example, is, in principle, limited to the territory of a State.[25] States are generally not permitted to enforce any decision, regardless of its nature, on the territory of another State, although exceptions may be negotiated between States.[26] With regard to adjudication, one could also say that States are not allowed to settle disputes on the territory of another State. One may recall in this regard that in order for a Scottish court to sit at 'Kamp Zeist' in the Netherlands to hear the cases against the Libyan nationals accused of blowing up an American aircraft in Scottish airspace, an agreement between the Netherlands and the United Kingdom (UK) had to be struck.[27] For prescriptive (or legislative)

---

[20] Cf., e.g., Akehurst 1972–1973, p. 145ff; Lowenfeld 1996, particularly pp. 15–136; Shaw 2008, p. 649ff; Wautelet 2004, p. 55.

[21] Supra Sect. 4.2.1.

[22] Mann 1984, p. 67. It should be noted that it has also been questioned if enforcement jurisdiction is a primary competence of a State in this regard. See Higgins 1984, p. 4.

[23] McLachlan 1993, p. 128.

[24] Brownlie 2008, p. 299; Cassese 2005, p. 49; Nollkaemper 2009, pp. 104–105; Lowe and Staker 2010, pp. 314–315.

[25] This was stated by the Permanent Court of International Justice in the *Lotus* case. See PCIJ, 7 September 1927, Series A no. 10, pp. 18–19 (*Lotus*).

[26] As an example, one could cite the fact that troops of NATO Member States stationed in another Member State are principally subject to the authorities in the home State, giving the home State enforcement jurisdiction in the host State as well as prescriptive jurisdiction. Cf. Lowe and Staker 2010, p. 317. See for examples regarding prescriptive jurisdiction the many contributions on this issue in Olmstead 1984.

[27] Verdrag tussen de Regering van het Koninkrijk der Nederlanden en de Regering van het Verenigd Koninkrijk van Groot-Brittannië en Noord-Ierland inzake de rechtszitting van een Schots Hof in Nederland, 18 September 1998 (Trb. 1998, 237; 1999, 1;1999, 208 en 2007-172) [Dutch version]. See also the Agreement concerning a Scottish Trial in the Netherlands, 18 September 1998, UKTS No. 43 (1999).

jurisdiction, though, there is more room for the extra-territorial assertion of jurisdiction compared to the other two types of jurisdiction, as States have applied their laws extra-territorially in several areas of law, particularly economic laws.[28]

The factors on which the assertion of jurisdiction can be based may also diverge depending on the specific area of the law concerned. Let us take legislative jurisdiction as an example, as this type of jurisdiction has the greatest potential to be assumed more generously than the other two types. Some bases of jurisdiction may be used regardless of the subject matter. The afore-mentioned territoriality principle and the nationality principle could be cited here as examples. It is practically undisputed that States have the right to extend the reach of their laws to their nationals, whether they are inhabitants of the State or not.[29] The protective principle—the assumption of jurisdiction over aliens who have undertaken acts abroad against the State exercising jurisdiction—is also used for a wide variety of offenses, although this basis is obviously more limited.[30] The universality principle, however, is much more controversial and mostly limited to criminal matters, more particularly very serious crimes, such as crimes which may be prosecuted by the International Criminal Court.[31]

Finally, it should be noted that the term jurisdiction in public international law is also used to denote the jurisdiction of international tribunals. In this vein, the term is used to describe the scope of the right of an international tribunal to hear cases. This usage of the term is similar to its use in private international law in the sense that jurisdiction then refers to the jurisdiction of a court instead of a State.

In sum, jurisdiction in public international law is concerned with the authority of the State to regulate conduct. This notion of jurisdiction can be differentiated in several specific types of jurisdiction, which are linked to the different competences of the State. These types of jurisdiction have their own characteristics and the limits placed on them by international law may consequently differ depending on the precise type of jurisdiction at hand. It should thus be stressed that the notion of jurisdiction in (public) international law is not unambiguous and may, in fact, refer to several distinguishable facets of jurisdiction.

4.2.3 The Notion of Jurisdiction in Article 1 ECHR

What does the notion of jurisdiction in Article 1 ECHR exactly mean? This has been the focus of quite some debate.[32] The Court has naturally been a major

---

[28] See in this regard the contributions in Olmstead 1984. Note that this is mostly the case in relation to civil cases and not necessarily criminal cases.

[29] See, e.g., Lowe and Staker 2010, pp. 323–325.

[30] See, e.g., Brownlie 2008, pp. 304–305.

[31] See, e.g., Nollkaemper 2009, pp. 108–110. But see supra Sect. 1.1 on the possibility of universal civil jurisdiction.

[32] See, e.g., Gondek 2009; Harris et al. 2009, p. 804ff; Lawson 2004, pp. 83–123; Milanović 2008, pp. 411–448; O'Boyle 2004, pp. 125–139; and Orakhelashvili 2003, pp. 529–568.

contributor to this debate, which has mostly been focused on the meaning of the requirement 'within their jurisdiction' and the issue of extra-territoriality, as will be shown below. Before delving into this debate and an examination of some of the Court's case law in this regard, it may be useful to take one step back and first to focus solely on the use of the word 'jurisdiction' in Article 1 ECHR.

It has been demonstrated above that the word 'jurisdiction' has multiple meanings in public international law. It is, for example, not only used to describe a State's authority to regulate conduct, but also to refer to the competence of international tribunals. This is where confusion may arise. One should note that jurisdiction in Article 1 ECHR refers to the jurisdiction of a State, or, more precisely, the jurisdiction of the Contracting Parties.[33] This much follows from the text of Article 1 ECHR, which explicitly states '[t]he High Contracting Parties shall (...)'. It thus does not refer to the jurisdiction of a court. In this sense this notion also differs from jurisdiction in private international law, as that notion refers to the jurisdiction of a court.

The question now, of course, is whether this notion of jurisdiction as found in Article 1 ECHR is the same notion of jurisdiction which exists in public international law. As will be further discussed below in the discussion on the extra-territoriality of the ECHR, the Court has held in *Banković* that this is, in fact, the case.[34] However, the Court's assumption in this regard raises a question. As has been demonstrated above, the notion of jurisdiction in public international law is not unequivocal—it has three different aspects (adjudicatory, prescriptive, and enforcement) and its characteristics may differ depending on the circumstances. The question therefore is which notion of jurisdiction in international law is the Court exactly referring to in *Banković*?[35] This does not become clear, which makes the Court's statement in this case concerning the relationship between the notion of jurisdiction in international law and Article 1 ECHR unhelpful at best.

How should the notion of jurisdiction in Article 1 ECHR, then, be interpreted exactly? This is not easy to establish and probably requires a separate study.[36] For the purpose of this book it is not necessary to answer this question exhaustively. It suffices to recall that the term jurisdiction in Article 1 ECHR does not refer to the jurisdiction of the Court, but to the jurisdiction of the Contracting Parties. It has been suggested that 'jurisdiction' in Article 1 ECHR merely refers to the power, or the authority of the Contracting Parties, which is admittedly not a defined legal term, but this mere factual approach to the term does appear to be the best fit.[37]

---

33 Milanović 2008, p. 415.

34 *Banković and Others v. Belgium and 16 Other Contracting States* (dec.) [GC], no. 52207/99, para 36, ECHR 2001-XI.

35 Cf. Milanović 2008, pp. 417–422.

36 See in this regard Milanović 2011.

37 Milanović 2008, p. 434ff. See also Loucaides 2006 and Judge Loucaides' critique of *Banković* in his concurring opinion in *Assanidze v. Georgia* [GC], no. 71503/01, ECHR 2004-II and partly dissenting opinion in *Ilaşcu and Others v. Moldova and Russia* [GC], no. 48787/99, ECHR 2004-VII.

It is possible to conclude with the observation that jurisdiction in Article 1 ECHR refers to a threshold: it is first necessary to establish that a Contracting Party has jurisdiction in order for the Court in Strasbourg to examine a complaint under the ECHR.[38] Even though the word 'jurisdiction' in Article 1 ECHR may not refer to the jurisdiction of the Court, the Court's jurisdiction is, of course, related to that Article.

4.2.4 Article 1 ECHR and the Extra-Territorial Application of the ECHR

The scope of the ECHR is contained in the phrase 'within their jurisdiction' in Article 1 ECHR. In order to examine the precise meaning of this phrase for the scope of the ECHR and, subsequently, the meaning of Article 1 ECHR for private international law, it is useful first to discuss briefly the *travaux préparatoires* concerning Article 1 ECHR (Sect. 4.2.4.1). Thereafter, the extra-territorial scope of the ECHR will be further discussed (Sect. 4.2.4.2). It will be shown that with regard to the applicability of the ECHR to events taking place outside the territories of the Contracting Parties, a distinction needs to be made between the actual extra-territorial application of the ECHR (Section "The Extra-Territorial Application of the ECHR") and the extra-territorial effect of the ECHR (Section "The Extra-Territorial Effect of the ECHR").

4.2.4.1 The '*Travaux Préparatoires*' Concerning Article 1 ECHR

The Court has assigned fluctuating value to the '*travaux préparatoires*' in interpreting the ECHR.[39] Moreover, one could remark that the Court has held that the *travaux préparatoires* are not decisive for the interpretation of Article 1 of the ECHR.[40] Nevertheless, a look at the creation of Article 1 ECHR and, particularly, the phrase 'within their jurisdiction', is certainly worthwhile, as it will become clear that the founding fathers of the ECHR have deliberately chosen 'within their jurisdiction' over more stringent alternatives. Accordingly, this legislative history may shed some light on the ensuing debate on the extra-territoriality of the ECHR.

The Council of Europe's Consultative Assembly included a different provision with regard to the scope of the ECHR in Article 1 in its first draft of the Convention:

> In this Convention, the Member States shall undertake to ensure to all persons residing within their territories (…).[41]

---

[38] See Milanović 2008, pp. 415–417. Cf. White and Ovey 2010, p. 89.

[39] See, e.g. Harris et al. 2009, pp. 16–17.

[40] *Loizidou v. Turkey* (preliminary objections), 23 March 1995, para 71, Series A-310.

[41] *Collected Edition of the 'Travaux préparatoires' of the European Convention on Human Rights*, part II, 8 September 1949, p. 276.

One immediately notices the striking difference between this version and the current provision: instead of 'within their jurisdiction', 'residing within their territories' had been proposed by the Consultative Assembly.[42] When this draft was discussed by the Governmental Sub-Committee, however, another proposal was brought forward: 'residing' would be replaced by 'living in', in order to expand the scope of the (future) instrument. This subsequently triggered a new proposal, which should be more familiar to the reader—to replace the words 'residing within' by 'within its jurisdiction'. Interestingly, the proposal to replace 'residing within' was preceded by the following explanatory words:

> Since the aim of the amendment is to widen as far as possible the categories of persons who are to benefit by the guarantees contained in the Convention, and since the words 'living in' might give rise to a certain ambiguity (...).[43]

Eventually, the Committee of Experts settled on the current 'within their jurisdiction', while explicitly refusing the overly restrictive term 'residing', particularly because it was of the opinion that there were good reasons to extend the guarantees in the ECHR to all persons in the territories of the Contracting Parties, 'even those who could not be considered as residing there in the legal sense of the word.'[44] It is noteworthy that the founding fathers rejected a restrictive phrasing of the scope of the ECHR in Article 1 ECHR, and even pushed for a definition which would be as inclusive as possible. On the other hand, one must concede that at no time during the negotiations did the founding fathers appear to have pondered the notion of the extra-territorial application of the ECHR and it is thus wise not to go too far in trying to decipher the drafters' intentions.

4.2.4.2 The Extra-Territorial Scope of the ECHR

It was thus clearly the drafters' intention not to overtly restrict the meaning of the phrase 'within their jurisdiction'. In a very early case, *Austria v. Italy*,[45] the Court confirmed that the nationality of applicants was not a factor in the interpretation of those words and that nationals of third states as well as stateless persons were included.[46] Shortly thereafter, the issue of whether the requirement of 'everyone

---

[42] One may also notice that the term 'persons' was used instead of 'everyone'. The latter term, which ended up in the final version, is at first sight more encompassing.

[43] *Collected Edition of the 'Travaux préparatoires' of the European Convention on Human Rights*, part II, 5 February 1950, p. 200.

[44] *Collected Edition of the 'Travaux préparatoires' of the European Convention on Human Rights*, Vol. II, 15 June 1950, pp. 236 and 260. Although Article 1 ECHR was changed after that meeting, the words 'within their jurisdiction' did not. For the text as adopted by the Conference of Senior Officials, see p. 218.

[45] *Austria v. Italy*, no. 788/60, Yearbook of the European Convention on Human Rights 1961.

[46] *Austria v. Italy*, no. 788/60, Yearbook of the European Convention on Human Rights 1961, p. 116.

within their jurisdiction' would limit the applicability of the ECHR to events occurring on the territories of the Contracting Parties came up for the first time.[47] The Court and the Commission have both dealt with cases concerning events actually taking place outside the territories of the Contracting Parties and cases in which events taking place within the territories of the Contracting Parties may have an effect outside the Contracting Parties. Both instances may be associated with the notion of extra-territoriality, but the two categories of cases should be distinguished. In its case law concerning the extra-territorial application of the ECHR, the Court has developed a two-track system. The Court makes a distinction between cases which concern the *extra-territorial effects* of the ECHR and cases in which the actual *extra-territorial application* of the ECHR is at hand.[48]

The Extra-Territorial Application of the ECHR

Cases concerning the extra-territorial application of the ECHR are those in which the Court has to decide whether the ECHR could also be applied to situations which occurred outside the territories of the Contracting Parties. An example is the well-known *Banković* case, which concerned the question of whether all the NATO Member States, which are also members of the Council of Europe, could be held responsible for the bombing of a building in Belgrade, Serbia, which was not a Contracting Party at the time. Five relatives of people who were killed during that attack and a survivor brought a complaint before the Court in Strasbourg. The Court first had to decide whether the facts of this case could come within the jurisdiction of the respondent States as a result of the extra-territorial act, i.e. the bombing of a radio tower outside the territories of the Contracting Parties. The Court ultimately held that this was not the case.

In deciding whether the facts could fall within the jurisdiction of the respondent States, the Court, seemingly following the suggestion of the seventeen respondent States,[49] took as its angle the ordinary meaning of 'jurisdiction' in public international law. This resulted in the Court's finding that this notion of jurisdiction in Article 1 ECHR is essentially territorial, and that other bases of jurisdiction are exceptional and require special justification.[50] The Court found confirmation hereof in the *travaux préparatoires*[51] and also made a reference to the *Soering*

[47] The issue came up for the first time before the Commission in *X v. the Federal Republic of Germany* (dec.), no. 1611/62, Yearbook of the European Convention on Human Rights 1965, pp. 159–168 (decision of 25 September 1965).

[48] See, e.g., *Banković and Others v. Belgium and 16 Other Contracting States* (dec.) [GC], no. 52207/99, para 68, ECHR 2001-XI.

[49] *Banković and Others v. Belgium and 16 Other Contracting States* (dec.) [GC], no. 52207/99, para 36, ECHR 2001-XI.

[50] *Banković and Others v. Belgium and 16 Other Contracting States* (dec.) [GC], no. 52207/99, para 61, ECHR 2001-XI.

[51] See supra Sect. 4.2.4.1.

case,[52] in which it, inter alia, had held that Article 1 ECHR 'sets a limit, notably territorial, on the reach of the Convention.'[53]

In *Banković*, the Court made every effort to distinguish the case from its previous case law with regard to Article 1 ECHR, as established in *Loizidou v. Turkey* (Preliminary Objections).[54] Ms Loizidou, a Cypriot national, lodged a complaint against Turkey, as she claimed to be the owner of certain plots of land situated in northern Cyprus which she could no longer peacefully enjoy since the Turkish invasion of northern Cyprus. She alleged that Turkish troops prevented her from returning to her land.

In this case, the Court recalled its own case law in which it had held that although Article 1 ECHR sets limits on the reach of the ECHR, it is not limited to the territories of the Contracting States. Thereafter, the Court held that, under certain circumstances, military action outside the territory of a State can also give rise to the responsibility of a State:

> Bearing in mind the object and purpose of the Convention, the responsibility of a Contracting Party may also arise when as a consequence of military action - whether lawful or unlawful - it exercises effective control of an area outside its national territory. The obligation to secure, in such an area, the rights and freedoms set out in the Convention derives from the fact of such control whether it be exercised directly, through its armed forces, or through a subordinate local administration.[55]

In *Loizidou*, the Court emphasised the object and purpose of the ECHR by referring to the Convention as 'a constitutional instrument of European public order (*ordre public*),'[56] in addition to its reliance on the concept of the exercise of 'effective control.'[57] The applicants in *Banković*, unsurprisingly, relied on *Loizidou* in their arguments, but the Court felt that the situation in *Banković* could be clearly distinguished from *Loizidou*, as the latter case fell within the legal space (the *espace jurisdique*) of the ECHR—both Cyprus and Turkey are members of the Council of Europe. Yugoslavia was not part of the legal space of the ECHR at the time. The Court held that '[t]he Convention was not designed to be applied

---

[52] *Soering v. the United Kingdom*, 7 July 1989, Series A-161.

[53] *Soering v. the United Kingdom*, 7 July 1989, para 86, Series A-161.

[54] *Loizidou v. Turkey* (preliminary objections), 23 March 1995, Series A no. 310.

[55] *Loizidou v. Turkey* (preliminary objections), paras 62, 23 March 1995, Series A no. 310.

[56] *Loizidou v. Turkey* (preliminary objections), 23 March 1995, Series A no. 310, para 75. The Court here thus refers to the notion of *ordre public*. This is, of course, a reference with a certain connotation for specialists of private international law (see on this notion in private international law supra Sect. 2.5). However, it should be noted that the Court here does not refer to a concept of private international law. See Kinsch 2004, pp. 202–205; Cf. Struycken 2009, pp. 51–52. But see *Neulinger and Shuruk v. Switzerland* [GC], no. 41615/07, para 133, ECHR 2010-. In this case concerning international child abduction the Court referred to the ECHR's special character as an instrument of European public order (*ordre public*) for the protection of individual human beings.

[57] See supra n. 55.

throughout the world, even in respect of the conduct of Contracting States.'[58] In connection with the applicants' invocation of *Loizidou* the Court also observed 'the essentially regional vocation of the Convention system',[59] an oft-cited notion of the Court, which will be revisited below.[60] With this the Court also rejected the applicants' suggestion in *Banković* of a specific application of 'effective control' and their reliance on the *orde public* mission of the ECHR.[61]

The Court not only had to distinguish its decision in *Banković* from its previous case law in *Loizidou*, but it also had to account for its more recent admissibility decision in the case of *Issa and Others v. Turkey*.[62] This case clearly concerned acts outside the legal space of the Contracting Parties, as it involved the alleged killing of Iraqi shepherds in Northern Iraq by Turkish troops, but it had been declared admissible by the Court. Here, the Court gave a rather straightforward and blunt explanation for the difference between *Banković* and this case: in the admissibility decision in *Issa* the respondent States had failed to argue that the Court did not have jurisdiction.[63] This is, of course, a rather odd argument. Was the Court, in such an important case, not prepared to give a ruling on its competence *ex officio*?[64]

The *Banković* decision of the Court has been much criticized.[65] Despite this criticism, it has to be acknowledged that this is an important case regarding the extra-territorial application of the ECHR, as the Court has since often repeated its stance in this case. However, it appears that this decision is not the final word on the extra-territorial application of the ECHR. After its decision in *Banković* the Court found in *Issa and Others v. Turkey*[66] that the concept of jurisdiction was not restricted to the territories of the Contracting Parties and that under exceptional circumstances—notably a situation in which a Contracting Party has 'effective control'—acts occurring outside the territory may entail the exercise of jurisdiction as found in Article 1 ECHR. This case was ultimately decided, though, on the fact that the applicants were unable to demonstrate the alleged facts in this case.[67]

---

[58] *Banković and Others v. Belgium and 16 Other Contracting States* (dec.) [GC], no. 52207/99, para 80, ECHR 2001-XI.

[59] Id.

[60] See infra Sect. 4.4.1.

[61] *Banković and Others v. Belgium and 16 Other Contracting States* (dec.) [GC], no. 52207/99, paras 75–80, ECHR 2001-XI.

[62] *Issa and Others v. Turkey* (dec.), no. 31821/96, 30 May 2000.

[63] See also another admissibility decision in a case concerning an extra-territorial act, the apprehension of the applicant in Kenya, in *Öcalan v. Turkey* (dec.), no. 46221/99, 14 December 2000, which the Court distinguished similarly.

[64] Lawson 2004, p. 115.

[65] See, e.g., Gondek 2009; Lawson 2004; Loucaides 2006, at pp. 391–407; and Orakhelashvili 2003.

[66] *Issa and Others v. Turkey*, no. 31821/96, 16 November 2004.

[67] *Issa and Others v. Turkey*, no. 31821/96, paras 76–82, 16 November 2004.

Since its findings in *Banković*, the Court has found that the arrest of a person in a third country by officials of a Contracting Party means that this person falls within the jurisdiction of that Contracting Party,[68] while applicants who are being held in a prison in a third country which is under the full control of the forces of a Contracting Party also falls within the jurisdiction in the sense of Article 1 ECHR.[69] Even in the exceptional circumstances where a Contracting Party assumes the authority for keeping part of a third country secure, this Contracting Party has jurisdiction under Article 1 ECHR with regard to civilians killed during security operations carried out by the forces of the Contracting Party in that area.[70] In all the afore-mentioned cases, however, the Contracting Party had some sort of physical control over the respective applicants.

More recently, for example, the Court has found that refugees travelling by boat who were picked up on the High Seas by a vessel sailing under the flag of a Contracting Party also came within the jurisdiction of this Contracting Party.[71] These cases are arguably all concerned with different categories of cases of the extra-territorial application of the ECHR and involve some sort of physical control, which may at least partly explain the different outcomes compared to that in *Banković*.[72] What is clear, however, is that even though *Banković* appeared to reduce the extra-territorial application of the ECHR, there are certainly plenty of scenarios remaining in which the ECHR is applicable extra-territorially.

The Extra-Territorial Effect of the ECHR

In cases concerning the extra-territorial effect of the ECHR, liability may be incurred by Contracting Parties by virtue of their taking action within their own territory (such as a decision to extradite or expel) which may consequently have an effect on non-Contracting Parties. An example of the phenomenon of the extra-territorial effect of the application of the ECHR in the Court's case law can be found in *Soering v. the United Kingdom*,[73] which may still be regarded as a leading case in the field of extradition.[74] Here the Court had to deal with the issue of

---

[68] *Öcalan v. Turkey* [GC], no. 46221/99, ECHR 2005-IV.

[69] *Al-Sadoon and Mufdi v. the United Kingdom*, no. 61498/08, ECHR 2010 (extracts). See also *Al-Jedda v. the United Kingdom* [GC], no. 27021/08, ECHR 2011.

[70] *Al-Skeini and Others v. the United Kingdom* [GC], no. 55721/07, ECHR 2011.

[71] *Hirsi Jamaa and Others v. Italy* [GC], no. 27765/09, 23 February 2012. See also *Women On Waves and Others v. Portugal*, no. 31276/05, 3 February 2009.

[72] There is rich literature on this subject. See for some recent theories on Article 1 ECHR, e.g., Miller 2009, pp. 1223–1246; Nigro 2010, pp. 11–30.

[73] *Soering v. the United Kingdom*, 7 July 1989, Series A no. 161.

[74] See generally on extradition and human rights Van der Wilt 2012, pp. 268–315.

whether it is possible for a Contracting Party to be responsible for an act that (possibly) occurs in another State which is not bound by the ECHR. In this particular case the question was whether the United Kingdom could be held responsible for the extradition of a person suspected of murder to the United States (US). The Court ultimately held that this was so in this case.

In reaching this finding, the Court started out by carefully sketching the Contracting Parties' obligations, noting that Article 1 ECHR

> sets a limit, notably territorial, on the reach of the Convention. (...) Further, the Convention does not govern the actions of States not Parties to it, nor does it purport to be a means of requiring the Contracting States to impose Convention standards on other States. Article 1 cannot be read as justifying a general principle to the effect that, notwithstanding its extradition obligations, a Contracting State may not surrender an individual unless satisfied that the conditions awaiting him in the country of destination are in full accord with each of the safeguards of the Convention.[75]

However, the Court subsequently observed that all this cannot absolve the Contracting Parties from responsibility under Article 3 ECHR 'for all and any foreseeable consequences of extradition suffered outside their jurisdiction',[76] and ultimately held that the decision of a Contracting Party to extradite an individual may indeed bring responsibility for the State 'where substantial grounds have been shown for believing that the person concerned, if extradited, faces a real risk of being subjected to torture or to inhuman or degrading treatment or punishment in the requesting country.'[77] While acknowledging that an assessment of the conditions in a State that is not a Contracting Party is inevitable in such cases, the Court did nevertheless emphasize this does not mean that one illicitly meddles with business that only concerns the extradition-requesting State and that there is thus 'no question of adjudicating on or establishing the responsibility of the receiving country (...).'[78]

The Court has taken analogous decisions in the field of expulsion, in which a similar principle applies, as it held in *Cruz Varas v. Sweden.*[79] This has been confirmed in *Daoudi v. France*,[80] a case concerning the expulsion of a suspected terrorist from France. *Drozd and Janousek v. France and Spain* offers another important example of a case concerning international judicial co-operation and the extra-territorial effect of the ECHR.[81]

---

[75] *Soering v. the United Kingdom*, 7 July 1989, Series A no. 161, para 86.

[76] Id.

[77] *Soering v. the United Kingdom*, 7 July 1989, Series A no. 161, para 91.

[78] Id.

[79] *Cruz Varas v. Sweden*, 20 March 1991, paras 69–70, Series A no. 201.

[80] *Daoudi v. France*, no. 19576/08, 3 December 2009.

[81] *Drozd and Janousek v. France and Spain*, 26 June 1992, Series A no. 240. The importance of this case for private international law is, incidentally, very much tied to Judge Matscher's concurring opinion in this case.

4.3 The Meaning of Article 1 ECHR for Private International Law

Having discussed Article 1 ECHR and the Court's interpretation thereof, it is now time to turn our attention to the issue with which this chapter is mainly concerned: what is the role of Article 1 ECHR with regard to issues of private international law? A related question is: what does the discussion concerning the possible extra-territorial scope of the ECHR exactly mean for private international law? It will be recalled that private international law is concerned with cross-border cases introducing foreign elements and deals with three main questions in this regard: the issue of jurisdiction, the issue of the applicable law, and, finally, the issue of the recognition and enforcement of foreign judgments. What is the role of Article 1 ECHR with regard to these three issues?

It is submitted here that if a court of one of the Contracting Parties has jurisdiction in the private international law sense to hear a case, then this automatically implies that the subjects in that case come within the jurisdiction of the Contracting Party and that the ECHR is applicable to such cases, even if the persons involved come from a non-Contracting Party and regardless even of whether the relevant facts took place within the jurisdiction of another State.[82] In this regard one could thus say that there is a link between jurisdiction in private international law—adjudicatory jurisdiction—and jurisdiction following from Article 1 ECHR. If a court of a Contracting Party asserts jurisdiction in the private international law sense, then its subsequent decision must be in conformity with the rights guaranteed in the ECHR.[83] It is interesting to note that with regard to the other two issues of private international law—the applicable law and the recognition and enforcement of foreign judgments—foreign elements (either a foreign applicable law or a foreign judgment possibly emanating from third countries) are introduced to the Contracting Parties. This raises the question of the extent to which one could speak of the extra-territoriality of the ECHR in this regard—meaning the extent to which the rights guaranteed in the ECHR may be applied to foreign law and judgments.

Long before the Court, at the beginning of the last decade, delivered a judgment concerning whether the ECHR could be applicable to the recognition of a foreign judgment emanating from a third State in *Pellegrini v. Italy*,[84] specialists in the field of private international law had noticed the possible analogy between the Court's reasoning in *Soering* and the applicability of the ECHR to the recognition of foreign judgments or the application of a foreign law emanating from a third country.[85] Although in the event of the recognition of a foreign judgment violating

---

[82] See *Markovic and Others v. Italy* [GC], no. 1398/03, ECHR 2006-XIV. See for a more extensive discussion of the relationship between Article 1 ECHR and jurisdiction in private international law infra Sect. 5.3.

[83] See further infra Chap. 5.

[84] *Pellegrini v. Italy*, no. 30882/96, *ECHR* 2001-VIII.

[85] See, e.g., Mayer 1991, pp. 653–655 and Van Loon 1993, pp. 145–146.

one of the rights guaranteed in the ECHR the violation has already taken place in that foreign country, it is the court of one of the Contracting Parties which would ultimately allow such a violation in the Contracting Party. It is this act of recognizing the foreign judgment which ultimately results in a violation of the ECHR.

The analogy is, of course, not perfect. It has been remarked that *Soering* turned on Article 3 ECHR, which prohibits torture and inhuman or degrading treatment, while private international law cases are generally not concerned with Article 3 ECHR.[86] However, in *Soering* the Court also considered that 'an issue might exceptionally be raised under Article 6 [ECHR] by an extradition decision in circumstances where the fugitive has suffered or risks suffering a flagrant denial of a fair trial in the requesting country.'[87] It has also been suggested that the above-cited passage indicates that the extra-territorial application of Article 6 ECHR is limited to the criminal sphere.[88] However, the Court's findings in *Pellegrini v. Italy* clearly indicate that this is not the case.

The Court's findings in *Pellegrini* with regard to the applicability of the ECHR should thus not have come as too great a surprise.[89] This case concerned the enforcement of a Vatican judgment annulling a marriage in Italy. The applicant alleged that she had not received a fair trial before the courts in the Vatican and that the subsequent enforcement of this judgment in Italy violated her rights under Article 6 ECHR. As the Vatican is not one of the Contracting Parties to the ECHR, for our purposes the most interesting question is whether the Court deemed that the ECHR could be applicable in this case. In its judgment the Court first noted that its task was not to examine whether the proceedings before the Vatican courts were contrary to Article 6 ECHR, as the Vatican is not a Contracting Party, but rather to examine whether the Italian courts duly satisfied themselves that the relevant proceedings fulfilled the guarantees of Article 6 ECHR. The Court added that such a review is required when the enforcement of a judgment emanating from a country that does not apply the ECHR is requested. After examining the reasoning of the Italian courts, the Court held that they had breached their duty to examine whether the proceedings had lived up to the standards of Article 6 ECHR.

It should be noted that the Court did not even mention Article 1 ECHR in *Pellegrini*, although it did treat the Vatican judgment as a judgment emanating from a country that has not signed the ECHR.[90] Apparently the applicability of the ECHR, following from its Article 1 ECHR, to such a situation may be regarded as a foregone conclusion. One could say that such a conclusion is completely in line

[86] See, e.g., Juratowitch 2007, p. 178.

[87] *Soering v. the United Kingdom*, 7 July 1989, para 113, Series A no. 161. Incidentally, the Court subsequently found that such a risk could not be construed from the facts in *Soering*.

[88] White and Ovey 2010, p. 275.

[89] This case has been much discussed, and one could say that other aspects of the Court's findings in this case were certainly surprising. See for annotations, e.g., Costa 2002, pp. 470–476; Flauss 2002; Pocar 2006, pp. 575–581. This case will be further discussed infra Sect. 8.2.

[90] Whether that in itself is completely justifiable can be the subject of debate. Italy and the Holy See clearly have a special relationship. See Kinsch 2004, p. 220.

with the Court's case law concerning extradition and expulsion, with which the recognition of a foreign judgment emanating from a third country may be said to correspond. There is also no reason to assume that the Court would reach a markedly different conclusion with regard to the application of a foreign law originating from a third country. The Court has confirmed as much in its decision in *Ammjadi v. Germany*,[91] in which it also did not comment on the applicability of the ECHR, despite the fact that the applicable law in this case originated from Iran, which, of course, is not a Contracting Party.[92]

One could remark that the application of a foreign law of a third country violating the ECHR by a court of a Contracting Party is not entirely similar to the recognition of a foreign judgment violating the ECHR. One could argue that when the court of a Contracting Party applies a foreign law violating the ECHR, this results in a direct violation of the ECHR, while the recognition of a foreign judgment by that same court results in a more indirect violation. After all, in the latter instance the actual violation would have already taken place in the country of origin of the judgment. However, one could wonder what the practical relevance of such a distinction is in the event that the foreign law or foreign judgment originates from a non-Contracting Party. In both these scenarios the violation of the ECHR by way of either applying the foreign law or recognizing or enforcing the foreign judgment is attributable to the Contracting Party in which the pertinent proceedings took place.[93]

The Court's judgment in *Pellegrini*, combined with its case law concerning extradition and expulsion, thus seem to indicate that the ECHR is generally applicable to cases concerning private international law issues, even if the foreign law or judgment introduced in the Contracting Parties has its origin in countries that are not signatories to the ECHR.[94] Consequently there appears to be little room for the invocation of the Court's case law concerning the extra-territorial application of the ECHR up to this point.

That is not to say that the applicability of the ECHR in these cases concerning issues of private international law is clear-cut from here on. There is, for example, much debate on what the Court's standard of control should be in such cases

---

[91] *Ammdjadi v. Germany* (dec.), no. 51625/08, 9 March 2010.

[92] See for a more detailed discussion of the case infra Chap. 6.

[93] Incidentally, the distinction may be of use in the event that the applicable law or foreign judgment emanates from another Contracting Party. In such an instance one could namely argue that when the judge of Contracting Party A applies the law of Contracting Party B, which subsequently results in a violation of the ECHR, State A is responsible for the violation of the ECHR. This would arguably not be the case when recognizing a foreign judgment emanating from another Contracting Party. See *X. v. Belgium and the Netherlands*, decision of 10 July 1975, *DR* 6, p. 77 and *Lindberg v. Sweden* (dec.), no. 48198/99, 15 January 2004. See for a more detailed discussion of this issue infra Sects. 6.2.1 and 8.3.

[94] Cf. Juratowitch 2007, p. 183; Kinsch 2004, pp. 203–205; Kinsch 2007, pp. 233–237.

concerning foreign elements.[95] In *Pellegrini* the Court made no mention of an attenuated standard with regard to the foreign proceedings, while in *Soering* and *Drozd and Janousek* the Court held that the Contracting Parties could only withhold their co-operation in the case of 'a flagrant denial of justice'. However, the standard of control in private international law cases is a separate issue, which will be discussed in subsequent chapters.[96]

The position of the Court concerning the applicability of the ECHR to private international law issues thus appears to be quite clear. However there is one more type of scenario that has yet to be fully discussed. One may recall that I started this discussion with a Dutch case concerning a request to judicially establish paternity—a request to which Surinamese law was applicable—over a child habitually residing in Surinam. This case may be considered as exemplary for cases in which their facts have little connection to the Contracting Party, except, of course, for the Contracting Party being the forum.

It should be noted that this is not the only conceivable case in which one could speak of there being little connection to a Contracting Party. One could, for example, envisage a case in which a couple living outside Europe might have immovable property in one of the Contracting Parties. The subject of the proceedings being immovable property would, in most countries, suffice for having jurisdiction to adjudicate such a case, but other than the property being in that country, there is little connection to the Contracting Party.[97] However it is not unimaginable that, for example, a succession according to Iranian law could result in an unequal share in the property between a brother and sister, which may violate the ECHR if this instrument is applicable to such a case.[98] The ultimate case would be one in which two parties have no link whatsoever with any of the Contracting Parties, other than having drafted a valid choice of forum clause selecting one of the Contracting Parties as the forum for their dispute, with the choice-of-law clause selecting a law of a non-Contracting Party. This admittedly far-fetched, but not entirely inconceivable, case would surely stretch the applicability of the ECHR to its limit.

The question, of course, is how to deal with such issues? Are these situations in which the Court's case law concerning the extra-territorial application of the

---

[95] See, e.g., Flauss 2002, pp. 73–75; Juratowitch 2007, p. 180ff; Kinsch 2007, p. 247ff. See also Judge Matscher's concurring opinion in *Drozd and Janousek* supra n. 81.

[96] See particularly Chaps. 6 and 8.

[97] It should be noted, though, that this head of jurisdiction has traditionally been regarded as an important (and exclusive) ground for jurisdiction in private international law. See, e.g., Article 22 of Council Regulation (EC) No. 44/2001 on Jurisdiction and the Recognition and Enforcement of Judgments in Civil and Commercial Matters, *OJ* 2001, L12/1. (Brussels I-Regulation) Cf. the Jenard Report. One could thus say that, while there may appear to be a limited connection between the parties involved and the forum, this may an important connection from the point of view of the forum State.

[98] Cf. the statement of facts of 27 May 2010 in *Hüseyinzade v. Turkey*, no. 4763/07 (lodged on 12 January 2007).

ECHR may be of any guidance, as was alluded to earlier? If so, this would severely limit the extra-territorial effect of the ECHR. It would, in fact, preclude the application of the ECHR in such cases. However, even though the link with the Contracting Party might be negligible at best, there appears, logically speaking, to be very little reason not to apply the ECHR to such cases. The reasoning which the Court used in its case law concerning extradition and expulsion (on the extra-territorial effects of the ECHR), and which was also followed in *Pellegrini* and *Ammdjadi*, holds up even in situations which have little connection to the Contracting Party. Even in those cases, it is still the judge of a court in a Contracting Party who would ultimately breach the ECHR by either applying a foreign law or recognizing a foreign judgment violating the ECHR.

This raises the following question: what are the outer limits of Article 1 ECHR in this regard? In what kind of situation would the ECHR no longer be applicable? The Court may have given us an indication in a recent case dealing with the aftermath of the undoubtedly well-known publication of twelve cartoons in the Danish newspaper *Politiken*,[99] which caused an international controversy. In this case, *Ben El Mahi and Others v. Denmark*,[100] the applicants were a Moroccan national living in Morocco and two Moroccan organizations. Their complaint concerned their contention that under Articles 9 ECHR (the right to freedom of thought, conscience, and religion) and 14 ECHR they had been discriminated against as Muslims by Denmark. Furthermore, by invoking Article 10 (the right to freedom of expression), they argued that Denmark had permitted the publication of the cartoons.

The Court first considered whether the applicants came within Denmark's jurisdiction, given that the first applicant lived in Morocco and the other two were based there. After summing up all of its case law by mostly referring to its various findings in the above-mentioned *Banković* case, the Court found that this was not so, as there 'is no jurisdictional link between any of the applicants and the relevant Member State, namely Denmark, or that they can come within the jurisdiction of Denmark on account of any extra-territorial act'.

What is not entirely clear from this case, however, is what the link is exactly between the applicants and Denmark. The Court noted that there 'is no jurisdictional link', and, if that is the case, then the conclusion that the applicants do not come within Denmark's jurisdiction is not exactly surprising. If the Court had held differently, then people and organizations from all over the world could quite randomly invoke the ECHR. However, in describing the circumstances of the case, the Court mentioned several Muslim organizations in Denmark reporting the newspaper to the police. It also mentioned several—otherwise unnamed—Muslim organizations instigating civil proceedings for defamation in Denmark. I would argue that if the applicants had been some of the organizations instigating proceedings in Denmark, then they would come within the jurisdiction of Denmark.

[99] Cf. Kinsch 2007, p. 230.

[100] *Ben El Mahi v. Denmark* (dec.), no. 5853/06, *ECHR* 2006-XV.

Does that not directly follow from the Court's reasoning with regard to Article 1 ECHR in *Soering* and *Pellegrini*?[101] It is not clear, however, from the relevant facts as they have been summed up by the Court in its decision, whether this was in fact the case.

In concluding this section concerning the meaning of Article 1 ECHR for private international law, I should reiterate that, in my opinion, the involvement of an individual in (international civil) proceedings in the territory of one of the Contracting Parties places that individual, in principle, under the jurisdiction of that State within the meaning of Article 1 ECHR. This is the case when an individual brings a case before a court of one of the Contracting Parties and that court makes a decision as to whether it has jurisdiction in the private international law sense. It should thus be clear that the mere bringing of proceedings in a case before a court of one of the Contracting Parties is, in principle, sufficient to come within the jurisdiction of a Contracting Party.[102]

4.4 The Consequences of the Applicability of Article 1 ECHR to Private International Law

In this part I will discuss the consequences of the above findings with regard to Article 1 ECHR and private international law. If one follows the Court's reasoning in *Soering* and *Pellegrini*, it will thus become clear that there is virtually no escaping the applicability of the ECHR to private international law cases. If a court of one of the Contracting Parties is competent to hear a private international law dispute, then that court will have to consider the possible impact of the ECHR on that case, regardless of the foreign elements. What does this mean? The discussion will commence with a review of some of the consequences of the findings above. Thereafter, the related discussion on the imperialism of the ECHR will be examined (Sect. 4.4.1). This will be followed by a discussion of the dangers of the

[101] See also the discussion of *Markovic and Others v. Italy* [GC], no. 1398/03, ECHR 2006-XIV infra Sect. 5.3.

[102] It should be noted, though, with regard to bringing (civil) proceedings in a Contracting Party, that the courts of the relevant Contracting Party may justifiably refuse to assume jurisdiction in the private international law sense. Even though Article 6 ECHR also contains the right of access to a court, there may be restrictions to this right of access. This issue will be discussed in the next chapter. See infra Chap. 5. It is also important to underscore that lodging proceedings in a Contracting Party with regard to an issue which is not at all attributable to the Contracting Party will result in the case being inadmissible. See, e.g., *Galić v. the Netherlands* (dec.) no. 22617/07, 9 June 2009 and *Blagojević v. the Netherlands* (dec.), no. 49032/07, 9 June 2009. These cases concerned applicants convicted by the ICTY, an international tribunal hosted by the Netherlands. The Court found that the sole fact that the ICTY is hosted in the Netherlands was not enough to attribute the matters complained about to the Netherlands, whereby it stressed that the case involved an international tribunal established by the Security Council of the United Nations and found that the applications were incompatible *ratione personae*.

proliferation of the rights guaranteed in the ECHR (Sect. 4.4.2). Finally, a few cases of the national courts of the Contracting Parties relating to the issues discussed in this chapter will be examined (Sect. 4.4.3).

First of all, one should concede that all this does give the ECHR an extra-territorial notion to a certain extent. This appears to be unavoidable. The ECHR will have an extra-territorial effect in the area of private international law in the sense that foreign laws and judgments originating from third States will—to a certain extent—be scrutinized as to their compliance with the ECHR, despite the State of origin of the law or judgment not being a Contracting Party to the ECHR. One could say that in this regard the ECHR is a sort of mandatory rule for private international law in the sense that the ECHR always applies to private international law cases.[103] If the judge of a Contracting Party has jurisdiction to hear an international (private law) case, the ECHR will be applicable to that international case to a certain extent.

It is, however, also important to underscore what all of this does not mean. The fact that the ECHR may be applicable to private international law disputes does not necessarily mean that there would be no possibility to account for the special nature of private international law cases, which is often a critique by specialists of private international law.[104] Even though the ECHR is applicable to a private international law case because such a case comes within the jurisdiction of a Contracting Party, there may still be room for maneuvering in this regard. The discussion concerning the possible attenuation of the requirements following from Article 6 ECHR with regard to the recognition of foreign judgments emanating from third States was briefly mentioned above, although the *Pellegrini* judgment appears to leave little room for such an interpretation.[105] However, with regard to family law situations and the possible impact of Article 8 ECHR, one could think of the so-called 'margin of appreciation' with which the impact of the ECHR on private international law may be softened.[106] These specific topics will be further discussed in the subsequent chapters, but it is nevertheless important to stress here that the mere fact that the ECHR is applicable in private international law disputes in the Contracting Parties does not mean that concerns specific to private international law can no longer be dealt with.[107] These should, in my opinion, merely be dealt with within the system of the ECHR.

This brings us to what is perhaps the greatest consequence of the impact of Article 1 ECHR on private international law, and that is its impact on the (relativity of the) public policy exception. Traditionally, fundamental rights in private

---

[103] See Mayer 1991; Cf. Gannagé 2001; Kiestra 2010, p. 30. See also infra Sect. 6.3.3.3.

[104] See, e.g., Kinsch 2004, pp. 214–218.

[105] See for a more detailed discussion of *Pellegrini* infra Sect. 8.2.

[106] See, e.g., Coester-Waltjen 1998, pp. 9–32; Engel 1989, p. 36ff; Van Loon 1993, pp. 146–147; Mayer 1991, pp. 660–661; Rutten 1998, p. 802ff. See with regard to the notion of the 'margin of appreciation' supra Sect. 3.5.2.

[107] See for examples of cases in which the rights guaranteed in the ECHR are softened in issues of private international law also further infra Sect. 4.4.3, and particularly Sect. 4.4.3.3.

international law cases have been protected by way of the intervention of so-called public order or public policy clauses (*ordre public*). The choice-of-law rules of the forum determine the law which is applicable to a case, but if the result of the application of that law would be manifestly incompatible with the fundamental principles of the forum, the public policy exception will be invoked in order to set aside that result.[108] An important characteristic of the public policy exception is its relative character. This naturally stems from the goals of private international law, which include respect for other legal cultures. This relative character is manifested by the fact that it is generally observed that the operation of the public policy exception is related to the proximity between the relevant case and the forum.

If a case has little or no connection to the forum, the public policy exception cannot be invoked—except for certain extreme cases in which the applicable law is so fundamentally against the values of the forum that the application of that law would never be permitted in the forum. If a case has more connections or links with the forum, the threshold for the application of the public policy exception is lower.[109] The public policy exception can be used as an instrument to prevent violations of the ECHR, as the ECHR undoubtedly belongs to the fundamental principles of the Contracting Parties.[110]

However, what happens if there is little connection between the issue and the forum? Normally the public policy exception would not then be invoked. However, not invoking the public policy exception because of the fact that there is little or no connection to the forum appears not to be permitted in light of Article 1 ECHR if one of the rights guaranteed in the ECHR is violated by either the application of a foreign law or the recognition or enforcement of a foreign judgment. As was stated above, this does not necessarily mean that all flexibility, which the use of the public policy exception would offer, is lost, but merely that such flexibility should be sought within the system of the ECHR. It may well be the case that there is room within the ECHR to reject the application of this instrument in full force, but a blanket rejection based on the links of a case with the forum and, consequently, the invocation of the public policy exception is asking for trouble, in my opinion.

4.4.1 Article 1 ECHR and the Debate on the 'Imperialism' of the ECHR

Related to the discussion concerning the relationship between Article 1 ECHR and private international law is a debate on the perceived dangers of what has been

---

[108] See for an extended discussion of the public policy exception, e.g., Lagarde 1994, Chap. 11. See also supra Sect. 2.5.

[109] See further supra Sect. 2.5.

[110] Cf. Stürner 2011, pp. 9–10. See also, e.g., Mills 2008, p. 214.

dubbed the 'imperialism'[111] of the rights guaranteed in the ECHR with regard to private international law and its possible solutions. This debate on the perils of the hegemony of the ECHR has particularly found acceptance in France.[112] The basic idea behind the alleged 'imperialism' of the ECHR is that the human rights contained therein are essentially an expression of the European-western legal culture, which would be incompatible with foreign legal norms of third countries.[113] Such criticism towards human rights, and the rights guaranteed in the ECHR in particular, is, incidentally, neither new nor limited to the area of private international law.[114]

In this particular debate on the relativism of human rights it is, however, important to carefully distinguish two different approaches of the proponents of such relativism concerning private international law: on the one hand, there are those that deny the universal nature of human rights altogether and that thus consequently support their restriction in private international law; on the other hand, there are those that denounce the inflation of the rights guaranteed in the ECHR by the Court in Strasbourg.[115] It should thus be noted that the first group denies the universality of human rights altogether, while the second group merely denounces the proliferation of human rights in the ECHR, which are not universally accepted. Such an increase is usually attributed to the interpretation of certain provisions in the ECHR by the Court, which has, for example, certainly not been reticent in its interpretation of Article 8 ECHR. The criticism of the second group is thus directed against rights which could never have been foreseen by the drafters of the ECHR and which are the result of the interpretation of the Court in Strasbourg.[116]

Critics of the proliferation of rights within the ECHR, who turn against the invocation of rights guaranteed in the ECHR which are not universally accepted, may feel strengthened in their arguments by a comment of the Court in the aforementioned *Banković* case. The Court explicitly stated that the ECHR has an 'essentially regional vocation'.[117] However, one should not forget the context in which this statement was made. This case concerned the issue of the possible application of the ECHR outside the Contracting Parties' territories. Such a statement cannot easily be read as a comment by the Court on the applicability of the ECHR in cases clearly falling within the jurisdiction of the Contracting Parties, even if such cases concern elements from third countries.

---

[111] Lequette 2004, p. 113.

[112] See Gannagé 2008, p. 265ff and the (French) authors cited there.

[113] See, e.g., Fulchiron 2010, p. 627.

[114] There is much debate on the universality and relativity of human rights. See, e.g., the debate between Donnely and Goodhart: Donnely 2007, pp. 281–306; Goodhart 2008, pp. 183–193; Donnely 2008, pp. 194–204.

[115] Gannagé 2008, pp. 269–270.

[116] Lequette 2004, p. 114.

[117] *Banković and Others v. Belgium and 16 Other Contracting States* (dec.) [GC], no. 52207/99, para 80, ECHR 2001-XI.

4.4.2 The Dangers of the Proliferation of Rights Guaranteed in the ECHR for Private International Law

The danger of an increasing number of situations in which the ECHR may be invoked in the area of private international law is that this will often lead to the non-invocation or the setting aside of legal norms of third countries. This will in effect be harmful to some of the objectives of private international law, such as the international harmony of decisions and the international mobility of people, which will be hindered if a status created in one country is not recognized in another.[118] If, for example, a divorce judgment between two spouses is not recognized in one of the Contracting Parties, because of the invocation of the ECHR, this will have the result that these spouses will be considered divorced in the country of origin of the divorce, while they are still legally married in the Contracting Party concerned. The result of this would thus be a limping legal situation.[119]

The main solution, which has been offered by the critics of the proliferation of the rights guaranteed in the ECHR in private international law, is the use of the public policy exception to deal with the rights guaranteed in the ECHR. This would offer the judge some flexibility when faced with the invocation of a certain right guaranteed in the ECHR. However, as was discussed above, it is at best questionable whether the use of the public policy exception in such a manner is permitted in light of Article 1 ECHR.[120] Gaudemet-Tallon has proposed a solution which consists of determining the scope of the application of the ECHR depending on the nature of the protected right.[121] She appears to call for, in essence, the introduction of a hierarchy with regard to the rights guaranteed in the ECHR, as she proposes to make a distinction between rights in the ECHR which have a universal vocation and rights which do not have such a vocation.[122]

The problem, discussed above, that stems from the possibly growing number of interventions in the area of private international law by the ECHR, is real. If legal solutions originating from third countries will be swept aside due to the invocation of the ECHR more and more often, this could indeed possibly lead to problems related to a lack of an international harmony of solutions. As indicated earlier, this international harmony of solutions helps avoid so-called limping international legal relationships. Moreover, the international mobility of persons could also be jeopardized.

However, in light of the obligations undertaken by the Contracting Parties, as set out in Article 1 ECHR, the use of the public policy exception is in all likelihood not the solution to this problem, as this runs the risk of running afoul of the prime

---

[118] See, e.g., Gannagé 2008, pp. 270–271. See with regard to the notion of the 'international harmony of decisions' supra Chap. 2.

[119] Cf. Fulchiron 2010, p. 627.

[120] See supra Sect. 4.4.

[121] Gaudemet-Tallon 2004, pp. 219–220.

[122] Gaudemet-Tallon 2004, pp. 219–220.

obligation to secure the rights for everyone within their jurisdiction. The solution offered by Gaudement-Tallon may also run into trouble with regard to Article 1 ECHR, but, moreover, attempting to determine which rights guaranteed in the ECHR truly have a universal vocation would appear to be very difficult. It is nearly impossible to determine the exact composition of such universally accepted rights. It should be noted that Gaudement-Tallon admits this herself.[123] As was indicated above, there may be other solutions to the issues discussed here. In my opinion there is room for such considerations within the rights guaranteed in the ECHR that are involved in cases of private international law. However, this will be further discussed in subsequent chapters.[124]

4.4.3 Jurisprudence of the National Courts of the Contracting Parties

This section will provide an overview of examples of how the foregoing issues have been handled by the courts of the Contracting Parties. Some of the cases mentioned below will be discussed again in subsequent chapters. These cases are solely being discussed in this chapter in relation to the issue with which it is mainly concerned: is the ECHR applicable at all to private international cases involving foreign norms emanating from third countries, and what is the role of Article 1 ECHR in this regard? The issues in the cases discussed below are of course not necessarily limited to this topic. However, for reasons of clarity, the discussion below will mostly be confined to this issue of the applicability of the ECHR to private international law following from its Article 1 ECHR. It should, incidentally, be noted that there is very little case law concerning private international law cases in which Article 1 ECHR and the applicability of the ECHR is explicitly discussed.

Three different aspects of the discussion on the role of Article 1 ECHR in issues of private international law will be further illustrated in this section. First, I will demonstrate that the Court's case law concerning the extra-territorial effect of the ECHR has been used explicitly by the House of Lords in private international law issues (Sect. 4.4.3.1). Thereafter, I will discuss some case law in which the pitfalls of using the public policy exception will be further shown (Sect. 4.4.3.2). The inevitable result of the findings in this chapter regarding Article 1 ECHR and issues of private international law—the extensive reach of the rights guaranteed in the ECHR in issues of private international law—is the final aspect of the discussion which will be examined here (Sect. 4.4.3.3).

---

[123] Gaudemet-Tallon 2004, p. 219.

[124] See particularly infra Sects. 6.3.2–6.3.3.

4.4.3.1 Private International Law Cases and the Extra-Territorial Effect of the ECHR

In England the—then—House of Lords (UKHL) was presented with a private international law case regarding an issue of possible international child abduction in which the applicability of the ECHR arose. In *Re J (a child)*,[125] the UKHL held with regard to the father's request for the return of the child to Saudi Arabia that the United Kingdom could be in breach of rights guaranteed in the ECHR 'where there is a real risk of particularly flagrant breaches.' In so finding, a reference was made to the *Ullah* case.[126] The UKHL in *Re J (a child)* thus acknowledged the applicability of the ECHR to this particular case, even though the possible violation of the ECHR could occur in Saudi Arabia, a non-Contracting Party.[127] It is interesting to note that in this issue of private international law, the UKHL, with a reference to *Ullah*, relied on the Court's case law concerning the extra-territorial effect of the ECHR. Then again, even though this case dealt with an issue of private international law, the case also resembled very closely the sort of removal cases with which the Court's case law regarding the extra-territorial effect is concerned,[128] as the possible breach of one of the rights guaranteed in the ECHR upon the child's return to a non-Contracting Party was at issue.

The *Ullah* case[129] did not concern an issue of private international law, but this case is generally regarded as providing a precedent for private international law cases.[130] In *Ullah* the UKHL had to decide whether Article 9 ECHR could be engaged in the case of the removal of an individual from the United Kingdom, which would allegedly lead to treatment of that individual violating the rights guaranteed in Article 9. The UKHL, per Lord Bingham, held with regard to the interpretation of Article 1 ECHR that a distinction should be made between 'domestic' and 'foreign' cases.[131] 'Domestic' cases are those in which a State has acted within its own territory in such a manner that it has infringed upon one of the rights guaranteed in the ECHR; 'foreign' cases are those in which the removal of a person from a State's territory will (possibly) lead to an infringement of the ECHR in that other territory.[132] *Soering* provided a precedent for the category of foreign cases, according to Lord Bingham.[133]

[125] *Re J (a child)* [2005] UKHL 40.

[126] *Re J (a child)* [2005] UKHL 40, no. 42. See with regard to *Ullah* infra n. 129.

[127] Incidentally, it was ultimately found that on the facts there was no such risk.

[128] See supra Sect. 'The Extra-Territorial Effect of the ECHR'.

[129] *R (Ullah) v. Special Adjudicator* [2004] UKHL 26.

[130] See, e.g., Fawcett 2007, p. 3ff; Juratowitch 2007, p. 179ff.

[131] See *R (Ullah) v. Special Adjudicator* [2004] UKHL 26, nos. 7 and 9.

[132] Id. With regard to this categorization Lord Bingham immediately admitted that the distinction was imperfect, as even in so-called 'foreign cases' the State naturally exercises authority over a person by virtue of the decision to remove him or her from the territory.

[133] One should note that this analysis ultimately provided only a partial answer. See *R (Ullah) v. Special Adjudicator* [2004] UKHL 26, no. 10.

This distinction between domestic and foreign cases is, incidentally, not entirely clear, because, as acknowledged by Lord Bingham, it is precisely this exercise of authority in so-called 'foreign' cases—namely the decision to extradite or expel—which leads to responsibility for a breach of the ECHR. In this sense the act which leads to responsibility takes place within the territory of the Contracting Party; this is only different in cases which concern a genuine extra-territorial act, where the act by definition takes place outside the territory of the Contracting Party.[134]

4.4.3.2 Article 1 ECHR and the Use of the Public Policy Exception

It is interesting to return once more to the Dutch case discussed in the beginning of this chapter with regard to the use of the public policy exception.[135] This case concerned a mother and child habitually resident in Surinam attempting to establish the paternity of a man living in the Netherlands. Surinamese law was the applicable law and the appeal court held that the normally applicable law could not be set aside save for exceptional circumstances. This decision could not be challenged in cassation (appeal), according to the *Hoge Raad*. The Advocate General in his conclusion also found that cassation was not possible, but he also posed the question of whether the applicants would have fallen within the jurisdiction of the Netherlands *ex* Article 1 ECHR had this case proceeded.

Interestingly enough, it should be noted that a few lower courts in the Netherlands had little hesitation in concluding that the ECHR was applicable in two cases in which the facts were remarkably similar to those of the case discussed previously.[136] Both cases concerned the request of a Moroccan mother to establish the paternity of a man residing in the Netherlands. In the first case the mother resided in Morocco, while in the second the mother was illegally residing in the Netherlands. In both cases the court—on the basis of the public policy exception—set aside the normally applicable Moroccan law, under which it was not possible to judicially establish paternity, and applied Dutch law instead. I should point out that in both these cases Article 1 ECHR was not discussed; both courts immediately raised Article 8 ECHR, presumably assuming that the ECHR was applicable to the case—which, in my opinion, is indeed the case.

---

[134] Cf. Juratowitch 2007, pp. 185–187.

[135] See supra Sect. 4.1.

[136] See Rb. 's-Gravenhage 3 November 2008, *NIPR* 2010, 23 and Hof 's-Hertogenbosch 27 November 2008, *NIPR* 2009, 95. These two cases, as well as the afore-mentioned case of the *HR*, were discussed in Kiestra 2010, pp. 27–30. See for a more recent example also Rb. Haarlem 11 December 2012, *NIPR* 2013, 24. In this case, which was decided on the basis of the 'new' article 10:97BW, the normally applicable Nigerian law was set aside on the basis of Article 8 ECHR, because the concept of the judicial establishment of paternity for children born out of wedlock does not exist under Nigerian law. In this case the mother, the child, and the presumed father all resided in the Netherlands. See for more on this case infra Sect. 6.3.3.2.

Such cases concerning the establishment of paternity have not been limited to the Netherlands.[137] The French *Cour de Cassation* has also dealt with an action for paternity of an Algerian child residing in Algeria against a Frenchman residing in France.[138] The normally applicable Algerian law prohibited such an action. The issue before the *Cour* was whether the principle of equality of filiations, which the court of appeal had expressly invoked in its decision, could be invoked by way of a reference to the public policy exception. The French *Cour* held that as the child had neither French nationality nor resided in France, the public policy exception could not be invoked. The outcome of this case has received a fair amount of praise in France, particularly in light of the debate concerning the imperialism of the ECHR discussed above.[139] However, it remains difficult to see how a court could find that the ECHR would not apply to these cases given the obligations following from Article 1 ECHR, which would make the *Cour de Cassation's* denial by way of finding that the public policy exception may not be invoked a questionable decision.[140]

In a more recent case, however, the *Cour de Cassation* appears to have reversed this course.[141] This case also concerned an action for paternity, which had to be decided on the basis of the law of the Ivory Coast. Here, though, it was merely found that the impossibility to do so would violate French public policy, while—contrary to the case discussed above—no mention was made of a further requirement of a connection between the child and France.[142] From the viewpoint of Article 1 ECHR, such a development is encouraging.

4.4.3.3 The Extensive Reach of the ECHR in Issues of Private International Law

There are two more cases which are interesting to discuss here, because they demonstrate the possibly extensive reach of the rights guaranteed in the ECHR in international civil proceedings, which is ultimately the result of Article 1 ECHR.

---

[137] It has also been suggested in the Swiss literature that Article 8 ECHR could be invoked by a child to establish a relationship with both parents in private international law cases, even though this issue appears not yet to have come up in the domestic case law. See Bucher 2011, pp. 588–589. See further infra Chap. 6.

[138] Cass. 1re civ., 10 May 2006.

[139] See for an overview, e.g., Gannagé 2008, pp. 266–267.

[140] One could, of course, argue that in this case the decision not to set aside the normally applicable Algerian law and consequently not to establish paternity could fall within the margin of appreciation which France has with regard to Article 8 ECHR. Regardless of how one may feel about this argument, though, the problem with the use of the public policy exception here in this manner is that its use precludes any discussion of the ECHR, and this is problematic from the point of view of Article 1 ECHR. See with regard to this case also infra Sect. 6.3.3.

[141] Cass. 1re civ., 26 October 2011, *JDI* 2012, p. 176 (note Guillaumé).

[142] See on this case Sindres 2012, pp. 887–901.

The first is an English case, *Douglas & Others v. Hello Ltd. & Others*.[143] In this case obligations following from Article 8 ECHR were deemed to be applicable, even though some of the relevant facts had taken place far from the English courts.

This rather complex case concerned the wedding reception of Mr Douglas and Ms Zeta-Jones (the Douglases), two very well-known movie actors. In November 2000 they were married in the Plaza Hotel in New York in the United States. There was a considerable amount of media interest in this event, particularly from the publishers of *OK!* and *Hello* magazines. Both publishers approached the couple to obtain the exclusive right to publish pictures of the wedding. The Douglases granted the right to publish to one publisher in order to protect their privacy, and reached an agreement with *OK!* magazine. However, *Hello* magazine later succeeded in acquiring unauthorized pictures of the wedding and published these more or less at the same time as the authorized ones in *OK!*.

The Douglases and the publishers of *OK!* filed a law-suit against the publishers of *Hello* and were awarded damages. All parties appealed against this decision. One of the issues (on appeal) was whether the Douglases could rely on their right to privacy following from Article 8 ECHR, as the wedding had taken place in the city of New York, which is, of course, outside the territories of the Contracting Parties.[144] The court ultimately decided that despite the wedding having taken place in New York, English law was the law applicable to the case and that the right to privacy, which is based on common law rights, after a discussion of the relevant principles found in the Strasbourg case law, was indeed applicable.[145] This case could thus be cited as an example of the possibly extensive reach of the rights guaranteed in the ECHR. It should be noted that although in the appeal before the House of Lords the Douglases still prevailed with regard to the breach of confidence, the importance of their right to privacy was significantly downplayed in the UKHL's decision.[146]

A final case, which is worth discussing because it raises a question regarding the possibly extensive reach of the ECHR in issues of private international law due to the extra-territorial effect of the Convention, is a Dutch case.[147] This case concerned a change of an arrangement regarding parental access between two divorced parents. After the divorce, the mother married another man and she moved to the United States with her new husband, taking the children with her. The former husband moved back to Denmark. The father had sought, before a Dutch appeal court, to change the arrangement they had originally agreed to after their divorce. The appeal court had changed the agreement. The mother

[143] [2005] EMLR 609, [2005] 4 All ER 128, [2005] 2 FCR 487, [2005] EMLR 28, [2005] 3 WLR 881, [2005] HRLR 27, [2005] EWCA Civ 595, [2006] QB 125.

[144] At no. 95ff.

[145] Cf. Janis et al. 2008, pp. 401–402. See with regard to this case also, e.g., Mak 2008, pp. 125–131.

[146] [2007] UKHL 2. See particularly Lord Hoffmann at no. 117ff.

[147] HR 19 October 2007, *NIPR* 2007, 267.

successfully argued before the *Hoge Raad* that the appeal court had set a more generous arrangement than the father had requested and the judgment was therefore quashed by the *Hoge Raad*.[148] What is of interest in relation to the scope of the ECHR is an argument raised by the mother. She argued that the new arrangement would violate her right to family life under Article 8 ECHR with her new husband in the US. This argument was not discussed by the *Hoge Raad*, which granted the mother's request for the reason mentioned above. However, the Advocate General did examine this claim and found that the mother could not rely on Article 8 ECHR, as she, her new husband, and the children resided in the US and were thus not within the jurisdiction of the Netherlands, as is required by Article 1 ECHR.

This case represents, in my opinion, the ultimate test regarding the scope of the ECHR. While the proceedings took place in a Contracting Party (the Netherlands), the applicant, who invoked a right guaranteed in the ECHR, no longer resided in a Contracting Party, as the family had moved to the United States. I should first emphasize that I will only discuss this case in relation to the issue concerning Article 1 ECHR. I will not venture further into the mother's claim concerning her rights under Article 8 ECHR, except to say that regardless of the international dimension of this case it seems, in principle, unlikely that a change to the arrangement for parental access would result in a violation of Article 8 ECHR.[149]

It should be clear that the connection between the forum and the case at hand is negligible. Above, I have stated that if proceedings take place in the Netherlands, these proceedings concerning issues of private international law fall within the jurisdiction of the Netherlands within the meaning of Article 1 ECHR and that thus any decision of a Dutch court should, in principle, also be in line with the guarantees of the ECHR. Should this still be the situation in a case such as this? This case really tests this finding. There are plenty of reasons to argue that the ECHR should not be applied to this case. What right to protection under the ECHR could a person residing in the United States possibly have? However, the reasoning discussed in this chapter regarding the role of Article 1 ECHR in connection with issues of private international law still holds up. If a Dutch court has jurisdiction in the private international law sense, this court should take a decision in accordance with the guarantees of the ECHR. If the decision of a Dutch court were to violate one of the rights guaranteed in the ECHR, even if this violation would actually

[148] One may wonder why a Dutch court still had jurisdiction, when the parties had since moved, respectively, to the United States and Denmark. The court based its jurisdiction on Article 8(1) of Council Regulation (EC) No. 2201/2003 concerning Jurisdiction and the Recognition and Enforcement of Judgments in Matrimonial Matters and the Matters of Parental Responsibility, *OJ* 2003, L 338/1 (Brussels II*bis*-Regulation), as the proceedings were initiated when the children still had their habitual residence in the Netherlands.

[149] It is unlikely that the Court would interfere in such a case on the basis of Article 8 ECHR. While a change of the arrangement on parental access may entail an interference with Article 8 ECHR, it follows from the Court's case law that a violation will only be found if no adequate steps are taken to enable access to a child. See, e.g., *Nuutinen v. Finland*, no. 32842/96, ECHR 2000-VIII.

take place in the United States, then the Netherlands could, in principle, still be responsible for this violation.[150]

While in this case the Netherlands may be held responsible if its courts were to take a decision violating one of the rights guaranteed in the ECHR, the Netherlands could presumably not be held responsible if its decision was not applied correctly, or not enforced at all, in the United States, as the Netherlands of course does not have the jurisdiction to enforce its decision in a third country. This latter situation should be distinguished from the one discussed directly above. If, for example, the Dutch courts were to decide on a visitation rights scheme which was subsequently not enforced in the United States by the authorities, this would not mean that the Netherlands would be responsible for a possible violation of Article 8 of the ECHR in this regard.[151]

4.4.3.4 Article 1 ECHR in National Case Law: Concluding Remarks

The scope of the ECHR, which can be found in Article 1 ECHR, is almost never explicitly discussed in private international law cases in the national legal orders of the Contracting Parties. In the cases discussed above, Article 1 ECHR was only explicitly referred to in a case concerning international child abduction, in which the requested return raised an issue, and in cases where the connection between the case at hand and the forum is limited. The international child abduction case, in which the requested return raised a possible issue under the ECHR, offered a direct parallel with the Court's case law concerning the extra-territorial effect of the ECHR where the decision to extradite or expel raised possible issues, and it is thus not surprising that Article 1 ECHR would be discussed in such cases. In cases

[150] One should, incidentally, note that it is unlikely at best that the United States would actually enforce a decision by the Dutch courts that would violate one of the rights guaranteed in the ECHR. Such a decision would presumably also violate the public policy of the United States.

[151] Cf. *Qama v. Albania and Italy*, no. 4604/09, 8 January 2013. In this case the applicant, an Albanian national, is the father of a son, also an Albanian national. The applicant's son went to Italy with his mother. The applicant followed at a later point. In 2002 the applicant was expelled from Italy, while the mother and son remained in Italy. Later that year the mother passed away. The applicant's sister in law was awarded custody over the child in Italy. The applicant's parental authority was suspended in these proceedings by the Italian judge. The child acquires a regular status in Italy. He does not want to have contact with his father. Later the father initiates proceedings in Albania. In this case an Albanian judge found that the father has visitation rights and awards these to the father. However, this right cannot be enforced by the Albanian authorities, as the child formally resides in Italy. Before the Court in Strasbourg the applicant alleges that both Albania and Italy have violated his rights under Article 8 ECHR. With regard to Italy the Court found that the applicant had failed to exhaust his local remedies. With regard to the complaint against Albania the Court held that it could not be held against Albania that it had failed to enforce the Albanian judgments regarding visitation rights. Article 8 ECHR does not entail an obligation for a Contracting Party to establish visiting rights between a parent and a child in the event that the child has moved out of the country and out of the jurisdiction of the Contracting Party, according to the Court. See with regard to this case further EHRC 2013/79 (note Kiestra).

which have so little connection to the forum that doubts arise as to whether the ECHR is applicable at all, it is also not surprising that Article 1 ECHR would be discussed—although, in my opinion, the ECHR is still applicable to these cases.

However, in cases concerning either the recognition of a foreign judgment or the application of a foreign law possibly originating from a third country, Article 1 ECHR is almost never discussed in jurisprudence at the national level. Nevertheless, this should not be interpreted as meaning that there is no role for Article 1 ECHR in such cases. In most cases concerning issues of private international law and third countries, and consequently norms originating from these third countries, courts will refer to the rights guaranteed in the ECHR in their assessment of either a foreign judgment or a foreign law—if circumstances so warrant. One could say in this regard that national courts merely skip the issue of the applicability of the ECHR to private international law cases, which is not that remarkable, as I have explained that it is virtually impossible to escape the applicability of the ECHR to private international law cases. Moreover, most issues of private international law clearly fall within the jurisdiction of the Contracting Parties. In that sense, one could argue that it is simply efficient to skip the issue of the applicability of the ECHR in private international law cases and that no harm is done.

However, the danger inherent to relegating the role of Article 1 ECHR to a mere afterthought has, hopefully, also become clear in this section. In many of the Contracting Parties, including England, the Netherlands, and Switzerland, the public policy exception is normally used in private international law cases in order to deal with the possible impact of the rights guaranteed in the ECHR in such cases.[152] However, if the use of this instrument were to lead to the application of the normally applicable law, which subsequently violates one of the rights guaranteed in the ECHR, one may wonder whether the Contracting Party in question has lived up to the obligations undertaken in Article 1 ECHR. A similar reason applies to the recognition and enforcement of a foreign judgment. The French case discussed above demonstrates that such a scenario is not inconceivable. However, as the national case law that will be discussed in subsequent chapters will clearly demonstrate, this has not stopped courts from using the public policy exception in private international law cases.

4.5 Conclusion

This chapter has considered the relationship between Article 1 ECHR and private international law. Article 1 ECHR defines the scope of this instrument with the phrase 'within their jurisdiction'. In order to examine the meaning of this phrase, the notion of 'jurisdiction' has been analyzed, and several of its aspects have been illuminated. It was found that the notion of jurisdiction in (public) international

[152] See with regard to the public policy exception supra Sect. 2.5. See also the national case law discussed in the subsequent chapters. See, e.g., Sect. 6.3.3.

law is generally concerned with the authority of a State to regulate conduct, but this notion has several distinguishable aspects, and its meaning is thus not always clear. While the Court, in its case law concerning the notion of jurisdiction in Article 1 ECHR, has held that the interpretation thereof should be based on the ordinary meaning of jurisdiction in international law, it should be clear that questions regarding this notion remain, as the meaning of jurisdiction in public international law is simply not unambiguous.

Thereafter the role of Article 1 ECHR with regard to private international law has been discussed. It has been found that when a court of one of the Contracting Parties either applies a foreign law or recognizes a foreign judgment originating from a third State, the ECHR is applicable to such cases. Even though such a third State has never signed the ECHR, it would ultimately be the court of one of the Contracting Parties whose application of a foreign law or recognition of a foreign judgment violating one of the rights guaranteed in the ECHR would breach the ECHR. This may be derived from the Court's case law concerning the extra-territorial effects of the ECHR, and has been confirmed by the little case law that specifically deals with issues of private international law. Even in circumstances in which there is only a negligible connection with the Contracting Party, the situation does not change appreciably. Such situations still come within the jurisdiction of the Contracting Party and the ECHR is thus applicable to such cases.

This does not mean that there cannot be any consideration of specific private international law issues, but only that such concerns should, in my opinion, be dealt with within the system of the ECHR. Therefore, one could question whether the public policy exception resulting in the non-application of the ECHR, because of the relative character of the exception, is permissible in light of Article 1 ECHR.

References

Akehurst M (1972–1973) Jurisdiction in international law. BYIL 46:145–257

Brownlie I (2008) Principles of public international law. Oxford University Press, Oxford

Bucher A (2000) La famille en droit international privé. Recueil des Cours 283:9–186

Bucher A (ed) (2011) Loi sur le droit international privé. Convention de Lugano, Helbing Lichtenhahn, Basel

Cassese A (2005) International law. Oxford University Press, Oxford

Coester-Waltjen D (1998) Die Wirkungskraft der Grundrechte bei Fällen mit Auslandsbezug—familien- und erbrechtlicher Bereich [The impact of fundamental right in cross-border cases—the area of family and inheritance law]. In: Coester-Waltjen D (ed) Die Wirkungskraft der Grundrechte bei Fällen mit Auslandsbezug [The impact of fundamental rights in cross-border cases]. C.F. Müller, Heidelberg, pp 9–32

Costa J-P (2002) Le Tribunal de la Rote et l'article 6 de la Convention européenne des droits de l'homme. Revue trimestrielle des droits de l'homme 13:470–476

Docquir B (1999) Le droit international privé à l'épreuve de la Convention européenne des droits de l'homme. Annales de Droit de Louvain 59:473–522

Donnely J (2007) The relative universality of human rights. Human Rights Q 27:281–306

Donnely J (2008) Human rights: both universal and relative (a reply to Michael Goodhart). Human Rights Q 30:194–204

Engel C (1989) Ausstrahlungen der Europäischen Menschenrechtskonvention auf das Kollisionsrecht [Emanations of the European Convention on Human Right on Conflict of Laws]. RabelsZ 53:3–51

Fawcett JJ (2007) The impact of article 6 (1) ECHR on private international law. ILCQ 56:1–48

Flauss J-F (2002) L'exequatur des jugements étrangers devant la Cour Européenne des Droits de l'Homme. In: Bieber R (ed) Mélanges en l'honneur de Bernard Dutoit, Librairie Droz, Genève, pp 69–87

Fulchiron H (2010) The French family judge encounters cultural pluralism. In: Foblets M-C (ed) Cultural diversity and the law: state responses from around the world. Bruylant, Brussels, pp 613–633

Gannagé L (2001) La hiérarchie des normes et les méthodes du droit international privé: étude de droit international privé de la famille. L.G.D.J, Paris

Gannagé L (2008) A propos de l'absolutisme des droits fondamentaux. In: Ancel JP (ed) Vers des nouveaux equilibres entre ordre juridiques: liber amicorum Hélène Gaudemet-Tallon, Dalloz, Paris, pp 265–284

Gaudemet-Tallon H (2004) Nationalité, statut personnel et droits de l'homme. In: Mansel H-P (ed) Festschrift für erik jayme. Sellier, Munich, pp 205–221

Gondek M (2009) The reach of human rights in a globalising world: extraterritorial application of human rights treaties. Intersentia, Antwerp

Goodhart M (2008) Neither relative nor universal: a response to Donnely. Human Rights Q 30:183–193

Harris DJ et al (eds) (2009) Law of the European convention on human rights. Oxford University Press, Oxford

Higgins R (1984) The legal bases of jurisdiction. In: Olmstead CJ (ed) Extra-territorial application of law and responses thereto. ESC Publishing, Oxford

Janis MW et al (2008) European human rights law: text and materials. Oxford University Press, Oxford

Juratowitch B (2007) The European convention on human rights and english private international law. J Private Int Law 3:173–199

Kiestra LR (2010) De betekenis van het EVRM voor de internationale gerechtelijke vaststelling van het vaderschap [The meaning of the ECHR for the international judicial determination of paternity]. NIPR 28:27–30

Kiestra LR (2011) Article 1 ECHR and private international law. NIPR 29:2–7

Kinsch P (2004) The impact of human rights on the application of foreign law and on the recognition of foreign judgments—a survey of the cases decided by the European human rights institutions. In: Einhorn T, Siehr K (eds) Intercontinental cooperation through private international law—Essays in memory of Peter E. Nygh. T.M.C. Asser Press, The Hague

Kinsch P (2007) Droits de l'homme, droits fondamentaux et droit international privé. Recueil des Cours 318:9–332. Martinus Nijhoff Publishers, Leiden

Lagarde P (1994) Public policy, international encyclopedia of comparative law, vol III. Mohr, Tübingen

Lawson RA (2004) Life after Bankovic: On the extraterritorial application of the European convention on human rights. In: Coomans F, Kamminga MT (eds) Extraterritorial application of human rights treaties. Intersentia, Antwerp, pp 83–123

Lequette Y (2004) Le droit international privé et les droits fondamentaux. In: Cabrillac R et al (eds) Libertés et droit fondamentaux, Dalloz, Paris, pp 97–118

Loucaides L (2006) Determining the extra-territorial effect of the European convention: facts, jurisprudence and the Bankovic case. Eur Hum Rights Law Rev 11:391–407

Lowe AV, Staker C (2010) Jurisdiction. In: Evans MD (ed) International law. Oxford University Press, Oxford, pp 313–339

Lowenfeld AF (1996) International litigation and the quest for reasonableness. Clarendon Press, Oxford

Mak C (2008) Fundamental rights in European contract law. A comparison of the impact of fundamental rights on contractual relationships in Germany, the Netherlands, Italy and England. Kluwer Law International, Alphen aan den Rijn

Mann FA (1964) The Doctrine of Jurisdiction in International Law. Recueil des cours 111:1–162
Mann FA (1984) The Doctrine of International Jurisdiction Revisited after twenty years. Recueil des cours 186:9–116
Mayer P (1991) La Convention européenne des droits de l'homme et l'application des normes étrangères. Rev crit dr int priv 98:651–665
McLachlan C (1993) The influence of international law on civil jurisdiction. Hague Yearb Int Law 6:125–144
Milanović M (2008) From compromise to principle: clarifying the concept of state jurisdiction in human right treaties. Hum Rights Law Rev 8:411–448
Milanović M (2011) Extraterritorial application of human rights treaties. Oxford University Press, Oxford
Miller S (2009) Revisiting extraterritorial jurisdiction: a territorial jurisdiction for extraterritorial jurisdiction under the European convention. EJIL 20:1223–1246
Mills A (2008) The dimensions of public policy in private international law. J Private Int Law 4:201–236
Nigro R (2010) The notion of 'jurisdiction' in Article 1: future scenarios for the extra-territorial application of the European convention on human rights. Ital Yearb Int Law 20:11–30
Nollkaemper PA (2009) Kern van het international publiekrecht [The essence of public international law]. Boom Juridische Uitgevers, Den Haag
O'Boyle M (2004) The European convention on human rights and extraterritorial jurisdiction: a comment on 'life after Bankovic'. In: Coomans F, Kamminga MT (eds) Extraterritorial application of human rights treaties. Intersentia, Antwerp, pp 125–139
Olmstead CJ (ed) (1984) Extra-territorial application of laws and responses thereto. ESC Publishing, Oxford
Orakhelashvili A (2003) Restrictive interpretation of human rights treaties in the recent jurisprudence of the European Court of Human Rights. EJIL 14:529–568
Pocar F (2006) Notes on the Pellegrini judgment of the European Court of Human Rights. In: Erauw J (ed) Liber Memorialis Petar Šarčević. Sellier, Munich, pp 575–581
Rutten SWE (1998) Mensenrechten en het ipr: scheiden of trouwen? [Human rights and private international law: to divorce or to marry?]. NJCM-Bull 23:797–811
Shaw MN (2008) International law. Cambridge University Press, Cambridge
Sindres D (2012) Vers la disparition de l'ordre public de proximité? JDI 139:887–901
Smit H (1961) The terms jurisdiction and competence in comparative law. AJCL 10:164–169
Struycken AVM (2009) Co-ordination and co-operation in respectful disagreement: general course on private international law. Recueil des Cours 311
Stürner M (2011) Extraterritorial application of the echr via private international law? a comment from the German perspective. NIPR 29:8–12
Thoma I (2007) Die Europäisierung und die Vergemeinschaftung des nationalen Ordre Public [The Europeanization and communitarization of domestic public policy]. Mohr Siebeck, Tübingen
van der Wilt H (2012) On the hierarchy between extradition and human rights. In: Vidmar J, De Wet E (eds) Hierarchy in international law: the place of human rights. Oxford University Press, Oxford, pp 268–315
van Loon JHA (1993) De wisselwerking tussen internationaal privaatrecht en rechten van de mens [The interaction between private international law and human rights]. In: van Dijk D et al (eds) Grensoverschrijdend privaatrecht: een bundel opstellen over privaatrecht in internationaal verband [Cross-border private law: a collection of essays on private law in an international context]. Kluwer, Deventer, pp 135–148
Wautelet P (2004) What has international private law achieved in meeting the challenges posed by globalization? In: Slot PJ, Bulterman M (eds) Globalisation and jurisdiction. Kluwer International Law, The Hague, pp 55–77
White RCA, Ovey C (2010) The European convention on human rights. Oxford University Press, Oxford

Chapter 5
Jurisdiction in Private International Law

Contents

L.R. Kiestra, *The Impact of the European Convention on Human Rights on Private International Law*, DOI 10.1007/978-94-6265-032-9_5

5.1 Introduction

As was first noted in Chap. 1, jurisdiction is one of the three main issues of private international law.[1] It concerns the issue of which court has adjudicatory or judicial competence in a private law conflict between parties in international litigation. There are many different reasons for States to assert jurisdiction in international litigation. The starting point here is that States have 'an inherent right and duty to dispense justice'.[2] This is one of the basic functions of a State. However, it is not a given in international litigation that a State will assert jurisdiction. If the facts of a case have little or no connection to the forum, there is a good chance that a court will refuse to assert jurisdiction. The courts of any country would quickly become overwhelmed if they were to allow litigants from all over the world to initiate proceedings there, and costs would soar. Then again, States cannot become too economical in this regard, because of this 'duty to dispense justice'.

There may also be more mundane reasons for a State to assert jurisdiction in international litigation. States may have an interest in attracting litigation in a particular field of law in order to develop legal rules and principles in that field of (international) law.[3] A State might also want to open its courts to promote important policies, such as, for example, human rights. However, as mentioned above, opening up one's courts to attract all sorts of litigation necessarily has its limits. In addition to practical issues, such as the capacity of courts and costs, there is also the danger in international litigation of concurrent litigation, which could ultimately lead to conflicting judgments in different countries. It is for the States to find some sort of balance with regard to the issue of jurisdiction in private international law.

Adjudication forms part of the exercise of State authority and States are bound by public international law in this exercise. However, as will be discussed further below, the standards established in international law with regard to the issue of jurisdiction in private international law are somewhat vague and appear not to be very restrictive.[4] The considerations concerning the assertion of jurisdiction in private international law mentioned so far are all given from the perspective of the State. Although these are important, they are not the only relevant considerations for the issue of jurisdiction in private international law. Private parties are, after all, still those seeking justice in matters of private international law and they have their own interests. This is where fundamental rights may come into play as a consideration in the exercise of jurisdiction in matters of private international law.

In this chapter the role of the ECHR with regard to the issue of jurisdiction in private international law will be examined. Before turning to the specific issue of the impact of the ECHR on jurisdiction in private international law, it is prudent to

---

1 See also supra Chap. 2.

2 Von Mehren 2002, p. 56.

3 Von Mehren 2007, p. 47.

4 See further infra Sect. 5.2.2.

first elaborate on the notion of jurisdiction in private international law and the different rules of jurisdiction of States. The impact of public international law on the issue of jurisdiction in private international law will also be included here (in Sect. 5.2). The discussion of the notion of jurisdiction in private international law will be followed by a brief word on whether the ECHR can be applicable at all to the (non-) assertion of jurisdiction. If a court of one of the Contracting Parties finds that it does not have jurisdiction, is it even possible for a litigant to invoke the ECHR against such a decision (Sect. 5.3)? Next, the heart of the matter will be discussed: what is the impact of the ECHR on the issue of jurisdiction in private international law? This broader question can be broken up into three separate parts (Sects. 5.4–5.6). The first part concerns the impact of the right of access to a court, which can be derived from Article 6(1) ECHR, on jurisdiction in private international law. This right can be invoked by a plaintiff in international litigation who would otherwise reasonably be left without a forum to seek justice. An important issue here is the extent of this right (Sect. 5.4). However, Article 6(1) ECHR can arguably also be invoked by a defendant. This could occur in the situation where a court exercises jurisdiction over a defendant on an exorbitant basis (Sect. 5.5). A final area where Article 6(1) ECHR may have an impact on jurisdiction in private international law is in strategic litigation, particularly to counter the abuse of procedural rights in international litigation (Sect. 5.6).

5.2 The Notion of Jurisdiction in Private International Law

In Chap. 4 the various possible meanings of the notion of jurisdiction were discussed fairly extensively.[5] Jurisdiction in private international law is concerned with the question of which court is competent to hear an international case. This is thus jurisdiction in the sense of adjudicatory jurisdiction. Adjudicatory, or judicial, jurisdiction in private international law deals with the conflict of jurisdictions. It should also be understood from the outset that jurisdiction in private international law is concerned with civil jurisdiction. Finally, it should be mentioned that adjudicatory jurisdiction is only concerned with the determination of which State may entertain an international case. Which court of the thus elected State subsequently claims jurisdiction is a matter of venue and is therefore an internal matter, and, in principle, not a concern of (private) international law.[6]

The rules of adjudicatory jurisdiction in private international law are of a procedural nature. It is a preliminary issue that necessarily needs to be dealt with before a decision on the merits may be taken. This field of (private international) law is—taken

[5] See supra Chap. 4.

[6] In some jurisdictions these two concepts are interwoven in the sense that the rules of venue also function as the rules of international jurisdiction.

together with the recognition and enforcement of foreign judgments—also referred to as international (civil) procedure or international procedural law. Although traditionally more attention has been paid to questions of choice of law in the literature on private international law, it should be pointed out that the outcome of international litigation often depends more on the choice of forum than on the choice of law.[7]

5.2.1 Jurisdictional Rules and Grounds of Jurisdiction

Every country has its own rules on jurisdiction and is generally free to decide when to assert jurisdiction in issues of private international law. This simple fact has, as a result, that there can be both negative conflicts of jurisdiction, where no State is willing is to assert jurisdiction in international proceedings, and positive conflicts of jurisdiction, where more than one State is willing to assert jurisdiction. States not only have national rules of jurisdiction,[8] but can also be party to international conventions in which jurisdictional rules are laid down.[9] The EU Member States are also bound by EU rules on jurisdiction in private international law, chief among them the Brussels I Regulation[10] on civil and commercial matters and the Brussels II *bis* Regulation regarding family matters.[11] The Brussels I Regulation is supplemented by the Lugano Convention,[12] which essentially extends the provisions of the former instrument to the European Free Trade Association (EFTA) countries. I shall therefore refer below to the Brussels (/Lugano) regime. The Brussels I Regulation distributes jurisdiction between the different EU Member States, which means that if the instrument is applicable, there will always be at least one Member State with jurisdiction.[13] However, as the Regulation is by and large only applicable to

[7] See, e.g., Hartley 2006, p. 27. See with regard to the increased attention for conflicts of jurisdiction over conflicts of laws McLachlan 2004, pp. 580–616.

[8] See with regard to the sources of private international law generally supra Chap. 2.

[9] An example would be the Hague Convention of 30 June 2005 on Choice of Court Agreements, which after long negotiations has finally been agreed upon, although it is yet to enter into force. See [www.hcch.net]. See further, e.g., Beaumont 2009, pp. 125–159.

[10] Council Regulation (EC) No. 44/2001 on Jurisdiction and the Recognition and Enforcement of Judgments in Civil and Commercial Matters, *OJ* 2001, L12/1. (Brussels I-Regulation). The Regulation replaces the 1968 Brussels Convention on Jurisdiction and the Enforcement of Judgments in Civil and Commercial Matters, *OJ* 1978, L 304/36. The consolidated version can be found in *OJ* 1998, C 27/1.

[11] Council Regulation (EC) No. 2201/2003 concerning Jurisdiction and the Recognition and Enforcement of Judgments in Matrimonial Matters and the Matters of Parental Responsibility, *OJ* 2003, L 338/1.

[12] Council Decision 2007/712/EC on the Signing on behalf of the Community, of the Convention on Jurisdiction and the Recognition and Enforcement of Judgments in Civil and Commercial Matters, *OJ* 2007, L 339/1. The 2007 Lugano Convention replaces the 1988 Lugano Convention, *OJ* 1988, L 329/1.

[13] See, e.g., Magnus and Mankowski 2012.

defendants domiciled in the EU, this brings disadvantages to parties from outside the EU.[14] In the recast of the Regulation this will partly change.[15] In the recast it is provided that national rules of jurisdiction may no longer be applied by the Member States to consumers and employees domiciled in third countries. Uniform rules of jurisdiction will also apply to parties domiciled outside the EU, where the (courts of) Member States have exclusive jurisdiction based on the new Regulation. This also applies in the event that the courts of Member States have jurisdiction based on an agreement between the parties.

Various grounds of jurisdiction are employed by States all over the world to assert jurisdiction in matters of private international law. This has to do with the fact that private international law is concerned with different underlying subjects of private law. What might be an appropriate connecting factor for the assumption of jurisdiction in a tort case is not necessarily reasonable in a family law matter. Bases of jurisdiction which are considered balanced with regard to one subject may be considered exorbitant as to another.

One could say that there are basically two bases of jurisdiction which are nearly always considered to be reasonable, regardless of the underlying subject matter. One is the head of jurisdiction based on the principle of *actor sequitur forum rei.*[16] This is also the general rule of jurisdiction in the Brussels I Regulation.[17] Even though this ground of jurisdiction is generally accepted, there are plenty of exceptions to this rule. The other almost universally accepted ground of jurisdiction is jurisdiction based on the consent of the parties. This consent may either be stated expressly by means of a jurisdiction agreement or implicitly by the parties by not questioning the jurisdiction of a court. The vast majority of legal systems in the world have recognized the autonomy of parties to agree on which court will decide their disputes.[18] Other bases of jurisdiction are not generally accepted and would thus need to be assessed on a case-by-case basis in order to determine whether they are balanced.

5.2.1.1 Exorbitant Bases of Jurisdiction

There is also a category of bases of jurisdiction which have been deemed exorbitant. These have also been dubbed 'jurisdictionally improper fora'.[19] Exorbitant

---

[14] See in this regard infra Sect. 5.5.2, pp. 88.

[15] Regulation (EU) No. 1215/2012 of the European Parliament and of the Council of 12 December 2012 on Jurisdiction and the Recognition and Enforcement of Judgments in Civil and Commercial Matters (Recast), *OJ* 2012, L 351/1. The Recast will apply from 10 January 2015 (see Article 81 of the Recast).

[16] See, e.g., Fernández Arroyo 2004, p. 169. But see De Winter 1968, p. 717.

[17] See Article 2 of the Brussels I Regulation supra n. 10.

[18] See, e.g., Wautelet 2004, p. 67. One could in this regard also cite the Hague Convention supra n. 9.

[19] Nadelmann 1961.

jurisdiction has been described as jurisdiction lacking 'reasonableness'.[20] In asserting jurisdiction, the interests of a State's own nationals or residents are of paramount importance, while the interests of other parties appear to have received little consideration.[21] A list of national rules of jurisdiction which are considered to be exorbitant can be found in the Brussels I Regulation. These shall not be applicable against persons domiciled in other EU Member States.[22] The list includes—among other things—grounds of jurisdiction based on the nationality of the plaintiff and jurisdiction based on the temporary presence in the country (the English tag jurisdiction).[23]

5.2.2 The Impact of Public International Law on Jurisdiction in Private International Law

It is useful to examine whether public international law provides rules which limit the adjudicatory jurisdiction of national courts in private international law. This is particularly so because there are some restrictions to the exercise of jurisdiction in private international law which may be derived from Article 6(1) ECHR, which have, however, also been presented as being restrictions following from public international law.[24] If these restrictions were indeed to follow from public international law, the possible meaning of Article 6(1) ECHR would be reduced in this regard. It is clear that as States are supposed to act in accordance with international law, the exercise of adjudicatory jurisdiction should be consistent with the principles of public international law. However, what the possible limits of public international law to the exercise of adjudicatory jurisdiction in private international law then exactly entail is a separate issue.

It has been argued that there are no rules of customary international law that limit the exercise of adjudicatory jurisdiction in private international law, except for rules on sovereign, diplomatic, and other immunities,[25] while States that deny foreigners the right of access to their courts may be guilty of denial of justice.[26] One could thus state that there are two important strands of the possible impact of public international law on jurisdiction in private international law. There is, first,

[20] Fernández Arroyo 2004, p. 170.

[21] De Winter 1968, p. 706. Cf. Kahn-Freund 1976, p. 34.

[22] See Article 3(2) (and Annex I) of the Brussels I Regulation supra n. 10.

[23] See Annex 1 to the Brussels I Regulation supra n. 10.

[24] These restrictions, which may follow from Article 6(1) ECHR, will be discussed infra Sects. 5.4 and 5.5.

[25] The limitations following immunities are well established, and will henceforth not be further discussed. See with regard to immunities in public international law, e.g., the recent case of the ICJ *Jurisdictional Immunities of the State (Germany v. Italy: Greece intervening)*, 3 February 2012. See with regard to this case, e.g., Hess 2012, pp. 201–206.

[26] Akehurst 1972–1973, p. 170.

the question of whether there are rules of public international law (other than immunities) that limit the ability of States to assert jurisdiction in private international law. The second strand entails the meaning of the doctrine of denial of justice. These two limitations are discussed below.

5.2.2.1 The Impact of Public International Law on the Assertion of Jurisdiction in Private International Law

The main evidence for the limited impact of public international law on the exercise of adjudicatory jurisdiction in private international law is the fact that the bases of jurisdiction in civil matters are more wide-ranging compared to bases of criminal jurisdiction, but protests by other States against these bases are virtually nonexistent.[27] However, others have contended that 'there is in principle no great difference between the problems created by the assertion of civil and criminal jurisdiction over aliens'.[28] It has been held that it is the function of international law to prescribe the limits within which a State may claim jurisdiction in private international law and the fundamental question that needs answering in a given case is whether, on the relevant facts, there is a sufficiently close connection between the facts and the legal system called upon to adjudicate the matter.[29] Many have argued that public international law prescribes that there should be a genuine link or close connection between the facts of a case and the court called upon to decide that case.[30] This 'rule' has also been dubbed the 'proximity' rule or the 'significant connection' rule.[31] In this regard it has also been held that 'the suggestion that the exercise of jurisdiction in civil matters, however exorbitant, can never be contrary to customary international law is both implausible and unattractive.'[32] Many have thus argued that public international law requires a significant connection between the facts of the case and the court asserting jurisdiction. However, not much evidence is cited in favor of the existence of such a rule.

The only relevant case of the Permanent Court of International Justice (the predecessor of the International Court of Justice) with regard to the assertion of jurisdiction, the *Lotus* case,[33] did not concern civil jurisdiction, but criminal jurisdiction. Nonetheless, it should be noted that this is quite a controversial case that has been much criticized for a variety of reasons.[34] It is also difficult to find an

[27] See Akehurst 1972–1973, p. 177. Cf. Shaw 2008, pp. 651–652.

[28] Brownlie 2008, p. 300.

[29] Mann 1984, p. 28. Cf. Mann 1964, pp. 44–47 and (on civil jurisdiction) p. 73ff. But see Matscher 1978, p. 157 (in reaction to Mann's work of 1964).

[30] See, e.g., Mann 1984; Meessen 1984, pp. 38–44.

[31] Kessedjian 1997, p. 23.

[32] Hill 2003, p. 43.

[33] See PCIJ, 7 September 1927, Series A No. 10 (*Lotus*).

[34] See, e.g., Higgins 1999, p. 100.

opinio iuris and state practice with regard to this significant connection rule, as many States still have legislation—national rules on jurisdiction—allowing them to claim jurisdiction in civil cases in which the link between the facts and the court is at best flimsy. One only needs to refer to the aforementioned exorbitant bases of jurisdiction.[35] State protests in this field are nevertheless rare.[36] They are, in issues of private international law, mostly limited to the regulation of international economic activity by way of giving laws extraterritorial reach in response to foreign conduct producing effects within the forum.[37] The exercise of extraterritorial jurisdiction has led to several disputes between the United States and the EU resulting in State protests and countermeasures.[38] One should, however, note that jurisdiction exercised in this sense concerns mostly prescriptive or legislative jurisdiction, although admittedly the demarcation between adjudicatory and prescriptive jurisdiction is not always clear.

Another argument often made in favor of the existence of public international law limitations on adjudicatory jurisdiction in private international law is the fact that judgments based on an exorbitant ground of jurisdiction are often not recognized or enforced by other States.[39] Thus one could argue that while States may not formally protest against judgments based on exorbitant grounds of jurisdiction, they do so implicitly by the refusal to recognize or enforce such judgments. It is questionable whether one may regard this as state practice in a public international law sense and that one could therefore consider this to be a public international law limitation to adjudicatory jurisdiction in private international law. Can one really equate the refusal to recognize and enforce foreign judgments based on exorbitant grounds of jurisdiction in private international law issues to state protest against the assertion of jurisdiction? This would entail a very indirect form of state protest.

However, in practice this question lacks urgency. Regardless of whether this is a limitation derived from public international law, it should be clear that this is, in fact, an important consideration for States and their courts in deciding whether it is prudent in a certain case to claim jurisdiction.[40] It is usually of little use to any party in an international situation to obtain a judgment that cannot be enforced in another country. In fact, it could easily be argued that the assertion of international jurisdiction by a State can only be effective if other States are willing to cooperate or are

---

35 See supra Sect. 5.2.1.1.

36 Cf. Joubert 2007, pp. 23–27, who appears to acknowledge this and concludes that public international law has only a limited role with regard to private international law, but who also points out that the increased attention for the importance of significant links may call into question this limited role. See in this regard also De Vareilles-Sommières 1997.

37 See, e.g., the many interesting contributions on this subject in Olmstead 1984; see also Kamminga 2012, particularly no. 17ff; Oxman 2012, particularly no. 52ff.

38 See, e.g., Sinclair 1984, pp. 217–222; April 1984, pp. 223–233.

39 Cf. Mayer 1979, pp. 1–29, pp. 349–388, p. 552.

40 An example of a national court being attentive to the question of whether the judgment will be recognized abroad is Hof's-Gravenhage, 21 December 2005. This case will be discussed in detail infra n. 181.

at least willing to refrain from thwarting the adjudicatory action.[41] Thus, it could be said that the internationally widespread practice of refusing to recognize or enforce foreign judgments based on a questionable ground for jurisdiction serves as a limitation for asserting adjudicatory jurisdiction in private international law.

In conclusion, one may state that the impact of public international law on the issue of adjudicatory jurisdiction appears to be limited, despite many authors claiming the opposite. There is little case law from international courts which gives us something to hold on to regarding the issue of adjudicatory jurisdiction in private international law. One may derive from the fact that States assume jurisdiction in cross-border civil matters where neither the facts nor the parties have a significant connection with the forum, and the fact that this leads to few state protests, that public international law offers limited restrictions to the assertion of adjudicatory jurisdiction in civil cases. However, if a State assumes jurisdiction under such circumstances, chances are that any judgment following from this will not be recognized or enforced in foreign countries. This is, of course, a serious limitation to the assumption of adjudicatory jurisdiction, but it is questionable whether this is a limitation that can be derived from public international law.

5.2.2.2 Denial of Justice

The doctrine of denial of justice has long been a part of public international law.[42] The exact meaning of the doctrine has long been discussed, but remains somewhat unclear.[43] The doctrine is generally regarded as a bar to a State's (non)-assertion of jurisdiction under international law, and although its exact content is not clearly defined, it is generally thought to pertain only to gross or manifest instances of injustices.[44] As such, its connotation with the issue of the right of access to a court should be clear.[45] What gross or manifest injustices exactly entail, though, is not clear. As will become apparent from the discussion below on the right of access to court, the problem with the doctrine of denial of justice is similar to some of the problems associated with the right of access *ex* Article 6(1) ECHR in private international law.[46] It is, as such, in my opinion, questionable whether, due to its vagueness, the doctrine of denial of justice can claim an independent role separate from Article 6(1) ECHR with regard to the right of access to a court in private international law.

---

41 Von Mehren and Trautman 1966, p. 1127. See also Schlosser 2000.

42 See, e.g., De Visscher 1935, pp. 363–442.

43 See, e.g., Adede 1976, pp. 73–95; Focarelli 2012; Paulsson 2005. See also Francioni 2007. See with regard to the doctrine in private international law: Corbion 2004.

44 See, e.g., Kessedjian 2007, p. 22; Cf. Focarelli 2012, at no. 13.

45 The Court in *Golder v. the United Kingdom* also expressly referred to a 'denial of justice'. See infra Sect. 5.4.1.

46 See infra Sect. 5.4.

5.3 The Applicability of the ECHR to Disputes Concerning Jurisdiction in Private International Law

Before turning to the impact of the ECHR on jurisdiction in private international law, it is first necessary to further elaborate on the question of whether the ECHR can be applicable at all to this issue. This question has been considered in more general terms in Chap. 4.[47] Here, the question of whether the ECHR can be applicable at all to the issue of jurisdiction in private international law will particularly be dealt with in relation to the impact of the right of access to court.[48] As will be demonstrated below, Article 6(1) ECHR—the right to a fair hearing—also entails the notion of the right of access to a court.[49]

It is easy to see how this right could impact upon the question of which national court is competent to hear an international case. However, if a court of one of the Contracting Parties finds that it has no jurisdiction to hear a case on the basis of its jurisdictional rules, is it then possible for a plaintiff habitually residing in another country to invoke one of the rights guaranteed in the ECHR? In particular, this question may arise with regard to a plaintiff habitually residing in a *third* country, i.e., a non-Contracting Party. Would there then be a responsibility for a Contracting Party to uphold the right of access to a court derived from the ECHR? One could argue that this instrument only applies if a Contracting Party has jurisdiction to hear the case. If a court has no jurisdiction in the private international law sense, how could it be expected to guarantee the rights contained in the ECHR?

Although this argument may appear to be sound, it is not. The authorities of the Contracting Parties are obligated to secure to everyone within their jurisdiction the rights and freedoms guaranteed in the ECHR, as Article 1 ECHR prescribes.[50] If a litigant of another Contracting Party or a third country brings proceedings before a court of one of the Contracting Parties, the decision of that court to either assert jurisdiction or not, based on the forum's jurisdictional rules, has to be in line with the ECHR. The moment the foreign litigant brings proceedings in a court of one of the Contracting Parties, he or she is within the jurisdiction of that Contracting Party in the sense of Article 1 ECHR. The jurisdictional rules of the forum cannot limit the applicability of the ECHR in this regard.[51] If this were different, the right of access to a court would become meaningless.

The Court seemingly confirmed this stance in *Markovic and Others v. Italy*.[52] This case was largely concerned with the same event that formed the background

[47] See supra Chap. 4

[48] See with regard to this issue also Guinchard 2005, p. 204ff.

[49] See infra Sect. 5.4.1.

[50] See further supra Chap. 4.

[51] Marchadier 2007, p. 45ff.

[52] *Markovic and Others v. Italy* [GC], no. 1398/03, ECHR 2006-XIV.

to the Court's decision in *Banković and Others v. Belgium and Others*,[53] i.e., the airstrike carried out by NATO forces on a building in Belgrade, Serbia.[54] The applicants in *Markovic* were all citizens of Serbia and Montenegro (not a Contracting Party at the time) who had initiated civil proceedings for damages in Italy against Italy on behalf of relatives who had died in the aforementioned attack. However, the Italian courts held that they had no jurisdiction to hear the case, as—in short—the impugned acts, acts of war, were not open to judicial review. In this case a number of interesting issues relating to both Article 1 and Article 6 ECHR were raised. One was whether the applicants came within the jurisdiction of Italy within the meaning of Article 1 ECHR. The Court held on this issue that while the extraterritorial nature of the events which allegedly underlay the applicants' action for damages may have an impact on the applicability of Article 6 ECHR and the outcome of the proceedings, it is beyond dispute that this does *not* affect the jurisdiction *ratione loci* and *ratione personae* of the respondent State. The Court came to the following conclusion, which would appear to leave little doubt:

> If civil proceedings are brought in the domestic courts, the State is required by Article 1 of the Convention to secure in those proceedings respect for the rights protected by Article 6 [ECHR]. The Court considers that, once a person brings a civil action in the courts or tribunals of a State, there indisputably exists, without prejudice to the outcome of the proceedings, a 'jurisdictional link' for the purposes of Article 1 [ECHR].[55]

This, of course, does not mean that courts of Contracting Parties would have to assert jurisdiction in the private international law sense in all cases. As will be further discussed below, Article 6(1) ECHR, the right of access to a court, requires regulation by the State and is therefore inherently limited. Such limitations may be allowed under Article 6(1) ECHR. However, such limitations to the right of access to a court are derived from Article 6(1) ECHR. The (courts of the) Contracting Parties cannot simply dismiss the invocation of Article 6(1) ECHR in this regard by finding that they have no jurisdiction in the private international law sense and by concluding that the ECHR therefore does not apply.

5.4 The Right of Access to a Court in Private International Law

Having sketched the background of the notion of jurisdiction in private international law, it is now time to turn to the core of this chapter, the impact of the ECHR on jurisdiction in private international law cases. The author submits that this is by and large limited to the impact of its Article 6(1) ECHR, which

---

[53] *Banković and Others v. Belgium and 16 Other Contracting States* (dec.) [GC], no. 52207/99, ECHR 2001-XI.

[54] See with regard to this case also supra Chap. 4.

[55] *Markovic and Others v. Italy* [GC], no. 1398/03, para 54, ECHR 2006-XIV.

guarantees the right to a fair trial. Three different manners in which this Article could have an impact on the issue of jurisdiction in private international law will be distinguished in this chapter. The first is concerned with the right of a *plaintiff* to have access to a court.[56] As demonstrated below, the right of access to a court has been derived by the Court from Article 6(1) ECHR. This right is examined in this section.

The examination of the right of access starts with an overview of the general case law of the Strasbourg Institutions regarding this right. It will be shown that the right of access to a court is not absolute. The overview of the Court's case law will thus continue with a discussion of some important limitations to this right, which could also have an impact on jurisdiction in private international law (Sect. 5.4.1). This general overview will be concluded with a discussion of the most relevant decisions concerning the right of access to a court in private international law, particularly the Commission's decision in *Gauthier v. Belgium*[57] (Sect. 5.4.2). A further analysis of the meaning of the right of access to a court for jurisdiction in private international law will follow. In this section the most important aspects of the right of access to a court are further examined, whereby developments in the case law of national courts are also analyzed (Sect. 5.4.3). Thereafter, it is observed that the right of access may also be engaged if this right is restricted because of procedural bars (Sect. 5.4.4). Finally, in order for the right of access to be effective, Contracting Parties may have to provide legal aid to (foreign) plaintiffs (Sect. 5.4.5).

5.4.1 General Overview of the Right of Access to a Court in the Case Law of the Strasbourg Institutions

Article 6(1) ECHR does not explicitly guarantee the right of access to a court, as it merely guarantees that '[i]n the determination of his civil rights and obligations or of any criminal charge against him, everyone is entitled to a fair and public hearing within a reasonable time by an independent and impartial tribunal established by law.' However, in an early case, *Golder v. the United Kingdom*,[58] the Court in Strasbourg made clear that the right of access to a court should also be understood to be part of the right to a fair trial.

This case concerned a detainee in an English prison whose right of access to a court was effectively barred by the decision of the Home Secretary to deny him leave to consult a solicitor. The Court recognized that '[t]he principle whereby a

[56] It should, incidentally, be clear from the outset that the right of access to a court *ex* Article 6(1) ECHR, or any other right guaranteed in the ECHR, does not entail a ground of universal civil jurisdiction for bringing claims concerning violations of the ECHR. See also supra Chap. 1.

[57] *Gauthier v. Belgium* (dec.), no. 12603/86, 6 March 1989.

[58] *Golder v. the United Kingdom*, 21 February 1975, Series A no. 18.

civil claim must be capable of being submitted to a judge ranks as one of the universally recognized fundamental principles of law; the same is true of the principle of international law which forbids the denial of justice. Article 6(1) [ECHR] must be read in light of these principles.'[59] Moreover, there would be no point in describing in detail the procedural guarantees that parties enjoy without first protecting 'that which alone makes it in fact possible to benefit from such guarantees, that is, access to a court. The fair, public and expeditious characteristics of judicial proceedings are of no value at all if there are no judicial proceedings.'[60]

In principle, a litigant may thus derive a right of access to a court from Article 6(1) ECHR. Although *Golder* does not concern an issue of private international law, there is no reason to assume that this right of access to a court would not apply in such cases. Article 6(1) ECHR after all applies to the determination of 'civil rights and obligations', which would appear to cover all issues with which private international law is concerned.[61] The Court has held that the rights and obligations of private parties, such as, for example, matters of contract law,[62] commercial law,[63] tort law,[64] family law,[65] and employment law[66] always concern civil rights and obligations. The Court has noted that this right of access to a court only extends to disputes over civil rights and obligations, which could at least on arguable grounds be recognized in domestic law, as Article 6(1) ECHR 'does not in itself guarantee any particular content for (civil) "rights and obligations" in the substantive law of the Contracting States'.[67] Article 6(1) thus does not create a right of access to a court where the substantive right sought is not recognized under the domestic law, as Article 6(1) ECHR does not in itself guarantee any

---

[59] *Golder v. the United Kingdom*, 21 February 1975, para 35, Series A no. 18.

[60] Id.

[61] It should be noted that the determination of 'civil rights and obligations' is not confined to relationships between private persons. In *König v. Germany*, 28 June 1978, paras 89–90, Series A no. 27, the Court held that in establishing whether a dispute concerns the determination of a civil right the character of the right was all that mattered. In *H. v. France,* 24 October 1989, Series A no. 162-A, the Court held that if the outcome of the case is conclusive for private law rights and obligations, then Article 6(1) ECHR applies.

[62] See, e.g., *Ringeisen v. Austria*, 16 July 1971, Series A no. 13.

[63] See, e.g., *Edificaciones March Gallego S.A. v. Spain*, 19 February 1998, *Reports of Judgments and Decisions* 1998-I.

[64] See, e.g., *Axen v. Germany*, 8 December 1983, Series A no. 72.

[65] See, e.g., *Rasmussen v. Denmark*, 28 November 1984, Series A no. 87. This also includes family law issues, which have a public law character in the sense that the authorities are involved in, e.g., parental access to children, adoption, and fostering. See respectively *P., C. and S. v. the United Kingdom*, no. 56547/00, ECHR 2002-VI; *Keegan v. Ireland*, 26 May 1994, Series A no. 290; *Eriksson v. Sweden*, 22 June 1989, Series A no. 156.

[66] See, e.g., *Buchholz v. Germany*, 6 May 1981, Series A no. 42.

[67] See, e.g., *James and Others v. the United Kingdom*, judgment of 21 February 1986, para 81, Series A no. 98 and *Powell and Rayner v. the United Kingdom*, judgment of 21 February 1990, para 36, Series A no. 172.

particular content of the civil rights and obligations of the substantive laws of the Contracting Parties.[68] One should note that this may give rise to a particular issue in private international law cases, as the substantive law in such a case—the applicable law—may very well be a foreign law.

The Court has found that the right of access to a court should not only exist in theory, but that it should also be effective.[69] Merely having the opportunity to go to court with a civil claim does not suffice if the court in question will not decide on the merits.[70] This effective right of access to a court also entails that the law regulating this access should not be so unclear or complex that it would result in legal uncertainty.[71] The effective right of access may, under certain circumstances, also imply that if a litigant lacking in funds wishes to bring proceedings of a complex nature which could not reasonably be successful without legal aid, there could be an obligation upon the State to provide such assistance if this is 'indispensable for an effective access to court'.[72] Whether or not legal aid is necessary for a fair trial depends on the circumstances of the case,[73] such as what would be at stake for the litigants, the complexities of the case, and the ability of the litigants to represent themselves.[74]

The Court in *Golder* held not only that access to a court is inherent to the right to a fair trial, but also noted that this right is not absolute.[75] As the right to a court by its very nature calls for regulation by the State, it may be subject to limitations. This presumably also applies to the right of access to a court in private international law. The Contracting Parties enjoy a certain margin of appreciation with regard to this regulation.[76] However, such limitations should not rob the right of its meaning and as such the very essence of the right should not be impaired.[77] The right of access must not only be theoretical, but also effective.[78]

---

[68] *Fayed v. the United Kingdom*, 21 September 1994, para 65, Series A no. 294-B.

[69] See, e.g., *Airey v. Ireland*. 9 October 1979, Series A no. 32; *Kutić v. Croatia*, no. 48778/99, ECHR 2002-II; and *Multiplex v. Croatia*, no. 58112/00, 10 July 2003.

[70] See, e.g., *Kutić v. Croatia*, no. 48778/99, ECHR 2002-II and *Multiplex v. Croatia*, no. 58112/00, 10 July 2003. However, the extent of the right in international proceedings would appear to be more limited. See infra Sect. 5.4.3ff.

[71] *De Geouffre de la Pradelle v. France,* 16 December 1992, para 33–34, Series A no. 253-B.

[72] *Airey v. Ireland*. 9 October 1979, para 26, Series A no. 32.

[73] *Steel and Morris v. the United Kingdom*, no. 68416/01, para 61, ECHR 2005-II. This case concerned two environmentalists who were sued for libel by McDonalds. As they defended their right to freedom of expression and had been sued for a huge sum of money, and the case itself was also quite complex, the Court found that Article 6(1) ECHR applied.

[74] See with regard to the latter, e.g., *McVicar v. the United Kingdom*, no. 46311/99, ECHR 2002-III, in which the applicant was deemed to be able to do without legal representation as a defendant in libel proceedings.

[75] *Golder v. the United Kingdom*, 21 February 1975, para 38, Series A no. 18.

[76] See with regard to this notion supra Sect. 3.5.2.

[77] See, e.g., *Ashingdane v. the United Kingdom,* 28 May 1985, para 59, Series A no. 93.

[78] See supra n. 69.

The Court has held that a limitation to the right of access is only compatible with Article 6(1) ECHR if the restriction pursues a legitimate aim and there is a reasonable relationship of proportionality between the means employed and the legitimate aim sought to be achieved.[79] One may note in this regard that these conditions are very similar to the system of restrictions in Articles 8–11 ECHR,[80] except for the fact that the requirement of 'prescribed by law' is not cited by the Court. Examples of a legitimate aim accepted by the Court include the good administration of justice,[81] restrictions aimed at preventing the judiciary from overflowing,[82] and international relations, which may require the granting of State immunity.[83]

The Court has further expanded on what kind of, and under what circumstances, restrictions to the right of access are permissible. Although most of the cases cited below do not specifically entail issues of the right of access to a court in private international law, one may assume that that the framework established by the Court in its case law concerning the right of access to a court is also relevant for cases concerning jurisdiction in private international law and the plaintiff's right of access to a court, even though the exact scope of the right in cross-border cases has to be further examined.

The Court has found that the right of access to a court is impaired when the rules regarding access no longer serve the aims of legal certainty and the sound administration of justice, but rather become an obstacle to the litigant who attempts to have his or her case heard before the competent court.[84] In many cases the restrictions in accessing a court are of a financial nature. The principle of proportionality has an important role in this regard. If, in determining the exact amount of the security that needs to be deposited, a court fails to take into account

---

[79] See e,g, *Tinnelly & Sons Ltd and Others and McElduff and Others v. the United Kingdom*, 10 July 1998, para 72, *Reports of Judgments and Decisions* 1998-IV. See for an overview of the Court's case law in this regard also *Fayed v. the United Kingdom*, 21 September 1994, para 68–83, Series A no. 294-B.

[80] See the Concurring Opinion of Judge Martens in *De Geouffre de la Pradelle v. France*, 16 December 1992, Series A no. 253-B, in which he argued that the test should be similar. In *Fayed v. the United Kingdom*, 21 September 1994, Series A no. 294-B, para 67, the Court indeed appears to tie these conditions concerning Article 6(1) ECHR to the restrictions it had formulated in *Handyside v. the United Kingdom*, 7 December 1976, Series A no. 24, para 41 regarding Article 8(2) ECHR. See with regard to the restrictions contained in Articles 8–11(2) also supra Sect. 3.5.1.2.

[81] *Tolstoy Miloslavsky v. the United Kingdom*, 13 July 1995, para 61, Series A no. 316-B. It is interesting to note that the good—or sound—administration of justice is one of the principles underlying the system of jurisdiction of the Brussels I Regulation. See Pontier and Burg 2004, pp. 160–162.

[82] *Brualla Gómez de la Torre v. Spain*, 19 December 1997, para 36, *Reports of Judgments and Decisions* 1997-VIII.

[83] See, e.g., *Al-Adsani v. the United Kingdom* [GC], no. 35763/97, para 54, ECHR 2001-XI. It will be recalled that immunities are not covered in this research. See supra Chap. 1.

[84] *Kart v. Turkey* [GC], no. 8917/05, para 79, ECHR 2009 (extracts).

the fact that the appellant has no financial means, this would essentially deprive him or her of their right of access to a court.[85] A similar line of reasoning applies to court fees, which are not ruled out entirely by the Court, but which should be proportionate.[86]

The Court has on occasion held that a restriction on the right of access to a court based on the nature of the litigant may have a legitimate aim. Here one could think of restrictions of access to children and mentally ill people. However, even though certain limitations to access may be permitted, a total lack of access is not.[87] The non-recognition of legal personality may also lead to a violation of the right of access to a court, as the Court held in *Canea Catholic Church v. Greece*,[88] in which the domestic courts denied the church legal personality.

5.4.2 The Right of Access in Private International Law in the Strasbourg Case Law

As has been indicated above, there appears to be only one case in which the Strasbourg Institutions have specifically examined an issue relating to the right of access to a court and the issue of jurisdiction in private international law. *Gauthier v. Belgium*[89] concerned a Belgian pilot, who worked for Air Zaire until he received a letter notifying him that he would be let go for economic reasons. The pilot brought proceedings against Air Zaire before the court in Brussels, Belgium. Air Zaire contended that the Belgian court had no jurisdiction, relying on the employment contract of the pilot which contained a jurisdiction clause favoring Léopoldville (now Kinshasa), the capital of Zaire (not a Contracting Party). In the first instance, the court set aside the jurisdiction clause, stating that it did not apply to the proceedings. Air Zaire appealed. On appeal the Belgian pilot argued that the

---

[85] See *Aït-Mouhoub v. France*, 28 October 1998, para 57-61, *Reports of Judgments and Decisions* 1998-VIII. Cf. *X v. Sweden* (dec.), no. 7973, 28 February 1979, in which the Commission examined the complaint of a Pakistani citizen who ran a carpet business and resided at the time of lodging the application in Sweden. The applicant instituted court proceedings against his bank in Sweden. The defendant bank requested the applicant to provide security for costs on the basis of the relevant Swedish law, which provided at the time that any alien, regardless of whether he lived in Sweden, could be asked to furnish security. The applicant declared himself unable to do so, which normally would have resulted in a rejection of the action. However, the bank withdrew its request and the parties reached an agreement. The applicant's complaint against the relevant Swedish law *in abstracto* was thereafter dismissed by the Commission. See also *Tolstoy Miloslavsky v. the United Kingdom*, 13 July 1995, para 61, Series A no. 316-B.

[86] See *Kreuz v. Poland*, no. 28249/95, paras 61–67, ECHR 2001-VI.

[87] See *Winterwerp v. the Netherlands*, 24 October 1979, para 75, Series A no. 33.

[88] *Canea Catholic Church v. Greece*, 16 December 1997, *Reports of Judgments and Decisions* 1997-VIII.

[89] *Gauthier v. Belgium* (dec.), no. 12603/86, 6 March 1989.

Belgian court had to reject the jurisdiction clause, because it pointed to a country with a judicial structure which would not necessarily guarantee the impartiality of the judiciary and the right to a fair trial. This argument was rejected by the Belgian court, which found that it was not for the court to assess the justice system of a foreign state, or to replace a jurisdiction clause freely entered into by the parties.

Before the Commission in Strasbourg the Belgian pilot relied, *inter alia*, on Article 6(1) ECHR, arguing that the Belgian courts, by finding that they lacked jurisdiction, had violated that provision. He argued that the declination of jurisdiction would lead to him being forced to turn to a court of a third country where the proceedings would not meet the guarantees of Article 6(1) ECHR. The Commission, however, noted that the lack of jurisdiction was not the result of a unilateral decision by Belgium, but rather a jurisdiction clause into which the pilot had entered. It considered that neither Article 6(1) ECHR—nor any other provision of the ECHR—prohibits the inclusion of such clauses. The Commission could not assume that in accepting the obligations of Article 6(1) ECHR the Contracting Parties have the obligation to prevent persons within their jurisdictions from entering into jurisdiction clauses.

An interesting argument with regard to the right of access to a court and jurisdiction in private international law is brought up in this case. Is it possible for a plaintiff to invoke the right of access to a court *ex* Article 6(1) ECHR in a situation where there is an alternative forum available in a third country where it is alleged that the proceedings would not meet the standards of Article 6 ECHR? Unfortunately the Commission did not really examine this issue here. Instead, the Commission focused on the fact that the parties had agreed upon a jurisdiction clause. Although one may not agree entirely with the reasoning employed by the Commission—one could question whether this case really came down to the obligation of Contracting Parties to prevent litigants from entering into jurisdiction clauses, or the applicability of Article 6(1) ECHR to such clauses—the outcome of the case is not unreasonable. If a plaintiff agrees to a jurisdiction clause selecting a certain jurisdiction, it stands to reason that this plaintiff cannot subsequently object to this jurisdiction based on the argument that one is unlikely to receive a fair trial there—provided that the parties freely entered into the agreement and that the circumstances in the chosen jurisdiction do not radically change afterwards.[90] In this regard one could also mention that the Court has generally found that it is possible to waive certain rights resulting from the right to a fair trial *ex* Article 6(1) ECHR.[91] One could argue that an applicant may waive certain rights *ex* Article 6(1) ECHR by virtue of entering into a jurisdiction clause, even though certain minimum requirements would arguably have to remain in place.

By zooming in on the jurisdiction clause and by noting that the pilot had himself cut off the road leading to the Belgian courts, the Commission at least

[90] Of course, this would in most jurisdictions presumably be a condition for the validity of the jurisdiction clause—or any agreement for that matter.

[91] See, e.g., *Pfeifer and Plankl v. Austria*, 25 February 1992, Series A no. 227.

leaves open the possibility that Article 6(1) ECHR would require a Contracting Party to open its courts to international civil proceedings where the only available forum for the plaintiff would result in proceedings that would not meet the standards of Article 6(1) ECHR. This possibility will be further examined below.[92] What the *Gauthier* case does make clear is that a plaintiff must not have contributed to the fact that only one open forum, of possibly questionable quality, is available, by agreeing to a jurisdiction clause.[93]

The Commission has, in *X v. Switzerland*,[94] had the opportunity to weigh in on a specific limitation to the right of access to a court in international civil proceedings. In this case the Commission had to examine time limits. This is an obvious limitation on the right of access to a court and it is generally categorized as falling under sound administration of justice and as such, in principle, an accepted limitation on the right of access.[95] However, time limits may be quite stringent for plaintiffs living outside the country (not an uncommon feature of private international law cases) where they wish to bring their claim. Nevertheless, the Commission has, in *X v. Switzerland*, which is admittedly an older case, established quite a strict approach in this regard.

The case concerned an applicant living in Norway who wished to bring an action in Switzerland relating to the partition of an inheritance. The applicant allegedly mailed his appeal more than a week before the deadline to the Swiss embassy in Oslo, believing that he had sent his appeal in time. The embassy allegedly forwarded the appeal the next day to the relevant court in Switzerland. However, the appeal did not reach the court until three weeks later and by then the deadline to appeal had passed. The Swiss court consequently rejected the appeal.

Before the Commission in Strasbourg the applicant invoked Article 6(1) ECHR against the Swiss decision. The Commission considered that Article 6(1) ECHR did indeed contain the right of access to a court. However, it also noted that this right does not restrain the Contracting Parties from setting up regulations regarding the access of litigants to appeal courts. Such regulations help guarantee ensuring the sound administration of justice. The Commission found that the Swiss regulations did not prevent the applicant from lodging the appeal in time. By his own admission the applicant still had plenty of time when he first received the decision and he had not demonstrated that the embassy had assured him that by mailing the appeal to them he had fulfilled the obligation to respect the time limit. Moreover, a provision in the Swiss civil procedure law would have allowed for a request for an extension, but the applicant had not availed himself of this possibility. The Commission consequently found the application to be manifestly ill-founded.[96]

---

[92] See infra Sect. 5.4.3.

[93] See also infra n. 132.

[94] *X. v. Switzerland* (dec.), no. 8407/78, 6 May 1980, D.R. 179.

[95] See supra Sect. 5.4.1.

[96] See with regard to the notion of 'manifestly ill-founded' supra Sect. 3.2.

As has been demonstrated above, the right of access to a court is a right which has been developed by the Court itself. It has been further elaborated upon by the Strasbourg Institutions and one could therefore say that it is a well-established right. Nevertheless, the Strasbourg Institutions have not yet really developed this right in relation to the issue of jurisdiction in private international law. There is not much that could be derived from the case law with certainty in this regard, leaving open many questions, which will be further discussed below. One thing that does stand out is that the applicants in both these cases contributed to their own undoing in the eyes of the Commission. This is not to say that this was an unjustifiable finding in these cases, but it is also clear that the Commission was not willing to take their cross-border dimension into real consideration, despite the unique challenges posed by such cases. As the discussion in the subsequent chapters will demonstrate, this almost appears to be a theme in relation to the impact of the ECHR on private international law.[97]

5.4.3 The Scope of the Right of Access to a Court and Jurisdiction in Private International Law

It has generally been accepted that the right of access to a court following from Article 6(1) ECHR is relevant to the issue of jurisdiction in private international law.[98] It is also clear that this right of access will mostly concern the plaintiff in international litigation. Defendants may also attempt to rely on Article 6(1) ECHR in issues regarding jurisdiction in private international law; not so much in relation to the right of access to a court, but rather the (general) right to a fair trial, as will be discussed further below.[99]

What does the right of access to a court, as derived from the Court's case law concerning Article 6(1) ECHR, exactly entail with regard to the issue of jurisdiction in private international law? It follows from the case law discussed above that this question has several aspects. There is, first of all, a right of access to a court on which plaintiffs in international litigation may rely when they are utterly unable to find a court. This is not very controversial (Sect. 5.4.3.1). An important question in this regard, though, is the extent of this right. Before delving further into this issue, it is first necessary to discuss whether it is possible for a Contracting Party to rely on proceedings in another country with regard to the right of access to a court in international proceedings (Sect. 5.4.3.2). After it has been established that this is indeed the case, the question of the extent of the right of access to a

---

[97] See, e.g., *Ammdjadi v. Germany* discussed in ch. 6.3; and *McDonald v. France* discussed in Sect. 7.2.

[98] See, e.g., Briggs and Rees 2009, pp. 19–20; Corbion 2004, p. 189ff; Gaudemet-Tallon 2006, pp. 173–189; Guinchard 2005, p. 200, p. 206ff; Kinsch 2007, p. 43ff; Marchadier 2007, p. 43ff, particularly at p. 66ff; Matscher1993a, b, pp. 79–80; Matscher 1998, p. 218.

[99] See infra Sect. 5.5.

court will be further examined. Three different scenarios will be discussed. The first has already been mentioned above, in relation to the *Gauthier* case:[100] what if there is an open forum available to the plaintiff abroad, but it is uncertain that the proceedings in this available forum would meet the (procedural) standards of Article 6(1) ECHR? One could argue that the right may entail the right of access to a court where the proceedings would be in line with the guarantees of Article 6(1) ECHR[101] (Sect. 5.4.3.3). It has also been argued that a denial of justice could occur in a situation where there is an open forum in another country, if it is clear that the plaintiff's substantive claim would be denied in this available forum[102] (Sect. 5.4.3.4). Similarly, the argument has been raised that the right of access to a court could also arise in the situation of an open forum in another country where it is clear that the decision rendered by this open forum would never be eligible for recognition and enforcement abroad, robbing the decision of its effectiveness in international litigation[103] (Sect. 5.4.3.5).

5.4.3.1 A Negative Conflict of Jurisdiction

In the first instance, there are thus two different imaginable situations in which a plaintiff's right of access to a court following from Article 6(1) ECHR may play a role in international litigation. First, a plaintiff could be faced with the situation that there is no court, regardless of the question of its location or quality, which has jurisdiction to hear his case. This situation should be distinguished from the situation in which courts of more than one country have jurisdiction to hear the case.[104] It will be recalled that this distinction is also referred to as the negative and positive conflicts of jurisdiction.[105]

That the right of access to a court is engaged in the former situation, where the plaintiff is unable to find a competent court, is quite clear.[106] If a court were to reject jurisdiction in such a situation, this would directly result in a denial of justice, which the Court in *Golder* held as being contrary to Article 6(1) ECHR.[107] This applies not only in the situation where there is no court of any country competent to hear the case in international litigation, but it also logically extends to the situation where there is realistically no other forum available to the plaintiff

---

[100] See supra n. 57.

[101] Matscher 1998, p. 218. But see Marchadier 2007, p. 84ff. See also Corbion 2004, p. 189ff.

[102] See Corbion 2004, p. 202ff and the authors cited there.

[103] See, e.g., Gaudemet-Tallon 2006, p. 174. Cf. Bucher 2011, p. 65.

[104] See in this regard infra 5.3.2ff.

[105] See supra Sect. 5.2.1.

[106] See, e.g., Kinsch 2007, pp. 44–45; Matscher 1998, p. 218. See generally the literature cited supra n. 98.

[107] See supra Sect. 5.4.1.

in international litigation due to extraordinary circumstances beyond the plaintiff's control, such as the normally competent court being unavailable because of war.[108] In such a case the refusal to assert jurisdiction would also directly lead to a denial of justice, as there would essentially be no other forum to which the plaintiff could turn. It is for this reason that many legal systems have incorporated a ground of jurisdiction based on necessity, often referred to as the *forum necessitatis*, for plaintiffs who otherwise have nowhere to turn.

The Right of Access to a Court: *Forum Necessitatis*

The ground of jurisdiction known as *forum necessitatis* entails a rule allowing national courts to assert jurisdiction on the ground that there is no other (viable) forum available abroad, and it can be found in one form or another in many legal orders.[109] It may thus be regarded as an elaboration of the right of access to a court.[110] The existence of such a rule would appear to prevent issues of there being no forum available for a plaintiff in private international law and the right of access to a court *ex* Article 6(1) ECHR. It is interesting to discuss the notion of *forum necessitatis* and the right of access to a court in the legal orders of England, the Netherlands, and Switzerland in this context.

With regard to the right of access to a court in private international law, one may still discern a fundamental difference between the English rules on jurisdiction, on the one hand, and the practice in the Netherlands and Switzerland, on the other. This is a divide that has not been completely closed by the Brussels I Regulation[111] and the Lugano Convention,[112] which have for a large part introduced similar rules with regard to jurisdiction for these three States.[113] One result of this divide is that England does not have a *forum necessitatis* rule, while both the Netherlands and Switzerland do have one.[114] One should nevertheless note that there are, in principle, few problems concerning the right of access to a court where there is no alternative foreign court available and the rules of jurisdiction in private international law in England, the Netherlands, and Switzerland.

Still, it is remarkable that while both the Netherlands and Switzerland have a *forum necessitatis* clause, England has no such rule.[115] This does not mean that

---

108 See, e.g., Briggs and Rees 2009, pp. 19–20.

109 See for an overview of the use of this ground of jurisdiction in the EU Member States Nuyts 2007a, pp. 64–66.

110 See Nuyts 2007a, pp. 21–22.

111 See supra n. 10.

112 See supra n. 12.

113 See also supra Chap. 2.

114 See Article 9 of *Burgerlijke Rechtsvordering* (Dutch Civil Procedure) and Article 3 of the Swiss Private International Law Act. Another distinction is the much more prominent place of *forum non conveniens* in England. See infra Sect. "Forum Non Conveniens".

115 See with regard to the rules on jurisdiction in England, e.g., Dicey et al. 2012, p. 371ff.

there are no differences between the *forum necessitatis* rules in the Netherlands and Switzerland.[116] The Netherlands has two different versions of the *forum necessitatis* rule, one of which does not require a connection with the forum, while the other does.[117] In Switzerland, a certain connection with the forum is always required.[118] Interestingly enough, in the Netherlands this ground of jurisdiction has only recently been introduced and its entrance coincided with the abolition of the ground of jurisdiction based on the domicile of the plaintiff in the forum, which is now considered to be an exorbitant base of jurisdiction.[119] This demonstrates the remarkable interaction between this *forum necessitatis* rule and other bases of exorbitant jurisdiction.[120] Before the abolition of this exorbitant ground of jurisdiction there was little need for a *forum necessitatis* clause, as plaintiffs domiciled in the Netherlands could always find a ground for jurisdiction.

This does, of course, beg the question why England has no such rule of jurisdiction, and whether this could become an issue in relation to the right of access to a court. The answer lies in the fact that the (traditional) rules on jurisdiction in England are largely less strict with regard to the assertion of jurisdiction compared to the Netherlands and Switzerland (thus leaving the rules on jurisdiction following from the Brussels Regulation and the Lugano Convention out of the discussion), and this would seem to lessen the need for a general *forum necessitatis* clause.[121] For example, the (traditional) general rule with regard to jurisdiction *in personam*[122] is that the foundation of the court's jurisdiction is the service of process.

[116] It could be noted in this regard that during the parliamentary proceedings leading up the new *forum necessitatis* clause in the Dutch Civil Procedure Code, reference was made explicitly to Article 3 of the Swiss Private International Law Act. See *Kamerstukken II* 1999/00, 26 885, nr. 3, p. 41ff (MvT).

[117] See Article 9 sub –b *Rv*. It should be noted that the *forum necessitatis* clause of Article 9 sub—c does require a certain connection with the Netherlands. See generally with regard to *forum necessitatis* in the Netherlands Ibili 2007, p. 107ff; Strikwerda 2012, pp. 234–235. See for an interesting Dutch case on *forum necessitatis*, e.g., Rb. 's-Gravenhage, 21 March 2012, LJN BV 9748.

[118] See Article 3 of the Swiss Private International Law Act. See generally with regard to this rule in Switzerland, e.g., Bucher 2011, pp. 62–66; Othenin-Girard 1999, pp. 251–285.

[119] Although it should be noted that while the Netherlands did not have such a rule in the Dutch Civil Procedure Code, courts occasionally filled in this gap. See, e.g., HR 26 October 1984, *NJ* 1985, 696.

[120] This interaction between the *forum necessitatis* rule and the previously incorporated exorbitant ground of jurisdiction of *forum actoris* in the Dutch Civil Procedure Code was acknowledged during the parliamentary proceedings. It was explicitly stated that the *forum necessitatis* should not result in the return of the *forum actoris*. See *Kamerstukken II* 1999/2000, 26 885, nr. 3, p. 41ff (MvT). Cf. Ibili 2007, pp. 121–122.

[121] See generally with regard to jurisdiction in England, e.g., Briggs and Rees 2009, p. 407ff; Dicey et al. 2012, p. 371ff; Cheshire et al. 2010, p. 199ff.

[122] In short, a claim *in personam* is a claim brought against someone to compel him or her to do something, such as pay a debt etc. It does not incidentally include most family law cases, such as filing for divorce. See Dicey et al. 2012, p. 371. In addition to an action *in personam*, there is the action *in rem*. The action *in rem* in English law concerns an action that lies with the Admirality court against certain *res*, particularly a ship, and other *res* associated with the ship, such as its cargo. See, e.g., Cheshire et al. 2010, p. 414ff.

Whenever in proceedings *in personam* a defendant can be legally served with process, the court has jurisdiction to hear the case against him or her. It should be noted that this admittedly rather broad power of English courts to hear a case is somewhat balanced by the discretionary power of the courts to decline or stay proceedings where the doctrine of *forum non conveniens* applies.[123]

However, an area where the jurisdiction of English courts is more limited is the area of family law.[124] For example, for divorce proceedings, an English court has jurisdiction if the court has jurisdiction under the Brussels II *bis* Regulation,[125] if no other court of one the parties to this Regulation has jurisdiction (i.e. EU Member States), and if one of the parties to the marriage is domiciled in England on the date of the start of the proceedings.[126] It is thus clear that a more substantial link with the forum is required in this case compared to the jurisdiction *in personam* discussed earlier.

This latter observation raises the question of whether this more strict framework of jurisdiction regarding family law, combined with the absence of *forum necessitatis*, could lead to an issue with the right of access to a court *ex* Article 6(1) ECHR. This appears to have never really arisen, although the English appeal court did discuss the possibility of the non-assertion of jurisdiction resulting in a violation of Article 6(1) ECHR in *Mark v. Mark*.[127] At issue was whether the English judge could entertain an application for divorce by a Nigerian woman who had essentially been abandoned by her Nigerian husband, who had returned to Nigeria but had made no arrangements for his wife to follow him. In the first instance it was decided that she could not be regarded as being habitually resident in England since she was 'an overstayer', and thus her presence was unlawful. However the divorce was granted on another ground, and the husband appealed against this decision.

The appeal court discussed, among other things, whether this deprivation of the wife's right to petition would be contrary to Article 6(1) ECHR, and considered that such a blanket restriction would indeed appear to be contrary to Article 6(1) ECHR, although it was also acknowledged that the State could impose conditions upon this access.[128] Ultimately, though, this case was not solely decided on human rights grounds.[129] It should be noted that the House of Lords eventually affirmed the Court of Appeal's decision to deny the husband's appeal against the divorce,

---

[123] See also infra Sect. 'Forum Non Conveniens'. See with regard to the doctrine in England, e.g., Dicey et al. 2012, p. 533ff. See generally, e.g., Brand and Jablonski 2007.

[124] It should be noted that many of the rules in this area have undergone significant changes with the continued European harmonization in this area.

[125] See supra n. 11.

[126] See Section 5(2) of the Domicile and Matrimonial Proceedings Act 1973.

[127] *Mark v. Mark* [2004] EWCA Civ. 168, [2005] Fam. 267.

[128] *Mark v. Mark* [2004] EWCA Civ. 168, [2005] Fam. 267, no. 40 (per Lord Thorpe LJ) and 71 (Waller LJ). Cf. Fawcett 2007, p. 6.

[129] See *Mark v. Mark* [2004] ECWA Civ 168, Nos. 37–39, and especially No. 38. The essential question for Lord Thorpe LJ was whether the public policy rule, which was set out by Lord Scarman in *R v. Barnet London Borough Council, ex p Nilish Shah* and held that only a person

but held that there was no need to find its decision on the Human Rights Act (and the right of access).[130]

In conclusion, one could thus state that it is generally accepted that when a plaintiff is absolutely unable to find a court in international proceedings anywhere in the world, this can be invoked in one of the Contracting Parties as a ground for jurisdiction based on the right of access to a court *ex* Article 6(1) ECHR. There is one caveat that should be mentioned. This does not apply to the plaintiff who is him or herself responsible for an otherwise available foreign court no longer being available. It will be recalled that this was established by the Commission in *Gauthier* in relation to a jurisdiction clause.[131] This was also the finding of the *Obergericht* Zürich in an old Swiss case.[132] An Italian national, domiciled in Zürich, brought proceedings before the local court, which he regarded as the *forum necessitatis* because his Italian lawyers had negligently allowed the time limits for the initiation of proceedings in Italy to run out. The Swiss court found that it had no jurisdiction on the basis of being the *forum necessitatis* under these circumstances, a decision that was upheld by the *Tribunal fédéral*.[133]

Forum Non Conveniens

Before moving on, it is necessary to examine one more doctrine—the *forum non conveniens*—which may impact upon the assertion of jurisdiction in private international law and could lead to a denial of access to a court. *Forum non conveniens* is a legal doctrine, mainly found in common law countries, that allows courts to decline jurisdiction even if that jurisdiction was formally prescribed by law and for which there would otherwise be a basis in deference to proceedings in a foreign court, where this court is considered to be a clearly more appropriate court for the proceedings.[134] If an English court were to exercise its discretion to stay the English proceedings, it is certainly conceivable that an issue with regard to Article 6(1) ECHR could arise. It is contended that there are three different scenarios in which such an issue may arise.[135]

(Footnote 129 continued)
lawfully in the UK could be regarded as being habitually resident in the UK, should now be recast in the light of the Human Rights Act 1998. See also No. 69 (Waller LJ) and No. 88 (Latham LJ).

[130] *Mark v. Mark* [2005] UKHL 42, No. 31. See with regard to this decision Briggs 2006, pp. 675–677.

[131] See supra 5.4.2.

[132] Obergericht Zürich, II. Zivilkammer, 1 May 1959, *Annuaire suisse de droit international* 1961, pp. 293–295. This case was delivered well before the entry of the Swiss Private International Law Act of 1987, but would still appear to be relevant with regard to the ground of jurisdiction of *forum necessitatis*.

[133] See ATF 85 II 305, 309.

[134] See supra n. 123.

[135] Fawcett 2007, pp. 9–10.

The first scenario is quite straightforward. If an English court stays the English proceedings in favor of proceedings abroad, it is clear that access to the English judge is denied. Could this result in a breach of Article 6(1) ECHR? One could argue that this is, in principle, not the case, as the English court will stay the proceedings in favor of another (foreign) court. This would thus leave open an alternative forum for the plaintiff. So, in principle, this is not a problem, although this may depend somewhat on the quality of the alternative forum, which leads us to the second scenario.[136]

The second scenario concerns the question of what if one could reasonably expect an unfair trial in the alternative forum abroad? The foreign court may, for example, be known for its lengthy and slow proceedings, or lack of an impartial judiciary. Would the staying of proceedings by an English court in favor of such a jurisdiction violate the right of access to a court? This issue has been discussed in *Lubbe v. Capre Plc.*,[137] in which it was held that the existing principles concerning the stay of proceedings, as contained in *Spiladia Maritime Corp v. Cansulex Ltd.*,[138] were in accordance with the guarantees provided by Article 6(1) ECHR.[139] However, had the court been inclined to stay the proceedings nevertheless, one could argue that Article 6(1) ECHR would have been violated.[140]

The third scenario in which an issue regarding Article 6(1) ECHR may arise concerns the length of the proceedings. As the consideration by a court to stay the proceedings, followed by the transfer of the case to a foreign court, would inevitably take up time, a stay on the ground of *forum non conveniens* could result in a breach of the right to a fair hearing within a reasonable amount of time.[141] This was one of the concerns put forward by Advocate General Leger in *Owusu v Jackson*[142] against this doctrine. Although the ECJ did not follow the Advocate General in this regard, it should be noted that the ECJ's eventual judgment in this case has largely, if not entirely, reduced the meaning of this rule of jurisdiction.[143]

Even before the ECJ's intervention concerning this legal doctrine, however, the doctrine had never received much enthusiasm from lawyers in civil law countries.[144] In the few cases in Europe where the doctrine is still relevant, it should be

[136] See also infra Sect. 5.4.3.

[137] *Lubbe v. Capre Plc* [2000] 1 WLR 1545.

[138] *Spiladia Maritime Corp v. Cansulex Ltd* [1987] AC 460.

[139] Lord Bingham opined: "I do not think article 6 [ECHR] supports any conclusion which is not already reached on application of *Spiladia* principles". (1561).

[140] Cf. Briggs and Rees 2009, p. 20.

[141] Fawcett 2007, p. 9.

[142] ECJ 1 March 2005, Case C-281/02, *Owusu v. Jackson*, ECR 2005, I-1383.

[143] See with regard to the meaning of this judgment to the future of the instrument, e.g., Duintjer-Tebbens 2006, pp. 95–103; Fentiman 2006, pp. 705–734; Rodger 2006, pp. 71–97.

[144] See, e.g., Van Lith 2009; see for an early example H. Gaudemet-Tallon 1991, p. 491ff. It could, incidentally, be noted that the old Dutch Civil Procedure Code did contain a more or less general provision on *forum non conveniens*. However, this rule disappeared with the introduction of the new Dutch Civil Procedure Code in 2002. See *Kamerstukken* II, 1999/2000, 26 855, nr. 3,

clear that Article 6(1) ECHR stands in the way of its invocation where such invocation would lead to a denial of access to the courts. However, as discussed above, the current interpretation of the doctrine would appear to be in line with Article 6(1) ECHR in this regard, save for a possible issue concerning the increased length of proceedings due to this doctrine, which could indeed be a concern.[145]

5.4.3.2 Denial of Access to Court Where a Foreign Court Is Available?

Turning to the issue of positive conflicts of jurisdiction, one could first wonder whether it is even possible to speak of a denial of access to a court if there is a foreign court available. Is the right of access to a court actually concerned with such a situation? Regardless of the quality and the level of independent judicial protection of the available foreign court, there is strictly speaking access to a (foreign) court in such a situation. One could consequently argue that the right of access to a court *ex* Article 6(1) ECHR is not applicable to such a situation, as there would be no infringement of this right. However, this mere availability of a foreign court raises the issue of whether it is possible for a Contracting Party to rely on this foreign court in a complaint about a lack of access to its courts in a private international law case.

Is it possible for a Contracting Party to rely on proceedings elsewhere in order to fulfill its own obligation to guarantee the right of access to a court? Proceedings elsewhere pose an obvious problem: it is difficult, if not impossible, for the Contracting Parties to exert control over such proceedings. Can they consequently rely on such foreign proceedings? It would be unrealistic in international proceedings to completely disregard foreign access to a court. The only alternative, after all, would be that everyone would have to be provided with access to a court in international cases, even in cases with little connection to the Contracting Party, which raises problems of its own.[146] It is thus submitted here that Contracting Parties may, in principle, rely on foreign proceedings in this regard.

However, this does have as a consequence that even though there is access to a foreign court, there would be no access to a court in the respondent Contracting Party. Thus one could argue that the right of access is still engaged in this situation and that there is a restriction to the right of access. As has been discussed above, such restrictions to the access to a court are allowed, but may not go so far as to endanger the very essence of the right of access, and they must pursue a legitimate

(Footnote 144 continued)
pp. 30–31. However, the doctrine has not entirely disappeared in Dutch civil procedure. In some family law disputes the Dutch judge may decline jurisdiction. See Article 4(3)–b and Article 5 *Rechtsvordering* [Dutch Civil Procedure Code]. However, the scope of these two exceptions is rather limited.

145 See with regard to England particularly *Lubbe v. Capre Plc* [2000] 1 WLR 1545.

146 See infra Sect. 5.5.

aim, while the measure restricting the access must also be proportionate to the legitimate aim pursued. In this test the requirement of having a legitimate aim would probably not pose much of a problem.[147] As stated above, disregarding foreign access would presumably not be a realistic option in international proceedings and would fulfill a legitimate aim. Whether one could thus speak of a violation of the right of access to a court where there was a foreign court available would consequently come down to the proportionality of such a decision.

In reviewing the proportionality of a Contracting Party's decision not to open up its courts in international proceedings in a case where foreign access is guaranteed, the Court could, in my opinion, take the quality of the proceedings in the available foreign court into consideration. Furthermore, it may even be possible to take into account the link between the case and the foreign court—the appropriateness of the ground of jurisdiction—even though this is a more theoretical possibility. The Court could also assess the reasonableness of expecting the litigant to subject himself to foreign proceedings. Alternatively, the Court could also suffice with the test it has introduced in cases concerning the right of access and immunities of international organizations. In such cases applicants were faced with the issue of being unable to sue the international organization because the organization could invoke immunity. The Court examined the issue in relation to the right of access to a court.

In *Waite and Kennedy v. Germany*[148] the Court had to deal with this issue. The two applicants' right of access to the German courts was essentially blocked in proceedings against their employer, the European Space Agency (ESA), because as an international organization, ESA could invoke immunity before the German courts. After finding that this restriction to the right of access served a legitimate aim, the Court held that an important factor in deciding whether this restriction would be permissible was the question of whether the applicants had 'a reasonable alternative means' to protect their rights.[149] It consequently noted that the ESA Convention offered several methods of settlement of private law issues, including staff matters, and that it was possible for the applicants to apply to the ESA Appeals Board, an institution independent from the ESA, which had jurisdiction to hear such disputes. This review satisfied the Court that the German courts had not overstepped their margin of appreciation and that there had not been a violation of Article 6(1) ECHR.

The Court could, in cases concerning the assertion of jurisdiction in private international law where a foreign court is available, thus similarly find that the mere availability of a foreign court would suffice. I will in this regard point out that the Court in *Waite and Kennedy* does not impose strict requirements concerning

---

[147] See supra 5.4.1.

[148] *Waite and Kennedy v. Germany* [GC], no. 26083/94, ECHR 1999-I. See also *Beer and Regan v. Germany* [GC], no. 28934/95, 18 February 1999, which was decided at the same time and is identical in its wording.

[149] *Waite and Kennedy v. Germany* [GC], no. 26083/94, para 68, ECHR 1999-I.

the alternative means of redress.[150] However, this method of review, in my opinion, does not suffice in international proceedings where a foreign court is available. It should first be noted that *Waite* was specifically concerned with the issue of the immunity of an international organization. This left the Court with considerably less room for maneuvering, as immunities are after all a generally accepted limitation to jurisdiction in international law.[151]

Moreover, as will be further discussed below, there are good arguments for the proposition that the right of access to a court in relation to jurisdiction in private international law will at least entail the right of access to a court of some procedural quality.[152] It will be recalled that in addition to procedural demands upon this available court, it has also been suggested that the available court should live up to even higher standards.[153] A number of scenarios will be examined further below. In the respective discussions national jurisprudence will also be considered.

5.4.3.3 The Proceedings in the Available Foreign Court Are Not in Accordance with the Guarantees of Article 6(1) ECHR

Does Article 6(1) ECHR, the right of access to a court, merely require that a trial is held somewhere, or does the right guarantee a court where the proceedings will meet the standards of a fair trial *ex* Article 6(1) ECHR? One should note that, in principle, this issue should only arise if the only court available to a plaintiff is the court of a third country. If a court of one of the other Contracting Parties is open, there should not be an issue in this regard, as presumably the proceedings would live up the standards of Article 6(1) ECHR.[154] But what if there is only a court of a third country available? This would guarantee a trial somewhere, but not necessarily that the proceedings there would meet the standards of Article 6(1) ECHR.

The Court in *Ashingdane v. the United Kingdom* held that the right of access to a court following from its judgment in *Golder* 'may be relied on by anyone who considers on arguable grounds that an interference with the exercise of his (civil) rights is unlawful and complains that he has not had the possibility of submitting that claim to a tribunal meeting the requirements of Article 6(1) [ECHR].'[155] However, this case did not concern the issue of jurisdiction in private international law and the required quality of the available court in a third country.

---

150 Cf. Kloth 2010, p. 141ff; De Wet 2006, p. 620.

151 See supra Sect. 5.2.2.

152 See infra Sect. 5.4.3.3.

153 See further infra Sect. 5.4.3.4.

154 This is nevertheless not always the case. See infra Sect. 5.6.1.

155 *Ashingdane v. the United Kingdom,* 28 May 1985, para 55, Series A no. 93 (referring to not only *Golder v. the United Kingdom*, para 36. Series A no. 18, but additionally to *Le Compte, Van Leuven and De Meyere v. Belgium*, 23 June 1981, Series A no. 43, para 44 and *Sporrong and Lönnroth v. Sweden*, 23 September 1982, Series A no. 52, para 81).

One could argue that it would be quite something for the Contracting Parties to be obligated to open their courts in all cases where there is a court of a third country competent to hear the case, but where it also is uncertain that the proceedings would be fair in the sense of Article 6(1) ECHR. Furthermore, it is easy to see that such a conception of the obligations under Article 6(1) ECHR would be less than well received in third countries, and it may also be difficult to assess the fairness of the foreign proceedings before they have actually taken place.[156] It is in any event doubtful whether this can be achieved at the jurisdictional stage of proceedings, rather than at the stage of recognition and enforcement.[157]

On the other hand, the right of access to a court does appear to entail more than merely the guarantee of a trial, regardless of the quality thereof. In this regard one could also cite the Court's finding that a right should not merely be theoretical, but also effective.[158] What is the value of having an available foreign court in the knowledge that one is unlikely to receive a fair trial there? Yet it would also be odd, and perhaps somewhat unrealistic, to demand that foreign courts live up to the standards of Article 6(1) ECHR.

A possible solution to this dilemma may have been given by the Court in a case concerning international child abduction, *Eskinazi and Chelouche v. Turkey*.[159] An application was made against the decision of the Turkish courts ordering the applicants to return to Israel. One of the arguments advanced by the applicants, based on Article 6(1) ECHR, was that a return to Israel would result in an Israeli rabbinical having jurisdiction over both the divorce case and the related issues over personal status. The Court thus had to a priori assess the proceedings in Israel. It found that in such circumstances, where no proceedings concerning the applicants' interests have yet been decided by a judicial decision in Israel, a Contracting Party is under the obligation to lend their assistance in the return, 'unless objective factors' caused the authorities to fear that the applicants 'risked suffering a flagrant denial of justice'[160]—a standard which the Court frequently invokes in cases with a cross-border dimension.[161] I would argue that a similar test could be used with regard to the right of access to a court in relation to the issue of allegedly unfair proceedings in the only available forum in international litigation.

---

156 Marchadier 2007, p. 86.

157 See in this regard also *Al-Bassam v. Al-Bassam* (infra n. 163).

158 See supra n. 69.

159 *Eskinazi and Chelouche v. Turkey* (dec.), no. 14600/05, ECHR 2005-XIII (extracts).

160 *Eskinazi and Chelouche v. Turkey* (dec.), no. 14600/05, ECHR 2005-XIII (extracts), under '2. The Court's assessment' (referring to *Mamatkulov and Askarov v. Turkey* [GC], nos. 46827/99 and 46951/99, para 88, ECHR 2005-I; *Einhorn v. France* (dec.), no. 71555/01, ECHR 2001-XI; *Drozd and Janousek v. France and Spain*, judgment of 26 June 1992, Series A no. 240, para 110; and *Soering v. the United Kingdom*, judgment of 7 July 1989, Series A no. 161, para 113). See with regard to the Court's case law concerning the extra-territorial effect of the ECHR also supra Chap. 4.

161 See supra Sects. 3.5.1.3 and 'The Extra-Territorial Effect of the ECHR' Chap. 4.

Whether the right of access to a court in private international law cases entails the right of access to a court in accordance with the demands of a fair trial *ex* Article 6(1) ECHR, and if so, what the standard of control should be, has not been definitely answered in the jurisprudence of national courts in the Contracting Parties. Nevertheless, the issue has arisen, and some interesting conclusions may be derived from the national case law.

Does Article 6(1) ECHR provide the plaintiff with an alternative forum if the plaintiff is unlikely to receive a fair trial in accordance with Article 6(1) ECHR in the only forum available in international civil litigation? In the English case of *Al-Bassam v. Al-Bassam*[162] such an argument was more or less raised before the Court of Appeal in relation to the refusal to grant an injunction. The claimant had requested the English judge to exercise his discretion to grant an anti-suit injunction regarding proceedings in Saudi Arabia. In the first instance such an injunction had been granted, in which the fear that the claimant would not receive a fair trial had been part of the equation. The Court of Appeal, however, held that while the concerns regarding a fair trial in Saudi Arabia were not unfounded, this was not a matter for the jurisdiction stage. This issue should not arise until a judgment had been given abroad, when the English court would have to decide on the recognition and enforcement of such a judgment.[163]

While this case concerns an injunction, the argument used here may still prove to be instructive. There is admittedly a distinction between a court allowing proceedings in the forum on the basis of the right of access *ex* Article 6(1) ECHR because proceedings abroad in the only forum available to the plaintiff would allegedly be unfair in the sense of Article 6(1), and granting an injunction prohibiting proceedings abroad for reasons of unfairness; the latter undoubtedly entails a more active approach, which raises questions with regard to Article 6(1) ECHR on its own.[164]

However, it is also easy to observe the parallel between these two situations. The reluctance of the English Appeal Court to defend Article 6(1) ECHR at the jurisdictional stage is an interesting objection to the argument that Article 6(1) ECHR requires access to a court where proceedings will take place in accordance with that provision. However, while it is correct that the recognition and enforcement of a foreign judgment violating Article 6(1) ECHR could be denied,[165] this would not help to ensure that the plaintiff would actually receive a fair trial. In such a case an argument for the right of access to a court could

[162] *Al-Bassam v. Al-Bassam*, [2004] EWCA Civ. 857.

[163] Cf. Fawcett 2007, at p. 13.

[164] See in this regard Fawcett 2007, p. 13. The argument of the Court of Appeal regarding the possibility to deny recognition and enforcement is indeed more relevant with regard to the refusal to grant an injunction.

[165] See further infra Sect. 8.2.

therefore be made, albeit only in the exceptional circumstances where it can be proven that there is the risk of a 'flagrant denial of justice'.[166]

Another English case which is instructive for the issue of whether the right of access to a court requires an available court that meets the standards of Article 6(1) ECHR is *OT Africa Line Ltd v. Hijazy (The Kribi)*.[167] This case also concerned an anti-suit injunction, but the argument was made that an anti-suit injunction would deny the defendants the right of access to a court in one of the other Contracting Parties. In this context it was held that 'Article 6 of the ECHR does not provide that a person is to have an unfettered choice of tribunal in which to pursue or defend his civil rights.'[168] According to Aikens J, Article 6 ECHR is not concerned with where this right would be exercised. The only relevant point is that a fair trial, in accordance with the guarantees provided for by Article 6 ECHR, should take place somewhere, regardless of its exact location. The argument here that an anti-suit injunction would deny the defendants' right of access to a court was thus denied, as England was still available as a forum. In this case the English court thus finds that the location of the trial is irrelevant, as long as a trial is held somewhere *and* in accordance with the guarantees of the right to a fair trial.[169] This latter part is, of course, an interesting finding. Then again, one should note that in this case England was still available as the (only) available forum, which may have made it easier for the court to make this observation.

In the Netherlands, the question of what to do if the plaintiff is unlikely to receive a trial to the standards of Article 6(1) ECHR in the only available forum could arise in relation to Article 9–c of the Dutch Civil Procedure Code.[170] This article provides that a Dutch court may assert jurisdiction even where a foreign court has jurisdiction to hear the case if it would be unacceptable to expect the plaintiff to bring his or her case before that foreign court. Article 9–c of the Dutch Civil Procedure Code does require a connection with the Netherlands. Plaintiffs invoke this article quite regularly, as would be expected, but courts in the Netherlands tend (justifiably so) to be quite reluctant in this regard.[171] Occasionally, plaintiffs will base their arguments as to why they cannot be expected to go to the foreign court on the right to a fair trial, although Article 6(1) ECHR is not always (expressly) invoked in this regard.[172] On a few occasions such arguments have been successful.[173]

---

[166] See supra the discussion of *Eskinazi* following n. 160.

[167] *OT Africa Line Ltd v. Hijazy (The Kribi)* [2001] 1 Lloyd's Report 76.

[168] *OT Africa Line Ltd v. Hijazy (The Kribi)* [2001] 1 Lloyd's Report 76, no. 42 (per Aikens J).

[169] See also Fawcett 2007, p. 7.

[170] See supra Sect. 5.4.3.

[171] Ibili 2007, pp. 125–126.

[172] See, e.g., Rb. 's-Gravenhage 12 January 2006, LJN AV2498. The district court held that it had jurisdiction, although this was not based on Article 9(c) *Rv*.

[173] See Ktg. Amsterdam, 5 January 1996, *NIPR* 1996, 145 in which pilots of Kuwait Airways, who (also) lived in the Netherlands, who had previously held the Iraqi nationality, successfully argued that they could not receive a fair trial in Kuwait, because of their previous nationality. The Dutch judge set aside the exclusive choice-of-court clause and asserted jurisdiction.

For Switzerland, the argument could be made that where proceedings before the only available foreign court would be demonstrably unfair, Swiss courts should assert jurisdiction on the basis of the *forum necessitatis* clause of Article 3 of the Swiss Private International Law Act, provided there was an argument that it could not reasonably be required that the foreign (available) court would be seized.[174] It has been argued that the *forum necessitatis* exception can be invoked when one could reasonably expect that the competent foreign court would not render a decision within a reasonable time.[175]

There is one more scenario that could be brought under this topic of the only available foreign court not meeting the standards of Article (1) ECHR. It is also possible that a foreign court is available, but that this foreign court is barely connected to the case and that it could be considered to have asserted jurisdiction based on an exorbitant or inappropriate ground of jurisdiction. It will be demonstrated below that the argument could be made that Article 6(1) ECHR may be invoked by a defendant against the unreasonable assertion of jurisdiction.[176] This argument could similarly be used by a plaintiff, who would then only have the option to litigate in a forum with only a negligible connection to the case. In that case there would only be available a foreign court whose jurisdiction was based on questionable grounds. However, it is submitted that this possibility is mostly theoretical, as it is hard to imagine a scenario in which there would only be a foreign court available with an insufficient link to the case. Moreover, there is a distinct possibility that the forum seized by the plaintiff in this manner could also be regarded as exorbitant. This argument appears not to have been raised before national courts.

5.4.3.4 The Right of Access and the Denial of Substantive Justice

Is it possible to speak of a denial of justice, which would run counter to the right of access to a court following from Article 6(1) ECHR, if a plaintiff before the normally competent court in another country was faced with the certainty that his claim would be denied there? The issue in such a case is not that the plaintiff does not have access to a court. However, the Court has consistently held, also particularly in relation to the right of access to a court, that the ECHR does not merely guarantee rights that are theoretical or illusory, but rather 'rights that are practical and effective'.[177] One could thus argue that for the rights guaranteed in Article

---

174 This is a condition for the application of the *forum necessitatis* exception in Switzerland. See generally on this condition Bucher 2011, pp. 65–66; Othenin-Girard 1999, pp. 272–275 and the works cited there.

175 See Othenin-Girard 1999, p. 272. See also *Tribunal fédéral*, 5 March 1991, *La Semaine judicidaire* 1991, p. 457, in which this possibility was essentially raised in a case concerning a divorce in the Netherlands.

176 See infra Sect. 5.5.

177 *Airey v. Ireland*. 9 October 1979, Series A no. 32, para 24.

6(1) ECHR to be effective, a court should also assert jurisdiction when it is certain that the normally competent (foreign) court would deny the plaintiff's (substantive) claim.

It is clear that such an interpretation of the right of access to a court would seriously extend this right. It has been argued that such an interpretation would go too far in the sense that the right of access to a court merely entails the right to a fair hearing, but not the right to be victorious.[178] One can only agree with this stance. It seems far-fetched that the procedural right of access to a court would also effectively entail the right to seek a court where one's claim would be awarded. It is also questionable whether this is something that can be dealt with at the jurisdictional stage of proceedings, as it would require going into the merits of a case.

It is, however, possible to make this dilemma more difficult. What if it was certain that the rejection of the claim before the normally competent court would result in a violation of one of the substantive rights guaranteed in the ECHR? What if, for example, it was beyond doubt that the custody of a child of divorcing parents would automatically be awarded to the father in the only available foreign court?[179] Could the mother argue, before a court of one of the Contracting Parties, a denial of justice based on Article 6(1) ECHR, possibly in conjunction with other rights guaranteed in the ECHR?

Although the situation of seeing that the action abroad would stand no chance of success would certainly infringe the plaintiff's effective right of access to a court, difficulties similar to the ones discussed immediately above would still be present. This would require delving into the merits of a case. One would thus essentially have to decide the case on the merits before deciding whether the court is (internationally) competent to hear the case. As discussed above, the right of access to a court under Article 6(1) ECHR is only concerned with procedural bars to this right, even though the demarcation between substantive and procedural obstacles in this regard is not always clear. Yet what is clear is that such a conception of the right of access to a court, including the right of access to a court where a certain outcome on the merits could be achieved, would more or less entail a substantive guarantee. This cannot be part of the mostly procedural right of the right of access to a court. However, despite these arguments against such a conception of the right of access, it is not entirely unheard of, as the Dutch case discussed directly below will demonstrate.

A remarkable decision concerning the ground of jurisdiction of *forum necessitatis* and the invocation of a substantive right was taken in the Netherlands by the *Gerechtshof* 's-Gravenhage.[180] The case concerned a joint application for a divorce by a Dutch wife and her Maltese husband who married in Malta. In the first instance their request was denied because the court held that it had no jurisdiction,

---

[178] Briggs and Rees 2009, p. 21.

[179] One could argue that this could constitute a violation of Article 8 ECHR (the right to private and family life) taken in conjunction with Article 14 ECHR (the prohibition of discrimination).

[180] *Gerechtshof* 's-Gravenhage, 21 December 2005, *EB* 2006, 32; *NJF* 2006, 154.

as the couple had their habitual residence in Malta. On appeal, the appeal court first confirmed that on the basis of the Brussels II Regulation,[181] Malta had exclusive jurisdiction. However, the appeal court went on to note that no divorce could be had (at the time) in Malta,[182] regardless of the question of whether Dutch or Maltese law would be the law applicable to the case. The appeal court in The Hague, noting that the ECJ has consistently held that fundamental rights form an integral part of the general principles of law and that the ECHR is of particular significance in this regard,[183] found that the jurisdictional rules of the Brussels II Regulation effectively barred the wife's right of access to a court, which is a right that is guaranteed in Article 6 ECHR. The court thus set aside the provisions of the Brussels II Regulation. In its consideration the court further noted that the case concerned a joint application and the husband would thus not be forced against his will to appear in proceedings in the Netherlands.

The court thereafter referred to the Dutch rules on jurisdiction and found that it had jurisdiction on the basis of Article 9–b *Rv*,[184] as it would be unreasonable to require the parties to initiate proceedings in another country. The court further observed that under Maltese law a foreign divorce will be recognized if that decision is taken by the competent court of either the place of habitual residence of one of the parties or the court of which one of the parties is a national. The appeal court noted that its decision would thus be recognized under Maltese law, and granted the application for a divorce.

This is quite a remarkable decision, which has led to mixed reactions.[185] A number of points can be made. It is, first, questionable whether a Dutch court is even permitted to refer to the *forum necessitatis* clause, which originates in the national Dutch rules on jurisdiction, once it has been established that the Brussels II Regulation is applicable to the case, even though no jurisdiction can be asserted on the basis of this instrument. What could the court have done instead? Neither the Brussels II Regulation, nor its successor the Brussels II *bis* Regulation, contain the escape route of a *forum necessitatis* clause. The appeal court could perhaps—although I imagine such an action would not be possible without the intervention of the relevant EU court in Luxembourg—have asserted jurisdiction referring to

[181] Regulation (EC) No 1347/2000 on jurisdiction and the recognition and enforcement of judgments in matrimonial matters and in matters of parental responsibility, *OJ* 2000, L 160/19. This regulation has been replaced by the Brussels II *bis* Regulation. See supra n. 11.

[182] After the majority of the Maltese population in a (non-binding) referendum voted for the legalization of divorce, the Maltese parliament has passed a law legalizing divorce. The law was due to take effect in October 2011.

[183] The Gerechtshof referred to ECJ 10 July 2003, *Booker Aquaculture and Hydo Seafood*, Cases C-20/00 and C-64/00, ECR 2003, I-7411.

[184] See supra n. 114.

[185] See with regard to this case, e.g., Boele-Woelki 2006, pp. 5503–5504; Ibili 2007, pp. 118, 147; Schmidt 2007, pp. 116–121. Boele-Woelki and Ibili agree with the substantive result reached by the court, even though they question the method used by the court. Schmidt, on the other hand, finds that the Dutch court could rely on its national rules, despite the Brussels II *bis* Regulation being applicable, but questions whether the result reached by the court is correct.

the right of access to a court *ex* Article 6(1) ECHR, which, as also noted by the appeal court itself, is part of the general principles of law and has a special position in this regard.[186] This would require, however, that Article 6(1) ECHR is actually relevant in this case, which, in my opinion, is not the case.

Does Article 6(1) ECHR guarantee the right of access to a court in the situation where there is only one forum open to the plaintiff and where it is certain that the plaintiff's action will be denied? Does it consequently matter what sort of action is concerned? As has been discussed above, it has been argued that Article 6(1) ECHR merely guarantees that there is a forum where proceedings in accordance with the guarantees derived from that provision could take place.[187] It is clear that in this case there was an open forum for the proceedings and there was, in principle, no reason to assume that the proceedings in Malta would not meet the procedural standards required by Article 6(1), as Malta is a Contracting Party to the ECHR. This also was not in question. The only problem was that the expected outcome of the proceedings in this forum was not compatible with the parties' wishes, as proceedings in Malta would not have resulted in the requested divorce at the time. This, nevertheless, does not mean that the right of access to a court *ex* Article 6(1) ECHR is violated. While one may be sympathetic to the result reached by the Dutch court in this case, the manner in which it arrived at this decision is highly questionable.

Let us take this argument one step further. Would it matter if litigating in the only available forum would result in a violation of one of the other (substantive) rights guaranteed in the ECHR? It should be noted that this was not at issue in the case discussed above, as the right to a divorce is not protected under the ECHR.[188] Yet even if a substantive right guaranteed in the ECHR was involved, it is difficult to see how the ECHR would force the Contracting Parties to open up their courts in such cases, and even more so in the event that the court of another Contracting Party was open. Even though the Court has held that rights must be effective, such an interpretation even in combination with another substantive right guaranteed in the ECHR would make this right more than effective.

It is perfectly understandable that States would want to keep open an option which could only be invoked under exceptional circumstances. It is, however, difficult to imagine that the Court would read into the right of access an obligation under Article 6(1) ECHR to do so, particularly also in light of the fact that under Article 6(1) ECHR the rights not only of the plaintiff in international civil

---

[186] Cf. Ibili 2007, p. 146. But see Schmidt 2007, p. 117, who argues that it would still be possible for a Dutch court to refer to its national rules on jurisdiction (including its *forum necessitatis* clause, if the Articles 3–5 of the Brussels II *bis* Regulation (see supra n. 11) do not point to a competent court, Article 7 would refer back to the national rules on jurisdiction of the court seized.

[187] See supra Sect. 5.4.3.3.

[188] See in this regard *Johnston and Others v. Ireland*, 18 December 1986, Series A no. 122.

proceedings should be considered, but also the rights of a defendant not to be forced to defend himself before a court based on exorbitant jurisdiction.[189]

In Switzerland, it would appear to be difficult to invoke Article 6(1) ECHR to gain access to the Swiss courts to obtain substantive justice which would be unavailable in the only normally available foreign court. It has been defended with regard to Article 3 of the Swiss Private International Law Act, which contains a *forum necessitatis* clause, that this ground of jurisdiction is not meant to be invoked in order to gain what cannot be obtained before a foreign court.[190]

It is interesting to note that on a few occasions, substantive rights guaranteed in the ECHR have been invoked in cases at the national level in order to enforce the right of access to a court—without any reference to the right of access to a court *ex* Article 6(1) ECHR. These attempts have all been unsuccessful, which is the correct approach, because, as the discussion up to this point also demonstrates, the substantive rights guaranteed in the ECHR do not entail a right of access to a court, while the procedural right of access *ex* Article 6(1), in principle, does not contain a right to a substantive solution.

An illustration may be found in a Dutch case before the *Hoge Raad* concerning a divorce in which the applicant invoked Article 8 ECHR (the right to family life) against the finding of the Dutch courts that they did not have jurisdiction.[191] The husband and wife were married in the Dutch Embassy in the United Arab Emirates. The husband was a Dutch national who usually resided in the Philippines. The wife was a Thai national who had never lived in the Netherlands and was also residing in the Philippines at the time of the proceedings. The District Court of Leeuwarden held that it had no jurisdiction to hear the case, on the basis of the Brussels II Regulation.[192] This was upheld on appeal, and the *Hoge Raad* also rejected the appeal.[193] The Advocate General, in his opinion, however, did briefly entertain the claimant's argument for jurisdiction based on Article 8 ECHR, but rejected this by merely pointing out that the Brussels II Regulation does not have a *forum necessitatis* provision.[194]

This case is, of course, somewhat reminiscent of the Dutch case concerning Malta discussed above, in which the Dutch court did assert jurisdiction.[195] In that case, however, Article 6(1) ECHR was at least invoked in relation to the claim of a right of access to a court. It is simply not possible to derive the right of access to court from a right other than Article 6(1) ECHR. In a Swiss case before the

[189] See further infra Sect. 5.5.

[190] See Bucher 2011, p. 64. Cf. Obergericht Zürich, BlZR 89 1990, no. 65, p. 139.

[191] HR 1 September 2006, *RvdW* 2006, 769; *JOL* 2006, 475; *JPF* 2006, 136 (note Oderkerk). See with regard to this case also Schmidt 2007.

[192] See supra n. 182.

[193] It did so on the basis of Article 81 RO, which states that if the complaint before the HR cannot lead to cassation and no important questions of law are brought up, the HR may dismiss the complaint without stating further reasons.

[194] See supra n. 192.

[195] See supra n. 181.

Tribunal fédéral an attempt to that effect by invoking Article 14 ECHR was therefore, in my opinion, also rightfully rejected by the Swiss court.[196]

5.4.3.5 Access to a Court and the Impossibility of a Judgment Being Recognized and Enforced

The last scenario that will be examined with regard to the denial of justice is whether this could apply when one faces the reality that the judgment delivered by the normally competent court abroad could not be recognized and enforced. This would render such a judgment meaningless. Could the right of access to a court create an obligation for the Contracting Party to open its courts if the foreign judgment would not be recognized? Any argument in this direction would also have to be based on the Court's case law regarding the right of access to a court being an effective right.[197] However, it is questionable whether it would be necessary to grant a plaintiff the right of access to a court pre-emptively, before any proceedings have taken place abroad in the normally competent court (unless, as discussed, it can be demonstrated that the proceedings would be blatantly unfair[198]). One should also note that the rights guaranteed in the ECHR, in principle, require Contracting Parties to recognize and enforce foreign judgments unless there are very compelling reasons not to do so.[199]

There is thus no immediate reason to allow proceedings on this basis. The argument could, however, be presented that should it nevertheless prove to be impossible to recognize and enforce a foreign judgment in the secondary forum (following fruitless foreign proceedings), a forum should be provided.

5.4.4 Restrictions to the Right of Access to a Court: Procedural Bars

As discussed above, the right of access to a court by its very nature requires regulation by the State, and may therefore be limited. A Contracting Party may not only regulate access to its courts in deference to other States in international civil litigation, but could also raise procedural bars to access within the forum particular to international litigation. The question is, of course, whether there are restrictions that are specific to international civil litigation in the forum and whether such restrictions would meet the requirements which the Court has developed in relation to the right of access to a court.

---

196 ATF, 19 April 2010, 5A_171/2010 (unpublished).

197 See supra n. 69.

198 See supra Sect. 5.4.3.3.

199 See infra Chap. 7.

Traditionally there has been one important restriction in this regard, and that is the so-called *cautio judicatum solvi*, or security for costs. This is an instrument used in international litigation and it can be found in many countries including England, the Netherlands, and Switzerland, even though it has largely lost its prominence, as will be further discussed below. Security for costs in international litigation entails that a claimant who is not habitually resident in the forum is obligated to deposit a certain amount in order to have his claim heard. This ensures that a defendant's possible costs relating to such international proceedings will be covered. Such costs could, in theory, be difficult to recover due to the fact that the claimant has no ties to the forum and/or no assets.

In *Tolstoy Miloslavsky v. the United Kingdom*[200] the Court examined the requirement to pay a sizable amount as security for costs as a condition for the applicant's appeal in relation to the right of access to a court. *Tolstoy* did not concern an international affair, but this judgment can nevertheless be applied to the use of this instrument in international proceedings.[201] It demonstrates that security for costs has a legitimate aim, while the proportionality of the restriction depends on the particular circumstances.[202] In this case the Court ultimately found that security for costs amounting to GBP 124,900, which had to be delivered within a short time frame (two weeks), did not result in a violation of Article 6(1) ECHR.[203] It will, however, be recalled that the financial means of the defendant must play an important role in this regard.[204] It is thus certainly conceivable that the *cautio judicatum solvi* is permissible in light of the right of access to a court, provided certain requirements are met.[205] However, possible issues relating to the *cautio* are not confined to the right of access to a court, as the national jurisprudence discussed below demonstrates.

The requirement of the *cautio judicatum solvi* has quite frequently been discussed by national courts with regard to its conformity with the demands of Article 6(1) ECHR. The *cautio* has, incidentally, not solely been discussed in relation to the right of access to a court *ex* Article 6(1) ECHR; it has been noted that there may also be issues relating to discrimination.[206]

---

[200] *Tolstoy Miloslavsky v. the United Kingdom*, 13 July 1995, para 61, Series A no. 316-B.

[201] See, e.g., infra n. 210.

[202] See also supra Sect. 5.4.1.

[203] But see the partly dissenting opinion of Judge Jambrek. He found that, while the security for costs order pursued a legitimate aim, it was disproportionate.

[204] See *Aït-Mouhoub v. France*, 28 October 1998, *Reports of Judgments and Decisions* 1998-VIII.

[205] See also Marchadier 2007, p. 70ff.

[206] It should be noted that several manifestations of the *cautio judicatium solvi* have, with regard to discrimination, come under fire from the European Court of Justice. See for an early example ECJ 1 July 1993, Case C 20/92, *Hubbard v. Hamburger*, ECR 1993, I-3777; see also Van Hoek, 2000, pp. 251–258; see also infra n. 213.

The *cautio judicatum solvi* is largely no longer permitted within the European Union with respect to nationals of a Member State of the European Union.[207] An order for security for costs may therefore only be made if the claimant is resident out of the jurisdiction, but not resident in a State where either the Brussels I Regulation or the Lugano Convention applies, while there must also be reason to believe that the claimant will be unable to repay the costs of the defendant if ordered to do so by the court. If a non-resident has sufficient assets in another country in which a judgment would be easily enforced, the power to order security would be inappropriate.[208]

In *Nasser v. United Bank of Kuwait*[209] the English Court of Appeal discussed Articles 6(1) and 14 ECHR in relation to the application for security of the costs of an appeal. The claimant was resident in the United States. The appeal court discussed *Tolstoy Miloslavsky*[210] in relation to Article 6 ECHR, while examining as to the issue of possible discrimination *ex* Article 14 ECHR the distinction between residents inside and outside the Brussels and Lugano regime States. The English appeal court held that although one cannot start with the inflexible assumption that anyone outside the Brussels and Lugano zone should deposit a security for costs, what matters is how great will be the burden of the defendant to enforce a judgment for costs against the plaintiff. The order for security for costs should be adapted to reflect the nature and size of the risk against which it is designed to protect. As it would probably be difficult for the defendant to secure enforcement in the United States, a certain amount for security for costs was justified in this case, according to the appeal court.

The appeal court in Amsterdam held that Article 224 of the Dutch Civil Procedure Code,[211] which requires everyone not residing in the Netherlands to deposit security for costs, is not discriminatory, because everybody residing outside of the Netherlands, including Dutch persons residing elsewhere, would have to comply with this requirement.[212] It should, incidentally, be noted that Article 6 EC Treaty[213] was invoked in this case, and not Article 14 ECHR.[214]

In older Dutch case law regarding the *cauto judicatum solvi*, which concerned an old provision,[215] the right of access to a court *ex* Article 6(1) ECHR was discussed.

---

[207] See ECJ 20 March 1997, Case C-323/95, *David Charles Hayes and Jeannette Karen Hayes v. Kronenberger GmbH.*, ECR 1997, I-1711.

[208] See Dicey et al. 2012, pp. 309–317.

[209] [2001] EWCA Civ 556, [2002] 1 All E.R. 401 (CA).

[210] See supra n. 81.

[211] Article 224 *Rv* [Dutch Civil Procedure Code].

[212] Hof Amsterdam, 17 July 2008, *NIPR* 2009, 31.

[213] Article 6 of the EC Treaty prohibited any discrimination on grounds of nationality.

[214] One should note that this article was also discussed in *Nasser* (supra n. 210).

[215] Article 152 *Rv* (oud) [(former) Dutch Civil Procedure]. This was the article of the former Dutch Civil Procedure Code, in which the rules concerning the *cautio judicatum solvi* were laid down. This article prescribed that all aliens could be required to pay security. This article has since been amended and the current article now uses residence as the connecting factor.

In one of these cases the district court held that the invocation of Article 6(1) ECHR against an order for security for costs was unsuccessful because the plaintiff had not sufficiently shown that it lacked the funds for the deposit.[216] A similar decision was reached in another case in which the district court held with regard to the plaintiffs' invocation of Article 6(1) ECHR and the claim that they lacked funds that merely declaring a lack of funds was not sufficient. Some tangible support for such a position is required. In this latter case the non-discrimination requirement was also discussed, albeit not in relation to Article 14 ECHR, but Article 26 of the International Covenant on Civil and Political Rights (ICCPR).[217] The district court held that the *cautio* did not violate the non-discrimination requirement because there was a reasonable and objective justification for it—in short, the fact that it would be very hard for the defendant company to recover its costs.[218]

In Switzerland, the *Tribunal fédéral* has also delivered a judgment on the *cautio judicatum solvi* and the right of access to a court.[219] In a complex case concerning a number of oil companies, one of the parties, X, at a certain point brought a suit against another party, Y, in Switzerland, eventually demanding USD 5 million. The defendants argued that the plaintiff should deposit a *cautio judicatum solvi*. In the first instance this action was denied, as the court found that X was domiciled in one of the States party to the Hague Convention on Civil Procedure.[220] However, the defendants later reiterated their objections in this regard, pointing out that X had changed his domicile to Mongolia, which is not a party to the aforementioned Hague Convention. They argued for a security of CHF 400,000. The plaintiff argued that the amount of CHF 400,000 was excessive and, relying on *inter alia* Article 6(1) ECHR, complained of an inadmissible restriction to the right of access to a court.

The *Tribunal fédéral* rejected this complaint, carefully outlining the Court's case law and its own previous jurisprudence. The *Tribunal* noted that the right of access to a court under Article 6(1) ECHR by its very nature requires regulation of the State, and this also applies for private international law cases. In this regard States enjoy a certain margin of appreciation, so they can provide certain limitations, provided these do not affect the substance of the right of access to courts, they pursue a legitimate aim, and there is a reasonable relationship of proportionality between the restrictions imposed and the purpose.[221] Thereafter, it

---

[216] Rb. Rotterdam, 22 March 2001, *NIPR* 2001, 300.

[217] Article 26 ICCPR states the following. 'All persons are equal before the law and are entitled without any discrimination to the equal protection of the law. In this respect, the law shall prohibit any discrimination and guarantee to all persons equal and effective protection against discrimination on any ground such as race, colour, sex, language, religion, political or other opinion, national or social origin, property, birth or other status.'

[218] Rb. Rotterdam, 11 January 2001, *NIPR* 2001, 146.

[219] ATF 132 I 134.

[220] The Hague Convention of 1 March 1954 on Civil Procedure, entry into force 12 April 1957.

[221] The Federal Tribunal cited in this regard *García Manibardo v. Spain*, no. 38695/97, para 36 , ECHR 2000-II, as well as *Patrono, Cascini and Stefanelli v. Italy*, no. 10180/04, para 58, 20 April 2006 and *Besseau v. France*, no. 73893/01, para 23, 7 March 2006.

observed that the Court has particularly recognized as a legitimate aim the claim of a defendant for the payment of security for costs so that the defendant does not face, in the event of dismissal of the appeal, the inability to recover his legal costs.[222] According to the jurisprudence of the Tribunal, similar principles apply to the right of access to courts as guaranteed by the Federal Constitution.[223] Applying the above-cited findings to the case at hand, the Tribunal held that the amount was not disproportionate and that Article 6(1) ECHR was thus not breached.

5.4.5 The Effectiveness of the Right of Access to a Court: Legal Aid

Above, it has been demonstrated that the Court's finding that the right of access to a court should be an effective right may be invoked as support for the argument that the right of access should be further extended.[224] Such a possible extension is not only limited to a possible extension of a denial of justice in situations in which there is another forum open, but could also have an impact on the position of a (foreign) plaintiff in issues of private international law.

It has been noted that in order to ensure that the right of access to a court is not merely a theoretical right, the Contracting Parties may have to offer legal aid in cases concerning complex issues where the assistance of a lawyer may be indispensable, as without representation such a case would be ineffective.[225] It is thus certainly conceivable that a Contracting Party would have to offer legal aid in cases concerning issues of private international law. In this regard, one could wonder whether it would be permitted to offer such legal aid only to nationals, and to exclude foreigners from such a legal aid scheme. This would be a difference in treatment regarding the right of access to a court, which could be forbidden under Article 6(1) ECHR taken in conjunction with Article 14 ECHR.

It is standard case law of the Court that a difference in treatment is discriminatory if there is 'no objective and reasonable justification' for that treatment, if it does not pursue a 'legitimate aim', or if there is not a 'reasonable relationship of proportionality between the means employed and the aim sought to be realized.'[226] One could attempt to justify not providing legal aid to foreigners by pointing to budgetary reasons. Then again, the Court has also found that only 'very weighty

---

222 Referring to *Tolstoy v. the United Kingdom* (supra n. 81) and *Kreuz v. Poland* (supra n. 86).

223 ATF 131 II 169, at no. 2.3.3.

224 See supra Sect. 5.4.3.3. Note that the extent to which this is actually possible is not clear.

225 See, e.g., *Airey v. Ireland*. 9 October 1979, Series A no. 32 and *Steel and Morris v. the United Kingdom*, no. 68416/01, ECHR 2005-II.

226 See, e.g., *James and Others v. the United Kingdom*, 21 February 1986, Series A no. 98; *Lithgow and Others v. the United Kingdom*, 8 July 1986, Series A no. 102; *Darby v. Sweden*, 23 October 1990, Series A no. 187.

reasons' would suffice for the Court to find the difference of treatment based solely on nationality to be compatible with the ECHR.[227] This, taken together with the fact that the Court has held that the absence of legal aid endangers the very essence of the right of access to a court, would, in my opinion, suggest that it is not possible to withhold legal aid to foreigners in complex cases.[228]

5.4.6 Preliminary Conclusions

In this section the impact of the right of access to a court on the issue of jurisdiction in private international law has been examined. The right of access, which has been derived from the right to a fair trial *ex* Article 6(1) ECHR by the Court in *Golder*, may be invoked by a plaintiff in international proceedings. It has been demonstrated that this right is, in principle, undisputed in the event that a plaintiff in international proceedings is unable to find a court in any country. However, it has been argued that the right of access may, under certain circumstances, also be invoked in the event that there would be a foreign court available. A number of scenarios have been reviewed.

It has been examined whether the right entails the right of access to a court in accordance with the procedural requirements of Article 6(1) ECHR. It has also been reviewed as to whether the right of access could be concerned with the situation in which it would be certain that the applicant's substantive claim would be denied. Finally, it has been examined whether the right of access could be invoked if it were certain that the judgment rendered by the only available foreign court would not be eligible for recognition and enforcement in the Contracting Party. In this examination the (little) relevant case law of the Court and the jurisprudence of national courts have been included. The author has argued that it is defensible that in determining whether the right of access to a court has been restricted in international proceedings, the procedural quality of the foreign proceedings may be considered by the court, even though this review would not be very strict.

It has further been found that the right of access to a court in international civil litigation is also concerned with procedural bars, such as, for example, the *cautio judicatum solvi*. Such restriction to the right of access to a court must have a legitimate aim, while the restriction must also be proportionate to the legitimate aim pursued. It has finally been determined in relation to the right of access to a court in private international law cases that there may be an obligation for Contracting Parties to offer legal aid, regardless of the nationality of the parties involved.

---

[227] *Gaygusuz v. Austria*, 16 September 1996, para 42, *Reports of Judgments and Decisions* 1996-IV.

[228] Cf. Marchadier 2007, p. 79.

5.5 The Invocation of Article 6(1) ECHR against the Assertion of Jurisdiction

In the previous section the impact of the right of access to a court, as derived from Article 6(1) ECHR, on the issue of jurisdiction in private international law has been discussed. Article 6(1) ECHR deployed in this manner should ensure that the plaintiff in international litigation will be able to find a forum. In this section, however, one will find an examination of the possibilities for the *defendant* to invoke Article 6(1) ECHR *against* the assertion of jurisdiction in private international law. Is it possible to invoke Article 6(1) ECHR against the unreasonable assertion of jurisdiction in international litigation? Does Article 6(1) ECHR provide a human rights check on the assertion of jurisdiction in private international law? As will become clear from the discussion in this section, there is little specific case law to support this stance. The discussion is thus mostly a theoretical one. However, as will be suggested below, there may be some situations in which Article 6(1) ECHR, constructed as a check on the unreasonable assertion of jurisdiction, may provide relief for defendants in untenable situations.

The examination of this issue will start with an overview of the relevant case law of the Strasbourg Institutions (Sect. 5.5.1). This will be followed by an examination of the different opinions that have been developed in the literature on this particular subject. As will be demonstrated below, the Due Process Clause of the US Constitution has been a source of inspiration for the role which Article 6(1) ECHR could perhaps play with regard to the assertion of jurisdiction on an exorbitant ground (Sect. 5.5.2). Thereafter, some consequences of this role for Article 6(1), and the role that Article 6(1) ECHR should ideally have, will be discussed (Sect. 5.5.3). Finally, some preliminary conclusions will be drawn (Sect. 5.5.4).

5.5.1 The Invocation of Article 6(1) ECHR against Jurisdiction in the Strasbourg Case Law

There is very little case law of the Strasbourg Institutions that specifically concerns the issue of (adjudicatory) jurisdiction in private international law. However, the Commission has on one occasion examined the assertion of jurisdiction in private international law from the perspective of Article 6(1) ECHR in an unpublished decision of 13 May 1976.[229] In the Digest of Strasbourg Case Law the following extract of the relevant part of the decision was given:

[229] Decision of the European Commission of Human Rights, no. 6200/73, 13 May 1976.

> The applicant claims that he and his daughter are Greek citizens and as such are subject only to the jurisdiction of the Greek courts. The applicant does not state on which Article of the Convention he relies for this part of his complaint. The Commission has examined the complaint from the point of view of Article 6 and concludes that the right given by that Article to a fair hearing by an impartial tribunal, confers no right on a person to select the particular tribunal by which his case will be heard.
>
> Assuming that, in certain cases, a problem concerning the jurisdiction and the criteria on which it may be based must be considered for the application of Article 6 of the Convention, one must recognize in the present case that the fact that the applicant's daughter lives with her mother in the United Kingdom, added to her mother's British nationality, constitutes for the jurisdiction of the British courts a sufficient link according to general principles of international law. An examination by the Commission of this complaint as it has been submitted, including an examination *ex officio*, does not therefore disclose any appearance of a violation of the rights and freedoms set out in the Convention and in particular in the above Article.'[230]

As will be further discussed below, this case is often cited as evidence for the idea that Article 6(1) ECHR could indeed play a due process-like role regarding the assertion of jurisdiction.[231] It is, particularly, the Commission's observation that the daughter living in the United Kingdom with her mother, coupled with the mother having British nationality, provided a 'sufficient link' with the forum for the British courts to assert jurisdiction that has sparked this idea. However, one could also observe that the Commission merely offers the fairly innocent remark here that there could be room for the application of Article 6 ECHR in regard to the criteria on which jurisdiction is based and that the domicile of the mother and daughter is in this case a sufficient link with the forum to assert jurisdiction.

Seven years later, the Commission had the opportunity to review another case, *H v. the United Kingdom*,[232] which could have been very interesting with regard to the assertion of jurisdiction by the English courts if not for the finding that the applicant had failed to comply with the six month rule of—then—Article 26 ECHR.[233] The applicant, an American citizen, was granted an oil exploration concession by the Libyan Government in 1957. The applicant exploited this concession jointly with British Petroleum (BP). After Iran seized three islands in the Persian Gulf following the withdrawal of the United Kingdom in that area, Libya allegedly expropriated BP's share of the concession in retaliation in December 1971. Libya subsequently exploited the concession jointly with the applicant until June 1973, when Libya also expropriated the applicant's half of the concession.

BP consequently issued proceedings against the applicant, the American citizen, in London, and contended that their agreement was governed by English law.

---

230 Decision of the European Commission of Human Rights, no. 6200/73, 13 May 1976, in 2 Digest of Strasbourg case law relating to the European Convention on Human Rights (Article 6) (Köln, Heymann 1984), p. 269.

231 See infra Sect. 5.5.2.

232 *H v. the United Kingdom*, no. 10000/82, decision of 4 July 1983, D.R. 33, p. 247.

233 Currently Article 35(1) ECHR. See supra Sect. 3.2.

BP claimed that it was entitled to restitution in respect of the exploration and development costs of the concession. The applicant challenged the propriety of the proceedings in England and argued that English law was not the proper law of the contract. Regardless, the High Court held in a judgment of 4 November 1975 that English law was the law applicable to the contract between the applicant and BP.[234] Leave to appeal this decision was granted to the applicant, but he decided against appealing on the advice of his counsel that such an appeal would be unsuccessful. In the case on the merits the applicant was eventually ordered to pay approximately USD 35 million. The proceedings did not end until the House of Lords' final decision of 2 August 1982.

Relying on Article 6(1) ECHR, the applicant complained in Strasbourg, *inter alia*, of the English court having exercised an extravagant jurisdiction over him by holding that English law was the law applicable to his contract with BP. In reviewing this matter the Commission noted that as far as the applicant's complaint related to the assumption of jurisdiction by the English courts, the applicant's proceedings against this decision effectively ended on 4 November 1975. The applicant contended that the assumption of jurisdiction was not his sole complaint and that the whole series of proceedings did not end until the House of Lords' decision of 2 August 1982, but to no avail. The Commission found that the jurisdiction of the English courts concerned 'a separate and separable preliminary issue, which was the subject of distinct proceedings',[235] and consequently found that the applicant's application in this regard was out of time.

It is unfortunate that the Commission did not get to the merits of this case concerning the issue of the alleged extravagant assertion of jurisdiction. It would have been interesting to see whether Article 6(1) ECHR could indeed have been successfully invoked against the assertion of jurisdiction in this case by the English courts. One could further wonder whether the Commission set a dangerous precedent by throwing out the claim with regard to jurisdiction on the basis of the six month time limit. Such an interpretation could severely limit one's chances of raising a preliminary argument such as the issue of jurisdiction before the Strasbourg Institutions, or would at least force litigants to raise such issues in Strasbourg before the case has been decided on the merits. Although the Commission may be right in finding that the issue of jurisdiction in private international law is a preliminary issue, it is, in my opinion, unfortunate to suggest that this is a separable part of the proceedings in the sense that an appeal should be raised in Strasbourg before the case has been decided on the merits. This would only add to the Court's case load. Then again, this is the normal practice, for example, before the ECJ in private international law cases regarding questions of jurisdiction. I would nevertheless contend that this is not a practical solution for the Court in Strasbourg.

---

[234] The jurisdiction of the English courts in this case over the defendant, who was not domiciled there, was derived from the fact that the contract was governed by English law.

[235] *H v. the United Kingdom* (dec.), no. 10000/82, 4 July 1983, D.R. 33, p. 255.

5.5.2 Article 6(1) ECHR and the Due Process Clause

Although there is little direct evidence in the case law discussed that Article 6(1) ECHR may be invoked against the assertion of jurisdiction where this jurisdiction is based on questionable grounds, it has been suggested in the literature by several writers that Article 6(1) ECHR could perform a role similar to that which the Due Process Clause of the US Constitution has in (inter-state cases within) the United States.[236] The Due Process Clause functions as a constitutional check on the assertion of jurisdiction by courts in the United States.[237] It is contended that Article 6(1) ECHR could, in a similar manner, be invoked against jurisdiction based on certain exorbitant rules of jurisdiction.[238]

While jurisdictional rules in the United States are essentially drawn up at the state level,[239] the US law on jurisdiction has primarily been created by the US Supreme Court, and is primarily concerned with inter-state litigation.[240] In the Supreme Court's decision in *Pennoyer v. Neff*,[241] Justice Field held that 'proceedings in a court of justice to determine the personal rights and obligations of parties over whom that court has no jurisdiction do not constitute due process of law.'[242] Although the Fourteenth Amendment (the Due Process Clause) was not ratified until 1868, it is said that this case brought 'the traditional sovereignty-based, international territorial rules of jurisdiction into the due process clause of the fourteenth amendment.'[243] Thus, from this point on the Fourteenth Amendment—the Due Process Clause—functioned as a boundary post for state court claims of adjudicatory jurisdiction.[244] In its subsequent case law this constitutional check has been further substantiated by the Supreme Court. In the well-known case of *International Shoe Co. v. Washington*[245] it was decided that the mere presence of a defendant was no longer enough to assume jurisdiction. The constitutionality of any exercise of 'general jurisdiction' should not be presumed solely on the basis of the presence of the defendant in the forum, but 'due process requires only that in order to subject a defendant to a judgment *in personam*, if he

---

236 See, e.g., Guinchard 2005, pp. 199–245; Juenger 1984a, p. 44ff; Kinsch 2007, pp. 65–67; Lagarde 1986, pp. 155–157; Matscher 1993, pp. 80–81; Nuyts 2005, p. 30ff; Schlosser 1991, p. 16.

237 There is a vast amount of literature on this particular subject. See, e.g., the works cited infra n. 244.

238 See in addition to the writers cited infra also Cohen 1989, p. 454ff.

239 Von Mehren 2002, p. 75.

240 Juenger 1984b, p. 1196.

241 95 US 714 (1877).

242 95 US at 733.

243 Whitten 1981, p. 835.

244 It should be noted that the implication of *Pennoyer v. Neff* did not become entirely clear until the *Riverside & Dan River Cotton Mills v. Menefee* decision of the Supreme Court in 1915. (237 US 189). Cf. Von Mehren 2007, p. 86.

245 326 US 310 (1945).

be not present within the territory of the forum, he have certain minimum contacts with it such that the maintenance of the suit does not offend "traditional notions of fair play and substantial justice."'[246]

It is this latter case of the US Supreme Court, *International Shoe*, which has spawned the debate on whether Article 6(1) ECHR could perform a similar role as a constitutional check on the assertion of jurisdiction in the Contracting Parties.[247] The immediate cause for the comparison between the Due Process Clause and Article 6(1) ECHR appears to be the similarity between the Commission's phrasing of the application of Article 6(1) ECHR in its admissibility decision of 13 May 1976[248] and the minimum contact test used by the US Supreme Court in *International Shoe*.[249] As has been set out above, the Commission found in the aforementioned decision with regard to the application of Article 6(1) ECHR 'that the fact that the applicant's daughter lives with her mother in the United Kingdom, added to her mother's British nationality, constitutes for the jurisdiction of the British courts a *sufficient link* according to general principles of international law.'[250]

It is this similarity between the use of 'sufficient link' and 'minimum contact' which has triggered the discussion of the similarities between the role of the Due Process Clause and Article 6(1) ECHR. However, not everyone agrees that Article 6(1) ECHR could assume a role similar to the Due Process Clause. It has been noted that '[t]he way in which Article 6(1) [ECHR] is drafted does not suggest a parallel with the US Constitution.'[251] Others do see such a parallel, but warn that while due process in the mold of Article 6 ECHR does play a role in European jurisdictional thinking, its role is the exact opposite to that played in the United States, 'as the Due Process clause in the United States protects the *defendant* against the unjustified *assertion* of jurisdiction, the trial principle in European law protects the *plaintiff* against the unjustified *denial* of jurisdiction.'[252] If one follows this line of reasoning, the role of Article 6(1) ECHR would be limited to providing access to a court, but nothing beyond that (at least not with regard to the issue of jurisdiction in private international law).

It is indeed true that there are some important distinctions between American and European thinking about jurisdiction.[253] In very general terms one could say that US courts are more plaintiff-friendly, while European jurisdictional practice favors the defendant. The difference between the role of the Due Process Clause and Article 6(1) ECHR can thus be explained by pointing out that both

[246] 326 US at 316.

[247] See supra n. 237.

[248] See supra n. 230.

[249] *International Shoe v. Washington*, 336 US 310, 316. See Kinsch 2007, pp. 66–67; Nuyts 2005, p. 52.

[250] Supra n. 231 [emphasis added].

[251] Hill 2003, p. 41.

[252] Michaels 2005–2006, p. 1053 [emphasis in original].

[253] See, e.g., Hay 1991, p. 281ff; Von Mehren 2002.

instruments, in a way, counterbalance the respective jurisdictional practices of courts in the United States and Europe.[254]

The analogy between the Due Process Clause and Article 6(1) ECHR is, in my opinion, certainly not perfect, as their respective roles are tailored to the jurisdictional regimes of, respectively, the United States and Europe. However, there is little need to get stuck in this comparison. The real issue is whether Article 6(1) ECHR can be invoked by the defendant against the unreasonable assertion of jurisdiction. There are certainly cases, imaginable in Europe, in which the defendant needs more protection; protection which could be provided by a more due process-like interpretation of the right to a fair trial *ex* Article 6(1) ECHR.

But on what argument should this be based, as the respective roles of the two instruments are clearly different? Article 6(1) ECHR guarantees the right to a fair trial. It does so not only for the plaintiff, but also for the defendant, as there must be a balance between the two parties in litigation.[255] The principle of equality of arms is an important element of the right to a fair trial.[256] If one looks at the right to a fair trial from this angle, it is only a small step to derive from Article 6(1) ECHR the defendant's right of access to a fair court.[257] In my opinion, the elements for such an interpretation of Article 6(1) ECHR are thus already present. It is therefore not unimaginable that Article 6(1) ECHR could be invoked against the assertion of jurisdiction on an exorbitant ground.

The next question would then be whether there is truly a need for such protection in the Contracting Parties, as defendants are generally favored in European jurisdictional thinking. In this regard it could be noted that exorbitant bases of jurisdiction have, of course, been outlawed under the Brussels/Lugano regime on jurisdiction.[258] However, this is not the case for defendants originating from States outside the EU Member States to the aforementioned instruments.[259] Many writers have already railed against this situation, but to little effect.[260] Perhaps a due process-like interpretation of Article 6 ECHR could bring relief in such situations.

---

[254] Michaels 2005–2006, p. 1054.

[255] See in this regard, e.g., *Steel and Morris v. the United Kingdom* supra n. 73. See also *Hentrich v. France*, 22 September 1994, Series A no. 296-A.

[256] See, e.g., *Dombo Beheer B.V. v. the Netherlands,* 27 October 1993, para 33, Series A no. 274.

[257] Cf. Nuyts 2005, p. 56ff; Kinsch 2007, p. 65ff.

[258] See Article 3 of, respectively, the 1968 Brussels Convention and the 1988 Lugano Convention on jurisdiction and enforcement of foreign judgments in civil and commercial matters.

[259] It should be noted that in the recast of the Brussels I Regulation the same rules will largely apply to defendants from within and outside of the EU. See supra n. 15. However, one could argue that with the new supplemental grounds of jurisdiction proposed, a new ground of exorbitant jurisdiction is created. This will depend on the interpretation of these articles, which for the moment appear to be broadly interpretable. See also Dickinson 2010, p. 280.

[260] See, e.g., Hartley 2008, pp. 19–23; Juenger 1984a, pp. 43–44; Schlosser 1991.

5.5.3 The Consequences of the Divergent Roles of Article 6(1) ECHR

In the first part of the examination of the impact of Article 6(1) ECHR on the issue of jurisdiction in private international law, the plaintiff's right of access to a court has been discussed.[261] In this part the possible role of Article 6(1) ECHR as a line of defense for the defendant against the assertion of jurisdiction, based on grounds that have little connection to the forum, has been reviewed. It is interesting to note that these two roles of Article 6(1) ECHR could intersect.

A court of a Contracting Party asserting jurisdiction based on a plaintiff's invocation of the right of access to a court, as he or she has nowhere else to turn to, may simultaneously result in a defendant being forced to defend himself or herself in a forum that has little or no connection to the case. This would, of course, be the kind of forum against which the defendant may invoke his or her right to a fair trial, as guaranteed in Article 6(1) ECHR.[262] All this would result in competing interests, remarkably derived from the same right. It would in this case fall upon the seized court of the Contracting Party to find a fair balance between these two competing rights.[263]

What this demonstrates is that it is ultimately necessary to find a balance in relation to the issue of jurisdiction in private international law between the distinct interests of the plaintiff and of the defendant, who may both rely on Article 6(1)ECHR in this regard. It would, however, primarily be the national and, where appropriate, the European legislator, who should find the necessary balance between these two interests, as both the plaintiff and the defendant ultimately require the ground of jurisdiction to be acceptable on objective grounds.[264] Article 6(1) ECHR should ideally be an important factor in this regard, which further calibrates the rules concerning jurisdiction in private international law of the Contracting Parties in the sense that there is equity between the interests of the plaintiff and the defendant in international civil proceedings.

5.5.4 Some Preliminary Conclusions

What does all this mean for the jurisdictional rules in the private international law regimes of the Contracting Parties? Even though this is not the place to review extensively all the jurisdictional rules of the Contracting Parties, it is possible to briefly touch upon some of the possible consequences of the impact of Article 6(1) ECHR on the issue of jurisdiction in private international law.

---

261 See supra Sect. 5.4.

262 See the discussion supra Sects. 5.5.1 and 5.5.2.

263 See generally on how the Court deals with competing rights supra Chap. 3.

264 Kinsch 2007, pp. 47–51.

It follows from the discussion of the right of access to a court in the first part of this chapter that Article 6(1) ECHR requires, under certain circumstances, that there is a court made available by a Contracting Party for a plaintiff in international proceedings in the event that he or she is otherwise unable to find a forum, even though the exact extent of this right is not yet clear.[265] It has nevertheless been argued that there is a good case for extending this right in the event that the only available court would offer no guarantees for a fair trial. One could in this regard note that many countries have a *forum necessitatis* exception, ensuring that a plaintiff has access to a court.

However, this right should not extend so far that it would violate a defendant's right to a fair trial, which is also guaranteed in Article 6(1) ECHR. In this light, the requirement of there being a sufficient link with the legal order, which can be found in the *forum necessitatis* exception in Switzerland, may thus be regarded as a sensible solution in light of Article 6(1) ECHR, although I would argue that this requirement of a significant link should be severed where a plaintiff runs the risk of being unable to find any forum and where simultaneously a defendant's right to a fair trial would not be endangered. The Dutch *forum necessitatis* clause, under certain circumstances, requires no link with the Dutch legal order.[266] This solution therefore carries the risk of violating a defendant's right to a fair trial. These divergent rights originating from Article 6(1) ECHR need to be carefully weighed by courts with regard to the issue of jurisdiction in private international law.

One may thus observe that the issue of jurisdiction in private international law requires a balanced system. States do not only have to account for the interests of other States, but the interests of private parties in international litigation are also of primary concern. In my opinion, Article 6(1) ECHR is the anchor that ensures that the system remains in balance in the Contracting Parties. This is particularly true because this Article not only contains the right of access to a court, which ensures that plaintiffs in private international law always have a forum in international litigation, but it arguably also includes checks on the assertion of jurisdiction. In the following section the important role of Article 6(1) will be further underscored, as it will be demonstrated that this Article can also be invoked against the abuse of procedural rules.

5.6 Article 6(1) ECHR as a Brake on Strategic Litigation

A last area in which Article 6(1) ECHR may have an impact on international civil jurisdiction is that of strategic maneuvering in international litigation. Strategic maneuvering in international litigation, in this context, is concerned with the manipulation of jurisdictional rules by one of the parties in order either to secure a

[265] See supra Sect. 5.4.1.

[266] See supra Sect. 'The Right of Access to a Court: *Forum Necessitatis*'.

more preferable forum, although this forum may not necessarily be the most appropriate, or—at worst—to willfully evade justice by seeking to obstruct or (endlessly) delay proceedings. This practice is also referred to as forum shopping.[267] Forum shopping, in principle, is not illegal. It is essentially nothing more than the plaintiff weighing his or her options among the available jurisdictions (with a sufficient link) to initiate proceedings, whereby it is only logical that the plaintiff would eventually settle on the forum that would offer the best prospects to him or her.[268] It could, as such, be regarded as unavoidable procedural behavior within true federal legal systems, such as the United States, and systems such as the Brussels regime, which is in many ways similar to a federal legal system.

Although forum shopping may be a normal consequence of a system where more than one forum is possibly open to a plaintiff, it cannot be denied that this phenomenon could also lead to the abuse of jurisdictional rules. It should be noted, for instance, that the jurisdictional rules laid down in the Brussels I Regulation are particularly vulnerable to such strategic litigating, because of the strict *lis pendens* rules of the Regulation[269] and its emphasis on legal certainty and the mutual trust in the judicial systems of other Member States, while *forum non conveniens*[270] or the use of injunctions are not allowed.[271]

While it is normally the plaintiff who has the right to choose where the proceedings will take place, a party aware of the fact that proceedings are likely to be brought against him or her can initiate proceedings for negative declaratory relief, thereby essentially establishing a role reversal: the presumed defendant would become the de facto plaintiff.[272] The advantage of selecting the best forum usually enjoyed by the plaintiff then thus transfers to the defendant. In many jurisdictions the possibility of bringing such claims for negative declarations is restricted,[273] but under the Brussels I Regulation there are no real obstacles to such claims.[274]

---

[267] See with regard to the notion of forum shopping, e.g., Lowenfeld 1997, pp. 314–324.

[268] As Lord Simon of Glaisdale eloquently put it in *The Atlantic Star* [1974] A.C. 436 at 471: '"Forum shopping" is a dirty word; but it is only a pejorative way of saying that, if you offer a plaintiff a choice of jurisdictions, he will naturally choose the one in which he thinks his case can be most favourably presented: this should be a matter neither for surprise nor indignation.'

[269] Articles 27–30 Brussels I Regulation. See on the notion of *lis pendens* in the Brussels I Regulation, e.g., Gebauer 2007, pp. 89–100. See more generally on this notion McLachlan 2008, pp. 203–553.

[270] See supra Sect. '*Forum Non Conveniens*'.

[271] Cf. Dickinson 2007, pp. 115-123. See also ECJ 9 December 2003, Case C-116/02 *Erich Gasser GmbH v. MISAT Srl*, ECR 2003, I-14693, para 67.

[272] See in this regard e.g. Von Mehren 1998, pp. 409–424.

[273] See, e.g., Bomhoff 2004, p. 1ff; Gebauer 2007.

[274] See ECJ 8 December 1987, Case C-144/86, *Gubisch Maschinenfabrik/Giulio Palumbo*, ECR 1987, I-4861 and ECJ 6 December 1994, Case C-406/92, *Tatry v. Maciej Rataj*, ECR 1994, I-5439. See also with regard to Article 5(3) Brussels I Regulation the recent case of the CJEU 25 October 2012, Case C-133/11, *Folien Ficher and Fofitec* (not yet published), in which the court held that an action for a negative declaration seeking to establish the absence of liability in a tort case could fall within the afore-mentioned article. With this finding the court, incidentally, went against the Opinion of the Advocate General.

Not only is it thus possible for a party who would normally be a defendant to choose the best forum, it is also conceivable that this party could further abuse the jurisdictional rules by bringing a case to court despite there being an exclusive choice-of-court clause selecting another court. It will be interesting to see to what extent Article 6(1) ECHR may function as a brake on tactical litigation in this regard.

Below, one will find an examination of the possible impact of Article 6(1) ECHR on the prevention of this abuse within the context of the jurisdictional provisions of the Brussels I Regulation, whereby particularly the rules regarding *lis pendens* will be examined. First, the state of the law will be presented (Sect. 5.6.1). Although the Strasbourg Institutions have not yet had the chance to decide a case on this issue, the ECJ has delivered an important and well-known judgment in which it has also considered the role of Article 6(1) ECHR. This will be followed by a further analysis of the possible impact of Article 6(1) ECHR on strategic litigation (Sect. 5.6.2).

5.6.1 The State of the Law: Gasser

Although the Strasbourg Institutions have not yet been asked to directly decide on this issue, the ECJ has, in *Gasser v. MISRAT*,[275] given an important and (in)famous judgment with regard to the abuse of jurisdictional rules in the Brussels I Regulation and the role of Article 6(1) ECHR. Gasser was an Austrian company that had entered into a contract with MISRAT, an Italian company. The contract allegedly included a choice-of-court agreement in favor of an Austrian court.[276] A dispute between the two companies arose and the Italian company first brought proceedings in Italy. This was followed by Gasser bringing proceedings in Austria. The Austrian courts eventually made a reference to the ECJ, asking whether the Italian proceedings prevented the Austrian courts from hearing the case. The ECJ held that this was indeed the case.

The UK Government, which made submissions to the court, argued that the strict principle of *lis pendens* should not apply in this case, due to there being an exclusive choice-of-court agreement in favor of Austria, which naturally precluded all other courts from having jurisdiction. Moreover, it was argued by the UK Government that the *lis pendens* provisions should be interpreted in conformity with Article 6(1) ECHR, whereby it pointed out the possibility for abuse of the strict application of the *lis pendens* rule.

The ECJ rejected these arguments. It observed with regard to the first argument that the second court seized is not in a better position to judge whether or not the

[275] Case C-116/02, *Erich Gasser GmbH v. MISAT Srl* [2003] ECR I-14693.

[276] This was actually disputed, but the case was considered by the ECJ on the assumption that the choice-of-court agreement was valid.

first court has jurisdiction.[277] Regarding the compatibility of the interpretation of the *lis pendens* rules with Article 6(1) ECHR, the ECJ held that the Brussels regime is 'necessarily based on the trust which the Contracting States accord to each other's legal systems and judicial institutions.'[278] The court added that the Brussels regime thus 'seeks to ensure legal certainty by allowing individuals to foresee with sufficient certainty which court will have jurisdiction.'[279]

5.6.2 Strategic Litigation and the Role of Article 6(1) ECHR

The *Gasser* judgment of the ECJ has been much discussed, and although the ECJ's position with regard to this issue may not have been completely surprising, the judgment was largely negatively received.[280] And, indeed, the ECJ does appear to leave the door open for unscrupulous litigants willing to manipulate the Brussels regime to their advantage. While the underlying motive of the rules of *lis pendens* in the Brussels I Regulation—namely the prevention of parallel proceedings, which brings along the risk of irreconcilable judgments—is in itself praiseworthy, one could question whether it is, in principle, allowed to subordinate the rights guaranteed in Article 6(1) ECHR to this goal.[281] It would certainly be interesting to see how the Court in Strasbourg would weigh these goals. Nonetheless, the ECJ's decision in *Gasser* at first sight would appear to leave little room for the invocation of Article 6(1) ECHR against such an abuse of jurisdictional rules, despite the fact that the ECJ has acknowledged over and over again that fundamental rights are considered to be part of the general principles of EU law and that the ECHR has a special position in this regard.[282]

It has, however, been suggested that the ECJ's decision in *Gasser* should perhaps not be interpreted as categorically denying the possible impact of Article 6(1) ECHR. It has been proposed that the court's findings are merely a response to the United Kingdom's argument that the second court seized should be able to take on the proceedings where proceedings 'generally' last an unreasonable time in the first court seized.[283] The sweeping nature of this statement was something that the ECJ could not accept in light of the principle of mutual trust. A more focused argument from the United Kingdom could perhaps have been more successful.

---

[277] Case C-116/02, *Erich Gasser GmbH v. MISAT Srl* [2003] ECR I-14693, para 48.

[278] Case C-116/02, *Erich Gasser GmbH v. MISAT Srl* [2003] ECR, I-14693, para 72.

[279] Id.

[280] See, e.g., Briggs 2005; Dickinson 2007; Hartley 2005, pp. 383–391; Nuyts 2007b, pp. 55–73; see generally the contributions in the latter book.

[281] Cf. Gaudemet-Tallon 2006, at p. 184ff.

[282] See, e.g., ECJ 28 March 2000, Case C-7/98, *Krombach v. Bamberski*, ECR 2000, I-1935. See with regard to this case further infra Sect. .8.2.2.1.

[283] Fawcett 2007, pp. 14–15; Cf. Nuyts 2007b supra n. 281, at p. 60.

Be that as it may—and it has to be acknowledged that the ECJ in *Gasser* may well have been deterred by the rather general nature of the arguments put forward, which would certainly have somewhat undermined the functioning of the Brussels regime in this regard—the ECJ's decision concerning Article 6(1) ECHR is still questionable. By allowing such procedural behavior, the ECJ—or rather the Austrian court, following the ECJ's lead—possibly not only violates the right to have a fair hearing within a reasonable time, but additionally the right of access to a court is endangered.

How would the Court assess the situation resulting from the finding in *Gasser* with regard to the right of access to a court? This right would appear to be directly engaged here.[284] By upholding the ECJ's decision and applying the strict *lis pendens* rules, the Austrian court would after all clearly infringe upon Gasser's right of access to a court. As has been discussed, the right of access to a court may be restricted, although this is only allowed if the very essence of the right is not endangered, if the right remains effective, if the restriction pursues a legitimate aim, and if there is a reasonable relationship of proportionality between the means used and the aim achieved.[285]

Does the decision of the Austrian court curtail the very essence of the right of access or its effectiveness, which would result in the restriction not being allowed at all? While there would indeed be no access to the Austrian court, at least until the matter would be resolved in Italy, this argument is difficult to sustain. As has been noted above, it is possible to rely on courts of other countries in international proceedings with regard to the right of access to a court.[286] It would consequently fall upon Gasser to make the case that this alternative is not a realistic option, as proceedings in Italy are known for their longevity, which the Court itself has confirmed on occasion.[287] Assuming that the Court would find that the Austrian court's decision to heed the ECJ's decision would indeed be a restriction on the right of access, one has to determine whether this restriction would consequently result in a violation of Article 6(1) ECHR. In this case the legitimate aim would in all likelihood not be an issue.[288] It would thus come down to the Court's assessment of the proportionality of the decision.

It is unclear how exactly the Court would decide in such a situation. What is clear is that such a case would be comparable to the scenario discussed above, in which the right of access is invoked when there is a foreign court available, but where the proceedings are not in line with the requirements of Article 6(1)

---

[284] Cf. Bomhoff 2004, p. 7ff.

[285] See supra Sect. 5.4.1.

[286] See supra Sect. 5.4.3.2.

[287] See, e.g., *Salesi v. Italy*, 26 February 1993, Series A no. 257-E. In response to the numerous breaches of the right to have judicial proceedings within a reasonable time in Italy, the so-called Pinto Act has been introduced, which enables claimants to have such violations remedied at the domestic level. This has, however, not solved all such problems. See, e.g., *Scordino v. Italy (no. 1)* [GC], no. 36813/9, ECHR 2006-V.

[288] See supra Sects. 5.4.1 and 5.4.3 See also supra n. 81.

ECHR.[289] It has been contended above that the Court could take the quality of the available foreign court into consideration in its decision regarding the proportionality of such a restriction to the right of access. As the Court has previously found proceedings in Italy to be lacking with regard to the requirement of a trial within a reasonable time,[290] it could thus be argued that as a result of the ECJ's finding in *Gasser*, Austria could have been held responsible for a violation of Article 6(1) ECHR before the Court in Strasbourg.[291] This would, of course, leave the Contracting Parties, who are also EU Members (with the exception of Denmark), with contradicting obligations under such circumstances.[292]

It should be noted that the issue with which *Gasser* was directly concerned has been resolved in the proposal for a new Brussels I Regulation in the sense that, despite the strict rules on *lis pendens*, the court which has exclusively been named in a jurisdiction clause will be allowed to first rule on its jurisdiction, even if a case has first been brought in another country.[293] While this is certainly a step in the

---

[289] See supra Sect. 5.4.3.

[290] See supra n. 288.

[291] Cf. Hartley 2005, pp. 389–390.

[292] In this regard one could note that—under admittedly entirely different circumstances—the Court has held, in a case of Community law possibly violating the rights guaranteed in the ECHR, that it was not necessary to examine whether the measure had been proportionate to the aim pursued, as it held that the protection of fundamental rights by Community law is, in principle, equivalent to the protection of the ECHR system. See *Bosphorus Hava Yolları Turizm ve Ticaret Anonim Şirketi v. Ireland* [GC], no. 45036/98, para 155, ECHR 2005-VI. This case concerned the issue of whether the implementation of a sanction regime by Ireland by way of EC Regulation 990/93 would violate Article 1 of Protocol No. 1 ECHR, the right to property. It is unclear whether the Court would follow a similar line of reasoning with regard to conflicting requirements under the Brussels I Regulation and Article 6(1) ECHR, but this is most likely. In a fairly recent case concerning, inter alia, the relationship between EU law and the ECHR in the context of an issue of private international law (international child abduction), *Povse v. Austria* (dec.), no. 3890/11, 18 June 2013, the Court indeed followed the equivalent protection doctrine it introduced in *Bosphorus*. This case concerned the enforcement of an Italian return order in Austria on the basis of the Brussels II*bis* Regulation. The applicants, the mother and daughter, argued that the enforcement of the return order had violated their rights under Article 8 ECHR. In this case the Austrian Supreme Court had asked for a preliminary ruling of the CJEU concerning the interpretation of the Brussels II*bis* Regulation. In its ruling the CJEU stated—in short—that there was no room for review of the return order by the Austrian Supreme Court. The Court held that the preliminary ruling left no discretion for Austria in ordering the return. The case therefore had to be distinguished from *M.S.S. v. Belgium and Greece* [GC], no. 30696/09, ECHR 2011 and *Michaud v. France,* no. 12323/11, ECHR 2012. Even though the CJEU did in its preliminary ruling not deal with the alleged violation of the fundamental rights of the applicants (which distinguished the case from *Bosphorus*), the Court was not convinced that the enforcement of the return order by Austria without review would rob the applicants of their rights. Under the EU system these rights simply had to be protected by the Italian courts. See with regard to this case further *EHRC* 2013/70 (note Kiestra).

[293] See, e.g., Amendment 121 by the European Parliament, 2010/0383(COD). See also Regulation (EU) No. 1215/2012 of the European Parliament and of the Council of 12 December 2012 on Jurisdiction and the Recognition and Enforcement of Judgments in Civil and Commercial Matters (Recast), *OJ* 2012, L 351/1.

right direction, which should preclude cases like *Gasser* from re-occurring, this does not provide a solution for the situation in which a case is deliberately brought before an ill-suited court, which does not have jurisdiction, to evade proceedings in the more suitable court in the absence of a jurisdiction clause. While in this latter scenario the willful evasion of a jurisdiction clause is absent, it would still be possible for cunning parties to slow down litigation by bringing proceedings first in a 'wrong' court.

There may be a turning point with regard to such strategic procedural behavior where the tactical use of the rules of jurisdiction becomes abusive. If a litigant stretches the limits of what is reasonable in international litigation, and the rules of international civil procedure do not put a stop to this,[294] it is certainly arguable that the right to a fair trial *ex* Article 6(1) ECHR could help to put a brake on such procedural behavior. It is important to remember that Article 6(1) ECHR ultimately entails an obligation for the Contracting Parties to guarantee a fair trial to all parties concerned.

5.7 Conclusion

In this chapter the impact of the ECHR on the issue of jurisdiction in private international law has been examined. Jurisdiction in private international law is concerned with the question of which court of which country has adjudicatory competence in international civil proceedings. It has been demonstrated that the impact of public international law on this subject is fairly limited.

In order to answer the question of what the impact of the ECHR on the issue of jurisdiction in private international law is, the question of whether the ECHR is at all applicable to this issue has first been revisited. The answer to this question can be found in Article 1 ECHR, which determines that the Contracting Parties are obligated to secure the rights and freedoms contained in the ECHR to everyone within their jurisdiction. If a litigant brings proceedings before a court of one the Contracting Parties, the decision of that court with regard to whether or not it should assert jurisdiction based on its jurisdictional rules must be in conformity with the ECHR, as the litigant is, in principle, within the jurisdiction of that Contracting Party in the sense of Article 1 ECHR from the moment of bringing the proceedings before the court of the Contracting Party. The jurisdictional rules of the forum therefore cannot limit the applicability of the ECHR in international

[294] It could be argued that solutions to this problem of international litigation should be sought elsewhere. One could think of sanctions derived from domestic or Community law against the abuse of procedural rights. However, the most salient approach to this problem is, in my opinion, connected to 'due process', which can be derived from Article 6 ECHR. See with regard to the abuse of procedure Briggs 2011, pp. 261–277. See for a response in the same book Cuniberti 2011, pp. 279–288. See also Normand 1999, pp. 237–248 and Mancini 1999, pp. 233–236.

civil proceedings. The Court has seemingly confirmed this stance in *Markovic and Others v. Italy*.

It has been demonstrated that the impact of the ECHR on the issue of jurisdiction in private international law is largely limited to the impact of Article 6(1) ECHR, which guarantees the right to a fair trial. There are three basic instances in which Article 6(1) ECHR may play a role with regard to the issue of jurisdiction in private international law that have been distinguished in this chapter. First, the right of access to a court, which can be derived from Article 6(1) ECHR, can be invoked by a *plaintiff* in international civil proceedings who is unable to find a court to hear his or her case. Second, the right to a fair trial may also be invoked by a *defendant* in international civil proceedings if he or she is summoned before a court that has asserted jurisdiction based on a so-called exorbitant or inappropriate ground of jurisdiction. Finally, the right to a fair trial may play a role in the area of strategic maneuvering in international litigation. These three instances have been elaborated upon in this chapter.

The right of access to a court may be invoked by a plaintiff in international civil proceedings. This right has been derived from the right to a fair trial *ex* Article 6(1) by the Court in *Golder v. the United Kingdom*. There are two scenarios, which may be distinguished, in which a plaintiff may have to rely on this right. First, a plaintiff could be faced with the situation that there is no court available to hear his or her case. This situation could occur not only in the event of a negative conflict of jurisdiction (meaning that no court anywhere is willing to assert jurisdiction), but also where the normally competent court is unavailable due to circumstances beyond a plaintiff's control, such as a situation of war. It has been demonstrated that it is generally accepted that the right of access to a court can be invoked in such a scenario, even though it follows from an examination of the case law of national courts that some connection with the forum State may still be required.

However, it has been contended that a plaintiff's right of access to a court may also apply when there is a foreign court available. This is a more controversial conception of the right of access to a court in private international law. The Strasbourg Institutions have not yet given an opinion on this conception. In the only case on this issue, *Gauthier v. Belgium*, the Commission has left this issue open. Nevertheless, in the Court's general case law on the right of access to a court, particularly in the Court's finding that this right must be effective, some support can be found for the proposition that the right could, under certain circumstances, also be applicable even where there is a foreign court available. It has been demonstrated that Contracting Parties may rely on foreign proceedings in fulfilling their obligation to guarantee the right of access to a court. It would be unrealistic to completely disregard foreign access to a court in international civil proceedings.

Three such scenarios have been distinguished and examined. It has been discussed whether the the right of access to court may be engaged if the proceedings in the only available foreign court would not meet the procedural standards of Article 6(1) ECHR. In other words, does the right entail the right of access to a court in accordance with the requirements of Article 6(1) ECHR? It is actually possible to distinguish two scenarios under this heading. A plaintiff may, first, face unfair proceedings in the only available court. As will be discussed further below, there is a good argument to be made that the right of access to a court may entail the right of access to a court where the proceedings meet a certain procedural standard. A second, more theoretical, possibility is that the only available foreign court would be an inappropriate court in the sense that there would no link between the case and the available court.

It has also been examined whether a denial of justice could occur if it would be certain that the plaintiff's (substantive) claim would be denied in the only available foreign court. Could a plaintiff rely on the right of access in such a situation? Furthermore, it has been examined whether the right of access could be invoked if it were certain that the judgment given in the only available foreign court could not be recognized and enforced in the Contracting Party.

The author has argued that if proceedings in the only available foreign court would allegedly be unfair in the sense of Article 6(1) ECHR, this could be taken into consideration by the Court in reviewing whether the right of access to a court in a Contracting Party should be granted, despite there being a foreign court available. This could be reviewed within the framework the Court usually applies to restrictions to the right of access to a court—whether a restriction to the right has a legitimate aim and whether the restriction was proportionate to the legitimate aim pursued. Ultimately, whether a decision not to grant access to the forum was proportionate should be reviewed. However, it is conceivable that the review of the quality of the foreign proceedings could not be very strict and that an attenuated standard would be used in the sense that only in the event of a flagrant denial of justice would access be granted. At least some support for the argument that access should be granted if proceedings in the only available court would be unfair in the sense of Article 6(1) of the ECHR can be found in all three legal orders that have been further examined.

It is more difficult to see how the right of access to a court could also include the right of access in the other two aforementioned scenarios. Even if it was certain that a plaintiff's claim would be rejected on the merits in the only available foreign court, it is hard to see how a plaintiff could derive a right to a substantive outcome in a case from the procedural right of access. Nevertheless, in one remarkable Dutch case, the right of access was deemed to be applicable in such a situation.

The last scenario concerns the right of access possibly being involved when it would be certain that the decision rendered in the only available forum would not be eligible for recognition and enforcement in the Contracting Party. It is questionable whether it would be necessary to pre-emptively grant a plaintiff the right of access before any proceedings have taken place abroad in the normally competent court. One should also note that the ECHR, in principle, requires Contracting Parties to recognize and enforce foreign judgments unless there are very compelling reasons not to do so.

The right to a fair trial may also be invoked by the defendant against the assertion of jurisdiction in international civil proceedings, where this jurisdiction is based on questionable grounds. It has been suggested in the literature that Article 6(1)

ECHR could play a role similar to the role that the Due Process Clause of the US Constitution fulfills with regard to the assertion of jurisdiction in private international law in the United States. Even though there are important differences between the rules on jurisdiction in Europe and the United States, which explain the different roles of Article 6(1) ECHR and the Due Process Clause, the Court's interpretation of the right to a fair trial would appear to allow for a due process-like role with regard to the defendant's right to a fair trial.

Article 6(1) ECHR may finally also have a role with regard to strategic litigation, where such procedural behavior could become abusive. In international civil proceedings it is perfectly normal for litigants, if they have a choice between different competent courts, to choose the one most favorable to their cause. However, it is possible that such strategic litigation could lead to abuse of jurisdictional rules. The Brussels regime is particularly vulnerable to this practice, because of the emphasis on legal certainty and mutual trust. It has been examined whether Article 6(1) ECHR may function as a brake on strategic litigation where this becomes abusive, and it has been found that there is some evidence for Article 6(1) ECHR having such a role. However, this has not yet been reflected in practice.

It is, in conclusion, interesting to reiterate that Article 6(1) ECHR can, with regard to the issue of jurisdiction in private international law, be invoked by both the plaintiff as well as the defendant in international proceedings. It should be clear that it is possible that these two rights, under certain circumstances, may clash. If one were to give in too easily to a plaintiff demanding the right of access to a court even though a foreign court would have jurisdiction, the defendant may be forced to defend him or herself in a court that has asserted jurisdiction on an exorbitant ground. This observation may point to the true role of Article 6(1) ECHR with regard to jurisdiction in private international law. Ideally, this right should ensure that the Contracting Parties use a balanced approach with regard to jurisdiction, taking into consideration both the interests of the plaintiff as well as the interests of the defendant in cross-border proceedings.

References

Adede AO (1976) A fresh look at the meaning of the doctrine of denial of justice under international law. Can Yearb Int Law 14:73–95

Akehurst M (1972–1973) Jurisdiction in international law. BYIL 46:145–257

April S (1984) Blocking statutes as a response to the extra-territorial application of law. In: Olmstead CJ (ed) Extra-territorial application of law and responses thereto. ESC Publishing, Oxford

Beaumont P (2009) Hague choice of court agreements convention 2005: background, negotiations, analysis and current status. J Private Int Law 5:125–159

Boele-Woelki K (2006) International Privaatrecht [Private International Law]. Ars Aequi 55:5503–5504

Bomhoff JA (2004) Het negatief declaratoir in de EEX-Verordening. Strategie, misbruik van procesrecht en de doorwerking van grondrechten in het Europese IPR [The negative declaratory in the Brussels-I regulation. Strategy, abuse of procedure and the impact of fundamental rights on European private international law]. NIPR 22:1–8

Brand RA, Jablonski SR (2007) Forum non conveniens: history, global practice, and future under the Hague convention on choice of court agreements. Oxford University Press, New York
Briggs A (2005) The impact of recent judgments of the European court on English procedural law and practice. Zeitschrift für Schweizerisches recht 124:231–262
Briggs A (2006) Decisions of British courts during 2005 involving questions of private international law. BYBIL 76:554–596
Briggs A (2011) The rejection of abuse in international civil procedure. In: Feria R de la, Vogenauer S, Prohibition of abuse of law. Hart Publishing, Oxford, pp 261–277
Briggs A, Rees P (2009) Civil jurisdiction and judgments. Informa, London
Brownlie I (2008) Principles of public international law. Oxford University Press, Oxford
Bucher A (ed) (2011) Loi sur le droit international privé. Convention de Lugano, Helbing Lichtenhahn, Basel
Cheshire GC et al (2010) Private international law. Oxford University Press, Oxford
Cohen D (1989) La convention européenne des droits de l'homme et le droit international privé. Rev.crit.dr.int.priv. 78:451–483
Corbion L (2004) Le déni de justice en droit international privé. Presses universitaires d'Aix-Marseille, Aix-en-Provence
Cuniberti G (2011) The discrete influence of abuse of law in international civil procedure. In: de la Feria R, Vogenauer S (eds) Prohibition of abuse of law. Hart Publishing, Oxford, pp 279–288
de Vareilles-Sommières P (1997) La compétence international de l'état en matière de droit privé: droit international public et droit international privé. LGDJ, Paris
De Wet E (2006) The emergence of international and regional value systems as a manifestation of the emerging international constitutional order. Leiden J Int. Law 19:611–632
De Winter LI (1968) Excessive jurisdiction in private international law. ILCQ 17:706–720
Dicey AV, Morris JHC, Collins LA (2012) The conflict of laws. Sweet & Maxwell, London
Dickinson A (2007) Legal certainty and the Brussels convention: too much of a good thing? In: de Vareilles-Sommières P (ed) Forum shopping in the European judicial area. Hart, Oxford, pp 115–123
Dickinson A (2010) Surveying the proposed Brussels I "bis" regulation: solid foundations but renovation needed. Yearb Private Int Law 12:247–309
Duintjer-Tebbens H (2006) From Jamaica with pain: enkele aantekeningen bij het arrest van 1 maart 2005 van het Hof van Justitie in de zaak Owusu [From Jamaica with pain: a few notes on the judgment of 1 March 2005 of the ECJ in the case Owusu]. In: Grinten P van der, Heukels T (eds) Crossing borders: essays in European and private international law, nationality law and islamic law in honour of Frans van der Velden. Kluwer, Deventer, p. 95–103
Fawcett JJ (2007) The impact of article 6(1) ECHR on private international law. ILCQ 56:1–48
Fentiman R (2006) Civil jurisdiction and third states: Owusu and after. CML Rev 43:705–734
Fernández Arroyo DP (2004) Exorbitant and exlusive grounds of jurisdiction in European private international law: will they ever survive? In: Mansel H-P (ed) Festschrift für Erik Jayme, vol I. Sellier European Law Publishers, Munich, pp 169–186
Focarelli C (2012) Denial of justice. In: Wolfrum R (ed) The Max Planck encyclopedia of public international law. Oxford University Press, Oxford. www.mpepil.com. Accessed Apr 2012
Francioni F (ed) (2007) Access to justice as a human right. Oxford University Press, Oxford
Gaudemet-Tallon H (1991) Forum non conveniens: une menace pour la convention de Bruxelles (a propos de trois arrets anglais récents). Rev.crit.dr.int.priv 80:491–524
Gaudemet-Tallon H (2006) Le "droit au juge" à l'épreuve des règles de compétence judiciaire internationale (matière civile et commercial). In: Léger P (ed) Le droit a la mesure de l'homme. Pedone, Paris, pp 173–189
Gebauer M (2007) Lis pendens, negative declaratory-judgments actions and the first-in-time principle. In: Gottschalk E et al (eds) Conflict of laws in a globalized world. Cambridge University Press, New York, pp 89–100
Guinchard E (2005) Procès équitable (article 6 CESDH) et droit international privé. In: Nuyts A, Watté N (eds) International civil litigation in Europe and relations with third states. Bruylant, Brussels, pp 199–245

Hartley TC (2005) Choice-of-court agreements, Lis Pendens, human rights and the realities of international business: reflections on the gasser case. In: Jobard-Bachellier M-N, Mayer P (eds) Le droit international privé: esprit et methodes. Mélanges en l'honneur de Paul Lagarde, Dalloz, Paris, pp 383–391

Hartley TC (2006) The modern approach to private international law. international litigation and transactions from a common-law perspective. Recueil des Cours 319:9–324

Hartley TC (2008) The Brussels regulation and non-community states. In: Basedow J (ed) Japanese and European private international law in comparative perspective. Mohr Siebeck, Tübingen, pp 19–25

Hay P (1991) Flexibility versus predictability and uniformity in choice of law. Reflections on current European and United States conflicts law. Recueil des Cours 226:282–412

Hess B (2012) Staatenimmunität und ius cogens im geltenden Völkerrecht: der international Gerichtshof zeigt die Grenze auf [Immunities of the state and ius cogens in current public international law: the ICJ illustrates the boundaries]. IPRax 32:201–206

Higgins R (1999) Allocating competence: jurisdiction (1993). In: Reisman WM (ed) Jurisdiction in international law. Ashgate, Dartmouth, p 263ff

Hill J (2003) The exercise of jurisdiction in private international law. In: Capps P et al (eds) Asserting jurisdiction. international and European legal perspectives. Hart Publishing, Portland

Ibili F (2007) Gewogen rechtsmacht in het IPR. Over forum (non) conveniens en forum necessitatis [Weighed jurisdiction in private international law. On forum (non) conveniens and forum necessitatis]. Kluwer, Deventer

Joubert N (2007) La notion de liens suffisants avec l'ordre juridique (Inlandsbeziehung) en droit international privé. LexisNexis Litec, Paris

Juenger FK (1984a) La Convention de Bruxelles du 27 septembre 1968 et la courtoise international. Réflexions d'un Américain. Rev.crit dr.int.priv. 37

Juenger FK (1984b) Judicial jurisdiction in the United States and in the European communities: a comparison. Mich Law Rev 82:1195–1212

Kahn-Freund O (1976) General problems of private international law. A.W. Sijthoff, Leyden

Kamminga MT (2012) Extraterritoriality. In: Wolfrum R (ed) The Max Planck encyclopedia of public international law. Oxford University Press, Oxford. www.mpepil.com. Accessed April 2012

Kessedjian C (1997) International jurisdiction and foreign judgments in civil and commercial matters, Preliminary Document No 7 of April 1997 for the attention of the special commission of June 1997 on the question of jurisdiction, and recognition and enforcement of foreign judgments in civil and commercial matters. www.hcch.net/index_en.php?act=conventions.publications&dtid=35&cid=98. Accessed Nov 2012

Kinsch P (2007) Droits de l'homme, droits fondamentaux et droit international privé. Recueil des Cours 318:9–332

Kloth M (2010) Immunities and the right of access to court under article 6 of the European convention on human rights. Martinus Nijhoff Publishers, Leiden

Lagarde P (1986) Le Principe de Proximité Dans Le Droit International Privé Contemporain. Cours général de droit international privé, Recueil des Cours 196

Lowenfeld AF (1997) Forum shopping, antisuit injunctions, negative declarations and related tools of international litigation. AJIL 91:314–324

Magnus U, Mankowski P (eds) (2012) Brussels I regulation. Sellier European Law Publishers, Munich

Mancini F (1999) Short note on abuse of procedure in community law. In: Taruffo M (ed) Abuse of procedural rights: comparative standards of procedural fairness. Kluwer Law International, The Hague, pp 233–236

Mann FA (1964) The doctrine of jurisdiction in international law. Recueil des Cours 111:1–162

Mann FA (1984) The doctrine of international jurisdiction revisited after 20 years. Recueil des Cours 186:9–116

Marchadier F (2007) Les objectifs généraux du droit international privé a l'épreuve de la convention européenne des droits de l'homme. Bruylant, Bruxelles
Matscher F (1978) Etude des règles de compétence judiciaire dans certaines conventions internationales. Recueil des Cours 161:127–228
Matscher F (1993) Die Einwirkungen der EMRK auf das Internationale Privat- und zivilprozessuale Verfahrensrecht. In: Matscher F (ed), Europa im Aufbruch: Festschrift für Fritz Schwind zum 80. Geburtstag, Manzsche Verlags- und Universitätsbuchhandlung, Wien, pp 71–85
Matscher F (1998) Le droit international privé face à la convention européenne des droits de l'homme, travaux du comité français de droit international privé (1995–1998), pp 211–234
Mayer P (1979) Droit international privé et droit international public sous l'angle de la notion de compétence. Rev.crit.dr.int.priv. 68: 1–29; 349–388; 537–583
McLachlan C (2004) International litigation and the reworking of the conflict of laws. LQR 120:580–616
McLachlan CC (2008) Lis pendens in international litigation. Recueil des Cours 336:203–553
Meessen KM (1984) International law limitations on state jurisdiction. In: Olmstead CJ (ed) Extra-territorial application of laws and responses thereto. ESC Publishing, Oxford, pp 38–44
Michaels R (2005–2006) Two paradigms of jurisdiction. Mich J Int Law 27:1003–1069
Nadelmann KH (1961) Jurisdictionally improper fora. In: Nadelmann KH et al XXth century comparative law and conflicts law. legal essays in honor of Hessel E. Yntema. A.W. Sythoff, Leyden, pp 321–335
Normand J (1999) Final report: the two approaches to the abuse of procedural rights. In: Taruffo M (ed) Abuse of procedural rights: comparative standards of procedural fairness. Kluwer Law International, The Hague, pp 237–248
Nuyts A (2005) Due process and fair trial: jurisdiction in the United States and in Europe compared, 2 CILE studies. In: Brand RA, Walter M (eds) Private law, private international law and judicial cooperation in the EU-US relationship, Thomson/West, Eagan MN, pp 27–73
Nuyts A (2007a) A study on residual jurisdiction (review of the member states' rules concerning the "residual jurisdiction" of their courts in civil and commercial matters pursuant to the Brussels I and II regulations), general report, final version dated 3 Sept 2007, pp 64–66. http://ec.europa.eu/civiljustice/news/docs/study_residual_jurisdiction_en.pdf. Accessed Oct 2012
Nuyts A (2007b) The enforcement of jurisdiction agreements further to gasser and the community principle of abuse of rights. In: De Vareilles-Sommières P (ed) Forum shopping in the European judicial area. Hart Publishing, Oxford, pp 55–73
Olmstead CJ (ed) (1984) Extra-territorial application of laws and responses thereto. ESC Publishing, Oxford
Othenin-Girard S (1999) Quelques observations sur le for de nécessité en droit international privé. RSDIE 9:251–285
Oxman BH (2012) Jurisdiction of states. In: Wolfrum R (ed) The Max Planck encyclopedia of public international law. Oxford University Press 2008-, online edition, www.mpepil.com. Accessed Apr 2012
Paulsson J (2005) Denial of justice in international law. Cambridge University Press, Cambridge
Pontier JA, Burg E (2004) EU principles on jurisdiction and recognition and enforcement of judgments in civil and commercial matters according to the case law of the European Court of Justice. T.M.C Asser Press, The Hague
Rodger BJ (2006) Forum non conveniens post Owusu. J Private Int Law 2:71–97
Schlosser P (1991) Jurisdiction in international litigation: the issue of human rights in relation to national law and to the Brussels convention. Rivista di diritto internazionale 74:5–34
Schlosser P (2000) Jurisdiction and international judicial and administrative co-operation. Recueil des Cours 284:9–428
Schmidt GE (2007) Forum necessitatis bij echtscheidingen. NIPR 25:116–121
Shaw MN (2008) International law. Cambridge University Press, Cambridge
Sinclair I (1984) The diplomatic response. In: Olmstead CJ (ed) Extra-territorial application of law and responses thereto. ESC Publishing, Oxford

Strikwerda L (2012) Inleiding tot het Nederlandse internationaal privaatrecht [Introduction to Dutch private international law]. Kluwer, Deventer

van Hoek AAH (2000) Artikel 12 EG-verdrag en het (internationale) procesrecht hernieuwde kritiek op de cautio judicatum solvi [Article 12 EC-treaty and (international) procedural law; renewed criticism of the cautio judicatum solvi]. NIPR 18:251–258

van Lith H (2009) International jurisdiction and commercial litigation. T.M.C Asser Press, The Hague

Visscher Ch de (1935) Le déni de justice en droit international. Recueil des Cours 52:363–442

von Mehren AT (1998) The transmogrification of defendants into plaintiffs: herein of declaratory judgments, forum shopping, and Lis Pendens. In: Basedow J (ed) Festschrift FürUlrich Drobnig. Mohr Siebeck, Tübingen, pp 409–424

von Mehren AT (2002) Theory and practice of adjudicatory authority in private international law: a comparative study of the doctrine, policies and practices of common- and civil-law systems. general course on private international law. Recueil des Cours 295:9–431

von Mehren AT (2007) Adjudicatory authority in private international law. Martinus Nijhoff Publishers, Leiden, A Comparative Study

von Mehren AT, Trautman DT (1966) Jurisdiction to adjudicate: a suggested analysis. Harvard Law Rev 79:1121–1179

Wautelet P (2004) What has international private law achieved in meeting the challenges posed by globalization? In: Slot PJ, Bulterman M (eds) Globalisation and jurisdiction. Kluwer International Law, The Hague, pp 55–77

Whitten R (1981) The constitutional limitations on state-court jurisdiction: a historical-interpretative reexamination of the full faith and credit and due process clauses. Creighton Law Rev 14:499–606

Chapter 6
Applicable Law

Contents

6.1 Introduction

The issue of the applicable law in private international law is concerned with the question of which law should be applied to a case where a court is presented with a claim concerning a foreign element.[1] In order to find the applicable law, a national court will refer to the choice of law rules of the forum. The result of the application of these (choice of law) rules will be that either the law of the forum (the *lex fori*),

---

[1] See also supra Chap. 2.

L.R. Kiestra, *The Impact of the European Convention on Human Rights on Private International Law*, DOI 10.1007/978-94-6265-032-9_6

the law of another country, or even uniform rules will be applied to the case.[2] If the facts of the case are closely connected to a foreign legal order, there is a good chance that foreign law will be the law applicable to the case. In this chapter, the impact of the European Convention on Human Rights (ECHR) on the issue of applicable law will be examined. It will be recalled that, for reasons set out in Chap. 1, this chapter will only be concerned with the impact of the rights guaranteed in the ECHR on the actual result of the application of the forum's choice of law rules—the applicable law; the possible impact on the choice of law rules of the forum will, in principle, not be covered here.[3]

What could the impact of the rights guaranteed in the ECHR on the issue of applicable law in private international law be? Remarkably, there is not much case law in which the Court has examined the impact of the rights guaranteed in the ECHR on the applicable law in private international law. The relationship between this issue of private international law and the rights guaranteed in the ECHR has nevertheless spawned a lively debate in the literature, in which several different aspects of the issue have been touched upon.[4]

Three different aspects of the discussion will be distinguished in this chapter. The classical example of the impact of the ECHR on the issue of applicable law is the scenario in which the application of the forum's choice of law rules would point to a foreign law whose application would subsequently violate one of the rights guaranteed in the ECHR. The application of a foreign law, as determined by a court of one of the Contracting Parties by virtue of their choice of law rules, could then result in a violation of one of the rights guaranteed in the ECHR. Yet even this relatively straightforward example raises a number of questions with regard to the impact of the ECHR, relating, inter alia, to the level of scrutiny that should be used with regard to the rights guaranteed in the ECHR.

This is, however, but one of the aspects of the debate concerning the impact of the ECHR on the issue of applicable law. In addition to being used as a *defensive mechanism against* the result of the application of a foreign law, the ECHR could also be invoked in order to *promote* the application of a foreign law. Related to this usage of the ECHR is, incidentally, the invocation of the ECHR against the application of the *lex fori* of one of the Contracting Parties in favor of a foreign

---

[2] For some areas of the law, international uniform laws have been established by a treaty. One could, for example, think of the United Nations Convention on Contracts for the International Sale of Goods. There is, in principle, a fourth option. A law which is not connected to any State, such as the *lex mercatoria*, may also be found to be the law applicable to the case. The discussion in this chapter on the impact of the ECHR on the applicable foreign law violating one of the rights guaranteed in the ECHR would, in principle, be equally relevant in the event that the application of such an international law would result in a violation of the ECHR.

[3] See supra Sect. 1.2. It was discussed there that the Court, in its case law, in principle, does not review laws *in abstracto*. But see the discussion of *Ammdjadi v. Germany* infra Sect. 4.3, in which the Court briefly touches upon this issue.

[4] See, e.g., Engel 1989, p. 36ff; Kinsch 2004b, p. 212ff, 2007, p. 165ff; Lequette 2004, p. 109ff; Marchadier 2007, p. 549ff; Matscher 1998, pp. 211–234; Mayer 1991, pp. 651–665; Oprea 2007, pp. 307–340. Further contributions to the debate will be cited infra.

applicable law. One could argue that some of the rights laid down in the ECHR provide a basis for such an argument.

It is interesting to note in relation to these two aspects of the impact of the ECHR on the issue of the applicable law that the substantive rights guaranteed in the ECHR play the leading role. The impact of the ECHR in this regard is confined to the material result of the application of the choice of law rules. Whereas issues of private international law are mostly thought of as procedural questions,[5] the impact of the ECHR on the issue of applicable law is thus largely a substantive issue—except for issues relating to the ascertainment of the content of the foreign applicable law.[6] This latter issue is the third and final aspect of the debate on the impact of the ECHR on the issue of applicable law and is thus concerned with the act of applying the selected (foreign) law by courts. This may also raise some issues with the ECHR, albeit not substantive ones, but rather procedural problems relating to Article 6(1) ECHR.

These three different aspects of the impact of the rights guaranteed in the ECHR on the issue of applicable law will be covered in this chapter. Before the examination of these three issues can start in earnest, it is first necessary to briefly return to the applicability of the ECHR to the issue of applicable law in private international law (in Sect. 6.2). Thereafter, the impact of the ECHR on the result of the application of a (foreign) law will be discussed (Sect. 6.3). The next section will feature the discussion of whether the ECHR can also be invoked in favor of the application of a foreign law, in which the invocation of the ECHR against the *lex fori* will be examined (Sect. 6.4). Finally, the impact of the ECHR on the act of applying law itself will be assessed (Sect. 6.5). The discussion will be finalized with a conclusion (Sect. 6.6).

6.2 The Applicability of the ECHR to the Issue of Applicable Law

Even though this issue has been discussed at length in Chap. 4, it may be useful to briefly recall the main findings of the discussion of the applicability of the ECHR to the issue of the application of a foreign law.[7]

---

[5] See with regard to the notion and characteristics of private international law supra Chap. 2.

[6] In this regard, one may thus observe a noticeable distinction from the issue of jurisdiction in private international law discussed previously. See supra Chap. 5. It will, incidentally, be demonstrated in the next chapters that with regard to the third issue of private international law, the recognition and enforcement of foreign judgments, both the procedural right of Article 6(1) ECHR as well as the substantive rights guaranteed in the ECHR may have an impact. See infra Chaps. 7 and 8.

[7] See for a more detailed discussion supra Chap. 4.

6.2.1 Responsibility When a Foreign Law Is Applied

As has been discussed, this question of the applicability of the standards guaranteed in the ECHR is particularly interesting in the event of the application of a foreign law originating from a third country, i.e., a non-Contracting Party. It is clear that the applicable law originating from a third country does not need to be in line with the standards provided by the ECHR, as the country responsible for the law is not a Contracting Party to the ECHR. Nevertheless, it has been found that when a court of one of the Contracting Parties applies a foreign law of a third country violating one of the rights guaranteed in the ECHR, it is ultimately this court that causes the violation of the ECHR by applying the repulsive foreign law in question. As Article 1 ECHR obligates the Contracting Parties to ensure all the rights and freedoms guaranteed in the ECHR to everyone within their jurisdiction, it should be clear that the ECHR is indeed applicable to this issue, regardless of whether the applicable foreign law originates from a third country or another Contracting Party.

Insofar as any doubts persisted with regard to the applicability of the ECHR to the issue of the application of a foreign law originating from a third country, the Court has fairly recently, in an admissibility decision in *Ammdjadi v. Germany*,[8] examined whether the application of Iranian law (a law originating from a third country) to a divorce between two Iranian nationals by the German courts violated the ECHR. Although ultimately no violation of the ECHR was found and the case was held to be manifestly inadmissible for reasons that will be further discussed below,[9] the Court's examination of the issues in this case implicitly demonstrates that the ECHR is indeed applicable to the issue of the application of a foreign law emanating from a third country. At no point in its examination did the Court suggest otherwise. It would ultimately have been the German courts' application of the Iranian law (allegedly) violating one of the rights guaranteed in the ECHR that would have led to a violation of the ECHR. One could note that some of the earliest case law of the Strasbourg Institutions in this regard already pointed in this direction.[10]

---

[8] *Ammdjadi v. Germany* (dec.), no. 51625/08, 9 March 2010.

[9] See infra Sect. 6.3.1.

[10] In an early case before the Commission, *X v. Luxembourg* (dec.), no. 5288/71, 10 July 1973, the application of Hungarian law by the Luxembourg courts played a minor role. Hungary was at the time not yet a Contracting Party. In this case, the Commission rejected an argument made by the Luxembourg authorities that the Commission was not competent to hear the case, because Hungarian law should have been applied to the case. The Commission quickly dismissed this argument by simply stating that the fact that, according to the Luxembourg rules of private international law, Luxembourg law was not the law applicable to the issue at hand was 'without relevance'.

6.2.2 Co-responsibility When the Law of Another Contracting Party Is Applied?

A related question in the sense that the answer is ultimately found in Article 1 ECHR is whether more than one of the Contracting Parties could be held responsible for a violation of the ECHR in the event that one Contracting Party applies the law of another Contracting Party. This is an issue that has occasionally been brought up in the literature.[11] As has been noted above, it is clear that the Contracting Party applying the repugnant foreign applicable law is responsible for the resulting breach of one of the rights guaranteed in the ECHR. However, one could in such a scenario wonder whether the Contracting Party whose repugnant law is applied by another Contracting Party could be held co-responsible for this violation. After all, its law should have been up to the standards of the ECHR in the first place. Yet the Commission has in two decisions confirmed that this cannot be the case.

In *X. v. Belgium and the Netherlands*[12] the Commission gave a first clear indication of its thinking concerning such shared responsibility when it decided *ex officio* to consider the complaint as being directed against Belgium, despite the fact that the applicant had targeted his complaint against the Netherlands. This case concerned an unmarried Dutch national, who lived in Belgium, and who wanted to adopt a child. According to the relevant Belgian choice-of-law rules at the time, the applicant's request was determined by the application of Dutch law. However, the Dutch law at the time did not permit an unmarried person to adopt. The applicant decided to target his complaint in Strasbourg against the Netherlands.

The Commission considered that this application should have been filed against Belgium. Although the Commission did not give extensive reasoning for its decision, it seems clear that it was of the opinion that, as a Belgian judge by virtue of Belgian choice-of-law rules regarding adoption had applied Dutch law, Belgium bore the responsibility for a possible violation of the ECHR, even though that violation would have been created by (the application of) Dutch law.

In *Gill and Malone v. the Netherlands and the United Kingdom*[13] the Commission confirmed the above reading of *X. v. Belgium and the Netherlands*. This case concerned a lengthy and complicated procedure regarding the establishment of paternity over a child. The applicants, Gill, a citizen of the United Kingdom, and Malone, an Irish national, were an unmarried couple whose daughter was born in Amsterdam when they unexpectedly had to discontinue their travels to the United Kingdom. When the father went to the Dutch authorities to declare his daughter's birth and ask that he be registered as the father and that his daughter be registered under the family name 'Gill', he was informed that that under British

[11] See, e.g., Kinsch 2004b, pp. 213–214.

[12] *X. v. Belgium and the Netherlands* (dec.), no. 6482/74, 10 July 1975, *DR* 6, p. 77.

[13] *Gill and Malone v. the Netherlands and the United Kingdom* (dec.), no. 24001/94, 11 April 1996.

law, as it was known to the authorities, his daughter could not be registered under his name and nor could he be registered as the father. To cut a long story short, this case ended up before the Commission in Strasbourg.

Could the United Kingdom be held responsible in this case? The United Kingdom submitted that regardless of whether the Dutch officials had applied and interpreted UK law correctly, the provisions of Dutch law were being challenged by the applicants. The Commission agreed with the United Kingdom that insofar as the complaint was targeted at the content of British family law, it was the Dutch authorities that, in accordance with the Dutch rules of private international law, took the relevant decisions regarding the recognition of paternity. The responsibility of the United Kingdom was therefore not directly engaged under these circumstances.

The Commission thus essentially confirmed the strong indication it had given in *X. v. Belgium and the Netherlands* that it is solely the Contracting Party applying the law of another Contracting Party that is responsible for a possible violation of the ECHR. There is no shared responsibility for such a possible violation. It ultimately comes down to the fact that the reason for the application—or eviction for that matter—of a foreign law is always found in the (system of private international law of the) forum and that the application—or non-application—of a foreign law is thus always the responsibility of that Contracting Party.[14] In this regard, the origin of the applicable law is therefore irrelevant. It is the Contracting Party actually applying the foreign law that could be held responsible for a possible violation of one of the rights guaranteed in the ECHR. However, this does not mean that the origin of the applicable law is completely immaterial. As the laws of all the Contracting Parties are supposed to be in line with the rights guaranteed in the ECHR, there is a case to be made that the origin of the law does matter with regard to the level of scrutiny to which Contracting Parties should adhere.[15]

6.3 The Impact of the ECHR on the Applicable (Foreign) Law in a Private International Law Dispute

Having demonstrated that in the case of a court of one the Contracting Parties applying a foreign law violating one of the rights guaranteed in the ECHR, this Contracting Party—and only this Contracting Party—could be held responsible, regardless of the origin of the applicable (foreign) law, it is time to turn to the other issues that surround the invocation of the ECHR against the normally applicable law. To be clear, the normally applicable law is not necessarily a foreign law. The application of the *lex fori* in an issue of private international law could, of course, also result in a violation of one of the rights guaranteed in the ECHR.

---

[14] Cf. Kinsch 2007, p. 205; Marchadier 2007, p. 564; Voltz 2002, pp. 217–219.

[15] See with regard to this particular topic infra Sect. 6.3.2.

However, this situation would not be markedly different from a non-private international law issue before the Court in Strasbourg in which the application of the law of the respondent Contracting Party would result in a violation of the ECHR, and as such this will thus not be discussed further, because it is not uniquely an issue of private international law unless the argument could be made that one of the rights guaranteed in the ECHR could be invoked in order to stave off the application of the *lex fori* in favor of a foreign law. This issue will be discussed below in relation to the invocation of the ECHR in order to *promote* the application of foreign law.[16]

It is one thing to conclude that nothing stands in the way of holding a Contracting Party responsible for the application of a foreign law violating one of the rights guaranteed in the ECHR by one of its national courts. However, as has been noted in the introduction to this chapter, this starting point raises a number of issues. The fact that a Contracting Party could be held responsible for the application of a foreign law infringing upon one of the rights guaranteed in the ECHR does not necessarily mean that such an act by one of the national courts of the Contracting Party will lead to a violation of one of the rights guaranteed in the ECHR. There may, for example, be good reasons to allow the application of a foreign law possibly interfering with one of the rights guaranteed in the ECHR.

It will be recalled that not every interference with a right guaranteed in the ECHR will necessarily lead to the finding of a violation of that right.[17] As has been previously discussed in Chap. 3, most rights guaranteed in the ECHR are not absolute, but may, under certain circumstances, be restricted. The extent to which it is possible to limit a right guaranteed in the ECHR depends on the nature of the right in question. In principle, the application of a foreign law by a court of one of the Contracting Parties could interfere with any of the rights guaranteed in the ECHR which are relevant in private law issues. Consequently, there is possibly a wide range of cases in which this issue could arise. It is submitted here that Article 8 ECHR (the right to private and family life) and Article 1 of Protocol No. 1 ECHR (the right to property) are the rights that are most likely to be invoked against the foreign applicable law, while the role of Article 10 ECHR (freedom of expression) is likely to gain in importance.

As has been noted in Chap. 3, both Article 8 ECHR and Article 1 of Protocol No. 1 ECHR are not absolute rights. In fact, the possibility to restrict these rights is already included in the text of the respective rights. One can find in Article 8(2) ECHR that an interference with this right may be allowed if this restriction has a foundation in national law, pursues a legitimate aim, and is necessary in a democratic society. It will be recalled that these conditions are cumulative.[18] It has been noted in Chap. 3 that this latter condition is of particular importance, as the

[16] See infra Sect. 6.4.

[17] See also supra Chap. 3.

[18] See supra Sect. 3.5.1.2.

Court will determine whether the restriction concerned a pressing social need, which entails that it was proportionate to the legitimate aim pursued.

It will be further demonstrated below that this condition of the proportionality of a restriction of Article 8 ECHR is the most important factor in determining whether the application of a foreign law results in a violation of this Article. With regard to the proportionality of the interference, Contracting Parties do enjoy a margin of appreciation.[19] A mostly similar framework applies to restrictions with regard to the right to property *ex* Article 1 of Protocol No. 1 ECHR: a restriction to this right is allowed if the restriction is prescribed by law, is in the public (or general) interest, and is necessary in a democratic society.[20] The proportionality of a measure interfering with the peaceful enjoyment of possessions also plays an important part here.

In order to examine the impact of the ECHR on the issue of the applicable foreign law, first the state of the law will have to be identified. Thus, first, the case law of the Strasbourg Institutions on this issue will be discussed (Sect. 6.3.1). Next, the impact of the ECHR on the issue of applicable law will be further analyzed by examining some of the ideas that have been developed in the literature, particularly the attenuation of the standards of the ECHR (Sect. 6.3.2). Thereafter, a few examples taken from the case law of the national courts of the Contracting Parties will be reviewed. Here one will also find a review of some of the issues surrounding the issue of applicable law identified in the preceding sections, particularly the manner of invocation of the ECHR in these cases (Sect. 6.3.3).

6.3.1 The Case Law of the Strasbourg Institutions

For all the debate on the issue of the applicable law and the impact of the ECHR, the case law of the Strasbourg Institutions that directly deals with this issue is rather limited. It is in effect limited to only a handful of cases, none of which may be regarded as providing a definitive precedent concerning the exact impact of the ECHR on the issue of applicable law in private international law.[21] There are two cases that need to be further discussed. Both merely concern admissibility decisions. Unfortunately, the Court has yet to deliver a judgment on the merits on the issue of applicable law. The first case, *Zvoristeanu v. France*,[22] was concerned with the impact of the ECHR in a case where the applicable foreign law originated

[19] See supra Sect. 3.5.2.

[20] See, e.g., Grgic 2007, pp. 12–15; Schutte 2004.

[21] See, in addition to the two cases discussed directly below, the cases of the Commission discussed supra Sect. 6.2.1 (i.e., *X v. Luxembourg*; *X. v. Belgium and the Netherlands*; and *Gill and Malone v. the Netherlands and the United Kingdom*).

[22] *Zvoristeanu v. France* (dec.), no. 47128/99, 7 November 2000.

from another Contracting Party. The more interesting case is the Court's fairly recent admissibility decision in *Ammdjadi v. Germany*.[23] Despite the fact that this latter case also merely concerned an admissibility decision, the Court has offered reasonably extensive reasoning regarding the impact of the ECHR on the issue of applicable law originating from a third country.

In *Zvoristeanu*, the applicant attempted to have her paternity established. The applicant's mother had married her natural father in Germany in a religious (mosaic) ceremony before a rabbi. Shortly after the marriage, the mother returned to France where the applicant was born. The applicant's birth was registered in France without the name of the father. The French courts applied German law to the applicant's request to establish paternity and denied it, inter alia, by finding that the (religious) marriage conducted between her parents in Germany was nonexistent under German law and thus could not produce any effects.

The applicant filed a complaint in Strasbourg, relying on Article 8 ECHR. The Court's reasoning to declare this case manifestly ill-founded was rather succinct.[24] The Court first briefly recapitulated its most important findings with regard to private and family life, as guaranteed in Article 8 ECHR.[25] The Court held that the assessment of the French courts' finding that the applicant could not rely on the effects of the invalid marriage under German law was neither arbitrary nor unreasonable. It noted further that with regard to the validity of a marriage, legal certainty and the security of family relationships have to be considered. Finally, the Court noted that the late initiation of the appropriate legal action had also contributed to the decision.

The Court in *Zvoristeanu* thus did not offer an extensive examination of the issue of applicable law originating from another Contracting Party. It merely set out its standard case law regarding Article 8 ECHR and emphasized that the decision of the French courts was not arbitrary. In support of this latter finding, the Court cited a number of reasons, in which the precise weight carried by these factors is uncertain. It is noteworthy that the Court appears to hold the fact that the applicant had waited a long time with her action against her. That the Court found fault in the applicant's procedural behavior is, remarkably enough, an oft-occurring phenomenon in cases concerning issues of private international law.[26]

Ammdjadi concerned a divorce before the German courts between two Iranian nationals residing in Germany. At the request of her husband, the couple was divorced by a decision of the district court in Köln. The German court applied Iranian law to the case. No motion for the compensation of pension rights was lodged at that time. Later, the former wife brought proceedings before the same court looking for the compensation of pension rights. However, on account of the

[23] *Ammdjadi v. Germany* (dec.), no. 51625/08, 9 March 2010.

[24] See with regard to the notion of manifestly ill-founded supra Sect. 3.2.

[25] The Court in this regard explicitly referred to *Keegan v. Ireland*, 26 May 1994, Series A no. 290 and *Kroon and Others v. the Netherlands*, 27 October 1994, Series A no. 297-C.

[26] See also, e.g., infra *Ammdjadi* and *MacDonald v. France* (discussed in Sect. 7.2).

fact that both parties had Iranian nationality and on the basis of the Agreement on Establishment between the German Reich and the Persian Empire of 17 February 1929, the German court found that Iranian law was applicable to the divorce and all of its consequences. The court further held that the fact that Iranian law did not know the concept of compensation of pension rights did not violate German *ordre public*. This assessment was upheld on appeal. The former wife subsequently lodged a complaint in Strasbourg on the basis of Article 8 ECHR, as well as Article 12 ECHR[27] and Article 1 of Protocol No. 1 ECHR, taken alone and in conjunction with Article 14 ECHR.

The Court noted with regard to Article 8 ECHR that although the compensation of pension rights is of a pecuniary nature, it is also the direct consequence of marital life and aims at the strengthening of the position of the weaker partner. It could as such be regarded as an expression of the respect of the State for family life. Therefore, the Court assumed that the facts fell within the scope of Article 8 ECHR. The Court further framed the case as raising the issue of whether this notion of respect for family life entailed an obligation for the German courts to disregard the Treaty between Germany and Iran by qualifying the compensation of pension rights as being part of German *ordre public*. The Court observed that the decision to give effect to the Treaty had a basis in national law and pursued a legitimate aim, namely upholding a treaty concluded between two States.

With regard to the proportionality of the decision of the German courts to find that the compensation rights did not form part of German *ordre public* and that the normally applicable foreign law thus should be applied to the case, the Court observed that the compensation of pension rights was only fairly recently introduced in Germany, while it is not known in many other countries—there is certainly no European consensus in this regard, as the manner in which financial protection is provided to the nonworking partner differs from country to country.

Moreover, Iranian law also provides a form of financial relief in this regard in the form of some alimony or the morning gift, according to the Court. The Court thus found that the ECHR cannot be interpreted as entailing the obligation to qualify the compensation of pension rights as being part of German *ordre public* in order to set aside the Treaty between Germany and Iran. According to the Court, the notion of respect for family cannot entail the obligation to grant a pecuniary privilege to one spouse, particularly where such financial relief would entail a pecuniary disadvantage to the other spouse. The application of Iranian law by the German courts thus did not result in a violation of Article 8 ECHR.

The applicant had also complained that the refusal to compensate the pension rights violated her rights under Article 1 of Protocol No. 1 ECHR, which guarantees the peaceful enjoyment of possessions. Referring to its case law concerning this notion of 'possessions', the Court found that the applicant must have had a

[27] As Article 12 ECHR is merely concerned with the right to marry and found a family, and as it is standard case law of the Court that this right does not entail the right to a divorce, it is clear that this Article is not applicable to this case, which deals solely with the consequences of a divorce. As such, this part of the complaint shall not be further discussed.

'legitimate expectation'.[28] As the compensation of pension rights was not available under the normally applicable Iranian law, while so far this compensation had not been classified as being part of German *ordre public*, the Court held that the applicant could not claim to have had such a 'legitimate expectation'. Therefore, the Court held this complaint to be incompatible *ratione materiae.*

Finally, with regard to Article 8 ECHR taken in conjunction with Article 14 ECHR, the Court noted that the difference in treatment stemmed from the fact that the applicant and her former husband both had Iranian nationality and that on the basis of the Treaty between Germany and Iran, Iranian law was the applicable law, while the application of German law was excluded. In this regard it was held, in a rather sweeping fashion, that:

> especially in conflict of laws cases, the differentiation for all family issues according to nationality and not to habitual residence is a well-known principle which aims at protecting a person's close connection with his or her home country. Therefore, even though the decisiveness of the habitual residence might arguably be considered preferable with regard to pension rights, the decisiveness of a person's nationality cannot be considered to be without "objective and reasonable justification". In this respect, it must also be noted that the applicant had been free to choose the application of German law, together with her husband, by notarial certification.

The Court's decision in *Ammdjadi* contains a number of interesting points.[29] It is, of course, first interesting to note that the Court was of the opinion that pension rights fell within the scope of Article 8 ECHR—pension rights may not be the first thing that come to mind if one considers the notion of family life. More directly relevant to the question of the impact of the ECHR on private international law is the manner in which the Court presented the main issue with regard to Article 8 ECHR in relation to the applicable Iranian law. The Court first noted that the decision to apply Iranian law on the basis of the bilateral treaty between the two countries had a basis in national law and pursued the legitimate aim of complying with an international obligation. In this regard, the Court thus appears to follow its regular scheme concerning restrictions under Article 8(2) ECHR,[30] although it by no means follows its framework carefully.

It is interesting to observe that the Court cites the fulfilment of an international obligation as the legitimate aim. The application of Iranian law indeed followed from a bilateral treaty between Germany and Iran. One should note, however, that if the application of Iranian law had resulted from national German choice of law rules (a national source), a different legitimate aim would have had to have been presented. This could consequently also have had an effect on the assessment of the proportionality, due to the connection between the legitimate aim pursued and

---

[28] The Court referred to its case law in *von Maltzan and Others v. Germany* (dec.) [GC], nos. 71916/01, 71917/01 and 10260/02, paras 74(c) and 112, ECHR 2005-V, and *Kopecký v. Slovakia* [GC], no. 44912/98, para 35(c), ECHR 2004-IX.

[29] See for a discussion of this decision also Kinsch, who focuses more on the right to nondiscrimination and choice-of-law rules. See Kinsch 2011, pp. 39–41.

[30] See supra Sect. 3.5.1.2.

the proportionality, which follows from the condition of the interference being necessary in a democratic society.[31]

The Court thereafter turned to the proportionality of the decision of the German courts not to set aside the applicable foreign law following from an international treaty by qualifying pension rights as being part of German *ordre public*. This is a somewhat odd presentation by the Court of the issue at hand. A more logical approach, in my opinion, would have been for the Court to consider whether the result of the application of Iranian law would infringe upon the applicant's rights guaranteed in Article 8 ECHR, and if so, whether this restriction of the applicant's rights would be in conformity with Article 8(2) ECHR. By immediately turning to whether the decision of the German courts not to qualify pension rights as being part of German *ordre public*, the Court, in my opinion, skips a step. While qualifying pension rights as being part of German *ordre public* would admittedly solve the potential problem of the application of Iranian law (allegedly) violating Article 8 ECHR, the interference with Article 8 ECHR, in principle, results from the application of Iranian law. This is what the Court should have focused on, in my opinion. It may be a subtle difference, and while in the present case, this difference would not have led to a different result, this may not always be the case.[32]

Instead, the Court thus essentially focused on whether Article 8 ECHR obligated the German courts to qualify pension rights as being part of German *ordre public*. In this regard, the Court offered a number of arguments: there is no emerging consensus on this issue in Europe, and the protection provided to non-working partners was only fairly recently introduced in Germany. Furthermore, the applicable Iranian law also provides a measure of financial relief in the form of the morning gift, according to the Court.[33] It is, unfortunately, difficult to assess how the Court exactly weighs these different reasons. Would the situation be different if one of these factors were missing? If there, for example, had been an emerging European consensus with regard to the compensation of pension rights, would there have been a violation of Article 8 ECHR, or would the presence of a form of financial relief in Iranian law still have sufficed for not finding a violation? This is difficult to tell from the Court's reasoning.

The Court's analysis concerning the right to property *ex* Article 1 of Protocol No. 1 ECHR appears to make a successful invocation of this right difficult. The Court found that the applicant should have had a 'legitimate expectation'. This criterion follows from the Court's case law concerning the notion of 'possessions'[34] and ensures that Article 1 of Protocol No. 1 ECHR not only applies to

---

[31] Id.

[32] See further infra Sect. 6.3.2.2.

[33] While the Court simply mentions this as one of the reasons for not having to find that Article 8 ECHR entails the obligation to compensation of the pension rights, it could be noted that domestic courts have struggled with how to deal with the notion of the morning gift. See Mehdi and Nielsen 2011.

[34] See, e.g., supra n. 28.

existing possessions, but also to claims, provided that the applicant has a 'legitimate expectation', and not mere hope. However, according to the Court, the applicant had no such expectation, because the compensation of pension rights was missing from the applicable Iranian law and it was not part of German *ordre public*. Yet the fact that such compensation was missing made the applicant invoke the right to property in the first place. If the compensation of pension rights had been part of German *ordre public*—resulting in 'legitimate expectations'—the applicant's actions before the German courts would most likely already have been successful. The successful invocation of Article 1 of Protocol No. 1 ECHR therefore appears to be difficult in such cases.

6.3.2 The Impact of the ECHR on the Applicable Foreign Law: Further Analysis

The virtual absence of directly relevant case law of the Strasbourg Institutions with regard to the issue of applicable law in private international law has certainly not stopped authors from discussing the possible impact of the ECHR on this issue.[35] The prolonged absence of an authoritative decision of the Court in this regard has resulted in important aspects of the debate on the impact of the ECHR on foreign applicable law being mostly developed in the literature. Authors have found inspiration as to the possible impact of the ECHR on the issue of applicable law in private international law cases in the Court's case law concerning the extraterritorial effects of the ECHR,[36] while a seminal decision by the German *Bundesverfassungsgericht* taken way back in 1971[37] also appears to have served as a model in this regard.[38]

In this latter case, often referred to as the *Spanierbeschluss*, the German Constitutional Court had to decide whether the application of Spanish law, which would result in a Spaniard not being able to marry a German woman in Germany because of the fact that the man's earlier divorce would not be recognized under Spanish law, would violate the right to marry, one of the fundamental rights laid down in the German *Grundgesetz*.[39] The German Constitutional Court held that

---

[35] See, e.g., the literature cited supra n. 4.

[36] See with regard to an overview of the Court's case law concerning the extraterritorial effects of the ECHR supra section "The Extra-Territorial Effect of the ECHR" in Chap. 4. See also infra Sect. 6.3.2.1.

[37] *NJW* 1971, p. 1508.

[38] This case is discussed by, e.g., Docquir 1999, p. 503ff; Kinsch 2007, p. 194; van Loon 1993, p. 135; Mayer 1991, p. 656.

[39] This case has been much discussed in the literature. See for a commentary in English, e.g., Juenger 1972, pp. 290–298; Hofmann 1994, p. 145ff; Weick 2003, p. 193ff. See also supra n. 38 and with regard to the (historical) debate on the use of connecting factors in private international law, supra Sect. 1.1.

this was indeed the case and in so finding discussed many issues that are also relevant for the impact of the ECHR on the issue of applicable law. Not only has this decision been cited as evidence of the fact that fundamental rights indeed have an impact on private international law before this issue was ever really raised before the Strasbourg Institutions, but the issue of the manner in which to ensure respect for fundamental rights was also discussed.

Three different facets of this debate may be distinguished. First of all, it has been discussed in relation to this case whether it is possible to invoke one of the rights guaranteed in the ECHR against the normally applicable foreign law, particularly where this foreign law originated from a third country. This issue has already been dealt with in relation to the ECHR above, where it was held that this is indeed the case.[40] The other two aspects will be examined below. They are, respectively, the standard of control that should be used in private international law disputes regarding a foreign applicable law possibly violating one of the rights guaranteed in the ECHR—whether or not the standards of the ECHR may be attenuated in such cases (Sect. 6.3.2.1)—and the manner in which the ECHR should be applied, which will be further explored in relation to the case law of national courts of the Contracting Parties (Sect. 6.3.3).

This latter issue concerns the question of how the ECHR should be invoked against the applicable foreign law possibly resulting in a violation of the ECHR—what techniques can be used by the national courts of the Contracting Parties. As will be discussed further below, there are, broadly speaking, two approaches: the use of the public policy exception, or the direct application of the right guaranteed in the ECHR against the foreign applicable law.[41] It should be noted, however, that it is difficult to entirely separate the issue of the attenuation from the technique used, as specialists of private international law, who favor the attenuation of the standards of the ECHR, frequently regard the public policy exception as the natural means to achieve this attenuation.

6.3.2.1 The Standard of Control with Regard to the Applicable Foreign Law

An important aspect of the debate on the impact of the rights guaranteed in the ECHR on the issue of applicable law is what the standard of control should be with regard to the scrutiny of the ECHR to the applicable foreign law. The standard of control concerns the issue of whether it is possible, and if so, whether it is desirable, to attenuate the standards of the rights guaranteed in the ECHR in private international law disputes in which a foreign law is the applicable law (either the law of another Contracting Party or the law of a third country). This issue is not confined to the issue of the applicable law in private international law.

40 See supra Sect. 6.2.

41 See further infra Sect. 6.3.3.3.

The same question may also be asked with regard to the recognition and enforcement of foreign judgments, even though this leads to a similar discussion to a certain extent.[42]

With regard to the standard of control it would, in principle, appear to be useful to make a distinction based on the origin of the applicable foreign law.[43] One could question how appropriate it is to subject foreign laws originating from third countries to the full scrutiny of the (qualified) rights guaranteed in the ECHR, whereas this may be different if the applicable foreign law emanates from another Contracting Party. In such a case, there is less reason to attenuate the standards of the ECHR.[44] After all, the laws of the other Contracting Parties should, in principle, already be in line with the requirements following from the ECHR.

In the development of the idea of the attenuation of the standards of the ECHR regarding the applicable foreign law of a third country, a few cases can be distinguished as the main sources of inspiration. When some of the ideas concerning the impact of the ECHR on issues of private international law were first developed in the literature, there was hardly any case law of the Strasbourg Institutions specifically dealing with issues of private international law. Yet specialists in the area of private international law had noticed the possible analogy between the Court's case law concerning the extraterritorial effect of the ECHR in *Soering v. the United Kingdom*[45] and *Drozd and Janousek v. France and Spain*[46] and the applicability of the ECHR to issues of private international law.[47] It will be recalled that in these cases, which were essentially concerned with international cooperation, the concept of 'a flagrant denial of justice' was introduced with regard to Article 6 ECHR.[48] In these cases, a reduced effect of Article 6 ECHR was thus introduced. It has consequently been suggested that a different standard should similarly be introduced in cases in which the law of a third country is applied.

Why should a different standard of the ECHR be applied to cases concerning private international law, and particularly to the applicable foreign law, more particularly the law of a third country? The idea behind the attenuation of the ECHR's standards in this regard is manifold, but in short it comes down to the question of whether laws from all over the world should be held up to European human rights standards, as guaranteed in the ECHR. Respect for the diversity of the world's legal cultures is one of the principles of private international law and thus a certain attenuation of the standards of the ECHR may be preferable. After all, if one were to insist on the full application of the rights guaranteed in the

---

42 See infra Sects. 8.2 and 8.3.

43 Cf. Marchadier 2007, p. 493ff. But see Matscher 1998, p. 222.

44 Cf. Kinsch 2004b, p. 214; Marchadier 2007, p. 493.

45 *Soering v. the United Kingdom*, 7 July 1989, Series A no. 161.

46 *Drozd and Janousek v. France and Spain*, 26 June 1992, Series A no. 240.

47 See, e.g., van Loon 1993, pp. 145–147; Mayer 1991, p. 653ff; Vonken 1993, pp. 172–174. See also supra Chap. 4.

48 See Sect. 3.5.1.3 and "The Extra-Territorial Effect of the ECHR" in Chap. 4.

ECHR in this regard, there may, in practice, be little room left for the application of a foreign law which fundamentally differs from the laws of the Contracting Parties. On this point one could also mention another goal of private international law, the international harmony of decisions, which is arguably predicated on a certain tolerance toward other legal cultures.[49] A lack of such harmony brings with it the real risk of limping legal relationships and could endanger the international mobility of persons.[50]

It has, additionally, been argued that by not allowing such leeway for a certain tolerance toward other legal cultures, one would run the risk of creating different blocks of States, each adhering to their own legal values, having little regard for norms originating from outside their legal atmosphere.[51] This risk has mostly been described in relation to issues stemming from the differences between European family law and Muslim law. Some authors have even approached this issue in terms of a clash of civilizations,[52] while it is also a driving force behind the debate on the 'imperialism' of the ECHR and fundamental rights in general.[53]

There are, however, also a number of arguments against the attenuation of the standards of the ECHR in issues of private international law. Although such attenuation may be justified to an extent, it should be observed—and this is an argument that perhaps has not been emphasized enough in the literature—that there are limitations inherent to the ECHR to this attenuation of standards. Moreover, the attenuation of standards with regard to the applicable foreign law originating from a third country inevitably creates inequality in the forum State.

The principle argument against attenuation is that it may not be allowed under the ECHR, or rather that it is only allowed insofar as it is permitted under the ECHR. As has been discussed extensively in Chap. 4, Article 1 ECHR explicitly guarantees that the rights and freedoms of everyone within the jurisdiction of the respective Contracting Parties will be guaranteed. This also applies to the application of a foreign law or the recognition and enforcement of a foreign judgment emanating from a third country.[54] The ECHR itself, of course, allows—under particular circumstances—for a certain attenuation: the so-called qualified rights, for example, expressly allow for an interference by the Contracting Party in order to secure certain interests, while an attenuation of the level of scrutiny of the ECHR is also possible and perhaps even desirable with regard to the limited right of Article 6(1) ECHR.[55]

---

[49] Cf. Van Hedel 2008, p. 132; Looschelders 2001, p. 475.

[50] See generally supra Chap. 2. It should further be noted that this problem is not confined to the issue of applicable law, but is also relevant with regard to the recognition and enforcement of foreign judgments. See further infra Chap. 8.

[51] See, e.g., Fulchiron 2002, p. 353ff.

[52] See, e.g., Najm 2003. See, however, for a critique of this approach Zaher 2010.

[53] See with regard to this debate supra Sect. 4.4.1.

[54] See supra Chap. 4.

[55] See particularly supra Sects. 3.5.1.2 and 3.5.1.3. See also Sect. 4.4.

Insofar as in issues of private international law these rights are concerned, a Contracting Party has some leeway to attenuate the standards of the ECHR in order to protect certain (private international law) interests and/or the rights of others in private international law cases. Furthermore, the Court has consistently held in reviewing the various obligations of the Contracting Parties under the ECHR that the Contracting Parties enjoy a certain margin of appreciation with regard to the obligations for which they have to strike a balance between the right of an individual (even in an international case) and the interests of society as a whole. One could state that the doctrine of the margin of appreciation is eminently suited for accommodating diversity within Europe.[56] It is certainly conceivable that there is room within this margin of appreciation also to protect private international law interests.[57] Such interests could therefore presumably be integrated to an extent in the system of restrictions which the Court uses with regard to interferences with qualified rights.

Another argument against the attenuation of the standards of the ECHR is that by attenuating the standards of the ECHR in such cases, one inevitably creates inequality. Cases which are concerned with foreign norms would be treated differently compared to purely domestic cases. One could perhaps argue that such inequality may be justifiable, because such situations are not analogous. However, the fact remains that the human rights guaranteed in the ECHR of some people (those involved in cross-border cases) before the court of a Contracting Party may be less protected than the rights of others (in purely domestic cases). One could wonder whether this creates a double standard with regard to the protection following from the ECHR and whether this is desirable.

6.3.2.2 Attenuation of the Standards of the ECHR in the Strasbourg Case Law?

As has been stated above, there is little case law of the Court that is directly relevant to the issue of applicable law in private international law.[58] What can nevertheless be derived from the Court's findings in these cases with regard to the possible attenuation of the standards of the ECHR? Does the Court adjust its level of scrutiny in cases concerning the applicable foreign law possibly violating the ECHR? There appears to be little evidence in the Court's case law directly concerned with the application of foreign law suggesting an attenuation of the standards.

In *Zvoristeanu*, discussed above, the Court examined the application of German law by the French courts. This was a case where the applicable law originated from another Contracting Party. It has already been stated that there is less reason to

[56] See Brems 2003, pp. 81–110.

[57] Cf. Engel 1989, pp. 38–41; Rutten 1998, p. 802ff; Vonken 1993, pp. 174–176.

[58] See supra Sect. 6.3.

insist on the attenuation of the standards of the ECHR in such a case. However, it has been argued that it cannot be completely ruled out that a certain attenuation of the standards may even be required in such cases, as the Court in its case law has generally indicated that the national characteristics should be taken into account.[59] This could be taken to mean that the standards of the ECHR even differ somewhat from Contracting Party to Contracting Party. This should then be taken into account with regard to the issue of an applicable law originating from another Contracting Party.

Returning to the Court's assessment in *Zvoristeanu*, it is difficult to infer much from this case in relation to the level of scrutiny concerning the applicable foreign law, as the Court's reasoning is rather limited. However, by merely finding that the decision of the French courts was neither arbitrary nor unreasonable, the Court does not appear to introduce a very rigorous test with regard to the issue of the application of a foreign law emanating from another Contracting Party.[60] This approach suggests quite the opposite, as the decision of the French courts escaped the strict scrutiny the Court usually applies to cases concerning Article 8 ECHR, whereby in the event of an interference with this right the Court would assess the conditions summed up in Article 8(2) ECHR and eventually turn to the proportionality of such a decision.[61] Here, the Court only quickly reviewed whether the decision of the French courts was arbitrary or unreasonable, which is quite a detached approach, but not incomprehensible, given the fact that this case concerns an admissibility decision. Moreover, the applicable law in question originated from another Contracting Party and thus should be in conformity with the rights guaranteed in the ECHR.[62]

The Court appears to use a different approach with regard to the applicable law originating from a third country in *Ammdjadi*. The Court's reasoning in this case has already been examined above.[63] What could one say specifically as to the level of scrutiny used in this case by the Court? The Court focused mostly on the complaint concerning Article 8 ECHR. It will be recalled that in its assessment of Article 8 ECHR, the Court presented the issue at hand as whether the decision of the German courts not to qualify compensation of pension rights as being part of German *ordre public* (which would have meant that such compensation would be deemed a fundamental value within Germany) was proportionate. The Court noted, inter alia, that there is no European consensus on the compensation of

---

59 Marchadier 2007, p. 495ff. The author cites *Podkolzina v. Latvia*, no. 46726/99, ECHR 2002-II as an example. One could in this regard also mention the doctrine of the margin of appreciation, which is (also) predicated on the idea that the national authorities are, in principle, better suited to evaluate local issues. See supra Sect. 3.5.2.

60 Cf. Marchadier 2007, p. 509ff.

61 See with regard to restrictions to Article 8 ECHR and the notion of proportionality in the Court's case law supra Sect. 3.5.1.2.

62 Cf. the reasoning used by the Court in *Gill and Malone v. the Netherlands and the United Kingdom* in the text following supra n. 13.

63 See supra Sect. 6.3.1.

pension rights and that Iranian law also provided for some sort of financial protection of the other spouse in order to reach the conclusion that the application was manifestly ill-founded.

One could say that in this case the Court at least scrutinized the decision of the German courts more closely compared to *Zvoristeanu* discussed above. The Court appeared to look more closely at the facts of the case and more or less followed its usual scheme with regard to the assessment of the conditions of Article 8(2) ECHR[64] by finding that the decision to apply foreign law had a basis in national law (Section 3(2) of the Introductory Act to the German Civil Code) and that this pursued a legitimate aim (giving effect to a treaty between Germany and Iran). It thereafter considered the proportionality of the decision.[65] However, the Court did find that the application was manifestly inadmissible. In this regard one could state that those in favor of attenuation could, of course, be satisfied with the rejection of the invocation of the ECHR against the result of the normally applicable foreign law.

Is it, however, possible to really discern an attenuation of the standards of the ECHR in this case—something which one may suspect, given the fact that the applicable law emanates from a third country? The Court clearly did not expressly mention an attenuation of the standards of the ECHR in this regard, such as, for example, it has done with regard to Article 6(1) ECHR and the recognition and enforcement of foreign judgments by introducing the notion of a 'flagrant denial of justice'.[66] One could argue, though, that by framing the relevant question as whether the German courts had violated Article 8 ECHR by finding that compensation rights did not form part of German *ordre public*, the Court raises the bar for finding a violation, as compared to when it would have merely required that the result of the application of Iranian law would not be in conformity with Article 8 ECHR. Moreover, the Court pointed to the fact that a form of financial relief for the other spouse is also available under Iranian law, a possibility of which it subsequently scarcely elaborates. This may suggest that any equivalent provision in the normally applicable foreign law would suffice for not finding a violation with regard to the ECHR.

It is questionable, though, whether this case lends itself to far-reaching conclusions with regard to the level of scrutiny. After all, the Court's reasoning is succinct. Moreover, while the Court notes that there is no European consensus as to the compensation of pension rights, one could question whether such compensation should be regarded as falling within the scope of Article 8 ECHR in the first place, even though the Court starts from the assumption that it does. The fact that the Court was unwilling to find a violation of Article 8 ECHR with regard to a

---

[64] See supra Sect. 6.3.1. See generally Sect. 3.5.1.2.

[65] Even though the Court does not mention this explicitly in its decision, the test of the proportionality of the decision follows from the requirement of whether a restriction is 'necessary in a democratic society', which can be found in Article 8(2) ECHR. See further supra Sect. 3.5.1.2.

[66] Although one should add that the Court has not consistently used this attenuated standard. See further infra Sect. 8.2.

right which is not generally deemed to be part of Article 8 ECHR is not that surprising. This case may simply not be the best example for finding a violation with regard to the foreign applicable law.

In conclusion, one could say that while there may be something to be said for the idea of the attenuation of the standards of the rights guaranteed in the ECHR with regard to the normally applicable foreign law originating from a third country possibly violating one of the rights guaranteed in the ECHR, there is not yet much evidence to be found in the Court's case law for such a stance. However, I would argue that even though some flexibility may be necessary in order to account for private international law interests, the room for maneuvering is limited. Such attenuation is only permitted insofar as it is allowed under the ECHR itself. In my opinion, the obligation following from Article 1 ECHR means that the room for attenuation is limited, even where the applicable law originates from a third country. This does not mean that there is no room at all here. It is, however, difficult to establish *in abstracto* what the limits inherent in the ECHR are in this regard. Nevertheless, this room should be sought within the system of restrictions possible under the right concerned that is guaranteed in the ECHR. What is thus clear is that the extent to which restrictions, and therefore attenuation, of a right guaranteed in the ECHR is allowed ultimately depends on which of the rights guaranteed in the ECHR is concerned in an issue of applicable law.

6.3.3 Jurisprudence of National Courts of the Contracting Parties

While in the case law of the Strasbourg Institutions no example of a case can yet be found in which the ECHR is successfully invoked against the normally applicable foreign law violating one of the rights guaranteed in the ECHR, there are some such examples in the jurisprudence of the national courts of the Contracting Parties. Moreover, the principle of the setting aside of the normally applicable foreign law violating fundamental rights has, for example, been accepted in the three legal orders, England, the Netherlands, and Switzerland, which will receive the most attention here, as the case law discussed in this section will demonstrate.

Below, one will first find a brief overview of the case law of national courts in which the principle of human rights guarantees standing in the way of the application of a foreign law violating such rights has been established (Sect. 6.3.3.1). Thereafter, the jurisprudence of national courts on the establishment of paternity will be discussed. This is an area of the law where the ECHR has successfully been invoked against the normally applicable foreign law. In this discussion, the issue of attenuation will also be further explored (Sect. 6.3.3.2). In conclusion, one will find a discussion on the *manner* in which fundamental rights, and the rights guaranteed in the ECHR in particular, are dealt with in issues relating to the applicable foreign law in private international law disputes before national courts of the Contracting Parties (Sect. 6.3.3.3).

6.3.3.1 The Invocation of the ECHR against the Applicable Foreign Law in the Jurisprudence of National Courts

While there may not be many concrete examples of the invocation of one of the rights guaranteed in the ECHR against the applicable foreign law—particularly not in English case law, and nor is it a frequent event in Swiss or Dutch case law—the principle of human rights standing in the way of the application of a foreign law violating such values seems to be generally accepted in England, the Netherlands, and Switzerland.

The classical example of the invocation of human rights in an issue of private international law in England may be *Oppenheimer v. Cattermole*.[67] In this case, the issue arose as to whether effect should be given in English law to a decree of the German government of 1941 stating that all Jewish refugees should be deprived of their German citizenship. In deciding whether giving effect to such a decree would violate English public policy, Lord Cross held that 'to my mind a law of this sort constitutes so grave an infringement of human rights that the courts of this country ought to refuse to recognize it as a law at all.'[68]

In *Kuwait Airways Corpn v. Iraqi Airways Co (Nos 4 and 5)*[69] Lord Cross was cited approvingly by Lord Nicholls, who mentioned foreign laws encompassing '[g]ross infringements of human rights' as an example of laws that would be contrary to English public policy.[70] It has been held with regard to foreign confiscatory decrees in *Williams & Humbert Ltd v. W&H Trade Marks (Jersey) Ltd*[71] that such foreign laws will be disregarded if they would offend principles of human rights.

In the Netherlands, the ECHR has occasionally been invoked against the normally applicable foreign law in a number of different contexts, particularly in cases concerning the establishment of paternity,[72] but one could, for example, also mention a case regarding the denial of paternity.[73]

---

[67] *Oppenheimer v. Cattermole* [1976] AC 249.

[68] *Oppenheimer v. Cattermole* [1976] AC 249, 278 (per Lord Cross).

[69] *Kuwait Airways Corpn v. Iraqi Airways Co (Nos 4 and 5)* [2002] 2 AC 883.

[70] *Kuwait Airways Corpn v. Iraqi Airways Co (Nos 4 and 5)* [2002] 2 AC 883, 18. See with regard to this case, e.g., Rogerson 2003, pp. 265–287.

[71] [1986] A.C. 368, 428 (per Lord Templeman).

[72] See infra Sect. 6.3.3.2.

[73] Rb. Amsterdam 23 November 2005, *NIPR* 2006, 14. See with regard to the impossibility to deny paternity under the foreign applicable law and the possible issues with the principle of equality also Rb. Haarlem 22 July 2008, *NIPR* 2008, 275.

In Switzerland, the *Tribunal fédéral* has stated in the *Bertl* case that human rights are part of Swiss *ordre public*.[74] Even though this case was concerned with procedural public policy, it has generally been accepted that human rights are fully integrated in the public policy exceptions regarding both applicable law and the recognition and enforcement of foreign judgments.[75]

The principle that human rights in general, and by extension the rights guaranteed in the ECHR, may be invoked against the normally applicable foreign law is well established in all three legal orders.[76] The discussion therefore is, also, not so much whether the rights guaranteed in the ECHR can be invoked against the applicable foreign law, but rather to what extent the rights guaranteed in the ECHR are protected. Nevertheless, there are not many cases in which the ECHR is actually invoked with regard to the issue of applicable law in private international law. For English case law this may, incidentally, be explained to a large part by the fact that England adheres to the *lex fori* tradition in international family law, which takes away a good number of potential cases. Most of the instances in which the ECHR is successfully invoked against the normally applicable law, and also the examples given here, pertain to issues of international family law. This is not unusual considering the fact that in this area of the law cultural differences are most clearly reflected. In particular, the possible incompatibility of family law originating from Muslim countries has been the subject of extensive debate.[77]

While national courts in both the Netherlands and Switzerland are, in principle, inclined to apply foreign law in international family law issues, England adheres to the *lex fori* tradition, which means that English courts apply the *lex fori*, English law, in such matters.[78] English courts will thus not be confronted with issues relating to the foreign applicable law in international family law cases, as foreign law will simply not be the law applied to such cases. This also explains why no English cases will be discussed in the next section.[79]

---

[74] ATF 103 Ia 199, 205.

[75] See, e.g., Bucher 2011, p. 249; Kinsch 2007, p. 214.

[76] See in addition to the case law discussed above, e.g., Bucher 2011, pp. 249–250; Cheshire et al. 2010, p. 145; Dicey et al. 2012, p. 99ff; Strikwerda 2012, pp. 55–56 (with regard to international human rights).

[77] See, e.g., Kinsch 2007, p. 258ff; Lagarde 2010, p. 525ff.

[78] See, e.g., *NG v KR*, [2008] EWHC 1532 (Fam), [2008] EWHC 1532 (Fam), [2009] 1 FLR 1478, [2009] 1 FCR 35, [2008] Fam Law 1082. This case will be further discussed infra Sect. 6.4.2.

[79] The issue of whether the application of the *lex fori* (instead of foreign law) may result in a violation of the ECHR will be discussed infra Sect. 6.4.

6.3.3.2 The Judicial Establishment of Paternity: And the Issue of Attenuation

In the Netherlands in recent years, a series of cases has been decided concerning the judicial establishment of paternity in which Article 8 ECHR was invoked against the normally applicable foreign law, because it was not possible to judicially establish paternity over the child(ren) under the respective applicable foreign laws originating from third countries.[80] In all these cases, the facts were more or less similar. All concerned a mother who wanted to establish the paternity of a man over her child. The relevant Dutch choice of law rules determined that a foreign law was applicable to the request.[81] However, under the relevant applicable foreign laws it was not possible to judicially establish paternity over a child. In all these cases, it was consequently argued that the application of the normally applicable foreign law, which would lead to a denial of the request, would violate Dutch public policy and/or Article 8 ECHR.[82]

It is interesting to note that the various Dutch courts did not come to the same conclusion in these cases, and even the courts which did reach similar conclusions did not use the same reasoning to reach that result. In all these cases, it was decided that the fact that the application of the normally applicable (foreign) law would result in a denial of the request did indeed violate Article 8 ECHR—with the notable exception of the one case that came before the Dutch *Hoge Raad*. Before turning (again) to the latter decision,[83] I will first examine the reasoning used by the lower courts that did find a violation of Article 8 ECHR.

In assessing whether the normally applicable foreign law would violate Article 8 ECHR, the *Gerechtshof* Amsterdam did not examine whether the application of the normally applicable Moroccan law would result in a violation of Article 8 ECHR, but instead chose to examine whether the relevant Dutch choice of law

[80] See, e.g., Hof Amsterdam 9 February 2006, *JPF* 2006, 71 (note Oderkerk), *NIPR* 2006, 98; Rb. 's-Gravenhage 3 November 2008, *NIPR* 2010, 23; Hof 's-Hertogenbosch 27 November 2008, *NIPR* 2009, 95; HR 12 December 2008, *NIPR* 2009, 1 (in which the judgment of Hof 's-Gravenhage 3 October 2007, *NIPR* 2008, 7 was not overturned). See for a more detailed discussion of particularly the last three cases Kiestra 2010, pp. 27–30. See also Rb. Haarlem 11 December 2012, *NIPR* 2013, 24; *JPF* 2013, 131 (note I. Curry-Sumner).

[81] The relevant Dutch choice of law rules with regard to the (international) establishment of paternity could at the time be found in the 'Wet conflictenrecht afstamming' 14 March 2002, *Stb.* 2002, 153. Nowadays, they may be found in the new codification of Dutch private international law in Boek 10 BW (see Article 10:97 BW).

[82] Although it is not explicitly mentioned in all the afore-mentioned cases, the Dutch courts appear to rely, with regard to the applicability of Article 8 ECHR to the judicial establishment of paternity, on the Court's findings in *Mikulić v. Croatia,* no. 53176/99, ECHR 2002-I. See particularly paras 52–55.

[83] See supra Sect. 4.1.

rule[84] violated Article 8 ECHR. [85] This is odd reasoning, as possible violations of a right guaranteed in the ECHR are usually raised through the public policy exception, which in Dutch law is normally only used against the result of the choice of law rules and not against the choice of law rules themselves.[86] The *Gerechtshof* Amsterdam ultimately found that the Dutch choice of law rules amounted to an unjustifiable infringement of the right to respect for family life following from Article 8 ECHR and subsequently applied Dutch law on the basis of Dutch public policy. The *Rechtbank* in The Hague found that the application of the normally applicable foreign law—in this case also Moroccan law—would violate Dutch public policy 'also seen in the light of Article 8 ECHR.'[87] The *Gerechtshof* 's-Hertogenbosch used reasoning similar to the appeal court in Amsterdam and also examined the relevant Dutch choice of law rule, but ultimately used more conventional reasoning by also finding that the normally applicable foreign law following the application of the Dutch choice of law rules violated Article 8 ECHR and that on the basis of Dutch public policy, Dutch law should be applied.[88]

In the case that reached the highest court in the Netherlands, no violation of either Dutch public policy or Article 8 ECHR was ultimately found with regard to the application of Surinamese law, which led to the denial of the request to judicially establish paternity.[89] It should be noted that the complaint before the *Hoge Raad* was rejected—in conformity with the Advocate General's conclusion—on the basis that the complaints put forward could not lead to cassation.[90] The appeal court had found that the normally applicable Surinamese law could only be set aside under exceptional circumstances and, according to the court, there were no such circumstances in this case, as the father could have recognized the child abroad.

In the more recent case before the *Rechtbank* Haarlem, the court sufficed with the observation that the fact that under the normally applicable law—Nigerian law—the judicial establishment of paternity was not possible, resulted in a

---

[84] Article 6 of the Wet conflictenrecht afstamming. [Parentage (Conflict of Laws) Act], 14 March 2002, *Stb.* 2002, 153. This law has since been replaced by Boek 10 *Burgerlijk Wetboek* See with regard to parentage, particularly Title 5, Article 10:92 BW onwards. *Vaststellings- en Invoeringswet Boek 10 Burgerlijk Wetboek* [Determination and Implementation Book 10 of the Dutch Civil Code], 19 May 2011, *Stb.* 2011, 272.

[85] Hof Amsterdam 9 February 2006, *JPF* 2006, 71 (note Oderkerk), *NIPR* 2006, 98.

[86] See Strikwerda 2012, pp. 52–54. Cf. note Oderkerk supra n. 85; Cf. van Hedel 2008, pp. 128–130.

[87] Rb. 's-Gravenhage 3 November 2008, *NIPR* 2010, 23 (translation provided by the author).

[88] Hof 's-Hertogenbosch 27 November 2008, *NIPR* 2009, 95.

[89] HR 12 December 2008, *NIPR* 2009, 1.

[90] Article 81 RO states that if the complaint before the *HR* cannot lead to cassation and no important questions of law are brought up, the *HR* may dismiss the complaint without stating further reasons.

violation of Article 8 ECHR.[91] Interestingly enough, no reference to the public policy exception was made in this case. Instead, Article 8 ECHR was applied directly.[92]

It is interesting to note that the Dutch courts came to different results despite ostensibly applying the same criterion to the issue at hand: does the fact that the normally applicable foreign law makes it impossible for the child to judicially establish his or her paternity require that this result should be set aside on the basis of Article 8 ECHR and/or the public policy exception? The *Hoge Raad* had no problem with the assessment that Article 8 ECHR would not be violated, because it would be possible for the man in that case to establish paternity within a reasonable time in Surinam. This is also how this case differs from the other cases, where it appeared that there really was no alternative to establish paternity.

Can one speak of attenuation of the standards of Article 8 ECHR in the cases discussed above? At first sight, there is little evidence of attenuation in the Dutch cases, with perhaps the exception of the case that came before the *Hoge Raad*. In the decision of the lower Dutch courts the normally applicable law, which did not allow for the establishment of paternity, was set aside, as this result was deemed to violate Article 8 ECHR. There was no noticeable attenuation introduced by the lower Dutch courts. Only in the decision of the *Gerechtshof* Den Haag, which was not dismissed by the *Hoge Raad*, may one discern a form of attenuation in the sense that the result of the application of the normally applicable foreign law was not set aside due to it not being entirely impossible to establish paternity under the applicable foreign law. In this regard, 'exceptional circumstances' were introduced as a guideline.

One could thus say that the latter court was attentive to the internationality of the case. However, this is, of course, also where the facts of the discussed cases differed: under the normally applicable law in the latter case it was possible to establish paternity, while the applicable laws in the other cases did not provide for this possibility at all. Thus, one could say that the principle of Article 8 ECHR standing in the way of the application of a foreign law rejecting the establishment of paternity was also accepted in the Surinam case, and that no real attenuation of the standards of Article 8 ECHR was introduced in this case.

In Switzerland, it has also been recognized that a child's right to know his or her filiation, which may be derived from Article 8 ECHR, could occasionally require the normally applicable law being set aside, where the result of the application of this foreign law following from the relevant choice of law rules[93] would lead to the nonrecognition of this right.[94] Here, it is interesting to note that this right can not only be derived from Article 8 ECHR, but also from Article 7 of

---

[91] Rb. Haarlem 11 December 2012, *NIPR* 2013, 24; *JPF* 2013, 131 (note Curry-Sumner).

[92] See further infra Sect. 6.3.3.3.

[93] See with regard to the provision concerning the applicable law on the establishment of paternity Article 68 of the Swiss Private International Law Act.

[94] Bucher 2011, pp. 588–589.

the Convention on the Rights of the Child,[95] as the right of a child to be raised by his or her parents implies the establishment of a paternity link.[96]

The *Tribunal fédéral* has held in two cases that Article 7 of the Convention on the Rights of the Child has direct effect in Switzerland.[97] It would thus also be possible to rely on this provision in Switzerland—at least for children under 18 years old. The issue of the establishment of paternity appears not to have arisen often in Swiss case law. An exception is an unpublished case of the *Tribunal cantonal Neuchâtel*,[98] reported on by Bucher, in which according to him the invocation of Article 8 ECHR could have provided a more elegant solution. Instead, the court manipulated the relevant choice of law rules by referring to the notion of *renvoi* in order to apply a foreign law, which made it possible to establish paternity.[99]

It will be recalled that the French *Cour de Cassation* has also examined a case concerning the establishment of paternity of an Algerian child residing in Algeria against a Frenchman residing in France.[100] In this case, the highest French court found that it was not possible to invoke the public policy exception against the applicable Algerian law, under which it is impossible to establish paternity, because it deemed that there was an insufficient connection of the case with the French legal order to do so.[101] This finding raises a number of issues. Below, the manner in which the rights guaranteed in the ECHR are applied to the issue of applicable law in private international law will be further examined,[102] but for the moment the discussion will be confined to the notion of attenuation.

One could say that in this case at least some attenuation of fundamental rights has been achieved. What is, however, the result of such attenuation of the fundamental rights concerned? In this particular case, the child is unable to establish paternity, resulting in the child not having a father, which will, of course, have further legal consequences. The other side of the coin is that by not setting aside the normally applicable Algerian law, the international harmony of solutions has been preserved. If French law had been applied in this case, there is more than a good chance that the resulting French decision would not have been recognized in Algeria. This would thus have resulted in the child having a father in France, but not in Algeria—a limping legal relationship. Private international law is also concerned with avoiding such limping relationships, and restraint in the

[95] Convention on the Rights of the Child, entry into force 2 September 1990 (UNTS).

[96] Bucher 2011, pp. 588–589.

[97] ATF 125 I 257, see 262; ATF 128 I 63, see 70ff.

[98] *Tribunal cantonal, Neuchâtel*, IIe Cour civile, 26 July 2001. See Bucher 2002, p. 285ff.

[99] Bucher 2002, p. 290ff. Bucher notes that referring to *renvoi* was actually not permissible in this case. Cf. Bucher 2011, p. 589.

[100] Cass. 1re civ., 10 May 2006. This case has also been discussed supra Chap. 4.

[101] This was, incidentally, not the first time such a decision had been taken. The principle was established in Cass. 1[re] civ., 10 February 1993, *Rev.crit dr.int.priv.* 1993, 620 (note Foyer). See Lagarde 2010, pp. 541–542.

[102] See infra Sect. 6.3.3.3.

application of fundamental rights, and the rights guaranteed in the ECHR in particular, helps avoid such situations. This could, for example, be accomplished by allowing Contracting Parties a wide margin of appreciation in the determination of whether under the particular circumstances—the internationality of the situation—the restriction of establishment of paternity would be proportionate to the legitimate aim pursued. However, in this particular case one could seriously question whether a child not having a father in either country is an ideal solution from the perspective of individual justice.[103]

It will finally be recalled that the *Cour de Cassation* appears to have altered its course with regard to the establishment of paternity, as in a similar case concerning the law of the Ivory Coast, the requirement of there being a link with the French legal order was no longer used.[104] The measure of attenuation, which was thus previously used, appears to be no longer in vogue and as a result the application of the foreign law emanating from a third country was denied based on its incompatibility with Article 8 ECHR.

The discussion above on the impact of the ECHR on the establishment of paternity, where this is impossible under the normally applicable foreign law, is an attempt to provide further insight into the consequences of the attenuation of the standard of control of the ECHR. Admittedly, Article 8 ECHR and the establishment of paternity is perhaps not the best example in this regard. There is not really a middle road to be taken for the establishment of paternity. One either establishes a family link, fully aware of the fact that this will probably lead to a limping family relationship because such a decision is unlikely to be recognized, particularly in the country of origin of the normally applicable foreign law, but possibly also in other countries, or one does not establish a family link—essentially interfering with a right guaranteed in Article 8 ECHR.

Yet this is invariably where the proposed attenuation of the standards guaranteed in the ECHR will lead. The attenuation of the standards of the ECHR will eventually lead to an infringement of a right deemed important enough to be protected in the ECHR. This may be permissible where such an infringement of the right in question would also be allowed in a purely internal matter. However, if one were solely to deviate from the standards of the ECHR for private international law purposes (with regard to third countries), one would create an inequality in the protection under the ECHR, which is, in my opinion, too high a price for any consideration relating to the protection of the system of private international law.

---

[103] Cf. Gannagé 2008.

[104] Cass. 1re civ., 26 October 2011, *JDI* 2012, p. 176 (note Guillaumé). See also supra Sect. 4.4.3.3.

6.3.3.3 The Manner of Invocation of Human Rights Against the Applicable Foreign Law

It is at this point of the discussion prudent to return to the issue of the manner of the invocation of human rights in cases before the national courts of the Contracting Parties concerning the issue of applicable law. Above, it has been stated that there are, broadly speaking, two different paths that national courts could follow regarding the manner of invocation of the rights guaranteed in the ECHR against the foreign applicable law violating these rights—the indirect route of use of the public policy exception, and the direct route of the direct application of the ECHR against the applicable foreign law.[105] In this section, first the techniques used in private international law will be further elaborated. Thereafter, the techniques used by the national courts of the Contracting Parties will be examined.

One should note that the manner in which the ECHR is applied by the national courts of the Contracting Parties to the applicable foreign law violating one of the rights guaranteed in the ECHR is, in principle, of no concern to the Strasbourg Institutions, as they are not concerned with the means used by the Contracting Parties to fulfill their obligations.[106] This would only be different if the method used by the national courts in one of the Contracting Parties would somehow lead to a violation of one of the rights guaranteed in the ECHR—if, for example, the method would offer insufficient protection.

The two possible techniques open to the national courts with regard to the applicable foreign law possibly violating one of the rights guaranteed in the ECHR were already distinguished by the German *Bundesverfassungsgericht* in the famous *Spanierbeschluss*.[107] The first solution—direct application—is modeled on the public law model of the direct application of the hierarchically higher norm, while the second solution—use of the public policy exception—is the traditional method of private international law.[108]

These two models could be regarded as the two extremes in the discussion. There are conceivable variations of these two solutions; variations positioned in between these two extremes. It will be recalled that the question of the manner of invocation of human rights standards in issues of applicable law is to a certain extent related to the issue of the standard of control.[109] As will become clear from the discussion below, authors fearing too much of an impact of the rights guaranteed in the ECHR on private international law will usually prefer the solution of the public policy exception as a gateway for human rights' concerns in private international law. Authors concerned about human rights' protection in private

---

[105] See supra Sect. 6.3.2.

[106] See supra Chap. 3.

[107] See supra n. 37.

[108] Kinsch 2007, p. 207ff.

[109] See supra Sect. 6.3.2.

international law becoming too lenient, however, will usually prefer the direct application of the ECHR.[110]

The public policy exception has historically been the preferred means of protection of fundamental rights in issues of private international law.[111] The choice to use this instrument to protect the rights guaranteed in the ECHR in issues of private international law is, therefore, in principle, rather obvious. Some authors have invoked this to justify the (continued) use of the public policy exception, by pointing out that this traditional method has proven itself to be effective over time in finding a balance between the protection of individuals and private international law interests.[112] The reason for using the public policy exception that is most often cited is that this instrument allows for more flexibility. Recourse to this technique will allow the national courts of the Contracting Parties to consider the impact of the ECHR on a case by case basis.[113] It has been argued in a similar vein that the use of the public policy exception would ultimately leave more room for the application of foreign law.[114]

It is also possible to directly apply one of the rights guaranteed in the ECHR in order to protect human rights' concerns in private international law. It should be understood that direct application in this regard only refers to the possibility to directly scrutinize the result of the applicable foreign law against one of the rights guaranteed in the ECHR without the intervention of the public policy exception. This discussion should therefore be separated from the manner in which the rights guaranteed in the ECHR are protected in the national legal orders and the differences between monist and dualist approaches in this regard.[115] It is, strictly speaking, not necessary to consider the rights guaranteed in the ECHR in the context of the public policy exception. In Chap. 4 it has been explained that due to the characteristics of the public policy exception, particularly its relative character, there may be—in cases in which there is only a weak link between the forum and the issue at hand—the possibility that the use of this instrument could lead to a violation of the ECHR.[116] The direct application of the rights guaranteed in the ECHR would eliminate this risk. This solution is, moreover, not entirely alien to private international law, as the direct application of the ECHR is reminiscent of the well-known (in private international law) instrument of (internationally) mandatory rules, or priority rules.[117]

---

[110] See, e.g. Lequette 2004, pp. 112–117.

[111] See Kinsch 2007, pp. 171–192 for an overview of the historical use of the public policy exception in this regard. See also Kinsch 2004a, pp. 419–435.

[112] Gaudemet-Tallon 2005, p. 394.

[113] Kinsch 2007, p. 207ff.

[114] See, e.g., van Hedel 2008, p. 132; Mayer 1991, p. 651ff; Najm 2003, p. 525ff.

[115] See on the status of the ECHR in the national legal order supra Sect. 3.3.

[116] See supra Sect. 4.4.3.2.

[117] Cf. Gannagé 2001, particularly p. 227ff. See also Kiestra 2010; Kinsch 2007, pp. 207–208.

Finally, it has also been suggested that both the traditional use of the public policy exception and direct application of the rights guaranteed in the ECHR are inadequate for the proper protection of the rights guaranteed in the ECHR in private international law, as the public policy exception would not be strict enough, while direct application would lead to a too rigorous defense of human rights.[118] The proposed solution to all this would be a refinement of the public policy exception—aimed at finding the middle ground.[119]

Before further discussing the solutions set out above, it is first necessary to observe that there can be no discussion on how human rights are actually implemented by national courts in issues of private international law. One need only to refer to the cases of national courts discussed above to demonstrate that in virtually all cases, reference was made to the public policy exception (*ordre public*) when assessing the foreign applicable law in relation to the rights guaranteed in the ECHR.[120] The method of the direct application of one of the rights guaranteed in the ECHR is almost never used in the case law of the national courts of the Contracting Parties. Rare exceptions can be found in France[121] and in the Netherlands.[122] It is clear that the manner of reasoning in these latter cases has attracted few followers.

One could, incidentally, note that even though the issue is not of its direct concern, the Court in its decision in *Ammdjadi* does not appear to be troubled by the use of the public policy exception to guarantee human rights in private international law. The Court after all explicitly referred to the use of German *ordre public* in its assessment of whether there had been a violation of Article 8 ECHR in this case.[123] However, one could question whether this should really be regarded as an endorsement of the use of the public policy exception. One could also say that in its reasoning the Court merely follows the route that is followed in the respondent Contracting Party. Then again, one may want to infer from this reasoning that the Court does not a priori reject its use either, for it could have chosen a different approach to the matter.

The fact that the public policy exception appears to be widely used as the point of entry of fundamental rights, and the rights guaranteed in the ECHR in particular,

---

[118] See, e.g., Hammje 1997, pp. 1–31

[119] Hammje 1997, p. 19ff.

[120] See also, e.g., the French (and German) case law discussed by Thoma 2011, pp. 13–18.

[121] *Cour de Paris* 14 June 1994, *Rev.crit.dr.int.priv.* 1995, 308 (note Lequette). The reasoning in this case has generally been negatively received, though, in the French literature. See, e.g., Lequette 2004, at p. 113ff; Najm 2003, p. 563ff.

[122] HR 15 April 1994, *NJ* 1994, 576. This appeared to be for a long time the only case relating to an issue of an applicable foreign law in which Article 8 ECHR was directly considered, instead of by way of the use of the public policy exception. Cf. Van Hedel 2008, p. 131ff. However, as noted above, in a case before the *Rechtbank* Haarlem Article 8 ECHR was fairly recently directly applied to the normally applicable foreign law (Nigerian law). See Rb. Haarlem 11 December 2012, *NIPR* 2013, 24; *JPF* 2013, 131 (note Curry-Sumner).

[123] See supra Sect. 6.3.1.

does not, of course, mean that this is the ideal method. The fact that national courts may be tempted on the basis of the relative character of the public policy exception to disregard the rights guaranteed in the ECHR without first fully examining the relevance of these rights is an important drawback of the use of the public policy exception. The direct application of the ECHR against the applicable foreign law would protect against possible shortcomings, and would thus be my preference.

However, the sharp distinction between these two solutions may be moot. As will be demonstrated below, there are indications to be found in the case law of the national courts of the Contracting Parties, as well as the doctrine, suggesting that the public policy exception would lose its relative character if it were to be used to protect human rights. If this were indeed to be the case, the most important argument against using the method of the use of the public policy exception would be eliminated. Yet this would also essentially remove the differences between these two solutions.

In, for example, the English cases of *Oppenheimer v. Cattermole*[124] and *Kuwait Airways Corpn v. Iraqi Airways Co (Nos 4 and 5)*[125] it was held that foreign laws leading to grave infringements of human rights should not be accepted at all.[126] One could thus state that in these cases there was little left of the relative character of the public policy exception, if anything at all. It could be observed, though, that both these cases did not specifically concern an issue with regard to the rights guaranteed in the ECHR, but rather human rights in general. However, in the Dutch doctrine, it has also been suggested that under certain circumstances, the public policy exception would assume an absolute character.[127] This has been described as the 'iron core' of the public policy exception.[128] In the Swiss doctrine, it has similarly been argued that while the public policy exception usually has a relative character and that its application then depends on the links of the case with the forum, the exception would be where it is used to protect values that are international in their scope, such as human rights.[129]

If one were to include the rights guaranteed in the ECHR in this 'iron core' of the public policy exception, which would result in the public policy exception always being applied when such rights are involved in a case, regardless of the links of this case with the forum, then the demarcation between the methods of the public policy exception and direct application essentially disappears. However, the proponents of the use of the public policy exception value the flexibility which the use of this medium provides in cases concerning fundamental rights in private international law. This flexibility would obviously be largely gone if one were to

[124] *Oppenheimer v. Cattermole* [1976] AC 249.

[125] *Kuwait Airways Corpn v. Iraqi Airways Co (Nos 4 and 5)* [2002] 2 AC 883.

[126] See with regard to these cases supra Sect. 6.3.3.1.

[127] See Strikwerda 2012, p. 53ff.

[128] Jessurun d'Oliveira 1975, pp. 239–261.

[129] Bucher 2004, p. 18.

accept that the rights guaranteed in the public policy exception would be part of the unwavering core of the public policy exception.

The problem in this debate is not so much the existence of this core of the public policy exception, but rather that not everyone would agree that (all of) the rights guaranteed in the ECHR are part of this core. This essentially brings this discussion back to the debate on the absoluteness of the rights guaranteed in the ECHR, considered earlier in Chap. 4.[130]

In conclusion of this debate on the manner in which the rights guaranteed in the ECHR are guaranteed with regard to the issue of applicable law in private international law, I should first reiterate that this is, in principle, a matter for the Contracting Parties themselves. The Court would only take action in the event that the technique used would lead to a result falling short of the required protection following from the ECHR. Thus, in most cases the manner of application is not important. Where the public policy exception is used as an intermediary to invoke one of the rights guaranteed in the ECHR, an issue is not likely to arise. Such an issue with the ECHR would only arise if the public policy exception would not lead to the setting aside of the foreign law violating one of the rights guaranteed in the ECHR, because of the insufficient connection between the case and the legal order. It is for this reason that I would favor a more direct application of the rights guaranteed in the ECHR against the normally applicable foreign law violating one of the rights guaranteed in the ECHR. If there was a need for some room for maneuvering with regard to specific private international law concerns, such room should be sought within the system of the ECHR. However, one should, in my opinion, be careful not to go too far in this regard, as this would lead to the diminished protection of individuals in cases concerning issues of private international law, which is difficult to justify.

6.4 The Application of the ECHR *Promoting* the Application of Foreign Law

Up to this point, the ECHR has only been discussed as a correcting device to the applicable foreign law. However, the application of a foreign law is, of course, not the only possible outcome when a country applies its choice of law rules in a private international law dispute. It is also possible, and arguably more likely, that the choice of law rules of the forum will determine that its own law, the *lex fori*, is the applicable law to the case. This leads us to the issue of whether it is also possible to invoke one of the rights guaranteed in the ECHR against the application of the *lex fori*, and argue that instead a foreign law should be applied.

In order to examine this issue, two separate streams that ultimately flow in the same waters have to be followed. On the one hand, there are some examples to be

130 See supra Sects. 4.4.1 and 4.4.2.

found in both the case law of the Strasbourg Institutions and the jurisprudence of national courts in the Contracting Parties of the invocation of one of the rights guaranteed in the ECHR against the application of the *lex fori*. In such cases, the argument is made that the application of the *lex fori* would violate one of the rights guaranteed in the ECHR. Of course, such an argument is not made in a vacuum. There has to be a law applicable to the case and by arguing against the application of the *lex fori* one thus ultimately ends up with an argument in favor of the application of foreign law. In the literature, the argument has been developed that some of the rights guaranteed in the ECHR actually entail the obligation to apply foreign law.[131] Even though this concerns a different line of argumentation to some extent, these lines eventually blend into each other somewhat, as the intended result of both arguments is the same: the application of foreign law instead of the *lex fori*.

Below, the case law of the Strasbourg Institutions will first be examined (Sect. 6.4.1). This will be followed by a review of some examples taken from the national jurisprudence of the Contracting Parties (Sect. 6.4.2). Thereafter, one will find an elaboration of the argument that some of the rights guaranteed in the ECHR could be interpreted as entailing the obligation to apply foreign law as it has been developed in the literature and the observation that there are few indications for such an interpretation of the ECHR (Sect. 6.4.3).

6.4.1 The Case Law of the Strasbourg Institutions

In *Batali v. Switzerland*,[132] the Commission had to examine several complaints of a Togolese man relating to his divorce, pronounced by the Swiss courts in accordance with Swiss law, from a Togolese woman. The marriage had been celebrated at the Togolese Embassy in Germany. The applicant, inter alia, argued that the Swiss courts had made serious errors by assuming jurisdiction and applying Swiss law to the divorce. He added that the Swiss divorce decision left him being divorced in Switzerland while he was still married in Togo, and that his family was split up according to two different legal orders.

Although the applicant thus admittedly raised some interesting issues, particularly with regard to application of the *lex fori*, which would allegedly lead to the divorce not being recognized in Togo, it should be noted that he did not rely on any specific provisions of the ECHR. The fact that the Commission made short shrift of the complaint may thus not be surprising. The Commission held in relation to the complaint concerning the Swiss divorce that—working on the assumption that the complaints raised an issue at all with regard to Articles 8 and 12 ECHR—it simply saw no lack of respect for the guarantees contained in these rights in this case.

---

131 Jayme 2003, p. 97. See further infra Sect. 6.4.3.

132 *Batali v. Switzerland*, no. 20765/92, 9 January 1995.

It is unfortunate that the Commission did not really examine this case, as important questions of private international law regarding limping legal relationships were raised. The Strasbourg Institutions have never examined this issue and its response to the complaints raised in this case would have been interesting.

A much more recent case of the Court, *Losonci Rose and Rose v. Switzerland*,[133] concerning the right to a name, provides us with an example of one in which the ECHR was successfully invoked against the application of the *lex fori*. This case concerned a couple, Laszlo Losonci Rose, a Hungarian national, and Iris Rose, who had both Swiss and French nationalities. The couple lived in Switzerland at the time. The applicants, who intended to get married, wanted to keep their own names after marriage, citing the difficulties of changing their names, respectively, under Hungarian and French law and the fact that the wife was well-known under her maiden name as reasons. The husband therefore applied for the application of Hungarian law to his surname. However, the couple's request and subsequent appeal were denied. Thus the applicants decided, in order to be able to marry, to choose the wife's surname as the family name under Swiss law. The couple got married and their names were thereafter registered as 'Rose' for the wife and 'Losonci Rose, né Losonci' for the husband.

After the marriage, the husband requested that his name be replaced by the single surname 'Losonci', as permitted under Hungarian law, while his wife's name would remain unchanged. However, the Swiss *Tribunal fédéral* ultimately found that after choosing the wife's surname, he no longer had the opportunity to have his name governed by Hungarian law. With regard to the applicants' complaint that the refusal was unconstitutional, as it violated the principle of equal treatment of the sexes, the Tribunal found that it was not permitted to introduce amendments that had already been rejected by the Federal Parliament.[134]

Relying on Articles 8 and 14 ECHR, the applicants claimed in Strasbourg that they had been discriminated against in the enjoyment of their family and private life. They argued in particular that had their sexes been reversed, there would not have been a problem, as they then could have chosen their preferred names: in the case of a woman of foreign origin, Swiss law would allow the woman's surname to be governed by her national law. It was clear before the Court that there was an inequality of treatment in this case. The Swiss authorities, however, claimed to have pursued the legitimate aim of reflecting family unity by way of a single 'family name'.

In assessing this argument, the Court noted that while Contracting Parties, in principle, have a wide discretion with regard to measures reflecting family unity, there had to be compelling reasons to justify a difference in treatment based on the ground of sex alone. The Court noted that there is a consensus emerging amongst the Contracting Parties concerning equality between spouses in the choice of the family name, while the activities of the United Nations are also heading in this

133 *Losonci Rose and Rose v. Switzerland*, no. 664/06, 9 November 2010.

134 *Tribunal federal*, 24 May 2005, 5A.4/2005 (unpublished). See with regard to this case Bucher 2007, pp. 315–321.

direction. The Court thus concluded that there had been a violation of Article 14 ECHR taken in conjunction with Article 8 ECHR.[135]

Although this case at first sight may appear to be an example of the successful invocation of one of the rights guaranteed in the ECHR *against* the *lex fori*, and thus simultaneously promoting the application of foreign law, one should be cautious in drawing this conclusion. It should be noted that this is first and foremost a discrimination case.[136] The Court ultimately did not per se find that people with a double nationality have on the basis of the ECHR the right to have their surname after marriage governed by their national law instead of the *lex fori*. The Court merely found that the Swiss rules on the determination of a person's name were discriminatory on the ground of sex alone, as the Swiss law did offer the opportunity to have the surname governed by the national law to a woman, but not to a man. However, it is worth emphasizing that it was the Swiss rules in this regard that offered this opportunity in the first place—at least to a woman, that is. Thus the Court could find that there had been an unjustified difference in treatment regarding the right of a person's name based on sex alone. However, it is doubtful that had Swiss law not offered this opportunity to women having a double nationality that on the basis of Article 8 ECHR a successful argument could have been made that a foreign law should have been applied instead of the *lex fori*.

6.4.2 Jurisprudence of the EU and the National Courts of the Contracting Parties

There is not much case law in which one of the rights guaranteed in the ECHR is invoked in order to argue in an issue of private international that the *lex fori* should be set aside in favor of foreign law. The argument raised in *Batali* that the application of the *lex fori* would lead to a limping legal relationship appears not to have been developed in the case law of national courts with regard to the rights guaranteed in the ECHR. However, one could say that the Court's case law in *Losonci* has found some support in national case law, although this national case law is not based on the rights guaranteed in the ECHR. Additionally, there have been some instances in which the ECHR has been invoked against the application of the *lex fori* in entirely different circumstances, albeit without much success.

There have been a number of cases in European and national case law regarding the law applicable to a name.[137] These cases particularly concerned the names of

[135] The Court further noted, in response to the fact that the *Tribunal fédéral* had held that it could not introduce any amendments that had previously been rejected by Parliament (see supra n. 134), that this had no bearing on Switzerland's international responsibility under the ECHR.

[136] See also Kinsch 2011, pp. 39, 41.

[137] See with regard to the right to a name, human rights, and EU law also Rossolilo 2010, pp. 143–156.

newborns where there were some facts linking the situation to more than one EU Member State. In these cases the rights guaranteed in the ECHR could arguably have been invoked, but the decisions were based on the case law of the ECJ in *Garcia Avello*[138] and *Grunkin-Paul.*[139] In a Dutch case, for example, the applicants, a Polish couple, succeeded in having Polish law applied to the last name of their children, who had both Dutch and Polish nationalities, even though the normally applicable law was the *lex fori*, Dutch law. The Polish couple had, inter alia, invoked Article 8 ECHR in this regard, but the Dutch court ultimately decided in their favor based on the ECJ's judgment in *Garcia Avello.*[140]

In a case before the English High Court, *NG v KR*,[141] Article 1 of Protocol No. 1 ECHR, the right to property, was invoked against the application of the *lex fori* to a prenuptial agreement. This case concerned the aftermath of a breakdown of the marriage between a (former) husband and wife, where the latter was very rich. At issue was the validity of a German prenuptial agreement between the parties which made no provision for either spouse upon divorce. The wife argued that under both the laws of Germany (where she was originally from) and France (where he was originally from) the agreement would be valid and enforced. Yet under English law the agreement was invalid. She submitted that it would be a violation of her human rights, particularly Article 1 of Protocol No. 1 ECHR, if the English court were to apply English law to the agreement and declare the agreement invalid.

The court, however, found that it is a central pillar of the English system of private international law that in the field of family law, England is a *lex fori* country.[142] It further held that while Article 1 of Protocol No. 1 ECHR was generally applicable, the right guaranteed in this Article was not infringed. It is interesting to observe that the English court explicitly relied on the margin of appreciation, the width of which it derived from *J.A. Pye (Oxford) Ltd and J.A. Pye (Oxford) Land Ltd v. the United Kingdom.*[143] While the Court in Strasbourg is not a proponent of national courts allotting themselves a margin of appreciation,[144] there is little evidence in this case to suggest that the English court should have found a violation of Article 1 of Protocol No. 1 ECHR in this case, as the interference with the wife's right to property would appear to meet the requirements set out in Article 1 of Protocol No. 1 ECHR.

---

[138] ECJ 2 October 2003, Case C-148/02, *Garcia Avello*, [2003] ECR, I-11613.

[139] ECJ 14 October 2008, Case C-353/06, *Grunkin and Paul*, [2008] ECR, I-7639.

[140] Rb. Amsterdam 23 September 2009, *NIPR* 2010, 21.

[141] [2008] EWHC 1532 (Fam), [2009] 1 FLR 1478, [2009] 1 FCR 35, [2008] Fam Law 1082.

[142] At 87.

[143] At 134. The English court particularly referred to *J.A. Pye (Oxford) Ltd and J.A. Pye (Oxford) Land Ltd v. the United Kingdom* [GC], no. 44302/02, paras 71, 74 and 75, ECHR 2007-III. It is interesting to note that *J.A. Pye* and the case law considered in this case with regard to the margin of appreciation are all concerned with the right to property, but cover a wide variety of subjects.

[144] See supra Sect. 3.5.2.

A case before the Swiss *Tribunal fédéral* between a husband and a wife, both Kosovo residents, concerned the appeal of the husband against the decision of a lower Swiss court to award the wife custody of their child.[145] In earlier criminal proceedings the husband had been convicted and imprisoned for sexual acts with children, sexual coercion, and rape. The husband, inter alia, invoked Articles 8 and 14 ECHR against the decision to award the mother custody, arguing, inter alia, that under their national law young children are usually awarded to their father.

The Swiss court found that awarding a child to one of the parents is a serious infringement of the right of the other parent to respect for his family life. Under certain circumstances such interference may be allowed, and the Tribunal found that Swiss law is, in this regard, up to the standards of the ECHR. With regard to the argument that the parties' national law usually awards children to their father, the Tribunal found that it matters little that the national law of the parties—which was not applicable to the case because Article 62(2) of the Swiss Private International Law Act determined that Swiss law was the applicable law—provided another solution. The Tribunal thus held that Article 8 ECHR had not been violated. The Tribunal further held that it was unable to see how any of this could lead to a difference in treatment between the parties and that the invocation of Article 14 ECHR had not been substantiated.

The prospects of the invocation of one of the rights guaranteed in the ECHR against the application of the *lex fori* in favor of a foreign law remain uncertain at best. This may not be altogether surprising, though. It is not difficult to see why national courts of the Contracting Parties would be less than inclined to find that the applicable *lex fori* would fall short and that the application of a foreign law would be required from the perspective of the ECHR. It follows from the Court's case law in *Losonci* that this is only different where in a private international law dispute the application of the *lex fori* would lead to a discriminatory result. However, in this case a violation of the ECHR was only found because the possibility to apply foreign law to a name depended on the sex of the applicant, a discriminatory situation which could not be justified by the authorities.

6.4.3 The Application of the ECHR Promoting the Application of Foreign Law: Debate in the Literature

In the literature, the thesis has been developed that Article 8 ECHR could also be regarded as entailing a right to the application of a foreign law.[146] Contrary to the situation concerning the issue of the recognition and enforcement of foreign

145 Judgment of the *Tribunal fédéral*, 5P.250/2001, 17 April 2002 (unpublished).

146 Jayme 2003. The author has further elaborated on this idea regarding cultural identity and the consequences thereof for private international law in Jayme 1995. See also Vonken 1998, pp. 106–107.

judgments, where the Court has found in several cases that the ECHR may also entail the obligation to recognize foreign judgments,[147] this issue has mostly been a theoretical discussion with regard to the issue of applicable law. Even though there are some examples to be found of the invocation of the ECHR against the *lex fori* in national case law, the argument that Article 8 ECHR would entail a right to the application of foreign law appears not to have been made.[148] In support of this claim a little known decision by the Commission, *G. and E. v. Norway*, has been pointed to by Jayme, the developer of the theory.[149]

The applicants were two Norwegian Lapps. They were part of a group that had protested in the vicinity of the Norwegian Parliament against the decision of the Norwegian government to construct a hydroelectric power station on their land. After refusing to leave the site of the protest, the police eventually removed the group by force and the two applicants were subsequently prosecuted and ultimately convicted for refusing to obey an order of the police. The applicants filed a number of complaints in Strasbourg, ranging from their arrest being an infringement of their right to freedom of expression (Article 10 ECHR) to complaints against the lack of protection of the Lapps as a minority.

The most important part of the decision, for our purposes, is the fact that the Commission considered that the applicants' complaints had to be partly examined under Article 8 ECHR. In this regard the Commission found the following:

> The Commission is of the opinion that, under Article 8, a minority group is, in principle, entitled to claim the right to respect for the particular lifestyle it may lead as being 'private life', 'family life' or 'home'.[150]

This consideration relating to Article 8 ECHR has been seized upon to pose the question of whether the ECHR also guarantees the right—or at least strengthens a claim thereto, one could add—to have a specific law applied to a judicial matter out of respect for the cultural identity of a person.[151] Others have added that one could easily extend such a right to legal cultures in general.[152] Thus a person could then argue that his or her law should be applied to a certain case out of respect for his or her legal culture.[153] It is interesting to note that this would essentially mean

---

[147] See infra Chap. 7.

[148] See the case law discussed supra Sects. 6.4.1 and 6.4.2.

[149] *G. and E. v. Norway*, no. 9278/81 & 9415/81 (joined), DR 35, p. 30 (decision of 3 October 1983).

[150] *G. and E. v. Norway*, DR 35, p. 35 (citations in original).

[151] Jayme 2003, p. 97. Cf. Looschelders 2001, pp. 468–469; Matscher 1998, p. 216; Rutten 1998, p. 801.

[152] van Loon 1993, p. 139.

[153] If one were to follow this line of reasoning, one could perhaps in the case of a religious-based law even attempt to base such a claim on Article 9 ECHR, which guarantees the right to freedom, thought, and religion. However, to my knowledge no such attempts have been made. I would, incidentally, argue that this line of reasoning offers little chance of success. The Court in its case law on Article 9 ECHR has given no indication that this right could entail the right to have one's religious-based law applied instead of the normally applicable law.

a return to the first principle that was used in Europe to determine what law should be applied to a person, namely that everyone had the right to have his or her own law applied to him or her.[154]

It should be noted, though, that the Strasbourg Institutions have never really moved the discussion in this direction. The Court has admittedly since confirmed that the protection of minority lifestyles is protected under Article 8 ECHR and it has even held that there are positive obligations for the State in this regard.[155] Thus the Contracting Parties not only have to abstain from interfering with minority lifestyles, but they also have to actively help preserve such lifestyles. Yet the Court has never stated that this respect for the cultural identity of a person could also entail the right to have a specific law applied. It would indeed be difficult to argue that this right to a cultural identity on the basis of Article 8 ECHR would take precedence over the laws of the forum.[156]

6.5 The Impact of the ECHR on the Act of Applying Foreign Law

In this part, an entirely different aspect of the issue of applicable law in private international law will be discussed, namely the act of applying foreign law. Problems related to the identification of the content of the applicable foreign law are a well-known problem of private international law.[157] A court, after having found in consultation with the choice of law rules of the forum that a foreign law is the law applicable to the case, is then faced with the question of how to find this foreign law. Even though this could be a difficult process, which may even require the help of third parties, courts have to be wary of unnecessary delays, which may result in a violation of the right to have a trial within a reasonable time, as prescribed by Article 6(1) ECHR.

In this part, the impact of the ECHR on this process will be discussed. First, the case law of the Strasbourg Institutions will be reviewed (Sect. 6.5.1). Next, a few examples taken from the case law of national legal orders will be discussed (Sect. 6.5.2). Finally, the practice regarding the act of applying foreign law by national courts of the Contracting Parties will be assessed in light of the requirements following from the ECHR (Sect. 6.5.3).

154 See, e.g., Pontier 2005, pp. 10–11.

155 See in this regard particularly *Chapman v. the United Kingdom* [GC], no. 27238/95, paras 93 and 96, ECHR 2001-I. The principles found in *Chapman* have been further developed in *Muñoz Díaz v. Spain*, no. 49151/07, ECHR 2009.

156 See Bucher 2000, pp. 92–93; Coester-Waltjen 1998, pp. 15–16; Kokott 1998, p. 91. See also Kinsch 2007, p. 148ff.

157 See, e.g., See, e.g., Bogdan 2011, p. 49.

6.5.1 The Case Law of the Strasbourg Institutions

There is only one case in which the Strasbourg Institutions were specifically concerned with procedural issues relating to the application of foreign law. In *Karalyos and Huber v. Hungary and Greece*[158] the Court examined certain aspects of the act of applying foreign law. The Court decided that a Contracting Party—in this case Hungary—cannot rely on the difficulties relating to the ascertainment of the foreign applicable law to explain very lengthy proceedings—in this particular case the length of the proceedings had risen to nine years, without the case even reaching an appeal court.

The case concerned a claim by a Hungarian illusionist and his wife, who entered into a contract with a Greek company to perform a show onboard a cruise ship. Unfortunately, on the same day that the Greek company shipped the illusionist's equipment onboard there was a fire which destroyed the applicants' equipment. The Greek company refused to pay for the damages. The illusionist subsequently brought an action before a Hungarian court. The court needed information on Greek law and a request was made through the appropriate Hungarian authorities to gather this information from their Greek counterparts on the basis of the Greek-Hungarian bilateral Treaty on Legal Assistance and the European Convention on Information on Foreign Law.

This started a back and forth between the Hungarian and Greek authorities, which yielded little. After several unsuccessful attempts by the Hungarian authorities to gather the required information, they suggested to the court that Hungarian law should be applied to the case. However, the court found that the information on Greek law was still required, as it held that the Greek authorities' refusal to provide information on a complex legal issue did not render it impossible to establish the content of the foreign law. The case was still pending before the Hungarian court during the proceedings in Strasbourg, where the applicants complained about the length of the proceedings against both Hungary and Greece.

Only the complaint against Hungary was held to be admissible.[159] The Court found, while acknowledging that there may have been difficult legal issues of

---

[158] *Karalyros and Huber v. Hungary and Greece,* no. 75116/01, 6 April 2004.

[159] One may note that the application was directed against both Hungary and Greece. However, the Court made short work of the complaint against Greece, as it declared the application inadmissible *ratione personae*. It noted in this regard that the proceedings were instituted in Hungary and not in Greece, and insofar as the complaint was directed at the reluctance of the Greek authorities to cooperate with the Hungarian authorities on the basis of the relevant international treaties, the Court held that any possible failure in this regard could not be the subject matter of a case before the Court. See *Karalyros and Huber v. Hungary and Greece*, no. 75116/01, para 40, 6 April 2004. The Court repeated that it is only competent to review the ECHR and not any other international agreement, as it had stated in *Calabro v. Italy*, no. 59895/00, 21 March 2002. Although the Court correctly decided that Greece could in this case not be held responsible for its failure to cooperate under these treaties, it should be noted with regard to international treaties that the Court has previously interpreted the ECHR in light of other

foreign law, that the length of the proceedings could not be explained by this fact alone. The Court considered that the defendants could not be reproached for their (in)action, as the Hungarian court was responsible for the proper administration of justice. The Court noted that it was 'regrettable' that the content of the relevant Greek law could not be established after a period of 9 years.[160] It was unclear to the Court why the Hungarian court did not try to locate an expert on this matter in Hungary, or why the Hungarian court did not apply Hungarian law as is allowed under the Hungarian International Private Law Decree. The Court also observed that the attempts made by the Hungarian authorities to gather the relevant information had not been conducted very efficiently.[161] All this led the Court to conclude that the delays in the case were mainly attributable to Hungary and that there had been a violation of Article 6(1) ECHR.

6.5.2 *Jurisprudence of the National Courts of the Contracting Parties*

There is little specific national jurisprudence relating to issues of the establishment of the applicable foreign law and the impact of the ECHR. In the Netherlands a case before the *Gerechtshof* Arnhem concerned a claim regarding a loan.[162] Australian law, particularly the law of Queensland, was the law applicable to the case. Before the appeal court issues concerning the gathering of evidence in Australia arose. Invoking the 1970 Hague Convention on the Taking of Evidence Abroad,[163] the claimant applied to have evidence heard in Australia by an Australian judge. The defendant argued that this would cost a lot of extra time and would be expensive. He argued that the costs of the proceedings should remain reasonable. The Dutch court considered that although it is the basic principle in the Netherlands that the judge should hear witnesses himself, under these circumstances an Australian judge performing these duties would have to suffice. Such a request cannot be dismissed solely on the basis of costs. The claimant was not abusing his procedural rights, according to the appeal court. The defendant's rights guaranteed in Article 6(1) ECHR which consisted of, inter alia, a fair trial, including effective access to a judge and a trial within a reasonable time, would not

(Footnote 159 continued)
international agreements. A pertinent example of this practice would be the Court's case law concerning international child abduction and the Hague Convention.

[160] *Karalyros and Huber v. Hungary and Greece*, no. 75116/01, para 35, 6 April 2004.

[161] The authorities had, for example, made some administrative errors, and did not resort to alternative and faster methods of communication than regular mail until 5 years had passed.

[162] Hof Arnhem 4 November 2003, *NIPR* 2004, 43.

[163] Convention on the Taking of Evidence Abroad in Civil or Commercial Matters, 18 March 1970, entry into force 7 October 1972 (UNTS).

be violated by having an Australian judge gather evidence in Australia, according to the appeal court.

While this case is not really concerned with the establishment of the content of foreign law, but rather with the more general issue of hearing experts abroad (although these experts may also advise the requesting court on issues of Australian law), it does demonstrate some of the issues with which a national court may be concerned when establishing the content of foreign law. Namely, there are two parties in a dispute, both of whom have procedural rights, inter alia, following from Article 6(1) ECHR. Where one party may want to get to the bottom of the exact content of the foreign law and would argue a denial of justice in the case of anything less, the opposing party may feel that such a search may lead to unreasonable costs and an unreasonable length of the proceedings.[164] It is up to the courts of the national legal orders in the first place to find a balance in this regard, guided by the requirements following from Article 6(1) ECHR, even though the Court in Strasbourg will ultimately decide such issues.

In Switzerland, the *Tribunal fédéral* has dealt with an interesting issue regarding the establishment of the content of foreign law.[165] This case concerned a dispute over the management of a family foundation, which had been set up by Swiss lawyers in Liechtenstein at the request of an Egyptian resident. The two lawyers became members of the board. After the Egyptian man passed away, one of the heirs filed a request before the Swiss courts to obtain all the records relating to the establishment of the foundation. The heir based his standing before the court on a report by the Swiss Institute of Comparative Law, which recognized his quality as an heir according to Egyptian law. The two lawyers were ordered to hand over the documents. The lawyers appealed against this decision. On appeal, the appeal court also turned to the Swiss Institute of Comparative Law to answer a question of Egyptian law. The two Swiss lawyers opposed the choice of the Institute as an expert, invoking, inter alia, Article 6(1) ECHR. Their protest against this decision was set aside by the appeal court.

Before the *Tribunal fédéral*, the lawyers again questioned the impartiality of the Institute, based on Article 6(1) ECHR. The *Tribunal fédéral* first emphasized that Article 16 of the Swiss Private International Law Act contains the obligation for the judge to establish *ex officio* the content of foreign law. For neighboring countries the judge should not, according to the *Tribunal fédéral*, routinely seek the advice of an expert, as the application of foreign law to concrete cases is within its expertise and not that of the expert. However, with regard to the law originating from non-neighboring countries, the advice of experts, such as the Swiss Institute, may be necessary, the *Tribunal fédéral* acknowledged. The appeal court had held that the scientific contribution of the Swiss Institute, which consisted of giving information on foreign law and responding to questions of the court, could not be compared to the advice given to a litigator. The *Tribunal fédéral* did not find this

[164] See with regard to the denial of justice supra Chap. 5.

[165] Judgment of the *Tribunal fédéral*, 1P.390/2004/col, 28 October 2004 (unpublished).

reasoning to be unsustainable and held that while generally speaking it is untenable that the same person would first give advice to one of the parties and thereafter would be asked to function as an independent expert in the same procedure, the Swiss Institute of Comparative Law cannot be equated with private counsel.

In this case, the role of expert institutes in establishing the content of foreign law was thus examined. The problem for courts, which are expected *ex officio* to establish the content of foreign law, is that they virtually cannot do so without the help of such institutes.[166] However, these institutes may also assist other parties in proceedings, which could lead to the awkward situation in which such an institute functions both as a witness for one of the parties and as an independent expert of the court. In Switzerland, the Federal Tribunal has decided that such a situation may be tenable, given the specific position of the Swiss Institute for Comparative Law.[167]

6.5.3 The Practice in National Legal Orders and the Impact of Article 6(1) ECHR

With regard to the particular issue of the establishment of the content of the foreign applicable law by national courts, it should be noted that there is a clear distinction in Europe regarding the position that foreign law has in the legal order. In continental Europe the starting point is generally that a court must apply foreign law *ex officio*, as foreign law is considered law just like the *lex fori*, while in England foreign law is treated as fact, which means that parties have to plead foreign law and offer proof.[168] Thus, if in England parties fail to argue that foreign law should be applied, the court will apply the *lex fori*, i.e., English law, while in continental Europe such failure, in principle, should have no effect, as the court is obligated to *ex officio* apply the foreign law.[169] This does not mean, however, that courts in continental Europe may not ask the parties to assist them in establishing the content of the foreign law. In the Netherlands, for example, courts may ask the

[166] Examples of such institutes are the 'Internationaal Juridisch Instituut' (International Legal Institute) in the Netherlands and the Swiss Institute for Comparative Law.

[167] See supra n. 165, at consideration no. 2.3.

[168] See, e.g., Esplugues Mota 2011; Geeroms 2004; Fentiman 1998.

[169] One could note that this difference has also led to issues regarding EU instruments on applicable law. As the issue could, e.g., not be resolved in relation to the Rome II Regulation, a review clause has been added providing for a further study on the effect of this issue. See Article 30 of Regulation (EC) No. 864/2007 on the law applicable to noncontractual obligations (Rome II), *OJ* 2007, L 199/40. The treatment of foreign law is also being monitored by the Hague Convention. See, e.g., Information Document no. 10 of April 2012 on Access to Foreign Law in Civil and Commercial Matters, http://www.hcch.net/upload/wop/gap2012info10en.pdf. Accessed March 2014. See for an interesting study on this issue also de Boer 1996, pp. 223–427.

parties for help in their task of establishing the content of the foreign law.[170] Switzerland has a similar practice for family law cases, and for pecuniary claims the judge can even impose the burden of proof on the parties.[171]

Given the status of foreign law in England, one would expect the possible impact of Article 6(1) ECHR on the issue of the establishment of the content of foreign law to be limited. If one of the parties were to plead that foreign law is applicable in a certain situation, but is unable to prove the content of this foreign law within a reasonable time, this should not lead to a delay in the proceedings, as an English court could simply apply English law without much further ado. However, this may be too simple. It should be noted that one of the prevalent methods of proof of foreign law[172]—by way of expert witnesses—has been criticized, because this method may lead to excessive delays and costs.[173] In order to prevent unnecessary delays and costs, English domestic courts have been given the power to control all expert evidence under the Civil Procedure Rules.[174]

In the Netherlands and Switzerland, however, the issue of a possible delay in the proceedings and the resulting issue with Article 6(1) ECHR due to a national court's inability to expeditiously establish the content of the applicable foreign law is more likely to arise, as in both countries the judge, in principle, has to apply foreign law *ex officio*.[175] However, in both countries there are several mechanisms to prevent such issues. As has already been discussed above, in both countries it is possible for national courts to ask for the assistance of the litigating parties in the establishment of the content of the applicable foreign law, whereby it should be noted that Swiss courts can be more forceful in claims for financial interest.[176]

There is also the European Convention on Information on Foreign Law,[177] a treaty of the Council of Europe that has been ratified not only by the Netherlands and Switzerland, but also by the United Kingdom.[178] Although the treaty is open for signature of all the Member States of the Council of Europe, and for accession by non-Member States, its impact is somewhat limited by the fact that only three non-Member States have ratified the treaty.[179] National courts in both countries may

---

170 However, national courts are in such an event not obligated to follow the parties' lead. See Strikwerda 2012, pp. 32–33 and the case law cited there.

171 See Article 16(1) of the Swiss Private International Law Act.

172 See generally with regard to how foreign law is proved Fentiman 1998, p. 173ff.

173 Cheshire et al. 2010, p. 114.

174 See Fentiman 1998, pp. 188–202; Cf. Cheshire et al. 2010, pp. 117–119.

175 In Switzerland this has, incidentally, fairly recently been confirmed in a number of judgments of the *Tribunal fédéral*. See ATF 131 III 153; ATF 131 III 511; ATF 132 III 609 and ATF 132 III 661.

176 See supra n. 171.

177 European Convention on Information on Foreign Law, CETS no. 62, London 7 June 1968.

178 A list of all signatories may be found at conventions.coe.int.

179 Belarus, Costa Rica, and Mexico.

also enlist the assistance of institutes specialized in issues of foreign law.[180] If, despite the above-mentioned mechanisms, it proves to be impossible to establish the content of the foreign applicable law, the Swiss Private International Law Act stipulates that Swiss law applies.[181] In the Netherlands, however, there is no such solution. Multiple solutions to this problem have been defended, but up until this point none of these have prevailed.[182] In light of the requirements following from Article 6(1) ECHR, and particularly the obligation to have a fair trial within a reasonable time, it may be useful to introduce a similar rule in the Netherlands.

6.6 Conclusion

In this chapter, the impact of the rights guaranteed in the ECHR on the issue of applicable law in private international law has been examined. This chapter has only been concerned with the impact of the ECHR on the result of the application of the forum's choice of law rules—the applicable law—as the Court's case law is the starting point of this research and the Court, in principle, does not concern itself with the examination of (private international law) rules *in abstracto*. Three separate issues relating to the impact of the ECHR on the issue have been distinguished: the invocation of the ECHR *against* the foreign applicable law; the invocation of the ECHR *promoting* the application of foreign law and against the *lex fori*; and, finally, the impact of the ECHR on the act of applying foreign law. This latter issue differs from the first two as it is concerned with a procedural issue, while the first two issues are concerned with the impact of the ECHR on the material result of the application of a foreign law. Consequently, the rights guaranteed in the ECHR that are concerned vary. With regard to the procedural issue of the act of applying foreign law, the procedural guarantees of Article 6(1) ECHR are relevant, while in principle any substantive right guaranteed in the ECHR could be invoked against either the result of the application of a foreign law or the *lex fori*.

Before turning to these three main questions regarding the impact of the ECHR on the issue of applicable law in private international law, first the question of whether the ECHR can be applied at all to this issue, particularly where the foreign law originates from a third country, has been revisited. In addition to confirming that this is indeed the case, some case law of the Commission regarding the responsibility of Contracting Parties for the application of a foreign law violating one of the rights guaranteed in the ECHR originating from another Contracting Party has been examined in this chapter. It has been demonstrated that solely the

[180] In the Netherlands the 'Internationaal Juridisch Instituut' (International Legal Institute) is frequently asked for assistance, while in Switzerland the Swiss Institute of Comparative law is often asked for advice.

[181] See Article 16(2) of the Swiss Private International Law Act.

[182] Strikwerda 2012, pp. 32–33.

Contracting Party whose courts have applied the repugnant foreign law can be held responsible in such a case. There can be no co-responsibility, even in the event of the foreign applicable law originating from another Contracting Party.

Even though the Court has yet to deliver a judgment on an issue of private international law in which the application of foreign law resulted in a violation of one of the rights guaranteed in the ECHR, it has generally been accepted that the application of a foreign law could result in a violation. However a number of interesting issues remain open. These issues, such as the level of scrutiny of the Court, the possible attenuation of the standards of the ECHR with regard to a foreign applicable law, in that there would remain more room for the application of an aberrant foreign law, and the techniques the national courts of the Contracting Parties could use in this regard, have been examined in this chapter.

The Court's case law concerning the impact of the ECHR on a foreign applicable law possibly violating one of the rights guaranteed in the ECHR is not yet crystallized. It has been argued that the best approach to such an issue would be to regard the foreign applicable law as interfering with one of the rights guaranteed, as a restriction to the right guaranteed in the ECHR. Whether such a restriction is permissible would consequently depend on the particular right concerned. Article 8 ECHR (the right to private and family life) and Article 1 of Protocol No. 1 ECHR (the right to property) are the most frequently invoked rights of the ECHR concerning the issue of applicable law. Both these rights are qualified rights and therefore not absolute. In assessing whether a foreign applicable law violates one of these rights guaranteed in the ECHR, the Court should follow its usual approach with regard to restrictions under these Articles. In relation to a restriction following from a foreign applicable law, the most important requirement would be the necessity in a democratic society and, in particular, the proportionality of the decision to apply foreign law. The margin of appreciation which Contracting Parties enjoy in this decision could then be used to properly weigh possible private international law concerns.

It has been argued by many that the standards of the ECHR should be attenuated with regard to a foreign applicable law, particularly where this foreign law would originate from a third country. While there may be good reasons for some attenuation, it is my contention that such an attenuation of the standards can only be allowed insofar as it is permissible under the ECHR. The extent to which such attenuation is thus possible with regard to a particular right guaranteed in the ECHR is therefore decisive here. It could also be noted that the few cases of the Court directly concerned with the invocation of one of the rights guaranteed in the ECHR against the applicable law do not offer much evidence for an attenuated standard in this regard.

The observations on Article 1 ECHR should also guide the discussion on the technique used by the national courts of the Contracting Parties. National courts can still use the public policy exception in deciding whether to set aside the normally applicable foreign law violating one of the rights guaranteed in the ECHR. There is no formal need to change course, as the Court in examining whether there has been a violation of the ECHR will only look at the result the national courts have reached in a certain case and not the method leading up to this result. However, the fact that attenuation of the standards of the ECHR in the issue of applicable law in private international law is only allowed insofar as permitted under the ECHR does entail that national courts would do well to take the ECHR into account, as the setting aside of the ECHR on the basis of the public policy exception for lack of a significant link with the forum could result in a violation of the ECHR. A form of the direct application of one of the rights guaranteed in the ECHR against the applicable foreign law would therefore appear to be a good idea, because such a technique would force national courts to put human rights concerns to the forefront and would consequently decrease the risk of human rights not being emphasized enough.

The rights guaranteed in the ECHR may not only be invoked against the normally applicable foreign law, but they could also be invoked against the most frequent outcome of the application by a court of the choice of law rules of the forum: the *lex fori*. However, it could be observed that the invocation of the rights guaranteed against the *lex fori* has not had much success before the Strasbourg Institutions or the national courts of the Contracting Parties. A notable exception is the Court's judgment in *Losonci*, although this case was more concerned with the discriminatory nature of the relevant Swiss private international law rules on names, as the application of the *lex fori* essentially took away a substantive result (a certain name) which could have been reached by applying a foreign law; this option would have been available if the applicant had been a woman. Under those circumstances it is possible to invoke the ECHR against the *lex fori*. However, in principle, the application of the *lex fori* over a foreign law would appear not to result in a violation of the ECHR.

The final part of this chapter has been concerned with an entirely different aspect of the impact of the ECHR on the issue of applicable law in private international law, namely the impact of the ECHR on the act of applying foreign law. It follows from the Court's case law on this subject that national courts should establish the content of the foreign applicable law in an expeditious manner. Otherwise, the Contracting Parties may be held responsible for the length of the proceedings, regardless of the difficulties national courts may face in the identification of the content of the foreign law. If all else fails, national courts should resort to the application of the *lex fori*. A review of the practice in the national legal orders under analysis has demonstrated that national courts generally have the tools to prevent such violations of Article 6 ECHR.

What, in conclusion, follows from the discussion on the impact of the ECHR on the issue of applicable law in this chapter is that the Convention's impact is mostly incidental. What I mean by that is that while it is certainly conceivable that the application of a foreign law could result in a violation of one of the rights guaranteed in the ECHR, this is an isolated occurrence which would not appear to have any long-term effects on the system of private international law. In fact, the private international law regimes of States have always taken into account the possibility to set aside a foreign applicable law.

Nevertheless, a reconsideration of the technique used by national courts of the Contracting Parties to scrutinize a foreign applicable law with regard to the rights guaranteed in the ECHR, or at least an increased awareness of the impact of these rights in relation to the use of the public policy exception, may be necessary. The observation on the impact of the ECHR being an isolated occurrence also applies to the invocation of the ECHR against the *lex fori*, albeit that it has been demonstrated that this is an even more rare scenario, as there is little evidence that the ECHR can be successfully invoked against the *lex fori*, except in cases where the invocation of the *lex fori* leads to a discriminatory result.

This may only be different with regard to the third aspect which has been distinguished in this chapter—the impact of the ECHR on the ascertainment of the applicable foreign law. While the national courts of Contracting Parties that have been examined in this chapter appear, in principle, to have the tools to deal with issues relating to the finding of the content of the foreign applicable law, this remains a difficult problem of private international law in general, and thus also deserves attention from the point of view of Article 6(1) of the ECHR.

References

Bogdan M (2011) General course on private international law. Recueil des Cours, vol 348. Martinus Nijhoff Publishers, Leiden

Brems E (2003) The margin of appreciation doctrine of the European Court of Human Rights: accomodating diversity within Europe. In: Forsythe DP, McMahon PC (eds) Human rights and diversity: area studies revisited. Nebraska University Press, Lincoln, pp 81–110

Bucher A (2000) La famille en droit international privé. Recueil des Cours 283:9–186

Bucher A (2002) Jurisprudence suisse en matière de droit international privé de la famille et des successions. RSDIE 12:267–316

Bucher A (2004) Le couple en droit international privé. Helbing & Lichtenhahn, Bâle

Bucher A (2007) Jurisprudence suisse en matière de droit international privé 2007. RSDIE 17:315–321

Bucher A (ed) (2011) Loi sur le droit international privé. Convention de Lugano, Helbing Lichtenhahn, Bâle

Cheshire GC et al (2010) private international law. Oxford University Press, Oxford

Coester-Waltjen D (1998) Die Wirkungskraft der Grundrechte bei Fällen mit Auslandsbezug—familien- und erbrechtlicher Bereich (The impact of fundamental right in cross-border cases—the area of family and inheritance law). In: Coester-Waltjen D (ed) Die Wirkungskraft der Grundrechte bei Fällen mit Auslandsbezug (The impact of fundamental rights in cross-border cases). C.F. Müller, Heidelberg, pp. 9–32

de Boer Th M (1996) Facultative choice of law. The procedural status of choice-of-law rules and foreign law. Recueil des Cours 257:223–427

Dicey AV, Morris JHC, Collins LA (2012) The conflict of laws. Sweet & Maxwell, London

Docquir B (1999) Le droit international privé à l'épreuve de la Convention européenne des droits de l'homme. Annales de Droit de Louvain 59:473–522

Engel C (1989) Ausstrahlungen der Europäischen Menschenrechtskonvention auf das Kollisionsrecht (Emanations of the European Convention on Human Right on Conflict of Laws). RabelsZ 53:3–51

Esplugues Mota CA (ed) (2011) Application of foreign law. Sellier, Munich

Fentiman R (1998) Foreign law in English courts: pleading, proof and choice of law. Oxford University Press, Oxford

Fulchiron H (2002) Droits fondamentaux et règles de droit international privé: conflits de droits, conflits de logiques? In: Sudre F (ed) Le droit au respect de vie familiale au sens de la Convention européenne des droits de l'homme. Bruylant, Bruxelles, pp 353–386

Gannagé L (2001) La hiérarchie des normes et les méthodes du droit international privé: étude de droit international privé de la famille. L.G.D.J, Paris

Gannagé L (2008) A propos de l'absolutisme des droits fondamentaux. In: Ancel JP (ed) Vers des nouveaux equilibres entre ordre juridiques: liber amicorum Hélène Gaudemet-Tallon. Dalloz, Paris, pp 265–284

Gaudemet-Tallon H (2005) Le pluralisme en droit international privé: richesses et faiblesses. Recueil des Cours 312:9–488

Geeroms S (2004) Foreign law in civil litigation: a comparative and functional analysis. Oxford University Press, Oxford

Grgic A (eds) (2007) The right to property under the European Convention on Human Rights. Human rights handbooks no. 10. Council of Europe, Strasbourg.

Hammje P (1997) Droits fondamentaux et ordre public. Rev.crit.dr.int.priv. 86:1–31.

Hofmann R (1994) Human rights and the ordre public clause of German private international law. Tel Aviv Univ Stud Law 12:145–155

Jayme E (1995) Identité culturelle et intégration: le droit international privé postmoderne. Recueil des Cours 251.

Jayme E (2003) Menschenrechte und Theorie des Internationalen Privatrechts (speech delivered on 24 January 1992). In: Jayme E (ed) Internationales Privatrecht und Völkerrecht [Private international law and international law]. C.F. Müller Verlag, Heidelberg, pp. 95–109

Jessurun d'Oliveira HU (1975) Openbare orde en rechtsvergelijking [Public policy and comparative law]. In: Jessurun d'Oliveira HU et al (eds) 't Exempel dwinght. Opstellen aangeboden door vrienden en vereerders and prof. mr. I. Kisch ter gelegenheid van zijn 70ste verjaardag. Tjeenk Willink, Zwolle, pp. 239–261.

Juenger FK (1972) The German Constitutional Court and the conflict of laws. AJCL 20:290–298

Kiestra LR (2010) De betekenis van het EVRM voor de internationale gerechtelijke vaststelling van het vaderschap [The meaning of the ECHR for the international judicial determination of paternity]. NIPR 28:27–30

Kinsch P (2004a) Sklavenbesitz, religiöse Ehehindernisse und entschädigungslose Enteignungen: zur Vorgeschichte der Frage nach der Einwerkung der Grund- und Mensenrechte auf die Anwendung ausländischen Rechts [Ownership of slaves, religious impediments to marriage, and uncompensated expropiation: the history of the question of the impact of fundamental- and human rights on the application of foreign law]. In: Mansel H-P et al (eds) Festschrift für Erik Jayme Band I. Sellier, Munich, pp. 419–435.

Kinsch P (2004b) The impact of human rights on the application of foreign law and on the recognition of foreign judgments—a survey of the cases decided by the European human rights institutions. In: Einhorn T, Siehr K (eds) Intercontinental cooperation through private international law—essays in memory of Peter E. Nygh. T.M.C. Asser Press, The Hague.

Kinsch P (2007) Droits de l'homme, droits fondamentaux et droit international privé. Recueil des Cours 318:9–332

Kinsch P (2011) Private international law topics before the European Court of Human Rights. Selected judgments and decision (2010–2011). Yearb Priv Int Law 13:39–41

Kokott J (1998) Grund- und Menschenrechte als Inhalt eines internationalen ordre public' [Fundamental and human rights as the content of an international public policy]. In: Coester-Waltjen D et al (eds) Die Wirkungskraft der Grundrechte bei Fällen mit Auslandsbezug. C.F. Müller, Heidelberg, pp. 71–114.

Lagarde P (2010) Reference to public order ("ordre public") in French private international law. In: Foblets M-C (ed) Cultural diversity and the law: state responses from around the world. Bruylant, Brussels, pp 521–546

Lequette Y (2004) Le droit international privé et les droits fondamentaux. In: Cabrillac R et al (eds) Libertés et droit fondamentaux. Dalloz, Paris, pp. 97–118

Looschelders D (2001) Die Ausstrahlung der Grund- und Menschenrechte auf das Internationale Privatrecht [The impact of fundamental- and human right on private international law]. RabelsZ 65:464–491

Marchadier F (2007) Les objectifs généraux du droit international privé à l'épreuve de la Convention européenne des droits de l'homme. Bruylant, Bruxelles

Matscher F (1998) Le droit international privé face à la Convention européenne des droits de l'homme, travaux du comité français de droit international privé (1995–1998), pp. 211–234

Mayer P (1991) La Convention européenne des droits de l'homme et l'application des normes étrangères. Rev.crit.dr.int.priv. 98:651–665.

Mehdi R, Nielson JS (eds) (2011) Embedding "Mahr" in the European legal system. DJØF Publishing, Copenhagen

Najm M-C (2003) Principes directeurs du droit international privé et conflits de civilizations: relations entre systèmes laïques et systèmes religieux. Dalloz, Paris

Oprea A (2007) La Convention europeénne des droits de l'homme et l'application des normes étrangère en droit international privé. Revista de drept internaţional privat şi drept privat comparat 2007:307–340

Pontier JA (2005) Europees conflictenrecht. Een complexe geschiedenis in vogelvlucht (European conflict of laws. A bird-eye's view of a complicated history). Vossiuspers, Amsterdam.

Rogerson P (2003) Kuwait Airways Corp v Iraqi Airways Corp: the territoriality principle in private international law—vice or virtue? Curr Leg Probl 56:265–287

Rossolilo G (2010) Personal identity at a crossroads between private international law, international protection of human rights and EU law. Yearb Priv Int Law 11:143–156

Rutten SWE (1998) Mensenrechten en het ipr: scheiden of trouwen? [Human rights and private international law: to divorce or to marry?]. NJCM-Bulletin 23:797–811

Schutte CB (2004) The European fundamental right of property: article 1 of protocol no. 1 to the European Convention on Human Rights: its origins, its workings and its impact on national legal orders. Kluwer, Deventer.

Strikwerda L (2012) Inleiding tot het Nederlandse Internationaal Privaatrecht [Introduction to Dutch private international law]. Kluwer, Deventer

Thoma I (2011) The ECHR and the ordre public exception in private international law. NIPR 29:13–18

van Hedel JHGE (2008) Het recht op eerbiediging van het familieleven ex artikel 8 EVRM en het conflictenrecht [The right to respect for family life ex Article 8 ECHR and the conflict of laws]. NIPR 26:125–133

van Loon JHA (1993) De wisselwerking tussen internationaal privaatrecht en rechten van de mens [The interaction between private international law and human rights]. In: Dijk D van et al (eds) Grensoverschrijdend privaatrecht: een bundel opstellen over privaatrecht in internationaal verband [Cross-border private law: a collection of essays on private law in an international context]. Kluwer, Deventer, pp. 135–148.

Voltz M (2002) Menschenrechte und ordre public im internationalen Privatrecht [Human rights and public policy in private international law]. Lang, Frankfurt am Main

Vonken APMJ (1993) De reflexwerking van de mensenrechten op het ipr [The reflex of human rights on private international law]. In: Cliteur PB, Vonken APMJ (eds) Doorwerking van mensenrechten [The impact of human rights]. Wolters-Noordhoff, Groningen, pp 153–185

Vonken APMJ (1998) De multiculturele samenleving en de bemiddelende rol van het internationaal privaatrecht en de mensenrechten. Iets over tolerantie, culturele identiteit en rechtspluralisme [The multicultural society and the mediating role of private international law and human rights. Something on tolerance, cultural identity and legal pluralism]. In: Cliteur PB (ed) Sociale cohesie en het recht [Social cohesion and the law]. Lelystad, Koninklijke Vermande, pp 97–166

Weick G (2003) Human rights and private international law. In MacEldowney J, Weick G (eds), Human rights in transition. Lang, Frankfurt am Main, pp. 193–200

Zaher K (2010) Conflict de civilisation et droit international privé. Harmattan, Paris

Chapter 7
The Recognition and Enforcement of Foreign Judgments: The Obligation to Recognize and Enforce Foreign Judgments

Contents

7.1 Introduction

The recognition and enforcement of foreign judgments is an important aspect of private international law.[1] Judgments rendered in one country have their effect, in principle, only in that country. In order for a judgment to have an effect in a foreign country, it first needs to be recognized in that foreign country. This effect of the recognition of a judgment is twofold: the judgment acquires *res judicata* effect, while the principle of *ne bis in idem* subsequently also applies: the matter is settled and can, in principle, not be re-litigated.[2] Whether it is subsequently

[1] See also infra Chap. 2.
[2] See, e.g., Schlosser 2000, p. 31; van Hoek 2003, pp. 337–338.

L.R. Kiestra, *The Impact of the European Convention on Human Rights on Private International Law*, DOI 10.1007/978-94-6265-032-9_7

necessary to enforce the judgment depends on the content of the judgment. The enforcement of a judgment is needed if a certain measure ensuring compliance with the judgment is required for the judgment to have an effect. For a declaratory judgment, such as a foreign family law judgment declaring a status, recognition suffices. However, judgments awarding a sum of money need to be enforced if the judgment debtor is unwilling to satisfy the judgment.

The rules relating to the recognition and enforcement of foreign judgments, in principle, differ from country to country. However there are also multilateral (and bilateral) treaties on the recognition and enforcement of judgments,[3] and for EU Member States, EU rules on recognition and enforcement are of great importance[4]; the Brussels/Lugano regime is particularly relevant for the EU and EFTA Member States in civil and commercial matters.[5] However, even though the exact composition of the regimes of States differs, the general rule with regard to recognition and enforcement of foreign judgments is in many States the same.[6] Foreign judgments should, in principle, be recognized and enforced, provided certain requirements are met. One should note that many international (and bilateral) treaties have a similar starting point, which is fairly obvious, as the goal of such treaties is to enhance international cooperation. The exact conditions a foreign judgment must satisfy in order to be recognized and enforced will depend on the legal regime concerned.

---

[3] See, e.g., the Hague Convention of 15 April 1958 concerning the recognition and enforcement of decisions relating to maintenance obligations towards children; the Hague Convention of 5 October 1961 concerning the Power of Authorities and the Law Applicable in respect of the Protection of Infants, *UNTS* 1969, p. 145ff; the Hague Convention of 1 July 1985 on the Law Applicable to Trusts and on their Recognition. The texts of these instruments can be found at www.hcch.net.

[4] See, e.g., Regulation (EU) No. 650/2012 on jurisdiction, applicable law, recognition and enforcement of decisions and acceptance and enforcement of authentic instruments in matters of successions and on the creation of a European Certificate of Succession, *OJ* 2012, L 201/107; Council Regulation (EC) No. 4/2009 on jurisdiction, applicable law, recognition and enforcement of decisions and cooperation in matters relating to maintenance obligations, *OJ* 2009, L 7/1; Council Regulation (EC) No. 2201/2003 concerning jurisdiction and the recognition and enforcement in matrimonial matters and the matters of parental responsibility, *OJ* 2003, L 338/1 "Brussels II *bis*" (repealing Regulation (EC) 1347/2000); Council Regulation (EC) No. 1346/2000 on insolvency proceedings, *OJ* 2000, L 160/1.

[5] This 'regime' consists of the so-called Brussels I Regulation, Council Regulation (EC) No. 44/2001 of 22 December 2000 on jurisdiction and the recognition and enforcement of judgments in civil and commercial matters, *OJ* 2001 L12/1 (a number of amendments and corrections have since been added to this text) and the Lugano Convention on jurisdiction and the recognition and enforcement of judgments in civil and commercial matters, *OJ* 2007 L339/3, which is practically identical to the Brussels I Regulation. The Lugano Convention has been adopted by Iceland, Norway, and Switzerland.

[6] See for a comparative study on the enforcement of foreign judgments Kerameus 1997, pp. 179–410.

The most common requirements for the recognition and enforcement of foreign judgments are that the foreign judgment should be final,[7] it should not violate either procedural or substantive public policy,[8] and not be contrary to another judgment between the parties.[9] Another important requirement in both international treaties and national legislation is the jurisdiction requirement, which in short entails that a foreign judgment will only be recognized if the court of the country of origin had adjudicatory jurisdiction on a reasonable basis.[10] Particularly in the event of a default judgment, the service of process will also be assessed by courts.[11] Other grounds of refusal, which are less frequently used, include fraud, or *fraude à la loi*,[12] and the choice-of-law requirement, which entails that a foreign judgment will only be recognized if the law that was applied to the merits of the case was the same law as the forum would have applied to the case.[13] A more liberal approach can be found within the European Union.[14] This has an effect that under, for example, the Brussels I Regulation,[15] a refusal may only be based on a limited number of grounds, which are explicitly defined in this instrument.[16]

What do the rights guaranteed in the ECHR mean for the recognition and enforcement of foreign civil judgments? It will be demonstrated in this chapter that the Court has, of the three main issues of private international law, delivered by far the most decisions on the issue of the recognition and enforcement of foreign judgments. It follows from the discussion of this case law that not only may an *obligation* for the Contracting Parties be derived from certain rights guaranteed in the ECHR to recognize and enforce a foreign judgment, but that there may also be an obligation requiring Contracting Parties to *deny* the recognition and enforcement of foreign judgments under certain circumstances.

Because of the volume of the Court's case law on the issue of the recognition and enforcement of foreign judgments, the examination of this issue will be divided into two chapters. In this chapter the obligation to recognize and enforce foreign judgments following from the rights guaranteed in the ECHR will be discussed. In the

---

7 See, e.g., the discussion of the requirements used in England, The Netherlands, and Switzerland infra Sect. 7.2.2.

8 Id.

9 See, e.g., Article 34(3) and (5) of the Brussels I Regulation (supra n. 5).

10 See, e.g., Article 23(2-a) of the Hague Convention of 19 October 1996 on Jurisdiction, Applicable Law, Recognition, Enforcement and Co-operation in Respect of Parental Responsibility and Measures for the Protection of Children. See also infra Sect. 7.2.2. See generally on the requirements for recognition and enforcement and particularly the jurisdictional requirement, e.g., von Mehren 1980, pp. 9–112.

11 See, e.g., Article 34(2) of the Brussels I Regulation (supra n. 5).

12 But see infra n. 23. See also, e.g., infra n. 77.

13 But see infra n. 113.

14 See further infra 8.2.4.

15 See supra n. 5.

16 See, particularly, Articles 34 and 35 of the Brussels I Regulation (supra n. 5). An even more liberal approach is proposed by the Commission. See further infra Sect. 8.2.4.

next, Chap. 8, the invocation of the rights guaranteed in the ECHR *against* recognition and enforcement of foreign judgments will be elaborated upon.

The obligation to recognize and enforce can be based on a number of different rights guaranteed in the ECHR. This discussion of the obligation therefore has three different strands. First, the general obligation following from Article 6(1) ECHR, which guarantees the (procedural) right to a fair trial, will be examined (in Sect. 7.2). Thereafter, the obligation to recognize and enforce judgments *ex* Article 1 of Protocol No. 1 ECHR, which guarantees the right to property, will be addressed (Sect. 7.3). Finally, it will be demonstrated that Article 8 ECHR, which guarantees, inter alia, the right to respect for private and family life, may also contain an obligation to recognize and enforce judgments (Sect. 7.4). All this will be followed by a conclusion (Sect. 7.5). Below, these rights will be examined separately. The separation of these Articles with regard to the recognition and enforcement of foreign judgments is somewhat forced, though, as it will be shown below that the general obligation following from Article 6(1) ECHR is often combined with a specific obligation from either Article 1 of Protocol No. 1 ECHR or Article 8 ECHR, or even both, depending on the subject matter of the issue. However, for analytical purposes it is nevertheless useful to make the distinction.

7.2 Article 6(1) ECHR and the Obligation to Recognize and Enforce

From the wording of Article 6(1) ECHR it is *prima facie* not clear whether the recognition and enforcement of (foreign) judgments would be covered at all. Nevertheless, one could say that the Court's starting point with regard to the recognition and enforcement of foreign judgments is that it would, in principle, be a violation of Article 6(1) ECHR not to recognize and enforce a foreign judgment. The Court's reasoning follows from a case concerning the execution of a domestic judgment, *Hornsby v. Greece*.[17] The Court decided that the execution of a judgment is also protected under Article 6(1) ECHR. The Greek government's main defense in this case was that the complaint could not fall within the scope of Article 6 ECHR, arguing that this right only guaranteed the fairness of the 'trial' in the literal sense. The Court, however, made clear that the government's interpretation would lead to an unacceptable confinement of Article 6 ECHR in the following—and later often repeated—consideration:

> However, that right would be illusory if a Contracting State's domestic legal system allowed a final, binding judicial decision to remain inoperative to the detriment of one party. It would be inconceivable that Article 6 para 1 should describe in detail procedural guarantees afforded to litigants - proceedings that are fair, public and expeditious - without protecting the implementation of judicial decisions; to construe Article 6 as being

[17] *Hornsby v. Greece*, 19 March 1997, *Reports of Judgments and Decisions* 1997-II.

concerned exclusively with access to a court and the conduct of proceedings would be likely to lead to situations incompatible with the principle of the rule of law which the Contracting States undertook to respect when they ratified the Convention. Execution of a judgment given by any court must therefore be regarded as an integral part of the "trial" for the purposes of Article 6.[18]

The Court has since reiterated its stance taken in *Hornsby* with regard to the need to comply with final judicial decisions in many subsequent cases concerning the failure of authorities to execute final, binding domestic decisions.[19] Although *Hornsby* and subsequent case law concerned domestic cases, there was, in principle, no reason to assume that this reasoning could not also extend to the recognition and enforcement of foreign judgments. This had also been argued in the literature well before the Court would find this to be the case.[20]

Initially, however, the Court appeared to approach this issue quite hesitantly in its admissibility decision in *Sylvester v. Austria*,[21] although it would eventually acknowledge that Article 6 ECHR applied to the recognition of an American judgment concerning divorce and a custody decision in Austria. It should be noted, however, that in this case the applicant complained about the length of the enforcement proceedings and not about the refusal to enforce the American judgment. The complaint was, incidentally, declared admissible by the Court.[22]

It would take a subsequent case concerning an American divorce judgment, *McDonald v. France*,[23] for the Court to finally embrace the applicability of its case law first established in *Hornsby* to the recognition and enforcement of foreign judgments. *McDonald v. France* concerned the divorce of McDonald, an American diplomat, and D, his French wife. He initiated divorce proceedings in France, but his request was denied in the first instance. He did not appeal, but brought a new set of divorce proceedings in his by then new place of residence, Florida. He was granted a divorce and subsequently married another French wife in the Ivory Coast. Later he requested *exequatur* of the Florida divorce in France. The *exequatur* was denied by the French courts and Mr. McDonald subsequently complained in Strasbourg on the basis of Articles 6(1) and Article 14 ECHR.

The Court for the first time considered the refusal to recognize a foreign judgment in light of Article 6(1) ECHR, as it had done with regard to the enforcement of a domestic judgment in *Hornsby*, but ultimately declared the application

[18] *Hornsby v. Greece*, 19 March 1997, para 40, *Reports of Judgments and Decisions* 1997-II (references omitted).

[19] See, e.g., *Burdov v. Russia*, no. 59498/00, ECHR 2002-III and *Jasiūnienė v. Lithuania*, no. 41510/98, 6 March 2003.

[20] See, e.g., Guinchard 2005, pp. 214–215; Marchadier 2007, p. 369ff; Matscher 1998, p. 222. Cf. Kinsch 2007, pp. 94–96.

[21] *Sylvester v. Austria* (dec.), no. 54640/00, 9 October 2003.

[22] In its subsequent judgment the Court found a violation of Article 6(1) in this respect. See *Sylvester v. Austria (no. 2)*, no. 54640/00, 3 February 2005. See with regard to the admissibility of claims generally supra Sect. 3.2.

[23] *McDonald v. France* (dec.), no. 18648/04, 29 April 2008.

inadmissible, because the French court had denied *exequatur* on the basis of '*fraude commise par le requérant*' and the Court held—in line with its earlier case law[24]—that nobody can complain about a situation to which they themselves had contributed. The applicant had committed this fraud by deliberately bypassing the French courts, while appeal was still open, by applying to an American court.

In *McDonald v. France* the Court thus fully embraced the principle that the refusal to recognize a foreign judgment may violate Article 6(1) ECHR, but it did not find a violation in this regard due to the applicant's own doing. It should be noted, though, that the Court acknowledged this in relation to the right to a fair trial.[25] Even though the Court ultimately found no violation of Article 6(1) ECHR, this case received quite some attention, particularly in France.[26] It was argued that the novelty of this case was that it was from now on possible to attach the right to the recognition and enforcement of a foreign judgment to the right of a fair trial *ex* Article 6(1) ECHR.[27] In a similar vein it was held that it followed from *McDonald* that Article 6(1) ECHR pertains to all stages of the proceedings, including the enforcement of the judgment, and that the origin of the judgment—whether a domestic or a foreign decision is concerned—is irrelevant in this regard.[28] The right to recognition and enforcement was thus clearly treated as being part of the procedural right to a fair trial.[29] In two subsequent cases, however, *Jovanoski v. the Former Yugoslav Republic of Macedonia*[30] and *Vrbica v. Croatia*,[31] the Court would also find a violation on account of Article 6(1) ECHR and the refusal to enforce a foreign judgment, but instead of relying on the (general) right to a fair trial, it based the violation on the right of access to a court *ex* Article 6(1) ECHR.

In 1991 Mr. Jovanoski, a Macedonian national, instituted enforcement proceedings against a Croatian company before a court in Macedonia. At first, part of the debt was paid. When the applicant thereafter attempted to enforce the remainder of the judgment during the years 1992–1993, communications were interrupted due to the conflict in Croatia and the case could not be resolved. The applicant claimed in Strasbourg that his rights under Article 6 ECHR had been

---

24 See, e.g., *Freimanis and Lidums v. Latvia* (dec.), no. 73443/01, 30 January 2003 and *Hussin v. Belgium* (dec.), no. 70807/01, 6 May 2004. See with regard to *Hussin* further infra Sect. 7.4.

25 The Court held the following in *McDonald v. France*: 'La Cour reconnaît que le refus d'accorder l'*exequatur* des jugements du tribunal américain a représenté une ingérence dans le droit au procès équitable du requérant. La Cour reconnaît que le refus d'accorder l'*exequatur* des jugements du tribunal américain a représenté une ingérence dans le droit au procès équitable du requérant'.

26 See *McDonald v. France*, *Rev.crit dr.int.priv.* 2008, p. 830ff (note Kinsch) and *McDonald v. France*, *Journal du droit international (Clunet)* 2008, p. 193ff (note Marchadier); see also Kinsch 2010, p. 267; Spielmann 2011, p. 774ff.

27 See note Kinsch 2008, p. 839 (supra n. 26).

28 See note Marchadier 2008, p. 196 (supra n. 26).

29 See also Kinsch 2010, p. 267ff.

30 *Jovanovski v. The Former Yugoslav Republic of Macedonia*, no. 31731/03, 7 January 2010.

31 *Vrbica v. Croatia*, no. 32540/05, 1 April 2010.

violated, as he had been denied the right of access to a court on account of the non-enforcement of his claim.

The Court held that even in light of the circumstances, the State (Macedonia) had failed to take adequate and effective measures to enforce the applicant's claim and thus found a violation of Article 6(1) ECHR. However, when it came to the assessment of the applicant's damages under Article 41 ECHR,[32] the Court held that it found persuasive the argument that the applicant could have sought to enforce the remainder of his claim before the Croatian courts. As the applicant had failed to do so, he was only awarded EUR 500 in respect of non-pecuniary damages, instead of the EUR 1,076,283 he had claimed in respect of pecuniary damages (which corresponded with the amount initially awarded in the Macedonian judgment plus interest).

In the case of *Vrbica v. Croatia* Mr. Vrbica, the applicant, had been awarded a monetary judgment in Montenegro against two Croatians for injuries sustained in a traffic incident. This judgment was subsequently recognized in Croatia. Shortly thereafter, the applicant filed for a rectification of this decision, as the decision mistakenly referred to a wrong case number. The Croatian court rectified the mistake later that month. The applicant had, meanwhile, already started enforcement proceedings in December 2001 (after the initial recognition of the Montenegrin judgment) before the very same court, but these proceedings proved to be unsuccessful, as the defendants successfully appealed by pointing out the incorrect case number. The Croatian court invited the applicant to resubmit the case, but the applicant failed to do so, as he figured that the court already had the correct case number. The court declared the pending, unaltered application for enforcement inadmissible. Later, the applicant once more attempted to get the judgment enforced, but this time the defendants successfully argued that by now the enforcement had become time-barred.

Mr. Vrbica subsequently filed a complaint in Strasbourg invoking not only Article 6(1) ECHR, but also Article 1 of Protocol No. 1 ECHR and Article 13 ECHR (the right to an effective remedy) taken in conjunction with Article 1 of Protocol No. 1 and Article 14 ECHR. With regard to Article 6 ECHR, the Court examined whether that decision had unduly limited the applicant's right to a court. As discussed in Chap. 5, it is standard case law of the Court that this right is not absolute and may be subject to limitations.[33] In assessing whether a limitation of the right of access to a court may be allowed, the Court follows a scheme similar to the one used with regard to restrictions in Article 8(2) ECHR.[34] Such limitations cannot reduce the access so much that the right of access is essentially thwarted;

---

[32] Article 41 ECHR reads as follows. 'If the Court finds that there has been a violation of the Convention or the Protocols thereto, and if the internal law of the High Contracting Party concerned allows only partial reparation to be made, the Court shall, if necessary, afford just satisfaction to the injured party.'

[33] See supra Sect. 5.4.1.

[34] Id.

moreover, such limitations must pursue a legitimate aim and be proportional to the aim pursued.[35]

The Court held in *Vrbica* that statutory periods serve several important purposes and that legal certainty in general is aided by such a limitation period. The Court has also on numerous occasions stated that the existence of such a period is not per se incompatible with the ECHR.[36] However, in this case the Court found that the restriction was not proportionate to the aim pursued. It did so by referring to its findings with regard to Article 1 of Protocol No. 1 ECHR.[37]

It is thus interesting to observe that in the cases of *Jovanoski* and *Vrbica*, the Court examined the issue of the enforcement of a foreign judgment from the perspective of the right of access to a court. As discussed in Chap. 5, this is a right that has been derived from the right to a fair trial by the Court in *Golder v. the United Kingdom*.[38] The finding of a violation of Article 6(1) based on the right of access to a court in *Vrbica* led two of the judges in this case, Judges Malinverni and Spielmann, to issuing concurring opinions, in which they both argued that it was not so much the applicant's right of access to a court that was unduly restricted, but rather the 'excessive formalism' and arbitrary interpretation of the relevant rules which led to a violation of the right to a fair trial *ex* Article 6(1) ECHR.[39] However, in a subsequent case concerning the enforcement of a foreign decision, *Romańczyk v. France*,[40] the Court once again approached the issue from the right of access to a court.[41]

Romańczyk concerned the enforcement in France of a maintenance order awarded to the applicant in Poland. Under the terms of the divorce in Poland between the applicant and her ex-husband and father of their two children (both Polish nationals), the latter was ordered to pay maintenance. The father lived in France. The applicant did not receive any payments and she subsequently made an application under the Convention of New York of 20 June 1956 on the Recovery Abroad of Maintenance (the New York Convention).[42] After a slow start to these proceedings, French police tracked down the debtor in 2004, and the French authorities informed the Polish authorities that he had signed a written undertaking to pay maintenance. In 2005 the Polish authorities informed the French authorities that the ex-husband had still not honored this commitment. The French authorities

---

35 *Vrbica v. Croatia*, no. 32540/05, para 63, 1 April 2010.

36 See, e.g., *Stubbings and Others v. the United Kingdom*, 22 October 1996, para 50, *Reports of Judgments and Decisions* 1996-IV.

37 See for the Court's findings in this regard infra Sect. 5.3.

38 *Golder v. the United Kingdom*, 21 February 1975, Series A no. 18. See further supra Sect. 5.4.

39 See paras 9–15 of the concurring opinion of Judge Malinverni and para 2ff of the concurring opinion of Judge Spielmann in *Vrbica* (supra n. 31).

40 *Romańczyk v. France,* no. 7618/05, 18 November 2010.

41 *Romańczyk v. France,* no. 7618/05, para 53, 18 November 2010.

42 Convention of New York of 20 June 1956 on the Recovery Abroad of Maintenance, *UNTS* vol. 268, p. 3.

did not follow up. Up until the procedure in Strasbourg the applicant had been unable to recover maintenance.

Invoking Article 6(1) ECHR, she filed a complaint against France, as the French authorities had been unable to procure the enforcement. She also complained about the excessive length of the proceedings. In this case the Court reiterated that the right to a court would be illusory if a State allowed a final, binding judgment to remain inoperative to the detriment of one party. While the French authorities argued that the obligation to act rested solely with the applicant, the Court found that France had a positive obligation to enforce the judgment, as the applicant had a right to the assistance of the authorities in the enforcement of the judgment under the New York Convention.

At issue was thus, according to the Court, whether the assistance of the French authorities had been adequate and sufficient. The Court found that this had not been the case. It particularly emphasized the fact that the French authorities had not followed up after being informed that the husband did not honor his written undertaking. The French government had argued that this was a trite administrative error, and that it would be contrary to the spirit of the ECHR that such an oversight by an individual would lead to a violation of the ECHR. However, although the Court accepted that a mere filing error could not lead to a violation of the ECHR, it found that this error could not be attributed to the applicant at all and that it had effectively thwarted the enforcement. The Court thus concluded that Article 6(1) ECHR had been violated.

The Court here therefore used a slightly different reasoning compared to the aforementioned cases of *Jovanoski* and *Vrbica*. Instead of only assessing the refusal, or perhaps rather the unwillingness, to recognize and enforce as an interference with the right of access to a court, the Court in *Romańczyk* held that France had a positive obligation to assist in the enforcement. This positive obligation for the State essentially followed from the New York Convention, an international treaty.[43] The different approach may thus be explained by the fact that the obligation to enforce in this case followed from an international commitment to do so. On the other hand, the Court's reasoning in *Jovanoski* and *Vrbica* similarly suggests that Contracting Parties should have a properly functioning system in place to assist in the enforcement of (foreign) judgments, even though it did not expressly discuss this in light of a positive obligation.

The Court has since confirmed its approach in *Romańczyk* with regard to judgments under the New York Convention in *Matrakas and Others v. Poland and Greece*.[44] In this case concerning the enforcement of three Polish maintenance orders in Greece under the New York Convention the applicants claimed under

[43] The Court also noted in this regard that it essentially followed its previous case law concerning the enforcement of judgments under the New York Convention. The Court cited *Huc v. Romania and Germany* (dec.), no. 7269/05, 1 December 2009; *Dinu v. Romania and France*, no 6152/02, 4 November 2008; *K. v. Italy*, no 38805/97, ECHR 2004-VIII; Zabawska *v. Germany* (dec.), no. 49935/99, 3 March 2006 and *W.K. v. Italy* (dec.), no. 38805/97, 25 June 2002.

[44] *Matrakas and Others v. Poland and Greece*, no. 47268/06, 7 November 2013.

Article 6(1) ECHR that both Poland and Greece had failed to effectively recover the maintenance payments and that the length of the proceedings had been excessive. With regard to the claim against Poland (the place of origin of the maintenance orders) the Court found that the claim was inadmissible, as the Polish court, which functioned as the Transmitting Agency under the New York Convention had acted diligently in the case. The few delays which could be attributed to the Polish authorities were not unreasonable, because of the complex procedure, according to the Court.

The claim against Greece is the more interesting for our purposes. The applicants argued that on account of the inactivity of the Greek authorities they had been unable to obtain the various maintenance orders awarded to them by Polish courts. In its assessment the Court started out by recalling that the 'right to a court' would illusory if a final, binding judicial decision would be allowed to remain unenforced. Even though a State cannot be responsible for the ineffectiveness of enforcement proceedings due to the insolvency of the debtor, a Contracting Party does have the positive obligation to have an effective system in place for the enforcement of judgments.[45] With a reference to *Romańczyk* the Court further noted that the failure to act with necessary diligence by the public authorities responsible for the enforcement may result in a violation of Article 6(1) ECHR. The Court observed that under the New York Convention the obligation to act does not rest solely on the claimant, but also on the State, which is under a positive obligation to assist the claimant in proceedings. The Court ultimately found with regard to all three claimants that the Greek authorities had failed to act with the required diligence. It thus found that there had been violation of Article 6(1) ECHR in respect of all three applicants.[46]

It is noteworthy that the Court's case law concerning the obligation to recognize a foreign (family law) judgment following from Article 6(1) ECHR has also been confirmed in *Négrépontis-Giannisis v. Greece*.[47] This case concerned the unjustified refusal by the Greek authorities to recognize a foreign adoption order. The Court noted that in order for a foreign decision to be recognized and enforced under Greek law, a number of conditions have to be met. One of these conditions is that the judgment must not violate Greek *ordre public* (public policy). However,

[45] The Court referred in this regard to *Fouklev v. Ukraine,* no. 71186/01, 7 June 2005.

[46] There is one more case, in which the Court found that the refusal to recognize a foreign judgment resulted in a violation of the right to access to a court ex Article 6(1) ECHR. In *Ateş Mimarlik Mühendislik A.Ş v. Turkey*, no. 33275/05, 25 September 2012 the Court held that the refusal by the Turkish courts to recognize a German judgment resulted in the very essence of the applicant's right to access to a court being impaired. The Court, incidentally, also found a violation of Article 6(1) ECHR on account of the excessive length of the proceedings. However, this concerns a fairly odd case, which appeared to hinge more on the interpretation of Turkish law, while it is at least arguable on the basis of the facts of the case that the Turkish courts should not have asserted jurisdiction in the first place. See in this regard also the partly dissenting opinion of Judges Popović, Karakaş and Pinto de Albuquerque.

[47] *Négrépontis-Giannisis v. Greece*, no. 56759/08, 3 May 2011.

the Court found that the interpretation by the Greek courts of the notion of *ordre public* should not be made in an arbitrary and disproportionate manner.

It is interesting to observe that the Court in this case explicitly refers to the private international law notion of *ordre public*, or public policy, which the Greek court invoked in order to deny the recognition and enforcement.[48] Taking into account the texts on which the Greek Supreme Court based its decision to refuse to give effect to the American decision and its conclusions under Article 8 ECHR, the Court held that the principle of proportionality had not been respected with regard to Article 6(1) ECHR and thus found a violation of this Article.[49]

It is important to note with regard to foreign family law judgments that there could be specific limitations to the invocation of Article 6(1) ECHR in cases where the rights of others, particularly children, are involved. For example, in *Pini and Others v. Romania*,[50] the Court examined the failure of the Romanian authorities to execute final, binding decisions concerning the adoption of two Romanian children by two Italian couples. In this case a Romanian educational centre, where the children stayed during the adoption proceedings, basically did everything to prevent the enforcement of the final adoption judgments. However, after all those years the minors involved expressed an unwillingness to move to Italy.

The Court examined the failure to enforce these judgments in light of both Articles 6(1) and Article 8 ECHR. Contrary to the complaint under Article 8 ECHR, the Court did find a violation of Article 6(1) ECHR on account of the failure of the authorities to enforce the final judgments. Citing the need for a swift solution in such cases,[51] as the mere passage of time can have irreparable consequences, the Court ultimately held that despite the delicate nature of the issue, the non-enforcement of the binding decisions contravened 'the principles of the rule of law and of legal certainty, notwithstanding the existence of special reasons potentially justifying it, the Government having cited the obligation on the respondent State with a view to its future accession to the European Union legal order'.[52] However, considering the fact that the minors did not want to move to Italy, the judgment amounted to nothing more than a Pyrrhic victory to the applicants.[53]

Finally, it is interesting to note with regard to the impact of Article 6(1) ECHR on the issue of the recognition and enforcement of foreign judgments that the Court has held that Article 6(1) ECHR is also applicable to *exequatur* proceedings

48 See with regard to the public policy exception infra Sects. 2.5 and 6.3.3.3.

49 *Négrépontis-Giannisis v. Greece*, no. 56759/08, paras 90–91, 3 May 2011. See for a more detailed discussion of this case infra Sect. 7.4.

50 *Pini and Others v. Romania*, nos. 78028/01 and 78030/01, ECHR 2004-V (extracts).

51 The Court cited in this regard, inter alia, *Maire v. Portugal*, no. 48206/99, ECHR 2003-VII.

52 *Pini and Others v. Romania*, nos. 78028/01 and 78030/01, para 187, ECHR 2004-V (extracts).

53 See infra Sect. 7.4 for a more detailed discussion of this case and the complaint under Article 8 ECHR.

concerning foreign judgments.[54] In *Saccoccia v. Austria*,[55] a case involving the enforcement of an American forfeiture order in Austria, the Court confirmed its admissibility decision in this case[56] in the sense that it held that the right to a fair trial following from Article 6(1) ECHR is also applicable to the execution phase of a foreign judgment.[57] *Exequatur* proceedings thus also have to meet all the fair trial requirements following from Article 6(1) ECHR. In *Saccoccia* no hearing had been held before taking over the execution of the American judgment. However, as the proceedings concerned merely technical issues of inter-State cooperation and no taking of further evidence was required, the Court found that there had not been a violation of Article 6(1) ECHR.[58]

In *Ern Makina Sanayi ve Ticaret A.Ş v. Turkey*, however, the Court had earlier found a violation of Article 6(1) ECHR in a case concerning *exequatur* proceedings regarding the enforcement of a Russian arbitral award in Turkey, in which the defendant had not been notified.[59] The fact that Article 6(1) ECHR is applicable to enforcement proceedings concerning foreign judgments means that the guarantee of a reasonable length of procedures is also applicable to such proceedings.[60] Whether or not such a violation can be found will naturally depend on the specific circumstances of the case. One could point to *Zabawska v. Germany*, a case concerning the enforcement of a Polish maintenance order in Germany, where no violation of Article 6 ECHR was found, despite the considerable lapse of time.[61]

7.2.1 The Obligation to Recognize and Enforce Following from Article 6(1) ECHR

It follows from the case law discussed above that the Court has derived an obligation to recognize and enforce foreign judgments from Article 6(1) ECHR. This right had already been deduced by the Court with regard to domestic judgments in

---

[54] Cf. Spielmann 2011, p. 770ff. See in this regard also Kinsch 2007, who before the Court's judgments in *Saccoccia* (infra n. 55) and *Ern Makina Sanayi ve Ticaret A.Ş* (infra n. 59) already noted—citing the Court's admissibility decision in *Ern Makina Sanayi ve Ticaret A.Ş v. Turkey* (dec.), no. 70830/01, 4 October 2005—that Article 6(1) ECHR (and Article 13 ECHR) could be applicable to such proceedings.

[55] *Saccoccia v. Austria*, no. 69917/01, 18 December 2008.

[56] *Saccoccia v. Austria* (dec.), no. 69917/01, 5 July 2007.

[57] *Saccoccia v. Austria*, no. 69917/01, paras 61–65, 18 December 2008.

[58] *Saccoccia v. Austria*, no. 69917/01, paras 70–80, see particularly paras 78–80, 18 December 2008.

[59] *Ern Makina Sanayi ve Ticaret A.Ş v. Turkey*, no. 70830/01, 3 May 2007.

[60] *K. v. Italy*, no. 38805/97, ECHR 2004-VIII and an older case of the Commission, *Kirchner v. Austria* (dec.), 12883/87, 14 October 1991.

[61] *Zabawska v. Germany* (dec.), no. 49935/99, 2 March 2006. See also supra n. 43.

Hornsby, but this right has been extended to foreign judgments. As Article 6(1) ECHR is concerned with virtually all civil judgments, the Court's finding of an obligation following from this Article introduces a general obligation to recognize and enforce foreign (civil) judgments, including foreign family law judgments.[62]

The Court has nevertheless not been consistent in how it has constructed this obligation. Originally, it based this obligation on the fact that recognition and enforcement must be part of the trial and it thus could be derived from the right to a fair trial.[63] In its more recent case law, though, it has based the obligation on the right of access to a court.[64] Moreover, the Court has also treated the obligation to enforce judgments as a positive obligation of the State.[65]

The precise construction of this obligation to recognize and enforce under Article 6(1) ECHR could be of interest in light of possible limitations to this obligation. It follows from the Court's case law that the obligation to recognize and enforce is not absolute. One could argue that the room for the Contracting Parties to maneuver with regard to the obligation following from Article 6(1) ECHR may differ depending on whether it is derived from the right to a fair trial, or from the right of access to a court, or whether this obligation concerns a positive obligation. However, even though the Court is not very precise in its assessment of the obligation to recognize and enforce, it is possible to observe important overlaps between the Court's different methods regarding limitations to this obligation. As has been noted above, it follows from the Court's case law that it deems it important that Contracting Parties have a system in place ensuring that (foreign) judgments will, in principle, be recognized and enforced.

A failure to recognize and enforce appears to be treated by the Court in most cases as a restriction to Article 6(1) ECHR. It further follows from the Court's case law that it reviews the proportionality of such a restriction in particular. This review, of course, fits in with the Court's general approach to restrictions to qualified rights, while it has previously been held that the Court also uses this approach with regard to the right of access to a court *ex* Article 6(1) ECHR.[66]

Whether a restriction to the obligation to recognize and enforce under Article 6(1) ECHR can thus be allowed will mostly depend on whether the restriction is proportionate to the legitimate aim pursued. In my opinion, the interests of others can, in principle, also be weighed by the Court in its assessment of the proportionality.[67] It follows that the restrictions which the Contracting Parties impose on the recognition and enforcement of foreign judgments in the framework of their

---

62 See with regard to the issue of whether Article 6(1) ECHR generally applies to issues of private international law supra Sect. 5.4.1.1.

63 See *Hornsby* and *McDonald* supra Sect. 7.2.

64 See *Jovanoski* and *Vrbica* supra Sects. 7.2–7.3.

65 See *Romańczyk* supra Sect. 7.2.

66 See generally on the system of restrictions supra Sect. 3.5.1. See with regard to the right to access to a court supra Sect. 5.4.1.

67 Even though the Court did not do so in *Pini* (see supra n. 50).

private international law regimes must also comply with this condition of proportionality. Thus these grounds of refusal in private international law must be proportionate to the legitimate aim pursued. Notably, this even applies to the substantive public policy exception, as the Court found in *Négrepontis*. This exception cannot be applied in a disproportionate and arbitrary manner. Yet there is no reason to assume that this, in principle, does not also apply to other private international law defenses against recognition and enforcement of foreign judgments.[68]

The one exception here is the condition of fraud. This is because the ECHR cannot be invoked against situations to which the applicant has contributed him or herself. Moreover, as will be further discussed in Chap. 8, human rights obligations may also stand in the way of the recognition and enforcement of foreign judgments.[69] It would stand to reason that there cannot be an obligation to recognize and enforce foreign judgments whose recognition would subsequently lead to a violation of one of the rights guaranteed in the ECHR. In this regard, one should also note that some of the requirements for the recognition and enforcement of foreign judgments, such as the proper service of documents and irreconcilable judgments, will presumably pass this test easily, as they contribute to a large part to the protection of rights guaranteed in Article 6(1) ECHR.[70]

7.2.2 Jurisprudence of National Courts of the Contracting Parties

Despite the Court's finding that an obligation to recognize and enforce foreign judgments follows from Article 6(1) ECHR, there is little relevant case law of the national courts in England, the Netherlands, or Switzerland to be found[71] in which this obligation is invoked in order to have a foreign judgment recognized and enforced.

There is one case worth mentioning, *Golubovich v. Golubovich*,[72] even though the obligation to recognize and enforce was not explicitly invoked. In this case one half of a couple, W, commenced divorce proceedings in England, while the other half, H, began divorce proceedings in Russia shortly thereafter. H prevented the grant of a divorce decree in England by producing a Russian divorce decree that turned out to be forged. Meanwhile, the English court issued a *Hemain*

[68] See for an overview supra Sect. 7.1.

[69] See infra Sects. 8.2–8.3.

[70] The proper service of documents certainly contributes to a fair trial under Article 6(1) ECHR, while the ground of refusal of irreconcilable judgments could be said to be vested in the general notion of the rule of law.

[71] See with regard to the choice of these legal orders supra Sect. 1.2.

[72] [2010] EWCA Civ 810.

injunction[73] preventing H from further action in the Russian courts. Contrary to the injunction, though, H obtained a divorce before the Russian courts. The Court of Appeal found that this divorce could be recognized in England and declined to refuse recognition on the basis of the public policy exception. The English court found that to deny recognition from another jurisdiction within the Council of Europe could only occur under truly exceptional circumstances. This was not deemed to be the case here.

This case clearly demonstrates the extent of the starting point, discussed above, that foreign judgments should, in principle, be recognized and enforced. Even under these circumstances, the English court found that this situation was not exceptional enough to make an exception to this principle. It is noteworthy that the English court emphasized the fact that the judgment originated from another Contracting Party, as if to suggest that this resulted in a stronger assumption that the judgment should be enforced.[74] However, one could say that it is quite remarkable that the English court was willing to recognize this judgment, considering the fraudulent behavior of one of the parties. As has been discussed above, the Court in *McDonald* saw it fit to deny an appeal for the recognition of a foreign judgment because of such fraudulent behavior.[75] Apparently the English public policy exception could not be invoked in order to prevent this. The English court in this case thus goes further in recognizing this judgment than the Court would require.

What could be the reason for the lack of case law concerning the obligation derived from Article 6(1) ECHR to recognize and enforce foreign judgments? First, most of the Court's case law on this issue is relatively recent. More importantly, however, is the fact that in England, the Netherlands, and Switzerland the starting point with regard to the recognition and enforcement of foreign judgments is that they will be recognized and enforced unless the foreign judgment does not meet the requirements to do so. For judgments in civil and commercial matters originating from other EU Member States or States party to the Lugano Convention, for example, the Brussels/Lugano regime applies in the aforementioned countries. The free movement of judgments is one of the purposes of the Brussels/Lugano regime and the grounds for refusal are limited.[76] The Brussels II *bis* Regulation, for example, has a similar starting point. Additionally, there are many bilateral treaties which follow a similar approach.

---

73 The so-called *Hemain* injunction is an interim injunction in international proceedings, which is sought for a limited time in order to preserve the *status quo*, while an application for a stay is made. The injunction thus precludes both parties from litigating on the substantive issues in either court involved. In *Hemain v. Hemain* [1988] 2 FLR 388, such an injunction was granted in respect of French proceedings (prior to the Brussels II Regulation).

74 As discussed above, the Court's case law in this regard suggests that the origin of the judgment is irrelevant. See supra Sect. 7.2.1.

75 See supra Sect. 7.2.

76 See, e.g., no. 6 of the preamble of the Brussels I Regulation (supra n. 5).

Although under the common law rules in England a few more obstacles may be raised against recognition and enforcement of foreign judgments compared to the Brussels/Lugano regime, the principle remains that foreign judgments will be recognized and enforced when the court of origin had proper jurisdiction, the foreign judgments are final, they were not obtained by way of fraud, and finally are not contrary to the principles of English public policy.[77] A comparable legal framework has been designed over time by the Dutch courts. Originally in the Netherlands, however, foreign judgments could not be recognized and enforced in the absence of a treaty stating otherwise.[78] This starting point is clearly in violation of the obligation to recognize and enforce following from Article 6(1) ECHR.[79] However, rules on the recognition and enforcement of foreign judgments have since been developed by the Dutch courts and, in principle, foreign judgments will be recognized, provided that at least three requirements are met: the foreign judge had jurisdiction to hear the case (based on internationally accepted standards of jurisdiction); there was a fair trial; and, finally, the foreign judgment does not violate Dutch public policy.[80] In Switzerland, the rules relating to recognition and enforcement are laid down in Article 25 of the Swiss Private International Law Act, in which much the same three requirements are included.[81]

This practice essentially means that the obligation to recognize and enforce foreign judgments following from Article 6(1) will in most cases be fulfilled and, if not, only because the foreign judgment did not satisfy one of a number of possible requirements following from the private international law regime of a Contracting Party. However, this is where the impact of the ECHR will be felt.

It is more than conceivable that some of these requirements for the recognition and enforcement will come under pressure in the future, as has been demonstrated by the Court with regard to (substantive) public policy in *Négrépontis*, for example.[82] Any reason put forward by a Contracting Party to deny recognition and enforcement, including traditional private international law defenses, must comply

---

[77] See generally with regard to the recognition and enforcement of foreign judgments in England, e.g., Briggs and Rees 2009, p. 665ff; Cheshire et al. 2010, p. 513ff; Dicey et al. 2012, p. 663ff.

[78] See Strikwerda 2012, p. 273ff.

[79] See also Kinsch 2007, pp. 105–106.

[80] Strikwerda 2012, pp. 279–280. Cf. Rosner 2004, p. 31ff. Some authors have argued that a fourth condition—finality of the judgment—should be added. See Rosner, p. 51ff and the Dutch authors cited there. Occasionally, the requirement that the foreign judgment should have a proper, understandable reasoning has been mentioned. See, e.g., Rb. Rotterdam 29 September 1989, *NIPR* 1992, 277. However, one could also argue that such a requirement would fall under the requirement of a fair trial, whereby it should be mentioned that a lack of reasons in a judgment will not always violate Article 6(1) ECHR. See, e.g., HR 18 March 2011, *RvdW* 2011, 392, which will be discussed infra Sect. 8.2.2.2.

[81] See generally with regard to the recognition and enforcement of foreign judgments in Switzerland, e.g., Dutoit 2005, p. 94ff; Siehr 2002, p. 672ff.

[82] See further infra Sect. 7.4. See also Bucher 2010a, p. 309, who foresees a similar development.

with the requirements regarding restrictions to Article 6(1) ECHR. At the very least, such a restriction must not have been arbitrary or disproportionate. While one could say that the substantive public policy exception in *Négrépontis* had been quite arbitrarily raised, as the Greek courts in this case referred back to ancient texts that were long thought to be irrelevant in this regard, it is nevertheless possible to infer more general consequences from this case. It is, for example, imaginable under the Court's reasoning that too much emphasis on national interests to the detriment of an applicant's interest in having a foreign judgment recognized and enforced may not be proportionate.

7.2.3 Preliminary Conclusions

The Court has found that Article 6(1) ECHR applies to enforcement proceedings and that the failure of the authorities to recognize and enforce foreign judgments may result in a violation of Article 6(1) ECHR. One could therefore say that Article 6(1) contains an obligation for Contracting Parties to facilitate the recognition and enforcement of foreign judgments. This obligation applies, in principle, to all civil judgments and one may thus infer that Article 6(1) ECHR contains a general obligation in this regard. However this obligation is not absolute. While the Court has used varying criteria to assess whether a restriction to the obligation to recognize and enforce a foreign judgment is permissible, the Court will at least assess whether the restriction was not arbitrary and was proportionate (to the legitimate aim pursued). It has been demonstrated that the proportionality requirement is usually the most important condition in this regard.

The obligation under Article 6(1) ECHR to recognize and enforce foreign judgments does not yet have a prominent role in the national case law of the Contracting Parties. This is most likely due to the fact that these countries adhere to a *favor recognitionis*: foreign judgments are, in principle, recognized and enforced under national or EU private international law, unless there are compelling reasons not to do so. Such reasons consist mainly of traditional private international law defenses—the aforementioned grounds of refusal—against recognition and enforcement, such as, for example, a jurisdiction requirement[83] or public policy. However, it follows from the Court's case law that any interference to the obligation to recognize and enforce based on these traditional private international law defenses must also meet the Court's demands with regard to restrictions under Article 6(1) ECHR. It has been demonstrated that the ground of refusal of fraud is an exception to this rule, while it should also not be forgotten that the grounds of refusal may also contribute to the protection of human rights, as

[83] But see further *Hussin v. Belgium* with regard to the jurisdiction requirement (with regard to Article 8 ECHR) infra n. 100.

it will be discussed in the next chapter that there may also be an obligation to refuse the recognition and enforcement of foreign judgments.

7.3 Article 1 of Protocol No. 1 ECHR and the Obligation to Recognize and Enforce

The obligation to enforce a judgment following from Article 1 of Protocol No. 1 ECHR, which guarantees the right to property,[84] was—just like the obligation derived from Article 6(1) ECHR—first developed in a purely domestic case. In a case concerning the failure of the authorities to execute a final judgment, *Burdov v. Russia*,[85] the applicant not only relied on Article 6(1) ECHR, but also complained of a violation of Article 1 of Protocol No. 1 ECHR. This domestic case concerned the Russian authorities' refusal to completely fulfill their obligations with regard to the compensation the applicant was awarded on account of his health issues following his part in emergency operations at the site of the Chernobyl nuclear plant disaster.

The Court examined the allegedly substantial and unjustified delays in the execution of the final judgments under both Article 6(1) and Article 1 of Protocol No. 1 ECHR. The Court held with regard to Article 6(1) ECHR, citing *Hornsby*,[86] that the authorities' failure to comply with the final decisions for years entailed a violation of the said Article. Furthermore, with regard to Article 1 of Protocol No. 1 ECHR, the Court first reiterated that a 'claim' could also constitute 'possessions',[87] as it had previously held in *Stran Greek Refineries and Stratis Andreadis v. Greece*.[88] It consequently found that by failing to comply with the judgments, the authorities had interfered with the applicant's rights following from Article 1 of Protocol No. 1 ECHR, while no justification for this interference had been presented.

With regard to the obligation *ex* Article 1 of Protocol No. 1 ECHR in relation to foreign judgments, the Court in *Vrbica*, in examining the complaint under this Article, relied on its judgment in *Burdov* in finding that the applicant's rights had been interfered with. The Court subsequently held that it found it untenable that instituting proceedings for the recognition of a foreign judgment did not interrupt the running of a statutory limitation period, as was held by the Croatian courts. Such a stance, according to the Court, makes it possible that a judgment creditor

---

[84] See generally with regard to Article 1 of Protocol No. 1 ECHR, e.g., Grgic 2007, pp. 12–15; Schutte 2004.

[85] *Burdov v. Russia*, no. 59498/00, ECHR 2002-III.

[86] *Burdov v. Russia*, no. 59498/00, para 34, ECHR 2002-III.

[87] *Burdov v. Russia*, no. 59498/00, para 40, ECHR 2002-III.

[88] *Stran Greek Refineries and Stratis Andreadis v. Greece*, judgment of 9 December 1994, Series A no. 301-B.

would lose the right to enforce a foreign judgment due to circumstances beyond the creditor's control, which cannot be brought in line with the principle of the rule of law.[89] The Court thus found that the interference was incompatible with the principle of lawfulness and it held that there had (also) been a violation of Article 1 of Protocol No. 1 ECHR.[90]

In this case the Court thus treated the non-enforcement of a foreign (monetary) judgment as a restriction to the right to property. As has been stated earlier, the right to property is not absolute.[91] Under Article 1 of Protocol No. 1 ECHR, however, such a restriction is only allowed if it is prescribed by law, is in the public interest, and is necessary in a democratic society. One should note that in this case the Court thus found, exceptionally, that the first condition—lawfulness—had not been met.

The (partial) non-enforcement of an arbitral award can also be a violation of Article 1 of Protocol No. 1 ECHR. *Kin Kin-Stib and Majkić v. Serbia*[92] concerned the enforcement of the remainder of an arbitral award. The Serbian government argued, inter alia, that it had done everything possible to enforce the award, but after the Serbian court had imposed the maximum amount of fines possible, there had effectively been no further attempts to enforce the remainder of the arbitration award as there appeared to be no more means available to enforce it under Serbian law. This failure to take the necessary measures to fully enforce the arbitration award, without providing any reasons for this failure, amounted to a violation of Article 1 of Protocol No. 1 ECHR, according to the Court.[93]

Even though Article 1 of Protocol No. 1 ECHR is concerned with property, it is possible for this Article to play a role in the recognition and enforcement of foreign family law judgments. In *Négrépontis* the Court held that the non-recognition of a family law judgment regarding one's status may also lead to a violation of Article 1 of Protocol No. 1 ECHR where one's position as an heir is concerned. Due to the non-recognition of a foreign adoption order by the Greek court on appeal, the applicant in *Négrépontis* lost his position as the sole heir to his adoptive father. The Court held that this amounted to a violation of Article 1 of Protocol No. 1 ECHR.[94]

---

[89] *Vrbica v. Croatia*, no. 32540/05, para 55, 1 April 2010.

[90] See also supra Sect. 7.2.

[91] See generally supra Sect. 3.5.1.2.

[92] *Kin Kin-Stib and Majkić v. Serbia*, no. 12312/05, 20 April 2010.

[93] *Kin Kin-Stib and Majkić v. Serbia*, paras 84–85, no. 12312/05, 20 April 2010. With regard to the alleged violation of Article 6(1) in this case, the Court considered it to be unnecessary to examine separately the same issue under Article 6(1) ECHR. The applicants had under Article 6(1) also complained about the failure to respect the *res judicata* effects of the arbitration awards. However, this complaint was incompatible *ratione temporis*, as Serbia had at the time of (the end of) the annulment proceedings not yet ratified the ECHR.

[94] *Négrépontis-Giannisis v. Greece*, no. 56759/08, paras 93–105, 3 May 2011. See also supra Sect. 7.2 and more extensively infra Sect. 7.4.

7.3.1 The Obligation Following from Article 1 of Protocol No. 1 ECHR

The impact of Article 1 of Protocol No.1 ECHR has to date hardly been discussed in the literature or the case law of the Contracting Parties.[95] The impact of the right to property on the enforcement of foreign judgments is a recent development. It should be emphasized that the right to property may, in principle, only come into play where the foreign judgment concerned falls within the scope of this right. However, as follows from the case law discussed above, this is not only the case where the enforcement of foreign money judgments is concerned, but may also be the case where a foreign judgment concerns a status acquired abroad, which may lead to possessions, such as the status of an heir. This, of course, enhances the importance of the right to property.

One may deduce from the Court's case law in *Vrbica* and *Kin-Stib and Majkic* that Article 1 of Protocol No. 1 ECHR, in principle, obligates a State to enforce a foreign monetary judgment, or at the very least obliges a State to have an effective framework for the enforcement of foreign judgments and arbitral awards in place. In both these cases the framework provided for the recognition and enforcement of foreign judgments fell short of the mark. As discussed above, a similar obligation can be deduced from Article 6(1) ECHR.[96] Of course there may be justifications for the non-enforcement of a foreign judgment. Article 1 of Protocol No. 1 ECHR, like Article 6(1) ECHR, leaves open that possibility.[97]

There is clearly some overlap between Article 6(1) and Article 1 of Protocol No. 1 ECHR. This also follows from the Court's finding in *Kin-Stib and Majkic*, in which it held, after finding a violation of Article 1 of Protocol No. 1 ECHR, that it was not necessary to separately examine the complaint under Article 6(1) ECHR, as it concerned the same issue. However, the distinction between these two rights should also be clear: Article 6(1) ECHR concerns a procedural right, while Article 1 of Protocol No. 1 ECHR is a substantive right. Moreover, the scope of Article 6(1) ECHR is larger. Not all judgments covered by Article 6(1) ECHR will also be covered by Article 1 of Protocol No. 1 ECHR. Finally, while the obligation following from these rights, as well as the manner in which the Court assesses interferences under these rights, is quite similar, there is a subtle difference with regard to the system of restrictions under the respective rights. As discussed above, although the Court's examination under Article 6(1) ECHR varies slightly, a restriction must, essentially, not be arbitrary and disproportionate. Under Article 1 of Protocol No. 1 ECHR the Court will, in principle, follow a somewhat stricter test, which follows from the Article itself, as Article 1 of Protocol No. 1 ECHR is a qualified right. This means that an interference with Article 1 of Protocol No. 1

[95] But see Spielmann 2011, p. 774ff, particularly at p. 783.

[96] See supra Sect. 7.2.1.

[97] Article 1 of Protocol No. 1 ECHR is not absolute. See supra Sect. 3.5.1.2.

ECHR should—compared to Article 6(1) ECHR—additionally have a basis in national law.

There may, however, be one more interesting distinction between these two rights with regard to the obligation to recognize which may be deduced from the Court's case law, and this concerns reparation *ex* Article 41 ECHR.[98] In *Jovanoski*, in which the enforcement of a monetary judgment was only examined in light of Article 6(1) ECHR, the successful applicant was awarded only a small amount in damages. In a case in which such a judgment was (also) examined in light of Article 1 of Protocol No. 1 ECHR, *Kin-Stib and Majkic*, however, the successful litigants were paid the entire sum of the judgment in question.[99]

7.3.2 Preliminary Conclusions

The failure on account of the authorities to enforce (part of) a foreign judgment or arbitral award concerning some sort of possession may (also) result in a violation of Article 1 of Protocol No. 1 ECHR, the right to property. However the obligation to enforce foreign judgments is not absolute. The Court's review in this regard is similar to its review under Article 6(1) ECHR, albeit slightly stricter. There is not much relevant case law of the national courts of the Contracting Parties on the impact of Article 1 of Protocol No. 1 ECHR in this regard, as is also the case concerning the obligation to enforce following from Article 6(1) ECHR. Here, too, one could point out that these developments are relatively recent. As was concluded for Article 6(1) ECHR, it is certainly conceivable that the requirements traditionally used in the Contracting Parties regarding recognition and enforcement will come under pressure.

7.4 Article 8 ECHR and the Obligation to Recognize Foreign Judgments

In addition to Articles 6(1) ECHR and Article 1 of Protocol No. 1 ECHR, there is one more right guaranteed in the ECHR that may entail an obligation for a Contracting Party to recognize a foreign judgment, and that is Article 8 ECHR, which, inter alia, guarantees the right to private and family life. After having initially rejected the argument that the failure to recognize a foreign family law judgment may violate Article 8 ECHR, the Court has in its most recent cases on

---

98 See supra n. 32.

99 However, this difference may also have depended on the particular circumstances of the cases. In *Vrbica* the case was re-opened, but this should, in principle, of course lead to enforcement after all.

this topic accepted that the non-recognition of such judgments may entail a violation of Article 8 ECHR.

In *Hussin v. Belgium*[100] the Court for the first time examined whether the non-recognition of a foreign family law judgment could possibly violate one of the substantive rights guaranteed in the ECHR, specifically Article 8 ECHR.[101] Mrs. Hussin, a Belgian national, was resident in Germany with her two children. The local youth Protection Agency in Germany, which had custody over the two children at the time, succeeded (on behalf of the children) in obtaining a judgment in the local court in Germany against G, a Belgian national and resident. The judgment held that G was the natural father of the children and ordered him to pay maintenance for the children. The German court based its jurisdiction on the Brussels Convention.[102]

Mrs. Hussin later attempted to have this judgment recognized in Belgium, where G resided, but ultimately failed in obtaining an *exequatur* of the German judgment in Belgium. The Belgian courts (all the way up to the Supreme Court) took another interpretation of the Brussels Convention and ultimately held that this instrument was inapplicable and that the German court could not assert jurisdiction under this Convention. Instead, the Belgian/German Convention of 1958 was held to be applicable, and it followed from this instrument that the German court was not competent to hear a case against a person domiciled in Belgium. It was ultimately held that none of the decisions obtained in Germany would receive *exequatur* in Belgium, as the jurisdiction requirement had not been met. Mrs. Hussin and her children subsequently complained in Strasbourg, invoking Article 8 ECHR and Article 1 of Protocol No. 1 ECHR (with regard to the maintenance order).

The Court first noted that its task did not include an examination of whether the Belgian courts' refusal to enforce the foreign judgment on account of the German court not having jurisdiction was justified; its task was not to decide on the rightfulness of the interpretation of the Brussels Convention. Rather, its task was to decide whether the refusal to enforce the German judgment was an interference of

[100] *Hussin v. Belgium* (dec.), no. 70807/01, 6 May 2004.

[101] It is worth mentioning that long before the Court would be called upon to examine whether the non-recognition of a foreign judgment could violate Article 8 ECHR, the Commission had already decided a case, *X. v. Sweden* (dec.), no. 172/56, *Documents and Decisions* 1955–1957, pp. 211–219, in which this was one of the issues. In this case the Commission had to decide whether the non-recognition in Sweden of a Polish judgment awarding the applicant a divorce and giving him custody of the child, followed by a Swedish decision granting the applicant's wife a divorce and giving her custody over the couple's child, violated Article 8 ECHR. The Commission ultimately decided that the application was inadmissible. However, it should be noted that the Commission in so deciding neither really discussed the private international law issue in this case, nor the complaint under Article 8 ECHR for that matter.

[102] The 1968 Brussels Convention on the Jurisdiction and Enforcement in Civil and Commercial Matters, *OJ* 1972 L 299/32, is the predecessor of the Brussels I Regulation, which has been discussed supra n. 5. Matters of status are excluded from the scope of the Brussels Convention, but this matter was also concerned with an issue of maintenance, which does fall within its scope.

the applicants' rights guaranteed in Article 8 ECHR and Article 1 of Protocol No. 1 ECHR. The Court found that the refusal to enforce the German judgment did indeed interfere with the applicants' rights guaranteed in both Article 8 and Article 1 of Protocol No. 1 ECHR.

Nevertheless, the Court held that the application was manifestly ill-founded.[103] It invoked in this regard the principle that no one can complain about a situation to which they themselves have contributed.[104] Reviewing the facts of the case, the Court found that the reason that the applicants were unable to have the German judgment enforced in Belgium—the reason for the Belgian refusal to enforce—was the fact that the applicants had initially brought their case before a court that did not have the competence to hear such a case. The Court concluded that the Belgian authorities could not be blamed for their refusal to enforce the German judgment, as this judgment had been rendered in disregard of the (proper) applicable rules on jurisdiction.

Before the Court's decision in *Hussin*, the possible impact of Article 8 ECHR in this regard had hardly been discussed in the literature, certainly if compared to issues concerning Article 6(1) ECHR.[105] The fact that the Court found that the non-recognition of a foreign family law judgment was indeed an interference of both Article 8 and Article 1 of Protocol No. 1 ECHR is thus an important finding and may have paved the way for the Court's subsequent findings, in particular in *Wagner* and *Négrepontis*, which are further discussed directly below. However, the reasoning consequently used by the Court in not finding a violation of these rights in *Hussin* is quite odd.[106]

By finding that Belgium had restricted the applicant's rights, the Court thus acknowledged that the obligations of a Contracting Party with regard to Article 8 ECHR are not confined to situations created by the Contracting Party itself or to situations which are already recognized in its legal order.[107] This may not be terribly surprising,[108] except perhaps for the fact that the Commission, in an old case, once had more or less expressed the opposite view.[109] However, despite the Court's acknowledgment of the importance of Article 8 ECHR (and also Article 1 of Protocol No. 1 ECHR) in *Hussin*, the application was found manifestly inadmissible.

However, it is first hard to see what Mrs. Hussin could have done differently in this case. Moreover, it is difficult to blame the applicants for the interpretation of

---

[103] See with regard to this notion supra Sect. 3.2.

[104] See also supra n. 24.

[105] But see Bucher 2000, particularly pp. 96–115. See also Matscher 1998, p. 221—noting the early decision of the Commission in *X. v. Sweden* (supra n. 101).

[106] Cf. Kinsch 2010, p. 262.

[107] Cf. generally Bucher 2011, p. 319; Franzina 2011, pp. 609–616.

[108] In Chap. 4 it has been discussed that the act of (not) recognizing a foreign judgment constitutes a situation within the jurisdiction of the Contracting Parties *ex* Article 1 ECHR. It consequently follows that this act may give rise to responsibility following a violation of one of the rights guaranteed in the ECHR.

[109] *X and Y v. the United Kingdom* (dec.), no. 7229/75, 15 December 1977.

the rules of international jurisdiction by the Belgian courts, which has been called 'dubious'.[110] Perhaps most importantly, by upholding the Belgian courts' decision to refuse the enforcement of the German judgment, the Court contributes to a limping legal relationship. In Germany the father of the children has been established, while this is not the case in Belgium. One could wonder whether this does not in itself violate Article 8 ECHR.[111] One could also wonder how the Court's findings in *Hussin* relate to its subsequent findings in *Wagner*, where the Court emphasized the importance of the legitimate expectations of the parties.[112]

In *Wagner and J.W.M.L. v. Luxembourg*[113] the Court had to decide whether the failure of the Luxembourg authorities to recognize the family ties between mother and child created by a Peruvian judgment (i.e., a judgment originating from a third country) pronouncing a full adoption, by not enforcing that Peruvian adoption judgment, would result in a violation of Article 8 ECHR. In addition to their complaint under Article 8 ECHR, the applicants had also alleged that by refusing to enforce the adoption judgment they had been unjustifiably discriminated against, resulting in a violation of Article 14 ECHR in conjunction with Article 8 ECHR. Finally, the applicants had also submitted that they had been deprived of a fair hearing under Article 6 ECHR, as the authorities had not fully considered their complaints in relation to Article 8 ECHR.[114]

The applicants were Jeanne Wagner and her adoptive daughter. At the time they both lived in Luxembourg. In 1996, under a Peruvian judgment, the mother had adopted the then 3-year-old girl, who had previously been declared abandoned. In 1997 the mother brought a civil action in Luxembourg seeking to have the Peruvian adoption judgment enforced in Luxembourg, in order, among other things, to have the child acquire Luxembourg nationality. However the district court dismissed the application, as it held that a court dealing with the enforcement of such a decision had to verify whether the adoption had been announced in accordance with Luxembourg law. The court thus used a choice-of-law test. Full adoption was not available to single women at the time under Luxembourg law. The mother appealed, relying in particular on the judgment being in violation of Article 8 ECHR. The appeal was dismissed, however, because, according to the higher court, the district court had rightfully dismissed the application on the basis that adoptions were subject to the law of the nationality of the adopter. These

[110] Kinsch 2010, p. 263.

[111] One could particularly wonder in this regard whether this takes the 'social reality of the situation' sufficiently into account. See, e.g., infra n. 118.

[112] See further infra the Court's findings in *Wagner*.

[113] *Wagner and J.W.M.L. v. Luxembourg*, no. 76240/01, ECHR 2007-VII (extracts).

[114] It should be noted that the Court in this case (also) found a violation of Article 6(1) ECHR, essentially because the Luxembourg courts had not given any reasons for the dismissal of the applicant's complaints based on Article 8 ECHR. However, as the complaint under Article 6(1) ECHR had otherwise little to do with private international law, it will not be further considered here.

conclusions were upheld by the *Cour de Cassation*, which held that Luxembourg law was applicable to the adoption.

With regard to the complaint under Article 8 ECHR, the Court first noted that there was de facto 'family life' between the mother and the adopted child. It thereafter considered that the refusal to declare the Peruvian decision enforceable amounted to an interference with the applicants' right to respect for their family life. This was in itself not a remarkable finding, as the Court had come to a similar conclusion concerning the recognition of a foreign (family law) judgment in *Hussin*.[115] However, this time the Court not only found an interference with Article 8 ECHR, but also a violation of this right.

In assessing whether the interference with Article 8 ECHR would amount to a violation, the Court essentially followed its usual approach regarding restrictions under this right—namely that it should be in accordance with the law, have a legitimate aim, and be necessary in a democratic society—which in short entails that the restriction must be proportionate to the legitimate aim pursued.[116] The Court first observed that the government's cautious approach in examining adoption decisions was not unreasonable. This served a legitimate aim, according to the Court. As for whether the government's measure had been 'necessary in a democratic society' under Article 8(2) ECHR, the Court noted that its task did not amount to defining the most appropriate response, but rather to review under the ECHR the decisions taken by the courts pursuant to their power of appreciation.

The Court used an all-encompassing approach, in the sense that it took quite a number of different factors into consideration. It noted that a broad consensus existed on the issue of adoption by unmarried persons. In most of the 47 Contracting Parties this is allowed without restrictions.[117] The Court further noted that up until recently, it had been the practice in Luxembourg to recognize automatically Peruvian judgments granting full adoption. Thus the applicants could reasonably have expected that the Peruvian judgment would be enforced. The Court took the view that the refusal to declare the judgment enforceable did not take account of the 'social reality of the situation'.[118] By not enforcing the decision, the family ties created in Peru could not officially be acknowledged in Luxembourg, which led to all kinds of problems in the applicants' day-to-day lives. Finally, the Court reiterated that in such cases the child's best interests had to take precedence, and thus found that there had been a violation of Article 8 ECHR.[119]

Once a violation of Article 8 ECHR is found, the Court usually no longer deems it necessary to review a complaint under Article 14 ECHR in conjunction with

---

[115] See supra n. 100.

[116] See with regard to the system of restrictions under Article 8 ECHR further supra Sect. 3.5.1.2 .

[117] *Wagner and J.W.M.L. v. Luxembourg*, no. 76240/01, paras 126, 129, ECHR 2007-VII (extracts).

[118] *Wagner and J.W.M.L. v. Luxembourg*, no. 76240/01, para 132, ECHR 2007-VII (extracts).

[119] *Wagner and J.W.M.L. v. Luxembourg*, no. 76240/01, para 133, ECHR 2007-VII (extracts).

Article 8 ECHR. However, in this instance, the Court did review that complaint separately. Not surprisingly, the Court also found a violation in this regard, as it held that the child had been penalized in her daily life because of her status as the adoptive child of an unmarried mother. This status resulted, for example, in her not having Luxembourg nationality, which necessitated applying regularly for residence permits and requesting visas for visiting certain countries. The Court did not see any justification for such discrimination, especially because earlier full adoption orders had automatically been granted in Luxembourg with respect to other Peruvian children.

How should one weigh the Court's findings in *Wagner*?[120] It should be clear that the impact of this judgment with regard to the recognition of not only foreign adoption judgments, but also foreign family law judgments determining one's status more generally, could potentially be enormous if one were to interpret this judgment as entailing a blanket obligation for the Contracting Parties to recognize and enforce such judgments. Interpreted in this manner, the *Wagner* judgment could be seen as introducing a new method of recognition for foreign family law judgments based on Article 8 ECHR replacing the traditional private international law methods.[121] The traditional private international law method entails that foreign family law judgments will, in principle, be recognized, provided that certain requirements are met.[122] Taken to the extreme, *Wagner* could entail that Contracting Parties are no longer allowed to deny recognition to such judgments in light of, in particular, the legitimate expectations of the parties and the social reality of the situation, and that the requirements, the grounds of refusal, following from the private international law regimes would no longer be valid. It has in this regard been argued that the *Wagner* judgment can be considered to be part of a general movement within European family law, a new methodology based on fundamental rights, in which the recognition of foreign situations trumps traditional private international law rules.[123]

However, one could, in my opinion, wonder whether such a far-reaching interpretation of this judgment can be justified.[124] Although one may easily argue that the Court's findings in *Wagner* need not necessarily be limited to foreign adoption judgments, it is at least arguable that the particular circumstances of the case have in large part contributed to the Court's judgment.[125]

---

[120] The *Wagner* judgment has been often discussed, primarily in the French literature. See for annotations, e.g., *Dalloz* 2007, p. 2700ff (note Marchadier) and *Rev.crit dr.int.priv.* 2007, p. 807ff (note Kinsch).

[121] See D'Avout 2010, p. 170ff.

[122] These requirements differ from country to country. See supra Sect. 5.1 for a brief presentation of the various requirements regarding foreign judgments.

[123] See Muir Watt 2008, pp. 1983–1998. The author invoked, in addition to fundamental rights, 'European citizenship' as a building block of this new methodology in the EU. See more generally Lagarde 2004, pp. 225–243.

[124] Cf. Franzina 2011.

[125] Cf. Kinsch 2010, p. 266. See also *Rev.crit dr.int.priv.* 2007, pp. 815–818 (note Kinsch; see supra n. 120).

The Court in *Wagner*, in its reasoning concerning Article 8 ECHR, named several factors which contributed to its finding that the decision of the Luxembourg courts to deny recognition was not proportionate. It noted that full adoption has been recognized in an overwhelming majority of the European States. This is essentially an argument against giving the respondent Contracting Party a wide margin of appreciation. The Court also clearly emphasized the legitimate expectations of the applicants. The mother had the legitimate expectation that the Peruvian judgment—and thus the status acquired abroad—would be recognized in Luxembourg, as that had, in fact, been the practice until the mother attempted to do so.[126] The impact of *Wagner* on the recognition and enforcement of foreign judgments determining a status may therefore largely depend on the extent to which the Court is willing to stretch its interpretation of the legitimate expectations of parties. This, in my opinion, does not necessarily mean that such a legitimate belief only exists in a case where recognition of a status acquired abroad is the current practice in a State, but there must at least be some reason to assume that recognition would be possible in order to invoke Article 8 ECHR. An individual must thus act 'in good faith'.[127]

Another important element of the Court's findings in *Wagner* concerns the fact that a status validly created in a foreign country may at a certain point become a 'social reality', as the Court puts it, which may consequently stand in the way of a denial of the recognition of such a foreign judgment.[128] If one were to focus more on this aspect of the Court's findings in *Wagner*, this may lead to many more occasions where a validly acquired status abroad will be able to circumvent traditional private international law rules regarding recognition/grounds for refusal, as it is easily imaginable that a status acquired abroad will attain such a status. The Court in this regard referred to the problems in the applicant's day-to-day life caused by ignoring this 'social reality', but these are arguably the concerns of limping legal relationships generally. Finally, the Court also referenced the best interests of the child, which remain an important consideration for the Court in such cases.

Since its judgment in *Wagner*, the Court has had the opportunity to expand on its findings with regard to the obligation to recognize foreign family law judgments

---

[126] See Kinsch 2010, p. 266, who notes that the legitimate expectation in this case may have been unique in the sense that, according to this author, the civil registry in Luxembourg did not apply the law as it stood correctly.

[127] *Wagner and J.W.M.L. v. Luxembourg*, no. 76240/01, para 130, ECHR 2007-VII (extracts).

[128] The *Wagner* judgment has in this regard also been hailed as 'an affirmation of the importance of the recognition of pre-existing family links, taking into consideration the best interest of the child, which should always predominate' by Judge Berro-Lefevre in a contribution to the Joint Council of Europe and European Commission Conference Challenges in adoption procedures in Europe: Ensuring the best interests of the child. This conference was held in Strasbourg from 30 November 2009 until 1 December 2009. The report of the Conference may be found at the website of the Council of Europe: http://www.coe.int/t/dghl/standardsetting/family/Adoption%20conference/Brochure%20conf%C3%A9rence%20Adoption_LR.pdf. Accessed March 2014.

(or rather a status acquired abroad).[129] In its admissibility decision in *Mary Green and Ajad Farhat v. Malta*[130] the Court found the applicants' invocation of Article 8 ECHR against the refusal by the Maltese authorities to register their marriage concluded in Libya to be manifestly ill-founded. The applicants were both Maltese nationals. In 1978 the first applicant, Mary Green, married Mr. X, a Maltese citizen, in accordance with the rites of the Catholic Church and Maltese law. In 1980 she went to Libya and converted to Islam. This had a consequence that her first marriage was deemed null and void. Later that year she married the second applicant in Libya in accordance with the rites of Islam. The applicants continued to live lawfully married in Libya for 20 years. In 2000 the couple returned to Malta to take care of the first applicant's ailing father. Several attempts were made to register the second marriage, but the Public Registry and thereafter the Maltese courts refused, as, in short, the first applicant had failed to prove that the first marriage had been annulled (the applicant's first husband had been unaware of any proceedings) and that her second marriage had not been polygamous, while she had also failed to establish that she was domiciled in Libya since she had retained her Maltese citizenship.

Before the Court in Strasbourg the applicants invoked Article 8 ECHR, and Article 8 ECHR taken in conjunction with Article 14 ECHR against the refusal to register the Libyan marriage, whereby the complaint with regard to Article 8 ECHR is of particular interest. The Court made short work of the invocation of Article 8 ECHR in this case. It found that even assuming that there had been an interference with Article 8 ECHR, there could be no breach of this Article. After setting out its general approach to interferences with Article 8 ECHR,[131] the Court found that the authorities' assessment that the applicant had not satisfied the legal requirements was not considered manifestly unreasonable. These legal requirements regarding the registration of marriages fell within the State's margin of appreciation. In the circumstances, the Court could not find that the respondent Contracting Party had failed to strike a fair balance, given 'the interests of the community in ensuring monogamous marriages' and those of the third party directly involved, the first husband. The interference could thus be held to be necessary in a democratic society.

Even though the Court dismissed the invocation of Article 8 ECHR against the refusal to register a foreign family law status, it is not difficult to rhyme this decision with the Court's judgment in *Wagner*.[132] The Court also referred to its usual scheme with regard to restrictions under Article 8 ECHR. While it does not really go into details, it is clear that in this case—just like it did extensively in

[129] See infra the discussion on the distinction between the recognition of a foreign family judgment and a status acquired abroad in a non-judicial manner directly following the examination of *Green and Farhat*.

[130] *Mary Green and Ajad Farhat v. Malta* (dec.), no. 38797/07, 6 July 2010.

[131] See supra Sect. 3.5.1.2

[132] See also Kinsch 2011a, pp. 42–44.

Wagner—the Court goes back to whether a refusal is necessary in a democratic society. This requirement leaves room for a balancing of interests. In *Green and Farhat* the Court's assessment of this requirement is simply different, which given the circumstances, is not hard to explain. Not only was *Wagner* concerned with a topic in which there was a European consensus, which has, of course, an impact on the margin of appreciation, but more importantly in *Green and Farhat* the interests of others played an important role, as the first applicant's first husband was still alive and domiciled in Malta, and had been unaware of any proceedings concerning the annulment of his marriage.

One could with regard to the recognition of a status acquired abroad, incidentally, wonder whether a more thorough distinction should be made between the recognition of a foreign family law judgment on the one hand, and the recognition of a status acquired abroad in a non-judicial manner on the other hand. One could argue that from the perspective of private international law there is a distinction between the two situations. The difference is that some changes in one's status require a judicial decision, such as, for example a divorce. In such a case in a cross-border affair the recognition of a foreign family law judgment is at stake. However, other status modifications, such as marriage, do not require a judicial decision. Consequently, one cannot in the latter situation in a cross-border affair (formally) refer to the recognition of a foreign family law judgment. Nevertheless, the term recognition is used in both situations. From the perspective of private international law one could say that both situations are different. Traditionally, in most countries the former category requires recognition in accordance with rules of private international law, while the latter category has a somewhat different recognition regime, which may differ depending on the exact status concerned (whether, for example, the recognition of a marriage or a name is concerned).

While admittedly a distinction between the two situations could be made from the perspective of private international law, this distinction does not add much with regard to the question of the impact of Article 8 ECHR on the recognition of a foreign status/judgment validly acquired abroad. It follows from the Court's case law, as discussed above, that the Court does not make a distinction between the two situations. *Green and Farhat*, for example, concerns the recognition of a marriage, and this case is thus formally speaking not concerned with the recognition of a foreign family law judgment. Yet, in its assessment of the question of whether the marriage should be recognized, the Court does not change its approach with regard to Article 8 ECHR. As stated above, despite the difference in outcome of the two cases, the Court's approach in *Green and Farhat* ties in well with its approach in *Wagner*. It is clear that Article 8 ECHR in principle prescribes a more recognition friendly framework, even though that does not necessarily mean that Contracting Parties can no longer require certain conditions to be met, as will also be further discussed below. This would appear to apply irrespective of whether the recognition of a foreign family judgment or the recognition of a status acquired abroad in a non-judicial manner is at stake. It is for this reason that the distinction is not further discussed in this chapter.[133] There is, incidentally, a lively debate in particularly the French and German literature on the method of recognition, and whether a status acquired abroad should be recognized automatically without too many formalities.[134] Interestingly enough, fundamental rights in general, and Article 8 ECHR in particular, are named as the catalysts of this debate.[135]

Négrépontis-Giannissis adds another piece to the discussion on the obligation *ex* Article 8 ECHR to recognize (and enforce) foreign family law judgments. This case concerned the refusal of the Greek courts to recognize an American adoption order. The applicant, Nikolas Négrépontis-Giannissis, was a Greek national born in 1964, who resided in Greece. In the 1980s, when the applicant was studying, he lived with his uncle, an orthodox monk, in the United States. In 1984 the applicant and his uncle started proceedings in the United States for the uncle to adopt him. The uncle indicated that he wanted an adoption because the applicant would thus become his legal heir. Later that year the adoption was pronounced by a court in Michigan. The following year the applicant returned to Greece. The applicant and his uncle visited each other on a regular basis. In 1996 the uncle returned to Greece, where he passed away 2 years later.

In the first instance the American adoption order was recognized in Greece and the adoption was declared to be final and legally enforceable in Greece in 1999. After this judgment the applicant initiated having his name changed, and was allowed to add his adoptive father's surname, Négrépontis, to his original last name of Giannissis. The recognition of the adoption order resulted, however, in the applicant being the only legal heir, which was to the prejudice of the brother and sisters of the applicant's uncle. The brother and sisters subsequently initiated proceedings challenging the recognition of the American adoption. This challenge was first denied, but it was overturned on appeal, as the appeal court found that monks were prohibited from carrying out legal acts relating to secular activities, such as adoption, because this was held to be incompatible with the monastic life and Greek *ordre public*. This decision was affirmed by the Greek Court of Cassation, which based the decision on canon law texts originating from the seventh and eighth centuries.

Before the Court in Strasbourg the applicant subsequently invoked Article 8 ECHR, Article 8 in conjunction with Article 14 ECHR, Article 6(1) ECHR, and Article 1 of Protocol No. 1 ECHR against the Greek court's refusal to recognize the American adoption order. The applicant alleged that the refusal by the Greek authorities to recognize his adoption in Greece and the obligation to change back his last name violated Article 8 ECHR. The Court first considered that it did not

---

[133] This also explains why a few Dutch cases concerning the registration of a name will be discussed in this chapter, even though these case are strictly speaking not concerned with the recognition of a foreign family law judgment. See infra Sect. 7.4.2.

[134] Lagarde has an important role in this debate: see Lagarde 2004, 2008. See further on this debate, e.g., Bollée 2007; Coester-Waltjen 2006; Mansel 2006; Mayer 2005; Melcher 2013; Muir Watt 2008, 2013; Pamboukis 2008.

[135] See, e.g., Muir Watt 2013, p. 416. See also supra n. 123.

see any reason why the relationship between the applicant and his adoptive father would not fall under 'family life'. The Court held that this case concerned two adults who were well aware of the consequences of the adoption procedure. Referring to its finding in *Wagner*, the Court thus found that the Greek authorities' decision amounted to an interference of Article 8 ECHR.

In assessing whether this interference was justified, the Court first turned to the issue of whether the interference was 'in accordance with the law', as Article 8(2) ECHR prescribes.[136] The Court acknowledged that the highest Greek court had based its rejection of the adoption order on certain provisions of the Greek Civil Code, which in short entail that a foreign judgment can only be enforceable in Greece if it does not conflict with Greek public policy. However, in finding that an adoption by a monk violated Greek public policy, the Greek court had referred to certain ancient articles of an ecclesiastical nature which dated back to the seventh and eighth centuries. Moreover, the Court found that in 1982 legislation was passed in Greece that permitted monks to marry, and there was no legislation that expressly did not permit monks to adopt. The Court also took into consideration the fact that the adoption order was already in place for 24 years and that it had been the express wish of the adoptive father to have a legitimate son who could inherit his property. Taking all this into account, the Court ultimately held that the interference—the refusal to recognize the foreign order—did not amount to a pressing social need, which is a requirement in relation to necessity in a democratic society.[137] Even if there had been a legitimate aim, the refusal to recognize the adoption order was disproportionate, as the refusal completely denied the adoptive son's status. The Court thus found a violation of Article 8 ECHR.

Similar to its judgment in *Wagner*, the Court in *Négrépontis* did not only find a violation in respect of Article 8 ECHR. As to the applicant's complaint that the Greek decision was discriminatory, because a biological child of his uncle could have maintained his inheritance rights invoking Article 8 ECHR taken in conjunction with Article 14 ECHR, the Court—referring to its earlier case law in this regard[138]—found a violation, because the Greek authorities could not provide reasons that justified the difference in treatment.[139]

It will, finally, be recalled that the Court in *Négrépontis* also found violations of both Article 6(1) ECHR and Article 1 of Protocol No. 1 ECHR. With regard to Article 6(1) ECHR the Court found that while it was, in principle, possible for the Greek courts to refuse to recognize a foreign adoption order where a foreign decision would violate public policy, the interpretation thereof cannot be made in

[136] See further on the system of restrictions regarding Article 8 ECHR supra Sect. 3.5.1.2.

[137] See supra Sect. 3.5.1.2.

[138] See, particularly, *Pla and Puncernau v. Andorra*, no. 69498/01, para 61, ECHR 2004-VIII.

[139] See *Négrépontis-Giannisis v. Greece*, no. 56759/08, paras 77–84, particularly paras 82–84, 3 May 2011.

an arbitrary and disproportionate manner.[140] As the refusal to recognize the foreign adoption order had consequences for the applicant's ability to inherit from his adoptive father, the Court—referring also to its findings with regard to Article 8 ECHR—found that there had also been a violation of Article 1 of Protocol No. 1 ECHR.[141]

Négrépontis-Giannisis is mostly a confirmation of what the Court had previously held in *Wagner*, even though the Court does give some more insights into what the obligation to recognize foreign family law judgments under Article 8 ECHR exactly entails.[142] Just like it had in *Wagner*, the Court in *Négrépontis-Giannisis* underscored the fact that the foreign judgment had been validly created abroad and that the relationship between the applicant and his adoptive father had become a social reality.[143] It could also be noted that the Court attached weight to the fact that the adoption had been valid for 24 years. In determining whether the interference of Article 8 ECHR could be justified under Article 8(2) ECHR the Court again, as it did in *Wagner*, grouped together a number of arguments before concluding that under the circumstances the reasoning used by the highest Greek court not to recognize the adoption did not amount to a pressing social need and that the non-recognition was disproportionate. Again, the particular circumstances of the case make it possible to interpret this judgment restrictively. After all, in its judgment the Court attached significant weight to the fact that the order had initially been declared legal, while it also criticized the peculiar use of the public policy exception.

It is interesting to further reflect on the fact the Court essentially rejected *in casu* the use of the public policy exception by the Greek courts, as the American adoption decree was ultimately rejected on the basis of the invocation of Greek public policy.[144] Even though this may come across as a very important restriction of the leeway that Contracting Parties may claim with regard to the recognition of foreign family law judgments under their private international law regimes, one should not overstate this particular finding. The public policy exception was invoked in this case by the Greek court because it was held that adoption by monks would violate public policy. However, as was also discussed above, this view was based on seventh- and eighth-century canon texts, while in 1982 a law had been passed allowing monks to marry. Moreover, there was no law prohibiting monks from adopting. It is not altogether surprising that given these circumstances, the Court did not condone the invocation of the public policy exception.

---

[140] *Négrépontis-Giannisis v. Greece*, no. 56759/08, paras 85–92, 3 May 2011. See also supra Sect. 7.2.

[141] *Négrépontis-Giannisis v. Greece*, no. 56759/08, paras 93–105, 3 May 2011. See also supra Sect. 7.3.

[142] Kinsch 2011b, pp. 818–819. See with regard to this case also Daelman 2011, pp. 70–73; Kinsch 2011a, pp. 44–45.

[143] *Négrépontis-Giannisis v. Greece*, no. 56759/08, paras 56 and 74, 3 May 2011 (citing *Wagner and J.W.M.L. v. Luxembourg*, no. 76240/01, paras 132–233, ECHR 2007-VII (extracts)).

[144] See also supra n. 48.

Nevertheless, it would go too far to regard the Court's decision in this respect as a general indictment of the use of (substantive) public policy as a barrier to the recognition of foreign family law judgments. There may be limits to its use, as *Négrépontis* clearly demonstrates, but one should not lose sight of the fact that the construction of the public policy exception by the Greek courts was quite peculiar. What should also be clear is that the invocation of the public policy exception by the courts of the Contracting Parties with regard to the recognition and enforcement of foreign judgments must meet the requirements that the Court prescribes in relation to restrictions to the rights guaranteed in the ECHR. An invocation of the public policy exception must thus be proportional.

Harroudj v. France[145] may, for now, be regarded as the Court's final piece of the discussion on the obligation *ex* Article 8 ECHR to recognize (and enforce) foreign family law judgments. However, this case should be distinguished from *Wagner* and *Négrépontis-Giannisis* because it does not concern the outright denial to recognize a foreign judgment, as the effects of the foreign judgments in this case were partly recognized.

The applicant was a French national who lived in France. In 2004 an Algerian court granted her the right, in accordance with Islamic law, to take into her legal care a child born in Algeria. This is known as *kafala*. The child had been abandoned at birth and her parents were unknown. The Algerian authorities granted legal authorization to change the child's last name to Harroudj. The child was brought to France in 2004.

In France, the applicant attempted to adopt the child, but this was denied by the French courts because the *kafala* gave the applicant parental authority over the child, which enabled her to take all the decisions in the child's interests, while also giving the child all the protection to which it was entitled under international treaties. Moreover, French private international law rules regarding adoption point to the law of the country of origin of the child, Algerian law. Algerian law does not allow adoption. Under Islamic law it is not possible to create family bonds comparable to those created by biological filiation. The form of guardianship of *kafala* available in Algeria entails a voluntary undertaking to provide for a child and to take care of his or her welfare and education. In France *kafala* is regarded as a form of guardianship, or delegation of parental authority, which does not create family bonds, gives no right to inherit, and no (automatic) right for the child to acquire the nationality of the guardian.

It should be noted that contrary to the situation set out above, French law does authorize adoption governed by Islamic law if the minor was born and habitually resides in France. Finally, it is possible for a child who has been under the care of a French national, but who cannot be adopted due to his or her status under Islamic law, to apply for French citizenship if they have lived in France for at least 5 years. On appeal before the French *Cour de Cassation* the mother argued that adoption

[145] *Harroudj v. France*, no. 43631/09, 4 October 2012. See with regard to this case also EHRC 2013/10 (note Voorhoeve); *Rev.crit dr.int.priv.* 2013, pp. 161–172 (note Corneloup).

was in the best interests of the child and that the denial of the adoption resulted in a difference in treatment based on the child's country of origin. The *Cour de Cassation* rejected these arguments by, inter alia, referring to the New York Convention on the Rights of the Child, in which *kafala* is explicitly acknowledged as protecting the child's best interests in the same way as adoption.

Before the Court in Strasbourg the applicant, relying on Article 8 ECHR, argued that the refusal to acknowledge family bonds between her and the child amounted to a disproportionate interference of her right to family life. She also complained under Article14 ECHR. Concurring with the French authorities, the Court first noted that the refusal to let the applicant adopt the child did not really amount to an interference with the applicant's family life. The Court remarked that it was more appropriate to discuss the complaint through the lens of a positive obligation.[146] The Court further immediately distinguished *Harroudj* from *Wagner*, as in *Harroudj* the situation was merely limited to not equating a *kafala* with an adoption and referring to the personal law of the child for determining whether an adoption is possible, while in *Wagner* the Luxembourg courts had ignored a status created validly abroad in an unreasonable manner, thereby violating Article 8 ECHR.

With regard to a possible positive obligation under Article 8 ECHR the Court first observed that France enjoyed a wide margin of appreciation on this issue, as there is no consensus between the Contracting Parties on how to deal with *kafala*. While none of the Contracting Parties, according to the Court, treat *kafala* as being equal to adoption, the approaches vary as to whether the law of the country of origin of the child constitutes an obstacle to adoption.[147] The Court further noted that, while the decision of France was in the first place based on the French law, it was also based on compliance with the New York Convention on the Rights of the Child, in which *kafala* is acknowledged as being on par with adoption.

The Court also observed that *kafala* was fully accepted in French law and produced effects similar to guardianship. Moreover, it was possible for the applicant to include the child in her will and to choose a legal guardian. The child had the possibility to acquire French nationality after a short time, after which it would even be possible for the child to be adopted, according to the Court. The Court concluded that the French authorities had struck a fair balance between the public interests and those of the applicant, thereby respecting cultural pluralism. In

---

[146] See *Harroudj v. France*, no. 43631/09, para 47, 4 October 2012. The Court, incidentally, noted earlier in its judgment that the principles regarding issues concerning a positive obligation under Article 8(1) ECHR and a negative obligation under the same Article and the extent to which possible interferences are allowed under Article 8(2) ECHR are similar. See *Harroudj v. France*, no. 43631/09, para 43, 4 October 2012. The fact that the Court uses a similar approach to these two issues also follows from its findings in *Wagner and J.M.W.L. v. Luxembourg*, no. 76240/01, 28 June 2007 (see supra n. 113).

[147] See *Harroudj v. France*, no. 43631/09, para 22, 4 October 2012.

light of this finding with regard to Article 8 ECHR the Court deemed that no separate issue arose under Article 14 ECHR.[148]

While the Court in both *Wagner* and *Négrépontis-Giannisis* appears to instill a more recognition-friendly framework with regard to the recognition and enforcement of foreign family law judgments, resulting in greater scrutiny of grounds for refusal of recognition, it is interesting to note that the Court in *Harroudj* did not find a violation of Article 8 ECHR. However, as noted above, this latter case did not concern the outright refusal to recognize a foreign judgment. Effect was given to the Algerian judgment in France, just not to the extent the applicant had in mind. The fact that some effect was given to the judgment appears to make a difference, in the Court's view. Moreover, the resulting disadvantages of not being adopted could be remedied by the mother by other means. The fact that *kafala* is recognized in international treaties as being in the best interests of the child appears to have persuaded the Court that in this case no violation of Article 8 ECHR had occurred.

The Court's judgment is thus understandable, even though the Court's finding does lead to a difference in treatment in the name of cultural pluralism. Finally, the invocation of cultural pluralism by the Court in this case is interesting. In the previously discussed cases in this research this never really appeared to be a consideration of the Court, at least not explicitly so.[149] It will be interesting to see whether this consideration will be limited to this case, or whether the Court will move in a new direction.

There are some other, final issues that could be discussed with regard to the obligation to recognize foreign family law judgments following from Article 8 ECHR. One of these is whether the origin of the foreign family law judgments is relevant. One could note that in *Hussin* the foreign judgment originated from Germany, another Contracting Party, while *Wagner* and *Négrépontis-Giannisis* were, respectively, concerned with a Peruvian and an American judgment (two non-Contracting Parties). However, in my opinion, the origin of the judgment is irrelevant. At issue is, after all, whether the *receiving* Contracting Party violates the right to family life by not recognizing the foreign family law judgment. It is only relevant whether the status following from this family law judgment has been validly acquired abroad and whether the applicant had a legitimate expectation that the status would be recognized. The origin of that judgment, however, is in itself not relevant.

What is, finally, particularly relevant with regard to the obligation to recognize foreign family law judgments following from Article 8 ECHR is the additional

---

[148] *Harroudj* will presumably not be the last case, in which the Court will have to examine the consequences of the refusal by the authorities to recognize *kafala*. See, e.g., the Statement of Facts in *Chbihi Loudoudi and Others v. Belgium*, no. 52265/10, introduced 25 August 2010 (available only in French).

[149] See, e.g., *Ammdjadi v. Germany*, discussed supra Sect. 6.3.1.

component that the recognition of such judgments may affect the rights of others—whose rights may also be protected under the same Article.[150] *Green and Farhat* is a pertinent example.[151] In such cases there may be interests that override the interest of the recognition and enforcement of a foreign judgment. This was also demonstrated in the Court's judgment in *Pini and Others v. Romania* in relation to a competing obligation under Article 6(1) ECHR.[152]

It will be recalled that *Pini* concerned the complaint of two Italian couples about a violation of both Articles 8 and 6 ECHR due to the failure to execute decisions of a Romanian court regarding the adoption of two Romanian minors. Because of this failure, the applicants had been deprived of virtually all contact with the two children. The Court found a violation of Article 6(1) ECHR.[153] With regard to the compliance with Article 8 ECHR the Court first reiterated that it had consistently held that the State's obligation to take positive measures includes the parents' right to measures facilitating the reunion with their children and the obligation of the State to take such action, although this obligation is not absolute, especially in the case in which parent(s) and child are strangers to each other.[154] Thus the decisive issue is whether the authorities took all the necessary steps to enable the applicants to establish family relations with the children they had adopted.

The Court held that the applicants could not enjoy absolute protection of Article 8 ECHR in this case, insofar as the children had a competing interest and that the children's interests should prevail. While the Court stated that it deplored the manner in which the adoption proceedings were conducted, in particular the lack of genuine contact between the parties to the adoption, it could not justify under these circumstances imposing on the Romanian authorities an absolute obligation to ensure that the children would go to Italy against their will. The Court thus did not find a violation of Article 8 ECHR in this respect.

Pini is something of a curious case, because the Court reached opposite conclusions with regard to the obligation to recognize under Articles 6(1) and 8 of the ECHR. It found a violation of Article 6(1) ECHR, but no violation of Article 8 ECHR. The latter result is perfectly understandable because of the two competing interests—that of the applicants, the prospective parents, and the children, who preferred to stay in Romania. As has been discussed above, in the balancing of interests, the interests of others play an important part. This balancing act is included in the requirement of necessity in a democratic society in Article 8(2) ECHR.

---

[150] The rights of others may also play a role with regard to the obligation to recognize and enforce under, respectively, Article 6(1) ECHR and Article 1 of Protocol No. 1 ECHR, but this issue will be more prevalent with regard to Article 8 ECHR.

[151] See supra n. 130.

[152] *Pini and Others v. Romania*, nos. 78028/01 and 78030/01, ECHR 2004-V (extracts).

[153] See supra Sect. 7.2.1.

[154] See *Pini and Others v. Romania*, nos. 78028/01 and 78030/01, paras 149–151 with references to the Court's established case law in this respect.

What remains difficult to understand, though, is how the Court could reach two opposite conclusions regarding Article 8 and Article 6 ECHR. If enforcing the final decisions would violate the rights of the children, how could the Court then still find a violation in respect of Article 6(1) ECHR?[155] The only thing that I could think of is that the Court wanted to make a statement with regard to the enforcement mechanism of the Romanian authorities, but even though such a signal may be important, it still leaves Romania with two competing obligations with which it could not have possibly complied simultaneously. It appears to follow from the Court's case law that where the rights of third parties are directly concerned, the obligation to recognize and enforce would, in principle, have to take a back seat.

7.4.1 *The Obligation to Recognize and Enforce Following from Article 8 ECHR*

What does the obligation to recognize foreign family law judgments exactly mean, particularly with regard to the traditional private international law rules on recognition and enforcement? It follows from the Court's case law that Article 8 ECHR, in principle, entails an obligation to recognize foreign family law judgments in which a status is acquired, but that this obligation is not absolute. This, incidentally, also applies to a status acquired abroad in a non-judicial manner. Therefore there is still room for private international law defenses against the recognition of foreign family law judgments. However, these must comply with the requirements following from Article 8 ECHR, which means that they must pursue a legitimate aim, have a basis in law, and be necessary in a democratic society. As we have seen before, the Court performs a balancing of interests, particularly in regard to this latter condition. In short, a decision to interfere with the obligation to recognize must be proportionate.

How does the Court weigh all of this? It has been noted that the Court takes into account a number of factors. However, the extent of the obligation to enforce will largely depend on how the Court will further interpret in future cases the legitimate expectations of parties in relation to the social reality of a situation which is created by a foreign family law judgment. In particular, an emphasis on this notion of the legitimate expectation of parties may limit the extent of the obligation to recognize under Article 8 ECHR and prevent this obligation becoming a semi-automatic override of traditional private international law defenses. One could argue that in both *Wagner* (where the practice to recognize and enforce was in place, until the applicants attempted to have the adoption recognized) and

[155] Cf. the Dissenting Opinion of Judge Thomassen joined by Judge Jungwiert in *Pini* (supra n. 50), who concludes that this is impossible. Incidentally, Judge Thomassen was of the opinion that in this case no family life existed between the applicants and the Romanian children.

Négrépontis (where the adoption was seemingly valid for 24 years) the parties had every reason to expect recognition of the status acquired abroad. It will be interesting to see what happens in the absence of such a strong presumption, where nevertheless the social reality created by the foreign judgment is hard to ignore.

In the balancing of interests with regard to the obligation to enforce, the protection of the rights of others appears to trump the obligation to recognize and enforce. Moreover, the best interests of the child is a transcending factor in the Court's case law, which may either help in finding a failure to recognize and enforce (*Wagner*), or override an obligation to enforce (*Pini*).

Finally, it follows from the Court's latest case on the obligation under Article 8 ECHR to recognize foreign family law judgments that a distinction should be made between the situation in which the recognition of a foreign family law judgment is refused and the situation in which some effect is given to such a judgment. One could argue that in the latter situation the scrutiny of the Court with regard to Article 8 ECHR will be less strict.

7.4.2 Jurisprudence of the National Courts of the Contracting Parties

There is not—yet—a lot of case law directly concerned with Article 8 ECHR and the obligation to recognize foreign family law judgments in the national case law of the Contracting Parties. The Court's case law in this regard is still quite recent, and developing. One may nevertheless already discern an increasing role for Article 8 ECHR in relation to the recognition and enforcement of foreign family law judgments. It will furthermore be demonstrated that the Court's case law concerning the obligation to recognize foreign family law judgments, in spite of traditional private international law rules opposing recognition, is not an isolated event, as long before the Court's findings in this regard the German *Bundesverfassungsgericht* had already decided such a case in a similar manner.[156] Below, some relevant decisions of national courts will be examined.

The English case of *Singh v. Entry Clearance Officer (New Delhi)*,[157] for example, concerned the issue of whether 'family life', as understood in Article 8(1) ECHR, could be established between the appellant, a 6 year old Indian boy, and his adoptive parents, who were settled in the United Kingdom (UK).[158] The Indian child had been adopted in India by an English couple of Indian descent in a

[156] See infra n. 171.

[157] *Singh v. Entry Clearance Officer (New Delhi)* [2004] EWCA Civ 1075, [2005] QB 608.

[158] It is, incidentally, interesting to compare this case to the aforementioned case of the Commission, *X and Y v. the United Kingdom*, no. 7229/75, 15 December 1977. The facts in both cases are remarkably similar, yet the outcome is not. It demonstrates the development of the interpretation of Article 8 ECHR.

Sikh religious ceremony. According to Indian law the adoption was valid and formally transferred parental rights from the natural parents to the adoptive parents. However, the adoption was not recognized by the UK. As a result of, inter alia, the non-recognition the child had been denied entry clearance to join his parents in the UK. However, it was held in this case that the relationship between the child and his adoptive parents was protected by Article 8 ECHR, while it was, incidentally, acknowledged that this situation had only come about because of the difference of views of what an adoption entails.[159]

In another English case, *Re N (Recognition of Foreign Adoption Order)*,[160] the impact of Article 8 ECHR on the obligation to recognize foreign adoption orders was also visible, as it was held in this case that the Adoption and Children Act 2002[161] should be read differently in order to respect the rights guaranteed in this Article. In this case a British man adopted the child of his Armenian partner in Armenia. The Armenian birth certificate was changed in order to name the British man as the child's father, but the name of the mother was also still on the certificate, which confirmed that the mother retained parental responsibility after the adoption. Upon relocation to England, the man sought a declaration before the courts recognizing the foreign adoption order. However, a literal interpretation of Section 67(3) of the Adoption and Children Act 2002 would appear to result in the mother losing parental responsibility. This was held to be in violation of Article 8 ECHR and the best interests of the child and, given that an English court would be able to make an adoption order without such an effect, it was held that the relevant section of the Adoption and Children Act 2002 should be read differently.

Dutch jurisprudence offers a few scattered examples of Article 8 ECHR being invoked in order to have a foreign family law judgment recognized. With regard to the recognition of foreign documents establishing the civil status of a person, Article 8 ECHR has been unsuccessfully invoked, even though Dutch courts have recognized the relevance of Article 8 in these cases. Before the *Gerechtshof* Amsterdam, for example, a man from Afghanistan requested the municipality to register the death certificate of his wife.[162] This death certificate, however, was deemed by the relevant Dutch authorities to be of questionable validity and the request was denied. The court in the first instance also rejected the man's request, as the validity of the document could not be established. On appeal Article 8 ECHR was, inter alia, discussed. The appeal court held that the refusal to register the certificate would indeed stand in the way of the man marrying in the Netherlands, which would interfere with his private life. However according to the

---

[159] See particularly [57] *per* Munby J.

[160] *Re N (Recognition of Foreign Adoption Order* [2009] EWHC 29 (Fam.), [2010] 1 FLR 1102.

[161] The Adoption and Children Act 2002.

[162] Hof Amsterdam 6 March 2003, *NIPR* 2005, 305. See also Rechtbank 's-Gravenhage, 22 April 2004, *NIPR* 2005, 224, in which a Dutch court in a somewhat similar case found, regarding the registration of a wedding certificate of a marriage between a Dutch man and his Afghan wife, that the decision not to register such a document did not interfere with his rights under Article 8 ECHR.

appeal court this interference was justified under Article 8(2) ECHR. The registration of the certificate was therefore denied.

An example of a successful invocation of Article 8 ECHR can be found in a case before the district court in Haarlem concerning the recognition of a Chinese adoption order.[163] The court recognized the adoption order on the basis of the criterion of the best interests of the child, which it basically derived from Article 8 ECHR.[164]

In a fairly recent case the Swiss *Tribunal fédéral* has refused the recognition of a Brazilian adoption order on the basis of Article 78(1) of the Swiss Private International Law Act.[165] The *Tribunal fédéral* concluded that as the adoption had been announced in Brazil in accordance with Brazilian law, the country of domicile at the time of the child, while the parents were at the time domiciled in Spain and had Swiss nationality, the requirements following from Article 78 of the Swiss Act had not been met.[166] The Swiss court held that Switzerland generally followed the principle of *favor recognitionis* and that, in principle, foreign adoptions are recognized. However, it held that the limitations following from the aforementioned Article were justified because the authorities of the State of domicile of the child are generally better qualified to examine whether the adoption corresponds with the best interests of the child and whether the prospective parents are able to take care of the child. As was indicated above, the child whose adoption had not been recognized has brought her case before the Court in Strasbourg, alleging violations of Article 8 ECHR and Article 8 in conjunction with Article 14 ECHR. The case is now pending.[167]

The cases discussed above could be cited as an acknowledgment by national courts of the Contracting Parties of an emerging obligation following from the Court's case law regarding Article 8 ECHR for Contracting Parties to (more easily) recognize foreign family judgments in which a status is validly acquired abroad. A clear exception to this trend can be found in the decision of the Swiss *Tribunal fédéral*, which found that the non-recognition of a foreign adoption did not violate Article 8 ECHR.[168] This decision has, however, been criticized, as it has been contended that this judgment is similar to the *Wagner* case, in which, of

[163] Rb. Haarlem 1 February 2005, *NIPR* 2005, 124.

[164] See also Rb. Alkmaar 16 January 2002, *NIPR* 2002, 170. Cf. HR 3 December 2004, NIPR 2005, 3 where Article 8 ECHR did not play a role and Rb. Utrecht 5 November 2003, *NIPR* 2004, 236, concerning a Russian adoption, which could not be recognized in the Netherlands.

[165] ATF 134 III 467, 470–475.

[166] Article 78(1) of the Swiss Private International Law Act reads as follows: Adoptions made abroad shall be recognized in Switzerland provided that they were pronounced in the State of domicile or the State of nationality of the adopted person or adopting spouses (translation provided by the author).

[167] *Michel v. Switzerland*, no. 3235/09. The case was introduced on 22 December 2008. See the Statement of Facts of 20 September 2010.

[168] ATF 134 III 467, 470–475.

course, a violation of, inter alia, Article 8 ECHR was found.[169] The same author has even, in more general terms, argued that the Swiss rules of private international law regarding the recognition of foreign adoption orders *ex* Article 78 of the Swiss Private International Law Act may, under certain circumstances, lead to a violation of Article 8 ECHR.[170]

There are, in my opinion, some differences between the Court's judgment in *Wagner* and the aforementioned decision of the Swiss *Tribunal fédéral*. It will therefore be interesting to see whether the obstacles to the recognition of the foreign adoption, as laid down in Article 78 of the Swiss Private International Law Act, and as applied by *Tribunal fédéral*, will pass the test of the Court. What makes this case different from *Wagner* is that the obstacle following from the Swiss Private International Law Act essentially concerns a jurisdiction test. One may recall that in *Hussin* the Court found that the applicant could not rely on Article 8 ECHR, because she could not complain about a situation to which she herself had contributed. It will be interesting to see whether the Court will focus once again on this aspect, which may become a hurdle in this case.

The Court could also go further down the path it chose in *Wagner* and also *Négrépontis-Giannissis*. However, while an emphasis on the 'social reality' of the situation could be regarded as an argument in favor of finding a violation of Article 8 ECHR in this case, one should also acknowledge that it cannot be said that the applicant really had a legitimate expectation that the adoption would be recognized, as the rules and practice with regard to the recognition of foreign adoption orders in Switzerland were clear. Moreover, as also acknowledged by the Court in *Wagner*, for example, there are, in principle, sound reasons for having stringent rules regarding the recognition of international adoptions. One could argue that the Swiss rules concerning the recognition of adoptions are particularly rigid, resulting in an undesirable outcome for the applicant in this specific case. However this is not a given, and a cautious approach by the Court in this case is certainly imaginable.

There have been other decisions that could be cited to support the thesis that a (family law) status has to be recognized where the parties (merely) had the legitimate expectation that their status would be recognized. Back in 1984, the German *Bundesverfassungsgericht*, for example, in the so-called *Wallace* case, found that a marriage concluded between an English military man and a German woman in Germany, but on an English military site in accordance with English law, would have to be recognized, despite the fact this marriage had formally never been validly concluded in Germany.[171]

After their marriage the couple settled in Germany. After the death of her husband in 1975, the wife attempted to make a pension claim for surviving

---

[169] Bucher 2010b, p. 203.

[170] But see Siehr 2004, pp. 778–779. This opinion was cited and followed by the *Tribunal fédéral*.

[171] *Bundesverfassungsgericht* 30 November 1982, *IPrax* 1984, p. 88ff.

spouses. At that time it was held that they had never been validly married. Until that time, though, the German authorities had never questioned the validity of the marriage. The *Bundesverfassungsgericht* finally held that the marriage should nevertheless be considered valid, citing, inter alia, the good faith of the parties, the fact that the German authorities had never before questioned the validity of the marriage, and the fact that the marriage had been validly concluded with regard to English law. In doing so, the *Bundesverfassungsgericht* effectively ignored the German choice of law rules. It has been argued that the German Court thus emphasized the 'social reality' of the situation, a notion which has, as has been discussed above, since been introduced by the Court in order to justify the obligation following from Article 8 ECHR to recognize foreign family law judgments in which a status is validly acquired abroad.[172]

One could thus argue that the Court does not stand alone with its case law concerning Article 8 ECHR containing an obligation to recognize and enforce foreign family law judgments in which a status has been acquired. It will be very interesting to see to what extent Contracting Parties will be obliged to recognize foreign family law judgments in the future. One could imagine that the recognition of some foreign family law judgments could be quite controversial in some (or all) of the Contracting Parties—for example, surrogacy judgments[173] and judgments pertaining to same sex relationships.[174]

How would the Court look at such judgments? If the 'social reality' which such judgments would undoubtedly create were to be emphasized by the Court, then there is a good case to be made that such judgments should be recognized, particularly where the rights of third parties do not play a role (and, admittedly, this could very well play a role, particularly with regard to surrogacy judgments). On the other hand it is also conceivable that the Court would find that parties could not have had a legitimate expectation, while it would also probably extend a wide margin of appreciation to the Contracting Parties with regard to such controversial judgments. After all, Contracting Parties have traditionally had a wide margin of appreciation in such cases. The social reality created by such international family law judgments may nevertheless eventually compel the Court to impose a more favorable view on the recognition of such judgments by the Contracting Parties. Although the extent of the Court's case law with regard to the obligation to

---

[172] Baratta 2010, p. 392. Cf. *Wagner* and *Négrépontis-Giannisis v. Greece* (cited above). See in the context of the protection of minority rights, *Muñoz Diaz v. Spain*, no. 49151/07, 8 December 2009, in which the Court found a violation of Article 1 of Protocol No. 1 ECHR taken in conjunction with Article 14 ECHR in a case with some remarkable similarities. This case also concerned a pension claim for surviving spouses. In this case the Spanish authorities refused to pay, because of an invalid marriage. The marriage had been concluded in Spain in accordance with Roma rites, but was never registered there. Nevertheless, the Court found a violation in this case.

[173] See in this regard, e.g., Struycken 2010. See also *Re: X & Y (Foreign Surrogacy)* [2008] EWHC 3030 (Fam). Cf. Baratta 2010, p. 393ff.

[174] See in this regard, e.g., *Schalk and Kopf v. Austria*, no. 30141/04, 24 June 2010. See also the Statement of Facts in *Orlandi and Others v. Italy* (and other applications), no. 26431/12.

recognize foreign family law judgments is not yet entirely clear, it appears that there should at least be an increased willingness to look favorably at recognition in such issues.

7.4.3 Preliminary Conclusions

It follows from the Court's case law that Article 8 ECHR clearly may entail an obligation for the Contracting Parties to recognize a foreign family law judgment granting a status or establishing a family relationship, provided that the judgment has been validly acquired abroad and that the parties had a legitimate expectation that the status established in the foreign family law judgment would be recognized. The Court will also take into account how a rejection relates to the social reality of the situation. Although it is clear that the Contracting Parties are not required to systematically recognize foreign family law judgments, it remains an open issue as to what sort of barriers erected in the shape of private international law rules of the Contracting Parties are permissible. What restrictions will be possible will be assessed in relation to the requirements of Article 8(2) ECHR and will mainly be examined by the Court in relation to the proportionality of a restriction to the obligation to enforce.

7.5 Conclusion

Article 6(1) ECHR, Article 1 of Protocol No. 1 ECHR, and Article 8 ECHR all entail an obligation for the courts of a Contracting Party to recognize and enforce foreign judgments, regardless of the origin of such judgments. Article 6(1) ECHR contains a general obligation in the sense that this Article, in principle, can apply to all sorts of civil judgments. Article 1 of Protocol No.1 and Article 8 ECHR offer a more specific obligation in this regard, as Article 1 of Protocol No.1 ECHR is only concerned with judgments pertaining to some kind of possession, even though this may include a status as heir, while Article 8 ECHR is solely concerned with family law judgments creating a status.

The obligation to recognize and enforce is not absolute. The Court will generally assess a refusal to recognize and enforce a foreign judgment as an interference with one of the aforementioned rights. Even though the Court's approach in this regard will differ somewhat depending on the exact right concerned, it has been demonstrated that the Court's approach is quite similar. For the obligation following from Article 1 of Protocol No. 1 and Article 8 ECHR, the Court will usually apply its scheme with regard to restrictions to qualified rights, entailing that a restriction to the obligation to recognize and enforce must be in accordance with the law, pursue a legitimate aim, and be necessary in a democratic society. It has been demonstrated that the principle of proportionality plays an important role in the consideration regarding the permissibility of a restriction to the obligation to recognize and enforce foreign judgments.

In some cases concerning Article 8 ECHR the Court has found that the obligation to recognize foreign family law judgments concerns a positive obligation. The emphasis with regard to interferences to a positive obligation is on whether the restriction was proportionate to the legitimate aim pursued. A similar test applies to interferences with the general obligation to recognize and enforce foreign judgments following from Article 6(1) ECHR. Restrictions under Article 6(1) must not be arbitrary and must be be proportionate to the legitimate aim pursued. In this test the principle of proportionality thus also plays an important role. The Contracting Parties enjoy a margin of appreciation in their assessment of whether a restriction to the obligation to recognize and enforce a foreign judgment is proportionate. The contours of the margin depend on the right guaranteed in the ECHR concerned.

What does all this mean for the private international law systems of the Contracting Parties with regard to the recognition and enforcement of foreign judgments? It has been discussed that England, the Netherlands, and Switzerland, like other countries, adhere more and more to *favor recognitionis*. This is partly due to international and European instruments, but the national rules of these legal orders also appear to be moving in this direction. This starting point, of course, fits perfectly with the obligation to recognize and enforce (foreign) judgments following from the ECHR. In the Netherlands, however, the official rule with regard to the enforcement of foreign judgments—in the absence of a treaty between the Netherlands and the country of origin of the foreign judgment—is that the judgment creditor, in principle, has to initiate new proceedings in the Netherlands, as enforcement is impossible. This starting point has been mitigated in legal practice. Nevertheless, one may question this starting point in light of the obligation to recognize and enforce.

However, the private international law regimes of States regarding the recognition and enforcement of foreign judgments do provide certain restrictions, depending on the applicable regime. For rules on recognition and enforcement one could say generally that foreign judgments will be recognized and enforced unless the foreign judgment would violate the public policy of the forum, the judgment is based on fraud, the court of origin did not have proper jurisdiction or did not apply the correct law, the judgment would be irreconcilable with other judgments in the forum state, or documents instituting the proceedings were not properly served.

It follows from the Court's case law concerning the obligation to recognize and enforce foreign judgments that these grounds of refusal flowing from the private international law regimes of the Contracting Parties can only be allowed if they comply with the Court's findings relating to the restrictions to the Articles concerned. The requirement of proportionality is especially important in this regard. A decision not to recognize and enforce must be proportionate to the legitimate aim pursued.

In principle, all the aforementioned private international law defenses may be found to provide an impermissible infringement on the obligation to recognize and enforce a foreign judgment. This has to be decided on a case by case basis. In its case law the Court has, for example, found that the invocation of the substantive public policy exception may result in a violation of the ECHR where this invocation would be arbitrary and would not be proportionate. The choice-of-law requirement has similarly been found to result in a violation of the obligation to recognize and enforce.

However, the condition of fraud, or *fraude à la loi*, appears to be more or less unaffected, as the Court has held that the ECHR cannot be invoked against a situation to which the applicant has contributed him or herself. The Court has also allowed the invocation of a jurisdiction requirement against the recognition of a foreign judgment on the basis of this latter criterion, as it found that the applicant had contributed to the invocation of this requirement by bringing the case to the wrong court.

Moreover, other grounds of refusal, such as the service of documents or the irreconcilability of decisions, would appear to easily meet the demands of the ECHR with regard to the obligation to recognize and enforce foreign judgments, as the service of documents is essential in ensuring a fair trial, while the irreconcilability of decisions is vested in the rule of law, as a State cannot recognize and enforce two contrary judgments in the same case. It is important to stress that the obligation to recognize and enforce a foreign judgment cannot be upheld if the recognition and enforcement of the judgment in question would result in a violation of one of the rights guaranteed in the ECHR. A final important factor in the determination of whether a refusal to recognize and enforce a foreign judgment would result in a violation is that the rights of others are an important justification for the Court.

It should, finally, be underscored that foreign family law judgments in which a status has been created have a special place in this regard. Such foreign judgments (also) fall under Article 8 ECHR and as the Court has found in *Wagner* and *Négrépontis*, there is a high(er) threshold for the denial of recognition of international family law judgments establishing a family link where parties have a legitimate expectation that the judgment will be recognized and social reality demands recognition. Traditional concerns of private international law, laid down, respectively, in the requirement that the foreign adoption should be in accordance with the *lex fori* (*Wagner*), and should not violate the public policy exception (*Négrépontis*), were set aside by the Court, as it held that such restrictions violated the applicants' rights under Article 8 ECHR. It has been discussed that these findings may usher in a new methodology for private international law in this regard.

It would go too far, however, in my opinion, to speak of a new methodology for private international law in this regard, because in both *Wagner* and *Négrépontis* the facts of the cases make it possible for the Court to interpret its own findings in subsequent cases in a more narrow fashion, as the applicants in these cases had a legitimate expectation that the judgments would be recognized. Nevertheless, the Court's jurisprudence in these cases is certainly a development toward an even more recognition-friendly framework for international foreign family law judgments. Even under such a framework with regard to Article 8 ECHR, an important ground of refusal would remain the rights of others, which may play an important role, particularly in international family law judgments, as, inter alia, follows from *Green and Farhat*. Moreover, where partial or sufficient effect is given to a foreign family law judgment, as was the case in *Harroudj*, the Court appears to be less inclined to find a violation of Article 8 ECHR.

References

Baratta R (2010) La reconnaissance internationale des situations juridiques personnelles et familiales. Recueil des Cours 348:253–499

Bollée S (2007) L'extension du domaine de la méthode de reconnaissance unilatérale. Rev. crit. dr. int. priv. 96:307–355

Briggs A, Rees P (2009) Civil jurisdiction and judgments. Informa, London

Bucher A (2000) La famille en droit international privé. Recueil des Cours 283:9–186

Bucher A (2010a) La dimension sociale du droit international privé: cours général. Recueil des Cours 341. Martinus Nijhoff Publishers, Leiden

Bucher A (2010b) Jurisprudence suisse en matière de droit international privé de la famille et des successions. RSDIE 20:189–245

Bucher A (ed) (2011) Loi sur le droit international prive convention de Lugano. Helbing Lichtenhahn, Basel

Cheshire GC, et al (2010) Private international law. Oxford University Press, Oxford

Coester-Waltjen D (2006) Anerkennung im internationalen Personen-, Familien- und Erbrecht und das Europaeische Kollisionsrecht. IPRax 26:392–400

D'Avout L (2010) Droits fondamentaux et coordination des ordres juridiques en droit privé. In: Dubout E, Touzé S (eds) Les droits fondamentaux: charnieres entre ordres et systems juridiques. Pedone, Paris, pp 165–198

Daelman C (2011) The interaction between human rights and private international law. Tijdschrift@ipr.be 2011:70–73

Dicey AV, Morris JHC, Collins LA (2012) The conflict of laws. Sweet & Maxwell, London

Dutoit B (2005) Droit international privé Suiss. Helbing & Lichtenhahn Verlag, Basel

Franzina P (2011) Some remarks on the relevance of article 8 of the ECHR to the recognition of family status judicially created abroad. Diritti umani e diritto internazionale 5:609–616

Grgic A (ed) (2007) The right to property under the European convention on human rights. Human rights handbooks no 10. Council of Europe, Strasbourg

Guinchard E (2005) Procès équitable (article 6 CESDH) et droit international privé. In: Nuyts A, Watté N (eds) International civil litigation in Europe and relations with third states. Bruylant, Brussels, pp 199–245

Kerameus KD (1997) Enforcement in the international context. Recueil des Cours 264:179–410

Kinsch P (2007) Droits de l'homme, droits fondamentaux et droit international privé. Recueil des Cours 318:9–332. Martinus Nijhoff Publishers, Leiden

Kinsch P (2010) Recognition in the forum of a status aquired abroad—private international law rules and European human rights law. In: Boele-Woelki K et al (eds), Convergence and divergence in private international law—liber amicorum Kurt Siehr. Eleven International Publishing, The Hague, pp 232–275

Kinsch P (2011a) Private international law topics before the European Court of Human Rights. Selected judgments and decision (2010–2011). Yearb Private Int Law 13:39–41

Kinsch P (2011b) La non-conformité du jugement étranger à l'ordre public international mise au diaspon de la Convention européenne des droits de l'homme. Rev. crit. dr. int. priv. 100:818–819

Lagarde P (2004) Développements futures du droit international privé dans une Europe en voie d'unification: quelques conjectures. RabelsZ 68:225–243

Lagarde P (2008) La reconnaissance mode d'emploi. In: Ancel J-P et al (eds) Vers de nouveaux équilibres entre ordres juridiques: liber amicorum Hélène Gaudemet-Tallon. Dalloz, Paris, pp 481–501

Mansel H-P (2006) Anerkennung als Grundprinzip des Europaeischen Rechtsraums. RabelsZ 70:651–731

Marchadier F (2007) Les objectifs generaux du droit international prive à l'épreuve de la convention europeenne des droits de l'homme. Bruylant, Bruxelles

Matscher F (1998) Le droit international privé face à la Convention européenne des droits de l'homme, Travaux du Comité français de droit international privé (1995–1998), pp 211–234

Mayer P (2005) Les méthodes de la reconnaissance en droit international privé. In: Jobard-Bachellier M-N, Mayer P (eds) Le droit international privé: esprit et méthodes. Mélanges en l'honneur de Paul Lagarde. Dalloz, Paris, pp 547–573

Melcher M (2013) (Mutual) Recognition of registered relationships via EU private international law. J Private Int Law 9:149–170

Muir Watt H (2008) European federalism and the "New Unilateralism". Tulane Law Rev 82:1983–1998

Muir Watt H (2013) Fundamental rights and recognition in private international law. Eur J Hum Rights 1:411–435

Pamboukis C (2008). La renaissance-métamorphose de la méthode de reconnaissance. Rev. crit. dr. int. priv. 97:513–560

Rosner N (2004) Cross-border recognition and enforcement of foreign money judgments in civil and commercial matters, Doctoral series, dissertation Groningen

Schlosser P (2000) Jurisdiction and international judicial and administrative co-operation. Recueil des Cours 284:9–428

Schutte CB (2004) The European fundamental right of property: article 1 of protocol no. 1 to the European Convention on Human Rights: its origins, its workings and its impact on national legal orders. Kluwer, Deventer

Siehr K (2002) Das Internationale Privatrecht der Schweiz [The private international law of Switzerland]. Schulthess, Zürich

Siehr K (2004) Art. 78. In: Girsberger D et al (eds) Zürcher Kommentar zum IPRG: Kommentar zum Bundesgesetz über dat Internationale Privatrecht (IPRG) vom 18. Dezember 1987, Schulthess, Zürich

Spielmann D (2011) La reconnaissance et l'exécution des decisions judiciaries étrangères et les exigencies de la convention des droits de l'homme. Un essai de synthèse. Revue trimestrielle des droits de l'homme 22:761–786

Strikwerda L (2012) Inleiding tot het Nederlandse internationaal privaatrecht [Introduction to Dutch private international law]. Kluwer, Deventer

Struycken AVM (2010) The Netherlands surrogacy, a new way to become mother? In: Boele-Woelki K et al (eds) Convergence and divergence in private international law—liber amicorum Kurt Siehr. Schulthess, Zürich, pp 359ff

van Hoek AAH (2003) Erkenning van vonnissen in het privaatrecht: een studie naar de grenzen van wederzijdse erkenning [Recognition of judgments in private law: a study on the limits of mutual recognition]. NIPR 21:337–350

von Mehren AT (1980) Recognition and enforcement of foreign judgments—general theory and the role of jurisdictional requirements. Recueil des Cours 167:9–112

Chapter 8
The Recognition and Enforcement of Foreign Judgments: The Invocation of the ECHR *Against* Recognition and Enforcement

Contents

8.1 Introduction

In the previous chapter, the discussion was limited to the obligation to recognize and enforce foreign judgments, which follows from some of the rights guaranteed in the ECHR. However, this does not mean that foreign judgments should always be recognized and enforced, regardless of the circumstances. Quite to the contrary, it is also possible to invoke the rights guaranteed in the ECHR against the

L.R. Kiestra, *The Impact of the European Convention on Human Rights on Private International Law*, DOI 10.1007/978-94-6265-032-9_8

recognition and enforcement of foreign judgments.[1] There may even be an obligation for the Contracting Parties to deny recognition and enforcement of foreign judgments violating one of the rights guaranteed in the ECHR. Below, it will be demonstrated that both Article 6(1) ECHR (in Sect. 8.2), as well as the substantive rights guaranteed in the ECHR (Sect. 8.3), may stand in the way of recognition and enforcement.

8.2 The Invocation of Article 6(1) ECHR *Against* Recognition and Enforcement

The Court's case law concerning the question of whether the ECHR contains an obligation to oppose the recognition and enforcement of foreign judgments goes back further than its jurisprudence concerning the obligation to recognize and enforce, even though this has not necessarily resulted in the former having crystallized. This will be demonstrated in the discussion of the Court's case law concerning Article 6(1) ECHR.

In *Pellegrini v. Italy*[2] the Court examined whether the enforcement of a foreign judgment originating from the Vatican regarding the annulment of a marriage would violate Article 6(1) ECHR, as the proceedings leading up to the judgment in the Vatican had been unfair. This case has already been discussed briefly in this research with regard to the meaning of Article 1 ECHR for private international law.[3] The applicant alleged that she had not received a fair trial before the courts in the Vatican and that the subsequent enforcement of this judgment in Italy violated her rights under Article 6 ECHR.

In 1962 Mrs. Pellegrini married Mr. Gigliozzi in a religious ceremony, which was also valid under the law. In 1987 Mrs. Pellegrini filed for a divorce in Italy. Her petition was granted and her husband was ordered to pay her maintenance. In the meantime, also in 1987, Mr. Gigliozzi sought to have the marriage annulled at a court of the Catholic Church on the ground of consanguinity (on account of his father and her mother being cousins). Mrs. Pellegrini was subsequently summoned to appear before an Ecclesiastical Court to answer some questions about her marriage. She went alone, unaware of the reason why she had been summoned, and had to answer questions about her consanguineous relationship with her husband. The Ecclesiastical Court consequently annulled the marriage on the ground of consanguinity.

Mrs. Pellegrini lodged an appeal against this decision with the 'Romana Rota'. She complained that she had not been told in advance what the hearing would be

---

[1] See for an introduction into the recognition and enforcement of foreign judgments supra Sect. 7.1. See further supra Chap. 2.

[2] *Pellegrini v. Italy*, no. 30882/96, *ECHR* 2001-VIII.

[3] See supra Sect. 4.3.

about. She had therefore been unable to prepare a defense and had also not been able to seek the advice of a lawyer. Her appeal was declared admissible and she was told that she had 20 days to submit her observations. She did that—still without the assistance of a lawyer—complaining, inter alia, that she neither had enough time nor the facilities to prepare her defense. She also stressed the fact that an annulment would have serious financial consequences. Nevertheless, her appeal was dismissed. Later, Mrs. Pellegrini was informed by the 'Romana Rota' that its judgment had been referred to the Florence Court of Appeal for a declaration of enforcement in Italy. Although in these Italian enforcement proceedings Mrs. Pellegrini again complained about the lack of a fair hearing, the Vatican judgment was declared enforceable in Italy.

Mrs. Pellegrini lodged a complaint against Italy in Strasbourg about a violation of her rights guaranteed in Article 6(1) ECHR. The Court first noted that its task was not to examine whether the proceedings before the Vatican courts were contrary to Article 6 ECHR, as the Vatican is not a Contracting Party, but rather that its task was to examine whether the Italian courts had duly satisfied themselves that the relevant proceedings fulfilled the guarantees of Article 6 ECHR. The Court added that such a review is required when the enforcement is requested of a judgment emanating from a country that does not apply the ECHR. After examining the reasoning of the Italian courts, the Court held that they had breached their duty to examine whether the proceedings met the standards of Article 6 ECHR and consequently found a violation of Article 6(1) ECHR.

In *Pellegrini* the Court thus found that Article 6(1) ECHR stands in the way of the recognition and enforcement of a foreign judgment emanating from a third country violating the procedural safeguards guaranteed in this Article. However the exact meaning of this judgment is still unclear, particularly because the Court in later judgments has appeared to somewhat distance itself from its findings in this case. This judgment has been much discussed because it has several noteworthy aspects.[4] The Court expressly treated the judgment emanating from the Vatican courts as a judgment from a country that does not apply the ECHR, even though it is questionable whether this is completely justifiable.[5] This raises the question of whether the origin of the foreign judgment—the judgment can either originate from a third country or from another Contracting Party—has consequences for the (standard of) control with regard to Article 6(1) ECHR.

The Court seems to introduce quite a strict standard with regard to foreign proceedings, as it makes no mention of an attenuated standard—taking into account the fact that the proceedings took place in a third country—which it had done in other cases concerning the right to a fair trial in relation to third countries.[6]

---

[4] See, e.g., Costa 2002, pp. 470–476; Flauss 2002; Pocar 2006, pp. 575–581; Sinopoli 2002, pp. 1157–1168. See also supra Sect. 4.3.

[5] See *Pellegrini v. Italy*, no. 30882/96, para 40, *ECHR* 2001-VIII. Italy and the Holy Sea, however, clearly have a special relationship, which is disregarded by the Court in its judgment. See for a critique Kinsch 2004, p. 220.

[6] See infra n. 9.

Instead, the Court thus appears to insist on full compliance with the procedural standards of the ECHR, as if the proceedings had taken place in Italy rather than in a State which has not ratified the ECHR.[7] However, as noted above, subsequent judgments of the Court have raised doubts as to the meaning of *Pellegrini* in this regard.

The confusion over the meaning of *Pellegrini* may even be traced back to a judgment delivered a mere 8 days before the Court handed down its judgment in the *Pellegrini* case. On that day the Grand Chamber of the Court delivered a judgment in *Prince Hans-Adam II of Liechtenstein v. Germany*,[8] in which it was indirectly concerned with the enforcement of a foreign judgment. In this case the Grand Chamber appeared to offer a different—less strict—standard with regard to the enforcement of foreign judgments by referring to case law in which a different standard was suggested. It has to be stressed that in *Prince Hans-Adam II* the Court did not directly deal with the question of the enforcement of a foreign judgment, although the issue did play a significant role in the case.

In *Prince Hans-Adam II* the applicant, the ruler of Liechtenstein, complained about the right of access to a court and the right to property (Articles 6 and 1 of Protocol No. I ECHR). The applicant's father had been the owner of a painting by Pieter van Laer, which had formed part of his family's art collection since at least 1767. It was displayed in one of the family's castles in Czechoslovakia. After the Second World War the painting was seized under the so-called 'Benes Decrees'. The father complained about this seizure, since this decree was only directed at the property of 'German and Hungarian persons and of those having committed treason and acted as enemies of the Czech and Slovak people', and he was not a German national. In 1951, however, the Bratislava Administrative Court (in Czechoslovakia) dismissed the appeal lodged by the father.

Forty years later the painting was lent to the municipality of Cologne by the Brno Historical Monuments Office. The applicant requested and received an interim injunction ordering the municipality of Cologne to hand over the painting to a bailiff at the end of the exhibition, pending the dispute over the property rights. The German courts, however, eventually rejected the claims of Prince Hans-Adam II regarding the painting on the basis of the Convention on the Settlement of Matters Arising out of the War and the Occupation of 1954, which excluded German jurisdiction over this case.

The Court in Strasbourg rejected the applicant's complaint about his right of access to a court, because it found that the exclusion of German jurisdiction was not unreasonable, given the particular status of the Federal Republic of Germany under public international law after the Second World War. In its judgment, however, the Court also had to consider the effect of the judgment of the Bratislava

---

[7] It will be recalled that it has been discussed in Chap. 4 that the ECHR is indeed applicable to the issue of the recognition and enforcement of foreign judgments emanating from third countries. See supra Sect. 4.3.

[8] *Prince Hans-Adam II of Liechtenstein v. Germany* [GC], no. 42527/98, ECHR 2001-VIII.

Administrative Court in Germany. This led to the following observation of the Court:

> [T]he Court observes that the German courts were not required to assess whether the standard of the Bratislava Administrative Court proceedings resulting in the decision of November 1951 was adequate, in particular if seen against the procedural safeguards of the Convention (see, *mutatis mutandis*, *Drozd and Janousek v. France and Spain*, judgment of 26 June 1992, Series A no. 240, p. 34, § 110).[9]

It is this reference to *Drozd and Janousek v. France and Spain*,[10] in the context of the effect of the foreign judgment in Germany, which has been seized upon by some authors to argue that a different standard with regard to the enforcement of foreign judgments is—or perhaps should be—used by the Court for the enforcement of foreign judgments emanating from third countries.[11]

In *Drozd and Janousek* the Court dealt, inter alia, with the issue of the enforcement of an Andorran criminal law judgment by France and Spain.[12] At the time Andorra was not yet a Contracting Party. In deciding whether these two countries could be held responsible for the allegedly unfair proceedings leading up to the judgments that were to be enforced, the Court held that Contracting Parties, in principle, were not required to impose their standards on third countries and that there was thus no obligation to verify whether the proceedings in Andorra were in line with Article 6 ECHR. Such an obligation would also seriously frustrate international cooperation in administrative justice, according to the Court. However, with a reference to the standard introduced earlier in *Soering v. the United Kingdom*,[13] the Court held that Contracting Parties are obliged to refuse cooperation 'if it emerges that the conviction is the result of a flagrant denial of justice.'[14] In these two cases the Court thus introduced the standard of 'a flagrant denial of justice'. However, despite the reference to this case in *Prince Hans-Adam II* with regard to the enforcement of a foreign judgment, no mention of such a standard was made by the Court in *Pellegrini*, which similarly concerned the enforcement of a foreign judgment originating from a third country.

One could say that it was certainly a surprise that this attenuated standard of 'a flagrant denial of justice' did not return in the Court's ruling in *Pellegrini*. It raises the question of whether it is, from now on, necessary to examine foreign

---

[9] *Prince Hans-Adam II of Liechtenstein v. Germany* [GC], no. 42527/98, para 64, ECHR 2001-VIII.

[10] *Drozd and Janousek v. France and Spain*, 26 June 1992, Series A no. 240.

[11] See, e.g., Kinsch 2004, p. 224ff. It will, incidentally, be recalled that *Drozd and Janousek* was the source of inspiration for many writers with regard to a possible attenuation of the standards of the ECHR in issues of private international law. See supra Sect. 6.3.2.

[12] See with regard to this case also supra section "The Extra-territorial Effect of the ECHR" in Chap. 4 and Sect. 6.3.2.

[13] *Soering v. the United Kingdom,* 7 July 1989, para 113, Series A no. 161. See with regard to this case also supra section "The Extra-territorial Effect of the ECHR" in Chap. 4.

[14] See *Drozd and Janousek* v. *France and Spain*, 26 June 1992, para 110, Series A, no. 240 (referring to *Soering*).

judgments as if they had not been delivered in a foreign country.[15] This is, of course, the unavoidable consequence of such an interpretation, which is seemingly hard to reconcile with the earlier held standard of control which called for action only in the case of 'a flagrant denial of justice'. Initially, *Pellegrini* was met approvingly and hailed as an important judgment.[16] It has since, however, been suggested by the Court that *Pellegrini* is not much of a departure from its previous case law.[17] Some authors have consequently argued that *Pellegrini* should be read together with the Court's decision in *Drozd and Janousek* and that it is clear from the Court's later cases that it prefers the standard of 'a flagrant denial of justice' with regard to judgments emanating from third countries.[18]

One of these instances where the Court suggested that *Pellegrini* fits in with its previous case law is its admissibility decision in *Lindberg v. Sweden*.[19] In this case the Court again had the opportunity to examine the enforcement of a foreign judgment, although this time in altogether different circumstances, because the case did not concern the procedural guarantees of Article 6(1) ECHR, but rather one of the substantive rights guaranteed in the ECHR, and the judgment originated from another Contracting Party instead of a third country.[20] Nevertheless, the Court, in reiterating its previous case law regarding the enforcement of foreign judgments (and Article 6 ECHR), found that:

> Comparable issues have previously been examined in the context of co-operation between States inside and outside the Convention territory, notably in the plenary *Drozd and Janousek v. France and Spain* judgment of 26 June 1992 (Series A no. 240) and the *Iribarne Pérez v. France* judgment of 24 October 1995 (Series A no. 325-B). Both cases concerned complaints about the enforcement in a Contracting State of a judgment by a court of a non-Contracting State (in Andorra - before joining the Council of Europe) reached in proceedings claimed to be at variance with due process. The Court attached decisive weight to whether the impugned conviction was the result of a "flagrant denial of justice" (see *Drozd and Janousek*, § 110; and *Iribarne Pérez*, § 31; see also *Pellegrini v. Italy*, no. 30882/96, ECHR 2001-VIII, even though no express mention was made of the said criterion in that judgment).[21]

Even though the Court acknowledged that no express mention was made of the criterion of a 'flagrant denial of justice', it could be argued that the Court here suggests that its judgment in *Pellegrini* does not differ significantly from the other mentioned cases.

---

[15] See, e.g., Costa 2002, p. 470ff; Flauss 2001, p. 1063; Kinsch 2004, p. 222; 2007, p. 292; Spielmann 2011, p. 764ff.

[16] Costa 2002, p. 470ff; Flauss 2001, p. 1064.

[17] See infra n. 21.

[18] See, e.g., Bucher 2010, p. 305; Kinsch 2007a, pp. 291–294, 302–317. See particularly no. 249, pp. 316–317; Marchadier 2007, pp. 454–455; Sinopoli 2002, p. 1158; Spielmann 2011, p. 767ff.

[19] *Lindberg v. Sweden* (dec.), no. 48198/99, 15 January 2004.

[20] This case will be discussed in more detail infra Sect. 8.3.1.

[21] See *Lindberg v. Sweden* under 'The court's assessment'.

However, in another case *post Pellegrini*, concerning the enforcement of a return order in an international child abduction case, *Eskinazi and Chelouche v. Turkey*,[22] the Court once more had the opportunity to further comment on the meaning of *Pellegrini*. In this case the mother, having both French and Turkish nationalities, complained on the basis of both Articles 6 and 8 ECHR against the enforcement of a judgment made by the Turkish courts on the basis of the Hague Child Abduction Convention ordering the return of her daughter to Israel (not a Contracting Party).

Invoking Article 6 ECHR, the mother argued that if her daughter were to return to Israel, the rabbinical courts would have jurisdiction over both the divorce and all matters pertaining to personal status, which would result in an unfair trial—the supervision over these courts by the Israeli Supreme Court (not a religious court) would be insufficient to prevent this. She further argued that she would miss the benefit of fair proceedings in the Turkish courts to which she had duly committed herself before her husband had started any proceedings.

With regard to this complaint the Court noted that it had previously held in *Pellegrini* that where the courts of one of the Contracting Parties are forced to enforce a judicial decision originating from a third country, these courts should duly satisfy themselves that the proceedings in that country are in line with the guarantees contained in Article 6 ECHR.[23] However, in *Eskinazi and Chelouche* the complaint concerned the possible—future—treatment in the Israeli courts. The Court felt that the test in this case, where the applicants' interests had not yet been decided by the Israeli courts (courts in a non-Contracting Party), should be whether 'the Turkish authorities had to lend their assistance with Caroline Chelouche's [the second applicant, the child] return unless objective factors caused them to fear that the child and, if applicable, her mother risked suffering a "flagrant denial of justice".'[24] The Court added, though, that a 'denial of justice' is prohibited by international law and that Turkey should thus make sure that this principle was respected with regard to its international commitments to Israel.[25]

It is interesting that in this case the Court appears to distinguish between the test with respect to the recognition and enforcement of judgments originating from third countries and the test with regard to proceedings in a third country that have yet to take place. In *Pellegrini* the Court was concerned with a judgment

---

22 *Eskinazi and Chelouche v. Turkey* (dec.), no. 14600/05, ECHR 2005-XIII (extracts). See also supra Sect. 5.4.3.3.

23 See *Eskinazi and Chelouche v. Turkey* (dec.), no. 14600/05, ECHR 2005-XIII (extracts) under C.

24 Id. The Court cited the following case law to support its observation: *Mamatkulov and Askarov v. Turkey* [GC], nos. 46827/99 and 46951/99, para 88, ECHR 2005-I; *Einhorn v. France* (dec.), no. 71555/01, ECHR 2001–XI; *Drozd and Janousek v. France and Spain*, judgment of 26 June 1992, para 110, Series A no. 240, para 110; and *Soering v. the United Kingdom*, judgment of 7 July 1989, para 113, Series A no. 161.

25 The Court referred to *Golder v. the United Kingdom*, judgment of 21 February 1975, para 35, Series A no. 18. See with regard to this case supra Sects. 5.4.1.1 and 5.4.1.2.

(allegedly) violating Article 6(1) ECHR that had already been rendered in a third country and, consequently, only had to be enforced in one of the Contracting Parties. In *Eskinazi and Chelouche*, however, the Court was occupied with a complaint about proceedings that had yet to take place. With regard to such proceedings the Court thus opts for its 'flagrant denial of justice' standard.

This scenario is markedly different from that in *Pellegrini*. The fact, though, that the Court makes this distinction between the two standards in this case could be cited as evidence that there is indeed a distinction between the two tests; otherwise the Court could have observed that the standards were similar, but it did not do so.[26]

Finally, one may deduce from the Court's admissibility in *Saccoccia v. Austria*[27] that the Court is aware of the competing standards,[28] as it first notes *Drozd* and thereafter explicitly refers to its 'subsequent' jurisprudence in *Pellegrini*, before observing that 'in the present case the Court is not called upon to decide in the abstract which level of review was required from a Convention point of view.'[29] Thus the Court is clearly familiar with the fact that it has created uncertainty with regard to the correct level of review for foreign judgments originating from third countries.

8.2.1 The Standard of Control Following from Article 6(1) ECHR with Regard to the Recognition and Enforcement of Foreign Judgments

What does the choice between the two standards discussed above entail? It has been presented as a choice between 'the optimal standard', insisting on full compliance with all the rights guaranteed in the ECHR, and the 'minimal standard' (an attenuated standard), insisting on merely the essential guarantees of a fair trial with regard to the recognition and enforcement of a foreign judgment.[30] It should be clear that even if one were to introduce an attenuated standard, it should not be possible to go below this minimal standard, as the ECHR contains certain minimum guarantees.[31] It is also important to keep in mind in the discussion of these standards what the goal of the protection of procedural safeguards is in the context of the recognition and enforcement of foreign judgments. The goal is to avoid

[26] But see Bucher 2010, p. 305.

[27] *Saccoccia v. Austria* (dec.), no. 69917/01, 5 July 2011.

[28] Spielmann 2011, p. 769.

[29] *Saccoccia v. Austria* (dec.), no. 69917/01, 5 July 2011. See under heading 2. Compliance with Article 6(1) in the decision.

[30] Kinsch 2007, p. 292.

[31] See generally supra Chap. 3.

giving effect to foreign judgments rendered in a manner which is so unfair that the eventual result—the (substantive) judgment—can no longer be trusted.[32]

There are a number of arguments in favor of introducing a less strict standard with regard to foreign judgments compared to domestic judgments. First, where foreign judgments originate from third countries, i.e., non-Contracting Parties, there is a good chance that the procedure leading up to that judgment is not precisely in line with the requirements following from Article 6 ECHR. The State of origin of the judgment has, after all, never signed the ECHR and is thus not obligated to adhere to its requirements, including the procedural safeguards following from Article 6 ECHR. Can one thus consequently ask these judgments to be precisely compatible with the standards of Article 6 ECHR—on penalty of the judgment not being recognized and enforced?[33] This may be a problematic proposition, as it could lead to an increase in the rejection of the enforcement of foreign judgments.

This, of course, does not mean that any judgment falling short of the standards set in Article 6(1) of the ECHR would be recognized and enforced. This is where the aforementioned standard of 'a flagrant denial of justice' would come in. If the foreign judgment were to fall short of this more lenient standard, and thus flagrantly violate Article 6(1) ECHR, then it cannot be recognized and enforced. It is instructive here to refer back to the concurring opinion of Judge Matscher in *Drozd and Janousek*.[34] He found that a Contracting Party may indeed incur responsibility for allowing the recognition and enforcement of a foreign judgment (originating from a third country), regardless of whether the judgment in question was a civil or a criminal law judgment. However, he added the following to this observation:

> This must clearly be a flagrant breach of Article 6 [ECHR] or, to put it differently, Article 6 [ECHR] has in its indirect applicability only a reduced effect, less than that which it would have if directly applicable (the theory of the "reduced effect" of ordre public with reference to the recognition of foreign judgments or other public acts is well known to international law).[35]

Judge Matscher thus clearly favors a reduced effect of Article 6(1) ECHR with regard to situations in which the ECHR is only indirectly applicable, as is the case when recognizing and enforcing foreign judgments emanating from third countries. It should be stressed that the refusal to recognize and enforce foreign judgments is not without consequences—it may ultimately lead to a difference between legal situations in two countries, which is something that should not be allowed readily. If courts are too eager to fend off foreign judgments, this will

---

[32] See, e.g., Fentiman 2010, p. 703.

[33] See in this regard, e.g., Mayer 1996, pp. 133–134; Guinchard 2005, pp. 219–220. .

[34] See also supra section "The Extra-territorial Effect of the ECHR" in Chap. 4.

[35] Concurring Opinion by Judge Matscher in *Drozd and Janousek*. It is, however, interesting to note that the reduced effect of public policy is restricted to substantive public policy and not to procedural public policy for the simple reason that, while the law applicable to a case may be a foreign law, the procedural rules are always governed by the *lex fori*. See Kinsch 2007, p. 293. He notes that this is an issue of terminology and that it is not impossible to attenuate the requirements of a fair trial with regard to the recognition and enforcement of foreign judgments.

undoubtedly lead to injustices for individuals, and may also lead to problems for States party to international instruments regarding the recognition and enforcement of foreign judgments.[36] Moreover, it has also been demonstrated above that in some cases the refusal may even lead to a violation of one of the rights guaranteed in the ECHR. However, with respect to this last argument, one should note that it appears, in principle, difficult to argue that there would be an obligation for Contracting Parties to recognize and enforce a foreign judgment violating Article 6(1) ECHR.

There are also arguments to be made in favor of insisting on full compliance with the standards of Article 6(1) ECHR, as the Court did in *Pellegrini*. By either recognizing or enforcing a foreign judgment of a third country, a State gives effect to such a judgment within its territory. In the event of the recognition or enforcement of a foreign judgment violating Article 6(1) ECHR, it would thus be a court of one of the Contracting Parties that would ultimately breach Article 6(1) ECHR by giving effect in the forum to such a judgment. One may refer to this as an indirect breach, as Judge Matscher did, but this may be a bit of a misnomer. It is, of course, clear that the court of the receiving State is not responsible in the first place for a fair trial in other countries. That is for the court of origin of the judgment. However, be that as it may, once the receiving court allows the recognition or enforcement of this foreign judgment that violates the rights guaranteed in Article 6(1) ECHR, one could argue that it takes ownership of that violation and makes the violation its own. After all, by recognizing and enforcing a foreign judgment a State gives effect to such a judgment in the forum—an effect it previously did not have. If that is the case, how fair would it be to the injured party to use a different standard with regard to Article 6(1) ECHR because of the fact that the proceedings concern a foreign judgment from a third State? Once this judgment has been recognized or enforced, the effect of such a judgment is essentially equal to that of a domestic judgment or a foreign judgment from another Contracting Party.

If one were to uphold the Court's line of reasoning in *Pellegrini* these difficulties would be avoided, because the courts would be obligated to scrutinize the foreign judgment in question in full—without having regard to the foreign nature of the judgment. Another issue concerning deviation from the regular standard of Article 6(1) ECHR is that one could easily argue that Article 6(1) ECHR already contains some sort of minimal guarantee for the Contracting Parties, which, considering the background of the ECHR, is not an argument that is easily dismissed.[37]

---

[36] Then again, many such instruments would probably include a (procedural) public policy exception, which would make it possible for such States to deny recognition to foreign judgments violating Article 6(1) ECHR. See supra Sect. 7.1. In the event that such an international treaty would not contain a public policy exception, one would, incidentally, be faced with the complicated situation of two conflicting international obligations. See supra Sect. 3.3.1.

[37] Kinsch 2007, p. 292; see also *Government of the United States of America v. Montgomery (No.2)* [2004] UKHL 37, *Rev.crit.dr.int.priv.* 2005, p. 321 (note Muir Watt); see with regard to a discussion of this case infra Sect. 8.2.2. See, for the background, the position of the ECHR in the legal orders of the Contracting Parties supra Sect. 3.3.

A final argument against the use of the standard of 'a flagrant denial of justice' concerns the substance of this standard.[38] What makes a violation of Article 6(1) ECHR so 'flagrant' that it cannot be tolerated with regard to a foreign judgment emanating from a third country? Even though the Court has in many instances used the phrase 'a flagrant denial of justice', it has never described what this notion exactly means.[39] However, if one were to take *Drozd and Janousek* as a starting point, one could question the usefulness of this criterion.

It will be recalled that *Drozd and Janousek* concerned (criminal) proceedings in Andorra.[40] These proceedings were far from perfect. After having been found guilty, the only appeal open to the applicants was an appeal to the same judges to reconsider their earlier ruling. A final—new—appeal procedure, although officially published in Andorra, appears not to have been communicated to the applicants.[41] They further alleged that the French judge on the Andorran court spoke little Spanish and even less Catalan, the language in which the proceeding was conducted and in which the judgment was delivered. The French authorities denied this allegation, stating that sufficient language skills were one of the requirements for the appointment of a judge in Andorra. The Spanish authorities added that a large part of the proceedings were usually conducted in either Spanish or French, depending on the defendants' language skills (in this case Drozd and Janousek both spoke Spanish), and that the applicants had at no point requested the assistance of an interpreter. The applicants also claimed that the witnesses had not been isolated before giving testimony, but this was denied by both governments.

It is hard to argue, given this description of the procedure in Andorra, that the proceedings were not deficient. They certainly did not live up to the standards guaranteed in Article 6(1) ECHR. Apparently, though, the deficiencies in these proceedings were not quite so bad that they constituted 'a flagrant denial of justice'. It is, in my opinion, not easy to reconcile the fact that the proceedings in *Drozd and Janousek* did not amount to 'a flagrant denial of justice' with the Court's findings in *Pellegrini*.[42] The proceedings in both cases showed remarkable deficiencies. The comparison between these two cases may not be entirely fair, in the sense that in *Drozd and Janousek* some of the facts were disputed, while this was not the case in *Pellegrini*. Moreover, one could say that *Drozd and Janousek* is a much older case

---

38 Cf. Juratowitch 2007, p. 182.

39 See in this regard also para 14 of the joint partly dissenting opinion of Judges Bratza, Bonello, and Hedigan in *Mamatkulov and Askarov v. Turkey* [GC], nos. 46827/99 and 46951/99, ECHR 2005-I, in which the following is, inter alia, stated: 'What constitutes a "flagrant" denial of justice has not been fully explained in the Court's jurisprudence, but the use of the adjective is clearly intended to impose a stringent test of unfairness going beyond mere irregularities or lack of safeguards in the trial procedures such as might result in a breach of Article 6 if occurring within the Contracting State itself.'

40 See supra n. 10.

41 *Drozd and Janousek v. France and Spain*, judgment of 26 June 1992, paras 18, 20, Series A no. 240.

42 See a description of the proceedings in *Pellegrini* supra n. 2.

and that the standards of the Court may thus have changed.[43] Nevertheless, if the proceedings with which *Drozd* was concerned did not amount to 'a flagrant denial of justice', one has to conclude that a violation of one's procedural rights in foreign proceedings is not easily categorised as being 'flagrant'.[44]

Pellegrini, in principle, leaves open the question of whether this standard also applies to foreign judgments originating from another Contracting Party.[45] The Court in *Pellegrini* explicitly notes, with regard to the review Contracting Parties have to perform, that this review 'is required where a decision in respect of which enforcement is requested emanates from the courts of a country which does not apply the Convention.'[46] This statement thus appears to entail an obligation to do so—at least with regard to judgments originating from courts of non-Contracting Parties.

Some authors have argued that this finding of the Court should be interpreted as meaning that there is no such obligation for foreign judgments originating from other Contracting Parties.[47] While it would, of course, be possible to review foreign judgments emanating from other Contracting Parties, there would not be an obligation to do so, because the Contracting Parties rendering such judgments could be held directly responsible before the Court in Strasbourg. Other authors, however, do not share this interpretation and to a greater or lesser extent find that the review following from *Pellegrini* regarding foreign judgments of third countries should also apply to foreign judgments originating from other Contracting Parties.[48]

While the Court has, in my opinion, left this question unanswered, I would argue that the standard of full compliance set in *Pellegrini* should certainly apply to foreign judgments emanating from other Contracting Parties. It is clear that the procedural safeguards of Article 6(1) ECHR should already be protected in other Contracting Parties, but this does not always happen.[49] The argument that possible violations of these safeguards should be directly dealt with within the Contracting Party, where these proceedings took place is, in principle, valid, but holds less

---

[43] Although that would make one wonder why the Court keeps referring back to this case without further comment.

[44] It should, incidentally, be noted that this argument has conversely been used in order to argue that the test used by the Court in *Pellegrini* should also be read as including the flagrant standard. This has, as discussed above, arguably retroactively also been contended by the Court in *Lindberg*. See Marchadier 2007, pp. 454–455. However, even though the Court appears to support this argument, the question remains—how it is possible that the proceedings in *Drozd* did not result in a flagrant violation, while the proceedings in *Pellegrini* did? In my opinion, it is difficult to rhyme these divergent results.

[45] Cf. Spielmann 2011, pp. 767–768.

[46] *Pellegrini v. Italy*, no. 30882/96, para 40, ECHR 2001-VIII.

[47] Kinsch 2004, pp. 227–228; Sinopoli 2002, p. 1162.

[48] Costa is of the opinion that the same standard should apply to all foreign judgments, regardless of their origin. See Costa 2002, at p. 475. See also Bucher 2010, p. 304. Fawcett finds that, although it is unclear, 'it is at least arguable that it does so.' See Fawcett 2007, p. 5. See also Hoek, van and Luchtman 2006, pp. 42–43.

[49] See the illustrations discussed supra Sects. 5.5.3.1 and 5.5.3.2.

sway with regard to violations of Article 6(1) ECHR.[50] One could, for example, not learn of proceedings in another Contracting Party in the event of inadequate notification, until one is faced with enforcement proceedings. By that time, appeal is usually no longer possible.[51] It may, for example, also be impossible to await proceedings in the country of origin regarding the unfairness of proceedings, as enforcement proceedings may have already been initiated elsewhere. Nevertheless, complaints concerning rights guaranteed in Article 6(1) ECHR should, in principle, be brought against the Contracting Party of origin of the judgment, as one otherwise runs the risk of being unable to complain successfully in Strasbourg.[52] Furthermore, even when the standard of full compliance with the procedural guarantees *ex* Article 6(1) ECHR is applied, it is always possible to consider possible procedural shortcomings of the applicant.

8.2.2 The Invocation of Article 6(1) ECHR Against Recognition and Enforcement: EU and National Jurisprudence

As the discussion below will demonstrate, national courts of the Contracting Parties have quite frequently invoked the right to a fair trial *ex* Article 6(1) ECHR or related notions against the recognition and enforcement of foreign judgments. It appears to be generally accepted that the absence of fair proceedings abroad will lead to the non-recognition or non-enforcement of the resulting foreign judgment. The discussion of some examples taken from the case law will, however, commence with a discussion of EU jurisprudence regarding the Brussels (/Lugano) regime, as the European Court of Justice (ECJ) has also been confronted with the impact of Article 6(1) ECHR on the enforcement of a foreign judgments (Sect. 8.2.2.1). Thereafter, one will find some illustrations regarding the invocation of the right to a fair trial against the recognition and enforcement taken from the national case law of the Contracting Parties (Sect. 8.2.2.2).

8.2.2.1 EU Jurisprudence

Krombach v. Bamberski[53] concerned the enforcement of a French judgment in Germany. The French proceedings were originally criminal proceedings. The defendant, Krombach, had been ordered to appear before the French courts, but he

---

[50] One should note that this may be different with regard to a violation of one of the substantive rights guaranteed in the ECHR. See *Lindberg v. Sweden* infra Sect. 8.3.

[51] See, e.g., *Maronier v. Larmer* infra n. 138.

[52] See also infra Sect. 8.3.1, particularly the text following n. 143 .

[53] ECJ 28 March 2000, Case C-7/98, *Krombach v. Bamberski*, [2000] ECR, I-1935.

had refused to do so. Consequently, the French courts had refused the defendant's request that his counsel be heard in his place, as he had not appeared in person. Krombach was sentenced *in absentia* to 15 years in prison, while he was also ordered to pay damages. Bamberski sought the enforcement of this latter (civil) award in Germany under the Brussels Convention.

The ECJ had to give a ruling on the interpretation of the public policy exception provided in Article 27 of the Brussels Convention (now Article 34(1) of the Brussels I Regulation),[54] particularly on whether a court of an EU Member State could take into account the fact that a defendant had been unable to have his defense presented, unless he appeared personally. The ECJ held that this was indeed the case, while noting that in setting limits on the public policy exception (recall that each forum State will, in principle, use its own version of the idea of public policy)[55] it had consistently held that fundamental norms are an integral part of the general principles that it takes into account and that the ECHR and the case law of the Court in Strasbourg are of particular significance in this regard.[56] The ECJ thus held that national courts could take into account the fact that the defendant's rights under Article 6(1) ECHR had been violated, as he had been unable to defend himself.[57]

The ECJ's decision in *Krombach* was followed in *Eurofood*, a case concerning the recognition of insolvency proceedings opened in another (EU) Member State, in which the ECJ found that a Member State may refuse to recognize the opening of insolvency proceedings in another Member State if that decision was taken in flagrant breach of the right to be heard.[58] However, in *Gambazzi*[59] the Court failed to speak out on any misgivings with regard to an English default judgment, but instead opted to leave the issue to the national court. This case concerned an English default judgment which was given against a defendant who, despite entering an appearance, was unable to defend himself due to the fact that he had failed to comply with a previous freezing order.[60]

---

[54] The Brussels I Regulation, Council Regulation (EC) No. 44/2001 of 22 December 2000 on jurisdiction and the recognition and enforcement of judgments in civil and commercial matters, *OJ* 2001 L12/1.

[55] See supra Sect. 2.5.

[56] See para 25 of *Krombach v. Bamberski* (supra n. 53).

[57] It is in this regard, incidentally, also interesting to note that the French (criminal) proceedings leading up to the enforcement proceedings in Germany have been condemned by the Court in Strasbourg. See *Krombach v. France*, no. 29731/96, ECHR 2000-II.

[58] ECJ 2 May 2006, Case C-341/04, *Eurofood IFSC*, ECR 2006, I-3813. See particularly paras 60–68. See with regard to public policy also ECJ 11 May 2000, Case C-38/98, *Régie Nationale des Usines Renault SA v. Maxicar SpA*, ECR 2000, I-2973.

[59] ECJ 2 April 2009, Case C-394/07, *Gambazzi*, ECR 2009, I-2563.

[60] One may note that from the perspective of the ECHR, it could be argued that the applicant had contributed to his inability to participate in the proceedings, which, as we have previously seen, could make the (successful) invocation of the ECHR difficult. See, e.g., *McDonald v. France* (supra Sect. 7.2).

In *Krombach* the ECJ thus acknowledged that the public policy exception in the Brussels (/Lugano) regime may be invoked against the recognition and enforcement of foreign judgments where the recognition and enforcement would lead to a manifest breach of a rule that is a fundamental part of the legal order of the State.[61] It will be recalled that all States falling under this Brussels/Lugano regime are also Contracting Parties to the ECHR. The ECJ in *Krombach* also emphasized that fundamental rights are an integral part of the principles of law that the ECJ aims to ensure and that the ECHR has a particular significance in this regard. While this case was, in principle, thus only concerned with the defendant's right to have his defense presented, one could easily argue that given the ECJ's emphasis of the significance of the rights guaranteed in the ECHR generally, and specifically the right to a fair trial, this finding may be interpreted more broadly.[62]

There are two issues that need to be further discussed in relation to the ECJ's findings in *Krombach* concerning the invocation of Article 6(1) ECHR against the recognition and enforcement of foreign judgments. These two issues have previously also been addressed in relation to the Court's case law.[63] First, the standard of control with regard to Article 6(1) ECHR will be discussed. Thereafter, the issue of whether Contracting Parties have an obligation to refuse the recognition and enforcement of foreign judgments emanating from other Contracting Parties will be examined.

In *Krombach* the issue of a possibly reduced effect of Article 6(1) ECHR was not discussed at all. It has been argued that this was, in fact, the standard of control with regard to Article 6(1) ECHR, which would be evidenced by the fact that the French decision in question was so clearly in violation of the rights guaranteed in Article 6(1) ECHR.[64] However, it could also be argued that there is no need for the attenuation of the standard of control with regard to Article 6(1) ECHR, as all the Member States of the EU are also Contracting Parties and therefore there is no need to deviate from the standards set in Article 6(1) ECHR. The latter is far more likely. Why would the standard of control possibly be mitigated in such cases? All the arguments regarding attenuation on the basis of the possible differences between legal systems are certainly not valid with regard to other Contracting Parties.

The second issue is whether there is an obligation to refuse the recognition and enforcement of foreign judgments. One should note that the ECJ in *Krombach* held that national courts are entitled to take a violation of the right to a fair trial into

---

[61] The *Krombach* case has been much discussed. See, e.g., Lowenfeld 2004, pp. 229–248; Strikwerda 2004, pp. 252–260.

[62] Whether it would possible to invoke one of the substantive rights guaranteed in the ECHR is difficult to say on the basis of *Krombach*. One of the issues that could make this difficult is the so-called local remedy argument. See further infra Sect. 8.3.1. See, however, also *Régie Nationale des Usines Renault SA v. Maxicar SpA*, Case C-38/98, ECR I-2973. In any event, the ECJ has held that it is ultimately up to the national courts to decide what public policy exactly entails. See *Gambazzi* (supra n. 59).

[63] See supra Sect. 8.2.1.

[64] Matscher 2004, p. 436.

account, but this does not indicate an obligation to do so. From the perspective of the ECJ there is thus no such obligation. It is merely a possibility. For an answer to this question, one would thus have to refer back to the Court's case law. It will be recalled that the Court's case law is also inconclusive, but I have argued that there indeed should be such an obligation.[65]

8.2.2.2 National Jurisprudence of the Contracting Parties

It is not too difficult to find examples of the invocation of Article 6(1) ECHR or a comparable notion against the recognition and enforcement of foreign judgments, as the fairness of the proceedings abroad is a requirement in all three legal orders under analysis. Below, a few such instances will be discussed.

The English courts have examined Article 6(1) ECHR as a bar to the recognition and enforcement of foreign judgments in a number of cases, some of which will be discussed below. English courts have, inter alia, dealt with the enforcement of a foreign judgment emanating from another Contracting Party as well as the enforcement of a foreign judgment originating from a third country.

Maronier v. Larmer[66] concerned the enforcement of a Dutch judgment in England on the basis of the Brussels Convention. Larmer was a dentist who worked in Rotterdam between 1978 and 1991. In 1983 Maronier, a patient, filed a complaint against him and was awarded a modest sum of money in a complaints procedure in the Netherlands. In 1984 Maronier started proceedings at the court in Rotterdam for a larger sum. These proceedings were stayed in 1986 at his request. Larmer moved to England in 1991. By that time, the proceedings had been dormant for 5 years. In 1998 the proceedings in the Netherlands were reactivated by Maronier. Larmer, however, was unaware that the proceedings had been reactivated and only became aware of the (now final) judgment against him when the order for registration was served on him in England.

In the first instance the order for registration was set aside. Maronier appealed against this decision, but the Court of Appeal held that the order had correctly been set aside in the first instance, as the respondent had not received a fair trial in the Netherlands, as required by Article 6(1) ECHR. The Court of Appeal therefore held that the recognition of the foreign judgment would violate the public policy requirement of Article 27(1) of the Brussels Convention. In doing so, the Court of Appeal considered—before discussing *Krombach*[67]—that courts 'should apply a strong presumption that the procedures of other signatories of the Human Rights Convention are compliant with Article 6 [ECHR].'[68] However, the Court of Appeal found that this presumption is not irrefutable.

---

[65] See further supra Sect. 8.2.1.

[66] *Maronier v. Larmer* [2002] EWCA Civ. 774, [2003] Q.B. 620.

[67] At [28–30].

[68] At [25].

In *Government of the United States of America v. Montgomery (No.2)*[69] the (then) House of Lords had to decide on whether the enforcement of an American judgment would violate Article 6(1) ECHR. Article 6(1) ECHR had been discussed before the Court of Appeal in this case, but no mention had been made of the two arguably most important judgments of the Court in this regard—*Drozd and Janousek* and *Pellegrini*.[70] These two cases were discussed before the House of Lords. The House of Lords ultimately held in this case, which concerned a judgment emanating from a third country, that a judgment originating from the United States could only be refused enforcement relying on Article 6(1) ECHR if the procedural shortcomings of such a judgment were 'flagrant'. It will be recalled, though, that in *Pellegrini* no reference was made to a 'flagrant denial of justice'.[71] Nonetheless, the House of Lords in *Montgomery* held that the Court's judgment in *Pellegrini* was not applicable by finding that the Court's ruling in *Pellegrini* relied on the special relationship between Italy and the Vatican.[72] However, as has been set out above, the Court in *Pellegrini* specifically treated the decision of the Vatican courts as a foreign judgment emanating from a third country,[73] which made this finding of the House of Lords at the time questionable.

The English case law concerning the recognition and enforcement of a foreign judgment violating Article 6(1) ECHR is thus not entirely unambiguous. In *Maronier v. Larmer* the English Court of Appeal found in a case concerning the enforcement of a judgment originating from another Contracting Party that the enforcement of this judgment would violate Article 6(1) ECHR and, therefore, public policy.[74] The findings of the Court of Appeal have been criticized, though, for taking 'human rights law less seriously' and reducing the impact of *Krombach*.[75] This critique was mostly aimed at the Court of Appeal's finding of there being 'a strong presumption that the procedures of other signatories of the Human Rights Convention are compliant with Article 6 [ECHR]',[76] as no mention of such a presumption was made in *Krombach*.[77]

However, in my opinion, the Court of Appeal's consideration has little impact, as—presumption or no presumption—it will always be for the defendant to demonstrate a violation of Article 6(1) ECHR. Since the Court of Appeal's

---

69 *Government of the United States of America v. Montgomery (No.2)* [2004] UKHL 37.

70 *Government of the United States of America v. Montgomery (No.2)* [2003] EWCA 392. It should be noted that *Soering v. the United Kingdom* was discussed by the Court of Appeal. See with regard to *Drozd and Janousek* and *Pellegrini* supra Sect. 8.2.1.

71 See supra Sect. 8.2.

72 *Government of the United States of America v. Montgomery (No.2)* [2004] UKHL 37 at [19] per Lord Carswell.

73 See supra n. 5.

74 See with regard to this case, e.g., Briggs 2003, pp. 470–472; Juratowitch 2007, pp. 188–189. See for a Dutch perspective on this case Kramer 2004, pp. 9–16.

75 Fawcett 2007, pp. 26–27.

76 *Maronier v. Larmer* [2002] EWCA Civ. 774, [2003] Q.B. 620, at [25].

77 See supra Sect. 8.2.2.1.

findings it has been held that such situations, where the foreign judgment emanates from another Contracting Party, offer 'little difficulty' to the English courts.[78] Indeed, there is, in principle, no reason to assume that a different standard regarding Article 6(1) ECHR should be applied in such a case where the country of origin is also a Contracting Party.

While the standard of control is clear where other Contracting Parties are concerned (full compliance), the situation is less clear where judgments emanating from third countries are at issue. As discussed above, the House of Lords in *Government of the United States of America v. Montgomery (No.2)*,[79] a case concerning a judgment emanating from a third country, held that such a judgment could only be refused, relying on Article 6(1) ECHR, if the procedural shortcomings of such a judgment were 'flagrant'. This finding has rightfully been criticized on account of the House of Lords' interpretation of *Pellegrini*.[80] At the time there was no indication that the 'flagrant' criterion should be used in such cases. However, could it be that the House of Lord's finding has been somewhat vindicated retrospectively in light of the Court's subsequent backing off of the standard it set in *Pellegrini*?[81] As was discussed above, it appears as if the Court has aimed to soften its stance with regard to its judgment in *Pellegrini*, even though its exact opinion has to be further clarified. Nevertheless, what is clear is that the House of Lord's (re)construction of *Pellegrini* at the time was incorrect.

In the more recent case *Merchant International Company v. Natsionalna Aktsionerna Kompaniya "Naftogaz Ukrayiny"*[82] concerning the invocation of Article 6(1) ECHR against the recognition and enforcement of a foreign judgment *Maronier* and *Montgomery* were again referred to and the approach followed in these two cases was essentially confirmed. What is most interesting is that Mr Justice David Steel articulated that the refusal to recognize a foreign judgment violating the ECHR is not so much an issue of public policy (or at least not alone), but rather of Section 6 of the Human Rights Act.[83] This case has a complicated factual background. This particular round of proceedings concerned one of many attempts by Merchant International Company (MIC) to recover a debt from *Natsionalna Aktsionerna Kompaniya* (NAK). In 2006 MIC finally obtained a judgment in its favor in Ukraine, but it was unable to enforce its judgment there. In 2010 MIC started proceedings in England to enforce its Ukrainian judgment. After NAK

[78] Dicey et al. 2012, p. 739.

[79] [2004] UKHL 37.

[80] See, e.g., Briggs 2005, pp. 537–543, see particularly p. 539ff; Dicey et al. 2012, pp. 739–740; Fawcett 2007, pp. 35–36; Juratowitch 2007, pp. 184–187.

[81] See supra Sect. 8.2.1.

[82] *Merchant International Company v. Natsionalna Aktsionerna Kompaniya 'Naftogaz Ukrayiny'* [2011] EWHC 1820 (Comm). This finding was upheld in appeal. See *Merchant International Company v. Natsionalna Aktsionerna Kompaniya 'Naftogaz Ukrayiny'* [2012] EWCA Civ 196.

[83] Citing Dicey et al. 2006, paras 14–149. See also, e.g., *Joint Stock Company (Aeroflot–Russian Airlines) v. Berezovsky & Anor* [2012] EWHC 3017 (Ch) at [53].

acknowledged service of the claim no defense was served and MIC entered judgment in default.

NAK subsequently sought to set aside this default judgment. During these latter proceedings NAK argued that the Ukrainian judgment should be set aside, as it in the meantime had applied to the Ukrainian Supreme Commercial Court, which had cancelled the judgment of 2006. MIC then argued that this latter Ukrainian judgment could not be recognized. In effect Article 6(1) ECHR was in this case thus invoked against a Ukrainian judgment setting aside an earlier Ukrainian judgment.

Mr Justice David Steel eventually found that the Ukrainian judgment setting aside the earlier judgment indeed violated Article 6(1) ECHR and thus could not be recognized.[84] He observed in this regard that the order of the Ukrainian Supreme Commercial Court reopening the case concerned a clear disregard of the principles of legal certainty. He, inter alia, noted that, while the case was re-opened on the basis of new facts calling the status of MIC in the original proceedings into question, NAK would be allowed to advance other points. Moreover, he observed that the original judgment had been in existence for 5 years and that the enforcement proceedings in England started more than a year ago. It was only after the failure by NAK to set aside service that the original judgment came under attack. Finally, the judge noted that the requirements of Article 6(1) ECHR should be approached carefully in this case concerning a state-owned entity, as follows from the Court's case law.[85]

This case concerned the recognition of a foreign judgment emanating from another Contracting Party (Ukraine). NAK, relying on *Montgomery*, had argued that recognition could only be refused in the event of a "flagrant" breach of Article 6(1) ECHR. Mr Justice held that even assuming that this stance would be correct that this case indeed concerned a flagrant breach. Moreover, he accepted in any event that *Montgomery* only applies to judgments originating from non-Contracting Parties. The standard of control regarding Article 6(1) ECHR thus differs in the English case law depending on the origin of a foreign judgment.

In concluding this discussion of English case law, one could state that it is generally accepted that a foreign judgment will not be recognized and enforced in England if the defendant has been denied a fair trial, regardless of the origin of the judgment.[86] It should, incidentally, be noted that a defendant's right to a fair trial is

---

[84] The setting aside of the newest Ukrainian judgment meant that the English default judgment would stand. NAK had argued that the re-opening of proceedings in Ukraine simply meant that there was no judgment to enforce and that the English default judgment had to be set aside. The judge did not agree, and in finding so, incidentally, referred to a Dutch case before the Amsterdam Court of Appeal dated April 2009. See Hof Amsterdam 28 April 2009, *JOR* 2009, 208—one of the many instalments of the Yukos-saga in the Netherlands. See for more instalments of the saga further infra.

[85] The Court's case law in *Pravednaya v. Russia*, no. 69529/01, 18 November 2004 and *Lizanets v. Ukraine*, no. 6725/03, 31 May 2007 was cited in this regard.

[86] See, e.g., Dicey et al. 2012, pp. 739–740.

not only embodied in Article 6(1) ECHR, but can also be founded upon common law principles.[87]

In the Netherlands, Article 6(1) ECHR has also occasionally been invoked against the recognition and enforcement of foreign judgments. The *Hoge Raad* has, for example, examined the enforcement of a German judgment, a so-called *Anerkenntnisurteil*, on the basis of Article 38 of the Brussels I Regulation in light of Article 6(1) ECHR.[88] In short, such a judgment entails a judgment by confession. In accordance with the relevant German rules, such a judgment does not give any reasons. In the Dutch enforcement proceedings in the first instance, the district court in Rotterdam had found that the judgment, which did not give any reasons, violated the fundamental principles of a fair trial and, thus, Dutch public policy. The enforcement was therefore denied on the basis of Article 34(1) of the Brussels I Regulation.

However, on appeal before the *Hoge Raad*, the court found that in the present case it could not be assumed that the lack of reasons was in violation of the right to a fair trial following from Article 6(1) ECHR. Whether or not the lack of reasons in a judgment leads to a violation of public policy depends on the specific circumstances of the case and the manner in which the case has been litigated, according to the court.[89] In the event of such a judgment by confession, a statement of reasons is not necessary, as the defendants have in such cases acknowledged the claim.

A pertinent example of the successful invocation of Article 6(1) ECHR against the enforcement of a foreign judgment in the Netherlands can be found in one of the many installments of the famous *Yukos* case, the fallout of which has led not only to many cases in the Netherlands,[90] but also in other parts of the world.[91] The district court in Amsterdam had, inter alia, to decide whether it could recognize the Russian judgment in which the bankruptcy of the Yukos company was declared.[92] Yukos Oil has been established in the Russian Federation in 1993 and was later privatized. It was the only shareholder of Yukos Finance, a company based in Amsterdam. In 2003 the Russian authorities, after initially having communicated that Yukos Oil did not owe the State any more taxes, re-examined this decision and found that the company owed the State a huge sum.

In the proceedings before the Russian courts, the Russian tax authority produced many pages of evidence, leaving the defense with virtually no time to review it all. Multiple requests for an extension were denied by the Russian court,

---

87 See, e.g., Fentiman 2010, p. 703.

88 HR 18 March 2011, *RvdW* 2011, 392.

89 HR 18 March 2011, *RvdW* 2011, 392. See no. 3.2.

90 See, e.g., Hof Amsterdam 10 May 2011, *RN* 2011, 82; Rb. Amsterdam 17 March 2011, *LJN* BP8070; HR 7 January 2011, *NJ* 2011, 134—just to name three fairly recent cases concerning *Yukos*.

91 See, Cordero Moss 2007, pp. 1–17 on proceedings concerning *Yukos* in Houston, Texas.

92 Rb. Amsterdam, 31 October 2007, *NIPR* 2007, 308.

which found in favor of the tax authority. Yukos, incidentally, filed an application in Strasbourg against this decision.[93] The Russian authorities, however, did not allow Yukos to await the result of these proceedings. The Russian tax procedures were followed by an insolvency procedure in Russia. In 2006 Yukos Oil was declared bankrupt by a Russian court.

In the subsequent Dutch procedure the court focused mainly on whether the insolvency judgment could be recognized in the Netherlands. The court held that it was clear in the tax proceedings in Russia the right to a fair trial *ex* Article 6(1) ECHR had been violated. The court concluded that this lack of fair proceedings ultimately stood in the way of the recognition of the bankruptcy judgment, as the tax assessments had been primarily responsible for the company's bankruptcy.

The Dutch *Rechtbank* Zwolle-Lelystad has refused to enforce a Norwegian alimony judgment on the basis of Article 6(1) ECHR.[94] The LBIO, the Dutch agency concerned with the collection of such judgments, requested the enforcement of a final Norwegian judgment against a man living in the Netherlands. The request was based on the 1973 Hague Convention on the Recognition and Enforcement of Decisions Relating to Maintenance Obligations.[95] Both the Netherlands and Norway are party to this Convention. The court agreed with the defendant that the execution of the Norwegian judgment in the Netherlands would violate Dutch public policy, as the man had not been heard in the Norwegian procedure. The man had, at the request of the Norwegian court, sent his last three pay stubs. The Norwegian court had subsequently based the amount of the alimony on this, without having a further hearing. The Dutch court held that the man could have expected to be properly heard in the proceedings and that the Norwegian proceedings had thus violated Article 6 ECHR.

In a final Dutch case before the *Hoge Raad*, which will be discussed here, Article 6(1) ECHR was not explicitly invoked, but this case may nevertheless be important with regard to the possibility to raise such a defense against the enforcement of a foreign judgment.[96] This case is concerned with the enforcement of an Austrian judgment. In proceedings in Austria the father requested the Austrian judge to lower the maintenance for his children to zero, as he was allegedly unfit to work. The Austrian judge ordered an inquiry. An expert reported

---

[93] *OAO Neftyanaya Kompaniya Yukos v. Russia*, no. 14902/04, 20 September 2011. The Court has recently held that in this case Russia did not misuse legal proceedings to destroy Yukos, but it did find violations of Article 6(1) and (3) ECHR, the right to a fair trial; Article 1 of Protocol No. 1 ECHR, the right to property, regarding the imposition and calculation of penalties in the 2000–2001 tax assessments; and Article 1 of Protocol No. 1 ECHR, in the sense that the enforcement proceedings were disproportionate. Neither a violation was found of Article 1 of Protocol No. 1 ECHR, with regard to the rest of the tax proceedings, nor with regard to Article 14 ECHR taken in conjunction with this Article. Unanimously, no violation of Article 18 ECHR was found.

[94] Rb. Zwolle-Lelystad, 20 July 2005, *NIPR* 2005, 327.

[95] Convention on the Recognition and Enforcement of Decisions Relating to Maintenance Obligations, concluded on 2 October 1973, entry into force 1 August 1976.

[96] See HR 5 April 2002, *NJ* 2004, 170 (note Vlas).

that the father was indeed unfit to work. The judge subsequently came to the conclusion that the man would be able to perform some tasks and that he could acquire a certain income. The father was ordered to pay maintenance. The Dutch proceedings concerned the enforcement of this decision based on a bilateral treaty between the Netherlands and Austria. At issue was whether this decision would violate Dutch public policy. The father had argued that the Austrian judge had not properly assessed his claim that he was unable to work and that the enforcement of the decision would thus violate Dutch public policy, as there had not been a fair hearing. However, the *Hoge Raad* held that the father could not invoke the public policy exception, as he had failed to appeal the decision in Austria, even though he was able to do so. Under such circumstances the public policy exception cannot be invoked against the enforcement of a foreign judgment, according to the *Hoge Raad*.[97]

This case raises the issue whether it is necessary to exhaust all remedies in the country of origin of the foreign judgment. The *Hoge Raad* essentially applies a local remedy rule. Above, I have argued in relation to proceedings before the Court in Strasbourg that, despite the basic obligation to direct complaints against the Contracting Party of origin of the foreign judgment, it should be possible to (fully) examine a foreign judgment emanating from another Contracting Party with regard to a possible violation of Article 6(1) ECHR.[98] Here a national court thus also applies a local remedy rule. By invoking this rule the *Hoge Raad* could prevent litigants from successfully invoking their rights under Article 6(1) ECHR, which could, in principle, lead to a violation of Article 6(1) ECHR. However, the Court would not necessarily frown upon this practice. In fact, it has already been demonstrated that the Court quite often invokes the rule that nobody can complain about a situation to which they themselves have contributed.[99] Moreover, it should be noted that the Court has not yet ruled on this particular situation. In *Pellegrini*, for example, the applicant did exhaust all possibilities before the Vatican courts.[100] However, I would argue that the application of a local remedy rule by a national court with regard to complaints concerning the procedural guarantees of Article 6(1) ECHR could, under circumstances, lead to a violation of Article 6(1) ECHR. Therefore, some caution should be exercised in this regard. It should, incidentally, be noted that the judgment of the *Hoge Raad* would appear to leave room for this. Having said all this, it would nevertheless be wise for a litigant to first exhaust all possibilities in the country of origin of the foreign judgment.

In the Netherlands one of the requirements for the recognition and enforcement of foreign judgments is that the foreign judgment does not violate public policy. Moreover, if the foreign proceedings do not meet the standards of what in the

---

97 See with regard to this case also van Hoek and Luchtman 2006, pp. 42–43.

98 See supra Sect. 8.1 This local remedy rule, incidentally, makes the invocation of one of the substantive rights guaranteed in the ECHR very difficult. See further infra Sect. 8.3.

99 Cf., e.g., *McDonald v. France* (dec.), no. 18648/04, 29 April 2008 (discussed supra Sect. 7.2).

100 See supra Sect. 8.1.

Netherlands would be deemed a fair trial, a foreign judgment cannot be recognized.[101] The impact of Article 6(1) ECHR in this regard is evidenced by the case law discussed above.[102] The finding in the *Yukos* case demonstrates that courts in the Netherlands are willing to go to great lengths with regard to Article 6(1) ECHR, in the sense that the Dutch court was unwilling to enforce a foreign judgment (the bankruptcy judgment) of which the underlying proceedings had not been unfair, but where the preceding tax proceedings leading to the bankruptcy were.[103]

In Swiss case law, Article 6(1) ECHR has also been discussed in relation to the recognition and enforcement of foreign judgments. In a case concerning the enforcement of an English judgment under the Lugano Convention, the Swiss *Tribunal fédéral* held that a violation of procedural public policy in the Swiss understanding can occur only if fundamental and generally accepted procedural principles have been violated. According to the Tribunal, these principles of a fair trial include in particular the right to be heard, the equal treatment of parties, respect for the law on evidence, and the right to defense, all as recognized in the ECHR.[104] In a later case the court held that the principle of independence and impartiality of the judge should also be included.[105]

In a case concerning the enforcement of an American default judgment which did not cite any reasons, the *Tribunal fédéral* found that the defendant could not rely on Article 6 ECHR with regard to this lack of reasoning, as the absence thereof does not always violate Swiss public policy.[106] If the defendant was aware of the trial and had the opportunity to participate, but knowingly relinquished this opportunity, such a default judgment does not violate Swiss public policy.

The *Tribunal fédéral* has further stated generally with regard to the recognition and enforcement of foreign judgments that 'Swiss public policy entails compliance with the fundamental procedural rules derived from the constitution, including the right to a fair trial and the right to be heard.'[107] This case concerned, incidentally, the recognition of a repudiation. Reference was also made to the equality of spouses, although the ECHR was not expressly discussed on this issue.[108] Procedural public

[101] Cf. Strikwerda 2012, p. 280; Cf. Rosner 2004, p. 31ff.

[102] But see Rosner 2004, p. 46ff, who is critical in relation to the usefulness of the standard of Article 6(1) ECHR.

[103] See with regard to this case Bos 2008, pp. 41–43.

[104] Judgment of the *Tribunal fédéral*, 4P.48/2002, 4 June 2002 (unpublished). See particularly 3.aa (referring to *Krombach* in support of its findings).

[105] Judgment of the *Tribunal fédéral*, 4A_305/2009, 5 October 2009 (unpublished), c.4, see particularly c.4.1. Both these cases, incidentally, refer with regard to the notion of a violation of public policy to ATF 126 III 249, a case concerning procedural public policy in relation to arbitration.

[106] ATF 116 II 625, 630–632.

[107] ATF 126 III 327, 330 (referring to ATF 126 III 101, 3–b, pp. 107–108 and ATF 122 III 344, 4a, pp. 348–349).

[108] See also infra Sects. 8.3.2 and 8.3.3.

policy has also been invoked against a repudiation which had not been notified to the spouse, who was consequently unaware of any proceedings.[109]

In Article 27(2) of the Swiss Private International Law Act it is it is explicitly stated that the recognition of a foreign decision must be denied if a party establishes that such a decision was given in violation of the fundamental principles concerning the Swiss concept of procedural law. This would include not having had the opportunity to defend oneself.[110] There has been some discussion in Switzerland whether the requirements enumerated in Article 27 of the Swiss Private International Law Act should be considered exhaustive, particularly in light of the new Swiss Constitution, in which the procedural guarantees were further strengthened.[111] In any event, the Swiss *Tribunal fédéral* has reiterated that 'Swiss public policy entails compliance with the fundamental procedural rules derived from the constitution, including the right to a fair trial and the right to be heard.'[112] It has been argued that this reference to a fair trial is consistent with the Court's approach in *Pellegrini*, except for the fact that the Swiss judge does not examine the requirements listed in Article 27(2) of the Swiss Private International Law Act *ex officio*.[113] In this regard the Swiss Act deviates from the previous practice of the Swiss *Tribunal fédéral*, which did examine such procedural safeguards *ex officio*.[114]

One could thus argue that, despite the wording of Article 27(2) of the Swiss Private International Law Act, the Swiss courts may have to return to this old practice in order to avoid a possible violation of Article 6(1) ECHR. On the other hand, one may question whether this issue would ever really become a problem before the Court in Strasbourg, as an applicant would have to demonstrate to the Court that he or she had already complained about the alleged violation in the national proceedings. It has been noted that Article 27(2) of the Swiss Private International Law Act is quite often invoked before the *Tribunal fédéral*, yet it is only rarely admitted.[115] While according to some the exact content of the requirements of Article 27(2) of the Swiss Act is somewhat vague, it appears to be clear that the requirements listed there should at least correspond with the minimal requirements of Article 6(1) ECHR.[116]

---

109 Cour de justice GE, 14 November 1991, SJ 1992, p. 219.

110 See Article 27(2)–b of the Swiss Private International Law Act.

111 See, e.g., Grisel 2002, p. 97ff. Cf. Volken 2004, p. 393.

112 ATF 126 III 330 ('l'ordre public Suisse exige le respect des règles fondamentales de la procedure déduite de la constitution, notamment le droit à un process equitable et celui d'être entendu') [referring to ATF 126 III 101, 3–b, pp. 107–108 and ATF 122 III 344, 4a, pp. 348–349].

113 Dutoit 2005, p. 105.

114 Id. Cf. Volken 2004, p. 394.

115 See ATF 111 Ia 12 as an example of a case in which it was admitted. Cf. Dutoit 2005, p. 108 and Volken 2004, pp. 394, 398.

116 See S. Othenin-Girard, *La reserve d'ordre public en droit international privé suisse* (Zürich, Schulthess 1999), p. 108.

8.2.3 The Manner of Invocation of Article 6(1) ECHR Regarding Recognition and Enforcement

A final issue that needs to be discussed in relation to the jurisprudence of the national courts of the Contracting Parties regarding the invocation of Article 6(1) ECHR against the recognition and enforcement of foreign judgments is the method used by national courts. It follows from the discussion of the jurisprudence above that national courts almost always refer to the public policy exception in order to invoke the right to a fair trial against the recognition and enforcement of foreign judgments. Article 6(1) ECHR is generally regarded as being a part of procedural public policy. However, it is interesting to pose the question as to whether it would also be possible to directly apply the rights guaranteed in the ECHR.[117] Could Article 6(1) ECHR have an autonomous role here? This is, of course, particularly interesting with regard to international instruments lacking such an exception.[118] This may additionally become an important issue because of the desire to further streamline the recognition and enforcement of foreign judgments within the European Union.[119]

8.2.4 The Abolition of the Exequatur Procedure

The importance of the role of the public policy exception and Article 6(1) ECHR is illustrated by the debate on the wisdom of the abolition of the *exequatur* procedure in the Recast of the Brussels I Regulation.[120] Ever since the so-called 'Tampere resolution',[121] the EU has moved toward the further simplification of the recognition and enforcement of foreign judgments within the EU and the (gradual) abolition of *exequatur* in several separate instruments. Instruments in which the *exequatur* procedure has been omitted include the European Enforcement Order

[117] See in this regard also the discussion infra Sect. 8.3.3 on the public policy exception and the invocation of the substantive rights guaranteed in the ECHR.

[118] This issue would, of course, also raise issues concerning hierarchy. See in this regard supra Sect. 3.3.1.

[119] See the Regulation of the European Parliament and of the Council on the Jurisdiction and the Recognition and Enforcement of Judgments in Civil and Commercial Matters (Recast), 2010/0383 (COD) PE-CONS 56/12. COM (2010) 748 final.

[120] See with regard to this debate, e.g., Beaumont and Johnston 2010, pp. 249–279 (a shorter version of this article has appeared in 30 *IPrax* (2010), p. 105); Cuniberti and Rueda 2011, pp. 286–316; Kramer 2011, pp. 633–641; Schilling 2011, pp. 31–40; Schlosser 2010, pp. 101–104.

[121] The often cited 'Tampere resolution' is not a binding resolution, but rather a summary provided by the Finnish presidency of the special meeting in Tampere in October 1999 concerning the area of security, freedom, and justice. See the document 'Tampere European Council 15 and 16 October 1999. Presidency Conclusions' www.europarl.europa.eu/summits/tam_en.htm, visited October 2012.

for Uncontested Claims,[122] the European Order for Payment Procedure,[123] and the European Small Claims Procedure.[124] These all deal with different types of judgments, although their general functioning is largely the same: judgments based on these instruments are immediately enforceable in other Member States, and may only be challenged in the Member State of origin on certain established grounds. They may explicitly not be challenged in the receiving Member State. In addition to these instruments concerning civil procedure, there is also an instrument relating to maintenance obligations, which basically extends similar rules to their enforcement.[125]

The issue that has become the focus of some debate is whether these instruments, or this movement in general toward automatic recognition and enforcement within the European Union, which may only be challenged in the State of origin, jeopardize the protection of (procedural) human rights, and particularly Article 6(1) ECHR.[126] Incidentally, it could be argued that these new EU instruments actually also promote human rights, as Article 6(1) ECHR also entails a right to enforcement of judgments. These new instruments in which the *exequatur* procedure is abolished would thus consequently protect the human rights of the creditors of judgments in the EU.[127] However this argument is somewhat unconvincing, because, as has been discussed above, Article 6(1) ECHR does not entail a blanket right to enforcement of (foreign) judgments; particularly if such a judgment were to violate Article 6(1) itself, it is unthinkable that one could invoke Article 6(1) ECHR to enforce this judgment.[128]

Moreover, one could hardy argue that these new instruments are necessary for the protection of the rights of creditors. While under the old regime (the current Brussels I Regulation) there is an *exequatur* procedure, this is not much of an inconvenience for creditors: it has been reported that the overwhelming majority of cases are successful and that a decision usually merely takes a few weeks.[129] Interestingly enough, the Commission uses this as an argument in favor of

---

[122] Regulation (EC) No. 805/2004 creating a European Enforcement Order for Uncontested Claims, *OJ* 2004, L 143/15.

[123] Regulation (EC) No. 1896/2006 creating a European Order for Payment Procedure, *OJ* 2006 L 399/1.

[124] Regulation (EC) No. 861/2007 establishing a European Small Claims Procedure, *OJ* 2007 L 1999/1.

[125] Regulation (EC) No. 4/2009 on Jurisdiction, Applicable Law, Recognition and Enforcement of Decisions and Cooperation in Matters relating to Maintenance Obligations, *OJ* 2009 L 7/1.

[126] See the contributions cited supra n. 120. See with regard to the aforementioned European Enforcement Order, the Payment Procedure and Small Claims Procedure: van Bochove 2007, pp. 331–339.

[127] See Cuniberti and Rueda 2011, p. 294.

[128] See supra Sect. 7.2 See also Cuniberti and Rueda 2011, p. 294 and the writers cited there.

[129] See the Report from the Commission to the European Parliament, the Council and the European Economic and Social Committee on the application of Council Regulation (EC) No. 44/2001, 21 April 2009 COM (2009) 174, http://ec.europa.eu/civiljustice/news/docs/report_judgements_en.pdf. Accessed March 2014.

abolishing *exequatur*: the vast majority of cases is successful, so these proceedings merely hinder the free movement of judgments within the EU. One could, of course, also argue the other way around: it is hardly an inconvenience for creditors, while in those rare cases in which the procedural safeguards following from Article 6(1) ECHR are violated, Article 6(1) ECHR may provide an escape hatch.

However, despite all this, the Commission initially envisaged the abolition of *exequatur* in the revised Brussels I Regulation. Without any form of *exequatur*, judgments would move freely within the EU. This would leave judgment debtors with less of an opportunity to challenge such judgments, even if the proceedings leading up to these judgments were contrary to Article 6(1) ECHR. Originally only a very limited possibility for debtors to challenge judgments was envisioned, which indeed raised questions with regard to Article 6(1) ECHR.[130] However, the Recast still offers a safety mechanism for the debtor in Article 45, which alleviates concerns with regard to Article 6(1) ECHR. Not only has a public policy exception been maintained,[131] but procedural guarantees have also been safeguarded.[132]

While a solution concerning Article 6(1) ECHR has thus been provided in the latest proposal of the Brussels I Regulation, issues in this regard may still occur in relation to the three aforementioned instruments in which *exequatur* proceedings have (already) been abolished.[133] Germany was, incidentally, so concerned about the possibility that the abolition of the public policy defense in the European Enforcement Order[134] would allow for the enforcement of foreign judgments violating the ECHR that it has retained defenses at the 'actual enforcement' stage if the debtor was unable to raise such a defense during the proceedings in the State of origin.[135] One may wonder whether the Commission welcomes this possibility. Despite the fact that *exequatur* would be abolished and that the public policy exception would be eliminated, one would still be left with a stage at which one could object to the enforcement of the judgment, albeit on a limited ground.

---

130 See the Green Paper on the Review of Council Regulation (EC) No. 44/2001 on Jurisdiction and the Recognition and Enforcement of Judgments in Civil and Commercial Matters, COM (2009) 175 and the contributions cited supra n. 120.

131 See Article 45(1)(a) of the Recast (supra n. 119). See also Article 46 Recast.

132 See Article 45(1)(b) of the Recast (supra n. 119). The irreconcilability of judgments has also been included in Article 45(1)(c).

133 See supra n. 122; 123; 124.

134 See supra n. 122.

135 Cuniberti 2008, p. 49ff, particularly p. 51. Cf. Beaumont and Johnston 2010, p. 271ff.

Nevertheless, I would argue that this, or a similar solution,[136] is absolutely necessary from the point of view of the protection of the rights guaranteed in Article 6(1) ECHR.[137]

8.2.5 Preliminary Conclusions

It is clear that on the basis of Article 6(1) ECHR Contracting Parties may refuse the recognition and enforcement of foreign judgments. It follows from the Court's judgment in *Pellegrini* that there is even an obligation to do so with regard to foreign judgments violating Article 6(1) ECHR originating from third countries. Moreover, there is a good argument to be made that this obligation also applies to judgments from other Contracting Parties, even though the Court has not yet spoken on this issue.

The exact standard that should be applied to foreign judgments is, however, unclear. The Court has in its jurisprudence following *Pellegrini* cast some doubt on the exact meaning of this judgment. Although the Court in *Pellegrini* insisted on full compliance with the rights guaranteed in Article 6 ECHR, it has been argued that it follows from the Court's subsequent case law (based on case law preceding *Pellegrini*) that the obligation to refuse enforcement of foreign judgments emanating from third countries only exists in cases in which there has been 'a flagrant denial of justice'.

One could say that the uncertainty with regard to the exact meaning of the Court's case law is, in a way, echoed in the case law of national courts of the Contracting Parties. While national courts have little trouble invoking the rights guaranteed in Article 6(1) ECHR against the recognition and enforcement of foreign judgments, there appears to remain at least some uncertainty in the case law concerning the issue of the standard of control.

---

136 See, e.g., Beaumont and Johnston 2010, p. 273, who argue (in relation to earlier plans regarding the Brussels I Regulation) for an exception similar to Article 20 of the Hague Child Abduction Convention, which allows for a refusal to return a child if such a return would be impermissible on the basis of 'the fundamental principles of the requested State relating to the protection of human rights and fundamental freedoms.'

137 See with regard to the necessity hereof also the ECJ's case law in *Krombach v. Bamberski* and the English case *Maronier v. Larmer*. Both cases concern the enforcement of a foreign judgment violating Article 6(1) ECHR based on the Brussels regime and are discussed supra Sects. 8.2.2.1 and 8.2.2.2.

8.3 The Invocation of the Substantive Rights Guaranteed in the ECHR Against the Recognition and Enforcement of Foreign Judgments

The invocation of Article 6 ECHR, which guarantees the procedural right to a fair trial, against the recognition and enforcement of foreign judgments has been discussed above. Whether or not it is possible to invoke one of the substantive rights guaranteed in the ECHR is a separate issue. Contrary to the situation in which one of the procedural rights of the ECHR is in play, one would not only have to look at the procedure which led to the foreign judgment, but also assess whether the application of that judgment would infringe one of the (substantive) rights guaranteed in the ECHR.

It follows from the Court's case law that with regard to the invocation of one of the substantive rights guaranteed in the ECHR against the recognition and enforcement of foreign judgments it is necessary to make a distinction depending on the origin of the judgment. Therefore, first the invocation of the ECHR against a foreign judgment emanating from another Contracting Party will be discussed (Sect. 8.3.1). Thereafter, the invocation against a foreign judgment originating from a non-Contracting Party will be examined (Sect. 8.3.2). This will be followed by a brief discussion of case law of the national courts of the Contracting Parties (Sect. 8.3.3).

8.3.1 The Invocation of Substantive Rights Guaranteed in the ECHR against a Judgment of Another Contracting Party

The issue of the invocation of substantive rights against recognition and enforcement has not been often discussed by the Court. By its own acknowledgment, many questions remain unanswered. In *Lindberg v. Sweden*,[138] the Court examined a case in which the applicant invoked one of the substantive rights of the ECHR to stave off the recognition of a Norwegian judgment in Sweden. *Lindberg* thus concerned the enforcement of judgment originating from another Contracting Party. The applicant complained under Article 13 ECHR (the right to an effective remedy) in conjunction with Article 10 ECHR (freedom of expression) that the Swedish Supreme Court had failed to carry out a proper review of his claim that the judgment of a Norwegian Court had violated his rights under Article 10 ECHR.

Lindberg, a Norwegian national residing in Sweden, had travelled aboard a seal hunting vessel in the capacity of seal hunting inspector. After the hunting season he wrote an inspection report. The *Bladet Tromsø*, a Norwegian newspaper,

[138] *Lindberg v. Sweden* (dec.), no. 48198/99, 15 January 2004.

published twenty-six articles on Mr. Lindberg's inspection, including the entire report. The report contained information about several breaches of the seal hunting regulations and received a lot of media attention. Thereafter, Mr. Lindberg also introduced a film entitled 'Seal Mourning', which contained footage shot by him of certain breaches of hunting regulations. Clips from the film were broadcast by a Norwegian television station and later the entire film was broadcast by a Swedish television station.

In reaction to all this, nineteen crew members of the ship brought—largely with success—a series of defamation proceedings in Norway against Mr. Lindberg and a number of media corporations and companies, including the *Bladet Tromsø*. The Norwegian Court ordered Mr. Lindberg to pay compensation to the nineteen crew members. Leave to appeal to the Norwegian Supreme Court was denied and the decision became final. Mr. Lindberg subsequently lodged an application with the former European Commission of Human Rights alleging violations of Articles 6, 10, and 13 ECHR. The Commission, however, declared the application inadmissible as it had been lodged out of time.[139]

Lindberg's case against Sweden was concerned with the Swedish courts' refusal to prevent the enforcement of the Norwegian judgment against him in Sweden. The crew members had requested the Swedish Enforcement Office to execute the award of compensation and costs made in the Norwegian judgment. The Enforcement Office ordered Mr. Lindberg to pay. Mr. Lindberg lodged a judicial appeal against that decision, arguing that the Norwegian judgment violated his freedom of expression under Article 10 ECHR. This appeal was, however, dismissed by successive courts in Sweden, which, inter alia, held that public policy considerations did not prevent the execution of the Norwegian judgment in Sweden.

Mr. Lindberg brought proceedings before the Court in Strasbourg. The Court first considered whether he actually had an arguable claim, since this is a requirement for the applicability of Article 13 ECHR. Although the Court showed great reservations as to whether this was the case, it ultimately found that that it did not need to decide on this issue and proceeded on the assumption that Article 13 ECHR was applicable.[140] The Court subsequently held that, for Article 13, it only needed to examine whether the scope of the review carried out by the Swedish courts was sufficient to conclude that the applicant had had an effective remedy in Sweden. After referring to the fact that it had previously decided comparable issues,[141] the Court ultimately held that it was not necessary to delve

---

[139] *Lindberg v. Norway* (dec.), no. 26604/95, 26 February 1997. Incidentally, the defamation case against the newspaper *Bladet Tromsø* and its former editor also went to Strasbourg and eventually reached the Grand Chamber, which found that there indeed had been a violation of Article 10 ECHR in this case. See *Bladet Tromsø and Stensaas v. Norway* [GC], no. 21980/93, ECHR 1999-III.

[140] See with regard to the reasoning of the Court on Article 13 ECHR in this case Spielmann 2011, p. 773.

[141] See supra n. 21.

into unanswered questions concerning the impact of the ECHR on the recognition and enforcement of foreign judgments. The Court stated:

> However, the Court does not deem it necessary for the purposes of its examination of the present case to determine the general issue concerning what standard should apply where the enforcing State as well as the State whose court gave the contested decision is a Contracting Party to the Convention and where the subject-matter is one of substance (i.e., here, the freedom of expression) rather than procedure. In the particular circumstances it suffices to note that the Swedish courts found that the requested enforcement (in respect of the award of compensation and costs made in the Norwegian judgment) was neither prevented by Swedish public order or any other obstacles under Swedish law. The Court, bearing in mind its findings above as to whether the applicant had an arguable claim, does not find that there were any compelling reasons against enforcement.

The Court thus recognizes that there are many interesting issues left unanswered up until this point with regard to the recognition and enforcement of foreign judgments. Alas, given the particular circumstances of *Lindberg*, as will be discussed hereafter, there was no need for the Court to delve deeper into this issue.

It should be reiterated that *Lindberg* concerned the recognition of a foreign judgment emanating from another Contracting Party. This appears to be decisive in the Court's decision: namely, the Court noted that any complaint directed against the findings of the Norwegian courts should have been addressed in an application pursued against Norway in Strasbourg, which the applicant, of course, had attempted to do.[142] To allow him to bring up this argument again in the Swedish proceedings would have amounted to a second chance, 'an undue possibility' in the words of the Court, which would carry 'the risk of upsetting the coherence of the division of roles between national review bodies and the European Court, making up the system of collective enforcement under the Convention.'[143]

The Court thus essentially applied the 'local remedy rule'—the necessity to first exhaust national procedures—which can be found not only in the ECHR[144] but also in international law,[145] and is equally recognized when it comes to the recognition and enforcement of foreign judgments.[146] The Court's finding could be interpreted as excluding any viable invocation of one of the substantive rights guaranteed in the ECHR against the recognition and enforcement of foreign

[142] See supra n. 139.

[143] *Lindberg v. Sweden* (dec.), no. 48198/99, 15 January 2004.

[144] See Article 35(1) ECHR. See with regard to this requirement also supra Sect. 3.2. This requirement is, incidentally, also included in a number of other human rights treaties. See, e.g., Article 46 of the Inter-American Convention on Human Rights and Article 5 of Optional Protocol I of the International Covenant on Civil and Political Rights.

[145] See, e.g., Amerasinghe 2004.

[146] See, e.g., the so-called Schlosser Report, an explanatory report on the Brussels Convention, *OJ* 1979, C 59/71, no. 192.

judgments originating from other Contracting Parties before the Court in Strasbourg. After all, in all these cases it would be possible (and necessary) to bring a complaint in Strasbourg instead of waiting for enforcement proceedings in another Contracting Party. This would, incidentally, be different with regard to the invocation of Article 6(1) ECHR, as in the absence of a fair trial the substantive issues have not been properly decided upon, and it may be impossible to rectify such a situation in the State of origin because, for example, one may not have been properly served and thus unaware of any proceedings, until it is too late.[147]

8.3.2 The Invocation of Substantive Rights Guaranteed in the ECHR against a Judgment of a Third Country

There are few cases in which substantive rights have been invoked against the recognition and enforcement of foreign judgments originating from a third country. One is a case concerning the recognition of an Algerian repudiation in France, although this case was ultimately struck out of the list as a friendly settlement had been reached. In *D.D. v. France*,[148] the Court had to consider whether a divorce in Algeria by way of repudiation could be recognized in France. The wife complained about the incompatibility of a repudiation with Article 5 of Protocol No. 7 ECHR, which guarantees equality between spouses. The Court ultimately decided to strike this case out of the list, but not before noting—and implicitly endorsing—the recent change in the case law of the French *Cour de Cassation* which no longer allowed the blanket recognition of such divorces, but instead found that even if the foreign decision had been the result of a fair and adversarial procedure, such a unilateral repudiation by the husband without giving any legal effect to possible opposition to such a decision by the woman would violate Article 5 of Protocol No. 7 ECHR.

Another case in which the invocation of one of the substantive rights guaranteed in the ECHR has been discussed is *Saccoccia v. Austria*,[149] a case considered previously in relation to the applicability of Article 6(1) ECHR to enforcement proceedings in Chap. 7.[150] The Court also examined the execution of an American forfeiture order in light of Article 1 of Protocol No. 1 ECHR. The applicant had asserted that he had been the owner of his assets and that the forfeiture order amounted to an interference of his right to property. However, the Court dismissed the arguments based on the right to property. The Court did agree with the applicant that the confiscation of his assets interfered with his right to peaceful enjoyment of his possessions. However, referring to its standard case law concerning Article 1 of Protocol No. 1 ECHR, it held that the forfeiture fell within the State's right 'to

---

[147] See, e.g., *Maronier v. Larmer*, supra n. 66.

[148] *D.D. v. France* (dec.), no. 3/02, 8 November 2005.

[149] *Saccoccia v. Austria*, no. 69917/01, 18 December 2008.

[150] See supra Sect. 7.2 (the case is discussed at the very end of Sect. 7.2).

enforce such laws as it deems necessary to control the use of property in accordance with the general interest.'[151] Moreover, the Court held that this interference had a basis in Austrian law. Finally, the Court established that the confiscation had the legitimate aim of enhancing international cooperation and making sure that the money made in drug trafficking was actually forfeited. The Court thus found, bearing in mind also the margin of appreciation of States in this regard, that the forfeiture order struck a fair balance between the applicant's rights under Article 1 of Protocol No. 1 ECHR and the interests of the community as a whole. There was thus no violation of Article 1 of Protocol No. 1 ECHR in this case.

Saccoccia thus concerns the invocation of one of the substantive rights guaranteed in the ECHR against the enforcement of a foreign judgment emanating from a third country.[152] What is the standard of control used by the Court in this regard? In its examination of the complaint under Article 1 of Protocol No. 1 ECHR, the Court appears not to really deviate from the standard it would have used in a purely national case.[153] It follows its standard approach with regard to interferences to the right to property.[154] The only reference to the international dimension of the case follows in the Court's assessment of the legitimate aim of the enforcement of the order. The Court cites, as the legitimate aim, the enhancement of international cooperation to ensure that assets derived from drug dealing were actually forfeited, which falls within the general interest of combating (international) drug trafficking.

The Court held that a fair balance had to be struck between the applicant's rights to peaceful enjoyment of his property and the general interest of combating drug trafficking, where the Contracting Parties enjoy a wide margin of appreciation. The Court thus does not appear to use a different standard than it would have used in a forfeiture procedure in a domestic case, although one should note that it extends a wide margin of appreciation to the Contracting Parties in this case on account of the fight against international drug trafficking and the difficulties authorities face here. Thus one may conclude that this is a very specific example of the invocation of one of the substantive rights guaranteed in the ECHR, and one that may be easily distinguished from other cases. Moreover the Court's assessment was, of course, limited to Article 1 of Protocol No. 1 ECHR. It can certainly not be excluded that the invocation of other substantive rights would lead to a different, possibly stricter sort of review.

When considering the impact on the recognition and enforcement of foreign judgments of the substantive rights guaranteed in the ECHR, one should not fail to mention that substantive rights may also be involved where the recognition and enforcement of a foreign judgment would infringe upon the rights of others. These

---

[151] *Saccoccia v. Austria*, no. 69917/01, para 86, 18 December 2008 (citing *AGOSI v. the United Kingdom*, 24 October 1986, para 48, Series A no. 108, and *Air Canada v. the United Kingdom*, 5 May 1995, paras 29–30, Series A no. 316–A).

[152] See with regard to this case also Spielmann 2011, p. 771.

[153] *Saccoccia v. Austria*, no. 69917/01, paras 85–92, 18 December 2008.

[154] See supra Sect. 7.3.1. See generally also supra Sect. 3.5.1.2.

rights of others may also be protected under the ECHR, and could consequently stand in the way of recognition and enforcement. Prime examples of such situations can, of course, be found in the area of international family law. Examples include cases concerning international child abduction where the rights of the stay-behind parent and the abducting parent, but above all the child(ren), may be in conflict with each other.[155]

In cases in which more than one of the rights guaranteed in the ECHR is involved, the Court generally has to perform a balancing test in which the interests of all involved are weighed.[156] The Court will thus review whether a fair balance has been struck. Such a test has to be performed *in concreto*, and the result thus depends on the specific circumstances of the case. However, one could note that in the aforementioned cases in which the rights of children were involved, the best interests of the child always prevailed.[157]

Even though the Court has in its case law at this point in time more or less discussed the different scenarios it distinguished in *Lindberg*, it has certainly not dealt with this topic exhaustively. Incidentally, in the literature this topic has generally been treated as similar to, and together with, the issue of the impact of the ECHR on the applicable foreign law.[158] It is true that the issue of the impact of substantive rights with regard to the recognition and enforcement of foreign judgments, particularly where these originate from third countries, raises similar questions, such as whether there should be attenuation of the standards of the ECHR and the manner of invocation of the rights guaranteed in the ECHR. These questions have been discussed in the previous chapter and a discussion here would roughly follow a similar path.[159]

However, one possible *caveat* should be discussed here. It may not be entirely correct to treat these two issues as entirely the same, as one should not overlook the differences between the application of a foreign law and the recognition and enforcement of foreign judgments violating one of the rights guaranteed in the ECHR, because this may have an impact on the standard of control. It has been remarked that there is, in principle, not much difference between either applying a foreign law or recognizing and enforcing a foreign judgment that possibly violates the ECHR.[160] This is correct in the sense that ultimately in both instances a court

155 It should be understood that in cases concerning international child abduction the ECHR can be invoked by both the parent whose child has been abducted and the abducting parent. Examples of the former situation include, e.g., *Iglesias Gil and A.U.I. v. Spain*, no. 56673/00, ECHR 2003-V and *Ignaccolo-Zenide v. Romania*, no. 31679/96, para 94, ECHR 2000-I. Examples of the latter situation include, e.g., *Maumousseau and Washington v. France*, no. 39388/05, ECHR 2007-XIII and *Neulinger and Shuruk v. Switzerland* [GC], no. 41615/07, ECHR 2010-. See also, e.g., *Pini*; discussed in more detail supra Sect. 7.4.

156 See generally supra Sect. 3.5.1.2.

157 Id.

158 See, e.g., Kinsch 2007, p. 165ff; Mayer 1991, pp. 651–665; Oprea 2007, pp. 307–340.

159 See supra Sect. 6.3.2.1.

160 See, e.g., Lequette 2004, p. 111; Mayer 1991, p. 657.

would in this way give effect to the repugnant foreign norm by either applying a foreign law or by recognizing and enforcing a foreign judgment.

However, one could interject that there is a crucial difference, in that in the case of the recognition and enforcement of foreign judgments, two competing obligations following from the ECHR may play a role: the obligation to recognize and enforce, and the obligation to deny such judgments in the event that they would violate the ECHR.[161] This does not apply to the issue of applicable law. It could therefore be argued that Contracting Parties should be even more careful with regard to denying enforcement to foreign judgments on the basis of the substantive rights guaranteed in the ECHR. However, this is not an incredibly useful distinction, because as has already been discussed above, it would appear obvious that there is no obligation to recognize and enforce foreign judgments where this would result in a violation of the ECHR.

8.3.3 The Invocation of Substantive Rights Guaranteed in the ECHR: National Jurisprudence

Perhaps surprisingly, there is not a lot of case law to be found in England, the Netherlands, or Switzerland in which the invocation of one of the substantive rights guaranteed in the ECHR against the recognition and enforcement of foreign judgments is explicitly discussed. In all three countries, though, the principle that public policy will oppose the recognition and enforcement of foreign judgments violating human rights has been generally accepted.[162] However, the exact interpretation of this principle and the role of the ECHR remain unclear.

There appear to be few cases in which one of the substantive rights guaranteed in the ECHR is successfully invoked against the recognition and enforcement of foreign judgments.[163] However, an example of the invocation of one of the substantive rights guaranteed in the ECHR against at least part of the effect of the recognition of a foreign judgment can be found in a Dutch case before the *Rechtbank* Utrecht.[164] In this case a Dutch woman married a Turkish man in Turkey. In accordance with the Turkish law on names her last name was altered. When registering her marriage upon her return in the Netherlands, the registrar registered her changed (Turkish) name. Her birth certificate was later also

161 See supra Sects. 7.2–7.4.

162 See, e.g., Dicey et al. 2012, p. 739. See additionally the examples discussed infra.

163 Cases concerning international child abduction are the exception hereto. See in the English case law, e.g., *Re J (A Child)* [2005] UKHL 40, although this case concerned mostly an issue of discrimination; see in the Dutch case law, e.g., Hof Amsterdam, 3 May 2011, *NIPR* 2011, 295; see also, e.g., *Neulinger and Shuruk v. Switzerland* [GC], no. 41615/07, ECHR 2010-.

164 Rechtbank Utrecht 31 October 2007, *NIPR* 2008, 33.

amended to reflect this. The woman argued that the change of her name made in the birth certificate was discriminatory.

The district court found that, in principle, a change in the last name as a result of a change in one's personal status outside of the Netherlands has to be recognized. In accordance with Turkish law, the woman received the last name of her husband; Turkish law did not at the time offer the possibility to the woman to keep her own name. However, the district court observed the judgment of the Court in Strasbourg in *Ünal Tekeli v. Turkey*, in which the Court held that the Turkish law in this regard violates Article 14 ECHR taken in conjunction with Article 8 ECHR.[165] Although this judgment, in principle, only binds the parties, it is an important source for interpretation of the ECHR, according to the district court. The district court found that the obligatory change in the woman's last name was a violation of the equality between man and woman and that the application of the relevant Turkish rules should be held to be in violation of Dutch public policy. The registrar was ordered to strike the change in the last name of the woman.

A similar case was decided by the *Gerechtshof* 's-Gravenhage.[166] This case concerned the registration of a Hungarian marriage in the Netherlands. According to the Hungarian marriage certificate, the woman had chosen the man's last name. She later claimed to have been unaware of the possibility to keep her own name under Hungarian law. The registrar registered the chosen name, but the district court ordered the name to be changed. The registrar appealed. The appeal court noted that the woman was insistent on keeping her own name, as a change in her family name would be reflected in her birth certificate. The appeal court held that the findings of the Court in Strasbourg in *Burghartz v. Switzerland*[167] and *Stjerna v. Finland*[168] indicated that the impossibility for the woman to choose her family name is discriminatory. In such instances, the registrar has to apply Dutch law to the choice of a name. Ultimately, the appeal court found that not allowing the woman in this case to choose her own last name amounted to an unjustified interference of her rights under Article 8(2) ECHR.

It is interesting to note with regard to these two Dutch cases that the relevant decisions emanated respectively from Turkey and Hungary, both Contracting Parties. It has been discussed that the invocation of one of the substantive rights guaranteed in the ECHR may be rebutted by the local remedy argument, which is also included in the ECHR.[169] Formally speaking, the Dutch courts in these cases thus could have argued that any complaints directed against the relevant Turkish and Hungarian rules regarding names should have been handled in Turkey and Hungary. In both these cases the women could have turned to the authorities in

[165] *Ünal Tekeli v. Turkey*, no. 29865/96, ECHR 2004-X (extracts). Cf. *Losonci Rose and Rose v. Switzerland*, no. 664/06, 9 November 2010. This latter judgment is discussed supra Sect. 6.4.

[166] Hof 's-Gravenhage 18 April 2007, *NIPR* 2007, 184.

[167] *Burghartz v. Switzerland*, judgment of 22 February 1994, Series A-280-B.

[168] *Stjerna v. Finland*, judgment of 25 November 1994, Series A-299-B.

[169] See supra Sect. 8.3.

these countries, but apparently they did not spring into action until their return to the Netherlands. Nevertheless, the Dutch courts did not hold this against the litigants. What distinguishes these cases from the Court's decision in *Lindberg*, though, is that in *Lindberg* enforcement was requested against the applicant. In these cases, the litigants themselves requested the recognition of the foreign decision, or to be more precise the recognition of their status acquired abroad, and only invoked the ECHR against one of the effects of the recognition (but not the recognition itself).

It is, in my opinion, certainly defensible that the national courts of Contracting Parties should not rely on this local remedy argument with regard to the recognition and enforcement of foreign judgments originating from a third country. While there may not be an obligation for national courts to deny recognition to such judgments, the recognition and enforcement would still result in the rights of a party under the ECHR being violated, which, in principle, should be avoided. It is therefore conceivable that national courts would deny recognition and enforcement in such cases, at least to a certain extent.

As has already been mentioned above, the Swiss *Tribunal fédéral* has, in a case concerning the recognition of a Lebanese repudiation, invoked both substantive and procedural public policy, as it held the recognition to be intolerably incompatible with the Swiss conceptions of justice.[170] Although in this regard reference was, inter alia, made to the equality of spouses, no express reference was made to this right as guaranteed in the ECHR. Incidentally, in its invocation of procedural public policy, the *Tribunal fédéral* also did not expressly rely on Article 6(1) ECHR, but rather on provisions containing similar rights in the Swiss Constitution. Regardless, the *Tribunal fédéral* has in the *Bertl* case found that human rights are an integral part of Swiss public policy.[171] It is, finally, interesting to note that with the exception of French case law, the rights guaranteed in the ECHR are not often invoked against the recognition of repudiations.[172]

8.4 Conclusion

In this chapter the second aspect of the impact of the ECHR on the issue of the recognition and enforcement of foreign judgments has been examined. This aspect concerns the role of the rights guaranteed in the ECHR opposing the recognition and enforcement of foreign judgments. It has been demonstrated that both the procedural right of Article 6(1) ECHR, which guarantees the right to a fair trial,

[170] ATF 126 III 327.

[171] ATF 103 Ia 199, 205 (*Bertl*).

[172] Cf. *D.D. v. France*, no. 3/02, decision of 8 November 2005 (discussed supra n. 148). See for an overview of how repudiations are treated in different countries, e.g., Foblets and Rutten 2006, pp. 195–213; Kruiniger 2008. See also Aldeeb and Bonomi 1999, pp. 149–230.

and the substantive rights guaranteed in the ECHR may be invoked against the recognition and enforcement of foreign judgments. It follows from the discussion of the case law in this chapter that the substantive rights of Article 8 ECHR, the right to family life, and Article 1 of Protocol No. 1 ECHR are particularly relevant in this regard, but in principle all the substantive rights guaranteed in the ECHR which may be invoked in private law cases can be applied to oppose recognition and enforcement of foreign judgments.

The most important questions in relation to the rules on recognition and enforcement of the Contracting Parties concern what exactly the standard of control should be with regard to the rights guaranteed in the ECHR. This standard of control will differ depending on whether Article 6(1) ECHR or one of the substantive rights guaranteed in the ECHR is concerned. The distinction between cases dealing with, on the one hand, the recognition and enforcement of foreign judgments originating from third countries and, on the other, cases dealing with judgments originating from other Contracting Parties, is also very important.

It has been discussed with regard to the impact of Article 6(1) ECHR that the Court in *Pellegrini* initially appeared to insist on full compliance with the procedural safeguards as set out in Article 6(1) ECHR, particularly for foreign judgments emanating from third countries. This means that in the assessment by a court of whether a fair trial preceded the judgment, a foreign judgment is treated as if it concerned a domestic judgment.

However, the Court may have changed its approach somewhat in subsequent case law by again referring to the standard of 'a flagrant denial of justice', to which it adhered in earlier case law. This standard, which the Court has introduced in cases regarding the extraterritorial effect of the ECHR, entails a threshold with regard to Article 6(1) ECHR in the sense that a violation of that provision may only be found in the event of 'a flagrant denial of justice'. However, what a 'flagrant denial of justice' exactly entails is unclear. Moreover, there are, in my opinion, good arguments to insist on full compliance with regard to procedural shortcomings in foreign proceedings.

Pellegrini is, in principle, concerned with the recognition and enforcement of foreign judgments emanating from third countries, and essentially leaves unanswered the question of whether the standard of full compliance would also apply to foreign judgments emanating from other Contracting Parties. However, as the procedural safeguards *ex* Article 6(1) ECHR should already be protected in other Contracting Parties, there is, in my opinion, no reason to mitigate the standard of control regarding Article 6(1) ECHR for foreign judgments originating from other Contracting Parties.

Another issue concerning the recognition and enforcement of foreign judgments originating from other Contracting Parties is the so-called 'local remedy' rule. Is it possible to invoke Article 6(1) ECHR against such foreign judgments? After all, should complaints directed against the procedure in the Contracting Party of origin of the judgment not also have been brought in that Contracting Party? This argument is, in principle, valid with regard to Article 6(1) ECHR, and it may thus be possible that the Court would deny such complaints for this reason, if they were ever to reach Strasbourg. Then again, there may be situations in which it would still appear to be possible to invoke Article 6(1) ECHR, for example when a party has not been properly notified of proceedings against him or her. It follows, incidentally, from the discussion of national case law on this topic that national courts are nevertheless willing to deny the recognition and enforcement of foreign judgments emanating from other Contracting Parties on this basis, but there is an exception.

There may be even more uncertainty with regard to the invocation of the substantive rights guaranteed in the ECHR. It follows from the Court's case law that a distinction should be made between judgments originating from other Contracting Parties and judgments originating from third countries. It would appear to be impossible to complain before the Court in Strasbourg about a foreign judgment emanating from another Contracting Party violating one of the substantive rights guaranteed in the ECHR, because of the local remedy argument. A complaint about such a violation should have been brought in the Contracting Party of the origin of the judgment. This does not, however, necessarily mean that the national courts of the Contracting Parties should recognize and enforce such judgments, as even though the applicant should have brought a complaint elsewhere, the Contracting Party would still give effect to a foreign judgment violating a right guaranteed in the ECHR.

The Court has added little on the invocation of substantive rights guaranteed in the ECHR against foreign judgments emanating from third countries. The only truly relevant case of the Court on this topic concerned the very specific issue of the combat against international drug trafficking. The Court found no violation of the right to property in this case, because Contracting Parties enjoy a wide margin of appreciation in this area. This case therefore does not really provide much clarity on the issue. Remarkably, in the national case law of England, the Netherlands, and Switzerland there is also not much case law to be found in which the substantive rights guaranteed in the ECHR are being invoked against the recognition and enforcement of foreign judgments. While the possibility of the invocation of these rights appears to be accepted, the national case law does not offer further guidance into the issues surrounding the invocation of these rights. It has been found, though, that these issues, in principle, will be similar to those concerning the invocation of the ECHR against the foreign applicable law violating the ECHR.

References

Aldeeb S, Bonomi A (eds) (1999) Le droit musulman de la famille et des successions à l'épreuve des orders juridiques occidentaux. Schulthess, Zurich

Amerasinghe CF (2004) Local remedies in international law. Cambridge University Press, Cambridge

Beaumont P, Johnston E (2010) Can exequatur be abolished in Brussels I whilst retaining a public policy defence? J Private Int Law 6:249–279

Bos TM (2008) Het faillissement van YUKOS en de beginselen van een behoorlijke procesorde [The insolveny of YUKOS and the principles of due process]. WPNR (Weekblad voor privaatrecht, notariaat en registratie) 139:41–43
Briggs A (2003) Decisions of British courts during 2002. Private international law. BYBIL 73:453–496
Briggs A (2005) Decisions of British courts during 2004. Private international law. BYBIL 75:537–593
Bucher A (2010) La dimension sociale du droit international privé: cours général. Recueil des Cours 341, Martinus Nijhoff Publishers, Leiden
Cordero Moss G (2007) Between private and public international law: exorbitant jurisdiction as illustrated by the Yukos case. Rev Cent East Eur Law 32:1–17
Costa J-P (2002) Le Tribunal de la Rote et l'article 6 de la Convention européenne des droits de l'homme. Revue trimestrielle des droits de l'homme 13:470–476
Cuniberti G (2008) The recognition of foreign judgments lacking reasons in Europe: access to justice, foreign court avoidance and efficiency. ICLQ 57:25–52
Cuniberti G, Rueda I (2011) Abolition of exequatur. Addressing the commission's concerns. RabelsZ 75:286–316
Dicey AV, Morris JHC, Collins LA (2012) The conflict of laws. Sweet & Maxwell, London
Dutoit B (2005) Droit international privé suiss. Helbing & Lichtenhahn, Basel
Fawcett JJ (2007) The impact of Article 6(1) ECHR on private international law. ILCQ 56:1–48
Fentiman R (2010) International commercial litigation. Oxford University Press, Oxford
Flauss J-F (2001) Chroniques: CEDH et droit du contentieux. L'actualité juridique droit administratif. Dalloz, Paris
Flauss J-F (2002) L'exequatur des jugements étrangers devant la cour européenne des droits de l'homme. In: Bieber R (ed) Mélanges en l'honneur de Bernard Dutoit. Librairie Droz, Genève, pp 69–87
Foblets MC, Rutten SWE (2006) De toelaatbaarheid van de verstoting: recente ontwikkelingen in het Nederlands, Frans en Belgisch internationaal privaatrecht [The admissibility of the repudiation: recent developments in Dutch, French and Belgian private international law]. In
Grisel E (2002) Le recours au tribunal fédéral en matière de reconnaissance et d'exécution des jugements étrangers. In: Bieber R (ed) Mélanges en l'honneur de Bernard Dutoit. Librairie Droz, Genève, pp 89–101
Guinchard E (2005) Procès equitable (article 6 CESDH) et droit international privé. In: Nuyts A, Watté N (eds) International civil litigation in Europe and relations with third states. Bruylant, Brussels, pp 199–245
Juratowitch B (2007) The European convention on human rights and English private international law. J Private Int Law 3:173–199
Kinsch P (2004) The impact of human rights on the application of foreign law and on the recognition of foreign judgments—a survey of the cases decided by the European human rights institutions. In: Einhorn T, Siehr K (eds) Intercontinental cooperation through private international law—essays in memory of Peter E. Nygh, T.M.C. Asser Press, The Hague, pp 197–228
Kinsch P (2007) Droits de l'homme, droits fondamentaux et droit international privé. Recueil des Cours 318:9–332
Kramer XE (2004) Europees procesrecht en fundamentele procedurele vereisten: de rol van artikel 6 EVRM ter invulling van de openbare orde toets onder het EEX [European procedural law and fundamental procedural demands: the role of article 6 ECHR in order to shape the public policy exception under the Brussels Convention]. NIPR 22:9–16
Kramer XE (2011) Abolition of exequatur under the Brussels I regulation: effecting and protecting right in the European judicial area. NIPR 29:633–641
Kruiniger P (2008) Marokkaanse verstotingsvormen in de Nederlandse rechtspraktijk: een juridische beschouwing over de Marokkaanse khul' en talaq in het kader van de erkenning in Nederland [Moroccan forms of repudiation in the Dutch legal practice: a legal examination on the Moroccan khul' and talaq in the context of the recognition in the Netherlands]. Celsus juridische uitgeverij, Tilburg

Lequette Y (2004) Le droit international privé et les droits fondamentaux. In: Cabrillac R et al (eds) Libertés et droit fondamentaux. Dalloz, Paris, pp 97–118
Lowenfeld AF (2004) Jurisdiction, enforcement, public policy and res judicata: the Krombach case'. In: Einhorn T, Siehr K (eds) Intercontinental cooperation through private international law—essays in memory of Peter E. Nygh, T.M.C. Asser Press, The Hague, pp 229–248
Marchadier F (2007) Les objectifs généraux du droit international privé à l'épreuve de la Convention européenne des droits de l'homme. Bruylant, Bruxelles
Matscher F (2004) Die indirekte Wirkung des Art. 6 EMRK bei der Anerkennung und Vollstreckung ausländischer Entscheidungen [The indirect effect of Article 6 ECHR with regard to the recognition of foreign judgments]. In: Bork R (ed), Recht und Risiko: Festschrift für Helmut Kollhosser zum 70. Geburtstag vol 2, VVW, Karlsruhe, pp 427–445
Mayer P (1991) La Convention européenne des droits de l'homme et l'application des normes étrangères. Rev.crit.dr.int.priv. 98:651–665
Mayer P (1996) Droit au proces equitable et conflit de juridictions,' Les Nouveaux développements du procès équitable au sens de la Convention, actes du colloque du 22 mars 1996 en la grande chambre de la cour de cassation, organisé par l'Institut des hautes études européennes. Bruylant, Bruxelles, pp 125–138
Oprea A (2007) La Convention europeénne des droits de l'homme et l'application des normes étrangère en droit international privé. Revista de drept internaţional privat şi drept privat comparat 2007:307–340
Othenin-Girard S (1999) La reserve d'ordre public en droit international privé suisse. Schulthess, Zurich
Pocar F (2006) Notes on the Pellegrini judgment of the European Court of Human Rights. In: Erauw J (ed) Liber memorialis Petar Šarčević. Sellier Munich, pp 575–581
Rosner N (2004) Cross-border recognition and enforcement of foreign money judgments in civil and commercial matters, Doctoral Series. Dissertation Groningen
Schilling T (2011) Das Exequatur und die EMRK [The exequatur and the ECHR]. IPRax 31:31–40
Schlosser PF (2010) The abolition of exequatur proceedings—including public policy review? IPRax 30:101–104
Sinopoli L (2002) Droit au procès equitable et exequatur: Strasbourg sonne les cloches à Rome. Gazette du Palais 122:1157–1168
Spielmann D (2011) La reconnaissance et l'exécution des decisions judiciaries étrangères et les exigencies de la convention des droits de l'homme. Un essai de synthèse. Revue trimestrielle des droits de l'homme 22:761–786
Strikwerda L (2004) De invloed van het EVRM op het Europese IPR [The impact of the ECHR on European private international law]. In: Corstens GJM et al (eds) Europeanisering van het Nederlands Recht [The Europeanization of Dutch law]. Kluwer, Deventer, pp 252–260
Strikwerda L (2012) Inleiding tot het Nederlandse internationaal privaatrecht [Introduction to Dutch Private International Law]. Kluwer, Deventer
van Bochove L (2007) Het ontbreken van de openbareorde-exceptie in de nieuwe generatie Europese procesrechtelijke verordeningen in het licht van artikel 6 lid 1 EVRM [The lack of a public policy exception in the new generation of European procedural regulations]. NIPR 25:331–339
van Hoek AAH, Luchtman M (2006) The European convention on human rights and transnational cooperation in criminal matters. In: van Hoek AAH et al (eds) Multilevel governance in enforcement and adjudication. Intersentia, Antwerp, pp 25–91
van der Grinten P, Heukels T (eds) (2006) Crossing borders: essays in European and private international law, nationality law and islamic law in honour of Frans van der Velden. Kluwer, Deventer, pp 195–213
Volken P (2004) Article 27. In: Girsberger D et al (eds) (2004) Zürcher Kommentar zum IPRG: Kommentar zum Bundesgesetz über das Internationale Privatrecht (IPRG) vom 18. Dezember 1987. Schulthess, Zürich

Chapter 9
Conclusions

Contents

9.1 Introduction

In this book the impact of the rights guaranteed in the ECHR on issues of private international law has been analyzed by an examination of the Court's case law and the case law of national courts. This book demonstrates that the impact of the rights guaranteed in the ECHR on private international law is considerable. This starts with the observation that most, if not all, of the issues with which private international law is concerned are, in principle, covered by the rights guaranteed in the ECHR, as follows from the Court's case law. Moreover, the Court has in the past few years delivered a number of decisions specifically dealing with issues of private international law. It has dealt with all three main issues of private international law: jurisdiction, applicable law, and the recognition and enforcement of foreign judgments. The Court's decisions have been more detailed and forthcoming in some areas than in other areas of private international law, but one may nevertheless distinguish a clear pattern. With these decisions the Court has given further evidence that private international law as an area of law is not immune to the rights guaranteed in the ECHR. It follows from the Court's case law that the result of the application of private international law rules, regardless of whether these are concerned with the issue of jurisdiction, applicable law, or the

L.R. Kiestra, *The Impact of the European Convention on Human Rights on Private International Law*, DOI 10.1007/978-94-6265-032-9_9

recognition and enforcement of foreign judgments, must always comply with the requirements following from the rights guaranteed in the ECHR. As has been discussed in this research, this may have some consequences for private international law.

The rights guaranteed in the ECHR should therefore be carefully considered by courts in relation to the three main issues of private international law. Even though the impact of fundamental rights on these issues is not a new phenomenon, it has been found in this book that the impact of the ECHR on issues of private international law, as determined by the Court in its case law, appears in certain respects not to have yet fully permeated at the national level, as some traditional private international law techniques are susceptible to leading to a violation of the ECHR. By way of conclusion, I will highlight the most important findings of this study in this chapter, before ending with some concluding remarks.

The role of Article 1 ECHR has proven to be an important preliminary issue in this research, and its role should not be underestimated in this discussion. In Article 1 ECHR the basic obligation undertaken by the Contracting Parties has been laid down, and it also defines the scope of the instrument with the phrase 'within their jurisdiction'. As private international law by its very nature introduces foreign elements to the legal orders of the Contracting Parties, which possibly emanate from third countries (i.e., non-Contracting Parties), one should turn to Article 1 ECHR to see whether the rights guaranteed in this instrument are applicable at all in issues of private international law. It has been demonstrated that it follows from the Court's case law concerning Article 1 ECHR that when a court of a Contracting Party either determines whether it is competent to hear an international case concerning an issue of private law, or recognizes and enforces a foreign judgment, the ECHR is applicable to such cases. This applies irrespective of whether a foreign law or judgment originates from either a Contracting or a non-Contracting Party (third country), or whether the case has a close connection to the Contracting Party concerned or little to none at all.

The fact that a third country has never signed the ECHR has no bearing on whether the ECHR is applicable to cases concerning the application of a foreign law or the recognition and enforcement of a foreign judgment emanating from a non-Contracting Party. It would, after all, ultimately be the court of one of the Contracting Parties whose determination of whether it has jurisdiction, whose application of a foreign law, or whose recognition of a foreign judgment violating one of the rights guaranteed in the ECHR would breach the ECHR. This could already be deduced from the Court's case law concerning the extraterritorial effects of the ECHR, and has since been confirmed by the case law that specifically deals with private international law. It has been demonstrated that even in circumstances in which an issue of private international law has only a negligible connection with the Contracting Party, the situation does not change appreciably. Such situations still come within the jurisdiction of the Contracting Party within the meaning of Article 1 ECHR.

This observation does have some consequences for issues of private international law, particularly where it is concerned with the application of a foreign law or the recognition and enforcement of foreign judgments of third countries possibly violating one of the rights guaranteed in the ECHR, as has been demonstrated in Chap. 4 and is further elaborated upon in Chaps. 6–8. It follows from this observation that it is only possible to restrict the rights guaranteed in the ECHR in such cases to the extent that this is permitted under the ECHR.

In this regard it should be noted that the most relevant rights guaranteed in the ECHR in the context of private international law—Articles 6(1) and ECHR and Article 1 of Protocol No. 1 ECHR—are not absolute rights. Under certain circumstances these rights may be restricted. The exact manner in which these rights may be restricted depends on the particular right guaranteed in the ECHR concerned, but it is important to note from the outset that it is, in principle, possible to take into account private international law concerns in this manner.

Traditionally, however, private international law has protected fundamental rights with regard to a foreign applicable law or the recognition and enforcement of a foreign judgment by means of the invocation of the public policy exception. One may question, though, whether the public policy exception resulting in the non-application of the ECHR, because of the relative character of the exception, is permissible in light of Article 1 ECHR. These observations will be further elaborated on below in relation to the separate discussions of the impact of the ECHR on the three main issues of private international law.

9.2 The Impact of the ECHR on the Issue of Jurisdiction in Private International Law

As discussed in Chap. 5, the impact of the ECHR on the issue of private international law is essentially limited to Article 6(1) ECHR, which guarantees the right to a fair trial. The impact of Article 6(1) ECHR has three distinct aspects. First, a plaintiff in international civil proceedings who is unable to find an open court may invoke the right of access to a court, which has been deduced from Article 6(1) ECHR by the Court in *Golder v. the United Kingdom.* Second, a defendant in such international proceedings can also at least attempt to rely on Article 6(1) ECHR, the right to a fair trial, if he or she is summoned before a court which has asserted jurisdiction based on a so-called exorbitant ground of jurisdiction. Third, the right to a fair trial may arguably also be invoked against the abuse of jurisdictional rules in international civil litigation.

The right of access to a court has the most profound impact on the issue of jurisdiction in private international law. The right of access to a court can be invoked by a plaintiff in international civil proceedings in two different situations. First, a plaintiff could be faced with the fact that no (functioning) court is competent to hear his or her case. This could either be due to there being a negative conflict of jurisdiction, or to the fact that the normally competent court is unavailable on account of circumstances beyond the control of the plaintiff, such as a situation of war or a natural disaster. It is undisputed that Article 6(1) ECHR obligates the Contracting Parties to open up their courts to plaintiffs under such circumstances. This has also found acceptance in the national legal practice of England, the Netherlands, and Switzerland. One may note also that the legislation of many Contracting Parties, which otherwise have hard and fast rules on jurisdiction, contains a *forum necessitatis* clause.

It has, however, been contended that a plaintiff's right of access to a court may also play a role in a situation in which there is, in principle, a court available to the plaintiff. This is without question a more controversial conception of the right of access to a court in private international law. The Strasbourg Institutions have not yet given an opinion on such a conception of the right of access to a court in private international law. In the only case in which this issue arose, *Gauthier v. Belgium*, the Commission did not really give an opinion. Nevertheless, in the Court's general case law on the right of access to a court, particularly in the Court's finding that this right must be effective, some support may be found for the proposition that the right of access to a court could, under certain circumstances, indeed entail an extended right of access.

Three possibilities to extend the right of access to a court to situations in which there is already an available court in international proceedings have been distinguished and discussed in this research. It has been contended that the right of access to court may be engaged if the proceedings in the only available foreign court would not meet the standards of Article 6(1) ECHR. The argument that a denial of justice could occur if it would be certain that the plaintiff's substantive claim would be denied in the only available foreign court has also been examined. Finally, the argument that the right of access could also play a role if it were certain that the judgment given in the only available foreign court could not be recognized and enforced in the Contracting Party has been discussed.

With regard to these three options, it should first be remarked that it is indeed possible for a Contracting Party to rely on foreign proceedings in fulfilling its obligation to guarantee the right of access to a court. It would be unrealistic to completely disregard foreign access to a court in international civil proceedings. Moreover, this would essentially entail that plaintiffs would always have the right of access to a court in the forum of their choosing, which simply cannot be the case. However, such reliance on foreign proceedings by the Contracting Parties with regard to their obligation concerning the right of access to a court would still result in there being no access to a court in the respondent Contracting Party. Thus one could say that not only is the right of access to a court engaged in such a situation, but also that this right of access is restricted.

It is, in my opinion, conceivable that a plaintiff's right of access to a court in international civil proceedings entails a right of access to a court in which proceedings must be deemed fair, or at least not at first sight result in a 'flagrant denial of justice'. Because denying access to the forum on account of there being a foreign court competent to hear the case would be a restriction of the right of access, it would be possible in the review of this restriction to take the quality of the foreign proceedings into consideration, particularly in relation to the proportionality requirement. However, such a review of the quality of the foreign proceedings cannot be too strict, because in such a situation an assessment has to be made of foreign proceedings which have yet to take place. Only exceptional circumstances could suffice for finding a violation of the right of access to a court in this regard. This also follows from the Court's case law in *Eskinazi and Chelouche v. Turkey*. Access to the forum may only be granted by the Contracting Party on the basis of the right of access to a court *ex* Article 6(1) ECHR if it would be clear that proceedings in the otherwise available court would lead to a flagrant denial of justice. It has similarly been accepted in some national case law of England, the Netherlands, and Switzerland that Article 6(1) ECHR entails the right of access to a court in accordance with the procedural standards of that provision.

It has been demonstrated that it would appear to be difficult to attach either a right to a substantive claim or the right to have a foreign judgment recognized and enforced to the right of access to a court. Even if it were certain that a plaintiff's claim would be rejected on the merits in the only available foreign court, it is hard to see how a plaintiff could derive a right to a substantive outcome in a case from the procedural right of access to a court. This would, after all, require a decision on the merits of a case before a decision on the preliminary question of jurisdiction has been taken. It is difficult to see how Article 6(1) ECHR could entail an obligation for a Contracting Party to do so. Moreover, asserting jurisdiction on this basis may result in proceedings on a basis which could be fought by the defendant on the grounds of the latter's rights under Article 6(1) ECHR, as will be discussed below.

It is similarly questionable whether it is necessary, on account of a decision yet to be rendered abroad, which might possibly not be recognized and enforced in the forum, to pre-emptively grant a plaintiff a right of access before any proceedings have taken place abroad in the normally competent court, unless, of course, the lack of fair proceedings were to be the culprit in this regard. The latter situation—lack of fair proceedings in the only available court—would match the scenario discussed above, in which a plaintiff is unable to find a court where proceedings would be fair. This latter situation can be distinguished because no pre-emptive assessment of the merits of a case is required. One should also note, with regard to the impossibility of the recognition and enforcement of foreign judgments, that the ECHR, in principle, requires Contracting Parties to recognize and enforce foreign judgments, as will be further discussed below.

In the jurisprudence of the national courts of the Contracting Parties under analysis it has been found that it has occasionally been held that a plaintiff's right of access to a court should entail a right of access where a fair trial could be had in accordance with the requirements of Article 6(1) ECHR. Remarkably, a Dutch court has even been willing to extend further the right of access to a court to a situation in which a substantive result could not be had in the available foreign court. However, as noted above, this would seem to stretch this right too far.

The second aspect of the impact of Article 6(1) ECHR on the issue of jurisdiction concerns the defendant in international civil proceedings. Article 6(1) ECHR may also be invoked *against* the assertion of jurisdiction, where jurisdiction is based on exorbitant or inappropriate grounds. It has been suggested in the literature that Article 6(1) ECHR could play a role similar to the role that the Due Process Clause of the US Constitution fulfills with regard to the assertion of jurisdiction in private international law in (intra-state cases in) the United States. Even though there are important differences between the rules on jurisdiction in Europe and in the United States, which explain the different roles of Article 6(1) ECHR and the Due Process Clause, the Court's interpretation of the right to a fair trial would appear to allow for a due process-like role with regard to the defendant's right to a fair trial. However, this right is until now more theoretical than practical, as little evidence can be found in the case law of the Court or in national case law of such an interpretation of the ECHR. Nevertheless, it would appear to be possible to construe such a due process-like right from the right to a fair trial.

Finally, Article 6(1) ECHR may also have a role with regard to strategic litigation, where such procedural behavior could become abusive. It is, in international civil proceedings, perfectly normal for litigants, if they have a choice between different competent courts, to choose the one most favorable to their cause. However, it is possible that such strategic litigation could lead to abuse. The Brussels regime is particularly vulnerable to this practice, due to its rules on *lis pendens*, overlapping jurisdictional rules, the possibility to sue for declaratory judgments, and the emphasis on legal certainty and mutual trust. It has been examined whether Article 6(1) ECHR may function as a brake on strategic litigation where this becomes abusive. The starting point of this discussion is the decision of the ECJ in *Gasser*. In this case an appeal to Article 6(1) ECHR was rejected by the ECJ, which cited, inter alia, the mutual trust of the Member States in each other's legal orders and legal certainty. It has been found, however, that Article 6(1) ECHR may play a more prominent role with regard to strategic litigation, even though, again, this is until now more of a theoretical possibility, as it has not yet been brought up in the case law.

In concluding a discussion on the impact of Article 6(1) ECHR on jurisdiction in private international law, it is possible to observe that Article 6(1) ECHR essentially requires the Contracting Parties to use a balanced approach with regard to this issue, which would include procedural maneuvering. After all, while the role of Article 6(1) for the plaintiff in international civil proceedings is quite clear, a good argument could be made that Article 6(1) ECHR could also be invoked by the defendant in such proceedings, in order to fight jurisdiction. This further demonstrates that Article 6(1) ECHR is an important factor in a balanced system of jurisdictional rules of the Contracting Parties.

9.3 The Impact of the ECHR on the Issue of Applicable Law

In examining the impact of the ECHR on the issue of applicable law in private international law, three different aspects have been distinguished in Chap. 6. The most important issue is the invocation of the rights guaranteed in the ECHR *against* the foreign applicable law violating the ECHR. Additionally, it has been examined whether one of the rights guaranteed in the ECHR can also be invoked against the *lex fori*, and whether the ECHR could thus also purport to favor the application of a foreign law over the *lex fori*. Finally, the act of applying foreign law by the national courts of the Contracting Parties has been examined and, in particular, whether the ECHR has an impact on issues relating to the identification of the content of the applicable foreign law.

This latter aspect is clearly different from the first two, as it is really a procedural issue and therefore only concerns Article 6(1) ECHR. The impact of the ECHR on the other two aspects of the issue of applicable law, however, is concerned with the impact on the material result of the application of either a foreign law or the *lex fori*. It follows that, in principle, all the substantive rights guaranteed in the ECHR capable of having an impact on issues of private law could be invoked. It has been demonstrated, though, that Article 8 ECHR (the right to private and family life) and Article 1 of Protocol No. 1 ECHR (the right to property) are particularly important rights in this regard.

It has been established that it is generally accepted that the application of a foreign law interfering with one of the rights guaranteed in the ECHR by a national court of one of the Contracting Parties may lead to a violation of the ECHR by the respondent Contracting Party. Nevertheless, the Court has never actually found a violation of the ECHR on this basis and has only dealt with a small number of admissibility decisions on this issue. Therefore, important questions on this topic remain unanswered by the Court.

One of the open questions is what the standard of control should be with regard to a foreign law applicable to a case possibly violating one of the rights guaranteed in the ECHR. Many have argued that the standard of control of the ECHR should be attenuated, particularly where the foreign applicable law originated from a third country. If a foreign applicable law of a third country were to be subjected to the full scrutiny of the ECHR there would be less room for the application of such foreign laws, as this would lead to the more frequent setting aside of the normally applicable foreign law. This could, in turn, lead to limping legal relationships (a relationship recognized in one country, but not in another), and it has even been argued by some that this would, on another level, result in different blocks of States each adhering to their own, different values.

While the attenuation of the standards of the ECHR in relation to the foreign applicable law may be desirable, because it would decrease the number of instances in which the application of a foreign law would be denied on the basis of its incompatibility with the ECHR, there are inherent limitations to the possibility of attenuation in this regard under the ECHR. This essentially follows from Article 1 ECHR. Restrictions to rights guaranteed in the ECHR are only permitted insofar as these are allowed under the respective rights guaranteed in the ECHR concerned. However, the rights guaranteed in the ECHR concerned with issues of private international law, and particularly the issue of applicable law, provide such leeway. This is because the rights concerned in issues of applicable law are usually so-called qualified rights, such as, for example, Article 8 ECHR and Article 1 of

Protocol No. 1 ECHR, which means that they are subject to interference by the Contracting Parties in order to secure certain interests.

It has been contended in this book that in assessing whether a foreign applicable law would possibly violate one of the rights guaranteed in the ECHR, the Court should follow its usual approach with regard to restrictions to (qualified) rights. Thus, after having determined that the foreign applicable law would interfere with one of the rights guaranteed in the ECHR, it should assess whether this restriction was in accordance with the law, had a legitimate aim, and whether it was necessary in a democratic society. This latter condition is often decisive. In accordance with its standard case law, the Court would determine whether the interference caused by the application of a foreign law fulfills a pressing social need. In reviewing this pressing social need the Court will evaluate whether the restriction was proportionate to the legitimate aim pursued and whether a less invasive measure could have been possible. The Contracting Parties enjoy a certain margin of appreciation in all of this, the extent of which will depend on the exact rights guaranteed in the ECHR concerned. It has been demonstrated that in its most relevant admissibility decision on the issue of applicable law, *Ammdjadi v. Germany*, the Court has more or less followed this approach.

As the Court has up until this point merely given a number of admissibility decisions in cases in which the issue of applicable law was a topic, it is not yet clear to what extent the Court would allow for the attenuation of the rights guaranteed in the ECHR in order to account for the international dimension of the issue of the application of a foreign law. However, in a first review of the available case law in this study, the Court does not appear to give much leeway in this regard.

A related issue concerning the invocation of the ECHR against the foreign applicable law is the manner in which the rights guaranteed in the ECHR are invoked by the national courts of the Contracting Parties. In almost all cases they use the public policy exception in private international law to consider the rights guaranteed in the ECHR with regard to the foreign applicable law. Formally speaking, there is no need to change course. The Court, after all, will only review the result the national court has reached with regard to the foreign applicable law and is, in principle, not concerned with the manner in which this result has been reached. However, there are dangers inherent to the use of the public policy exception with regard to the impact of the rights guaranteed in the ECHR on the issue of applicable law in private international law.

The use of the public policy exception in this regard may lead to the setting aside of the rights guaranteed in the ECHR in cases which lack a sufficient link with the forum. The relative character, which is generally ascribed to the public policy exception, could then result in the public policy exception not being applicable, which may, in turn, result in the right guaranteed in the ECHR not being applied to a case. However, as has been discussed, it follows from Article 1 ECHR that the ECHR is even applicable in cases which have only a negligible connection with the forum. Therefore, an attenuation of the standards of the ECHR by way of the use of the public policy exception could result in a violation of the ECHR.

A second aspect of the impact of the ECHR on the issue of applicable law that has been examined in this research is the possible invocation of the rights guaranteed in the ECHR *against* the *lex fori* in favor of the application of foreign law. This is a scenario that has been raised in the literature, where it has been argued that this could be a possibility under the ECHR. However, it has been demonstrated that there is little indication to be found in the case law of the Strasbourg Institutions for such a conception of the ECHR.

There is one exception, though. In *Losonci Rose v. Switzerland* the Court held that the application of the *lex fori* resulted in a violation of Article 8 ECHR taken in conjunction with Article 14 ECHR, as the application of the *lex fori* by the authorities essentially took away the possibility of a husband to choose his preferred last name in accordance with his national (foreign) law after his marriage; this option would have been available if the applicant had been a woman. However, as this latter observation also demonstrates, this case was more concerned with the (result of) discriminatory nature of the relevant Swiss private international law rules and not so much with the possibility to invoke the ECHR against the application of the *lex fori* in favor of the application of foreign law.

With regard to the third aspect of the impact of the ECHR on the issue of applicable law, it follows from the Court's case law that national courts should establish the content of the foreign applicable law in an expeditious manner. Otherwise, the Contracting Parties may be held responsible for a violation of Article 6(1) ECHR due to the length of the proceedings. The difficulties national courts may face in the identification of the content of the foreign law are hardly a mitigating factor. If the complexities in finding the content of the foreign applicable law are too difficult to overcome another solution must be found, which could, for example, include the national courts of the Contracting Parties resorting to the application of the *lex fori*, because it is paramount that a decision is taken within a reasonable time, as Article 6(1) ECHR prescribes. A review of the practice in the national legal orders under analysis has demonstrated that national courts, in principle, have all the tools required to prevent such violations of Article 6 ECHR, as the national courts in question are allowed to apply the *lex fori* if it proves to be impossible to establish the content of the normally applicable foreign law within a reasonable time.

In conclusion, one could say that the impact of the ECHR on the issue of applicable law will largely be limited to the invocation of one of the (substantive) rights guaranteed in the ECHR against a foreign applicable law possibly violating this right and the impact of Article 6(1) ECHR on the ascertainment of the content of the foreign applicable law. While questions remain concerning the extent to which rights guaranteed in the ECHR may be limited in the name of the internationality of a case or the origin of the foreign law, particularly laws originating from third countries, it should be noted that the national courts of the Contracting Parties are, in principle, well prepared for the possibility that a foreign law may violate fundamental norms of the forum.

Nevertheless, I would argue that national courts should take human rights more seriously in the sense that the use of the public policy exception in relation to the rights guaranteed in the ECHR against a foreign applicable law interfering with one of the rights guaranteed in the ECHR may result in a violation of the ECHR. This risk could, in my opinion, be mitigated by more directly examining the possibly repugnant foreign law in light of the right guaranteed in the ECHR concerned by examining the extent to which restrictions to the rights guaranteed in the ECHR may be permissible.

9.4 The Impact of the ECHR on the Recognition and Enforcement of Foreign Judgments

The impact of the rights guaranteed in the ECHR on the recognition and enforcement of foreign judgments has two distinct aspects, as the ECHR may contain both the obligation to recognize and enforce foreign judgments and the opposite obligation to deny recognition and enforcement of foreign judgments. These obligations have been examined separately in Chaps. 7 and 8. It has been established that Article 6(1) ECHR, Article 1 of Protocol No. 1 ECHR, and Article 8 ECHR may entail an obligation for the authorities of the Contracting Parties to facilitate the recognition and enforcement of foreign judgments, while in the absence of fair proceedings abroad Article 6 ECHR may obligate Contracting Parties to deny recognition and enforcement. It is, finally, also possible that a substantive right guaranteed in the ECHR would stand in the way of the recognition and enforcement of a foreign judgment.

Article 6(1) ECHR contains a general obligation to recognize and enforce foreign judgments in the sense that it applies to all kinds of foreign judgments, regardless of whether they originate from other Contracting Parties or from third countries. This obligation is not absolute. While the Court has not always been consistent in its case law, it appears to examine a failure to recognize and enforce a foreign judgment in relation to Article 6(1) ECHR mostly as an interference with the right of access to a court. It has been demonstrated that the Court's assessment entails that such a failure is only allowed if it has a legitimate aim—it must not be arbitrary—and is proportionate to this legitimate aim pursued. The proportionality requirement is usually the most important requirement in this regard.

It follows from the Court's case law that the rules of private international law in the Contracting Parties concerned with the recognition and enforcement of foreign judgments must comply with the framework developed by the Court, discussed above. Any interference with the obligation to recognize and enforce based on traditional private international law defenses, such as, for example, the (substantive) public policy requirement, requirements as to jurisdiction, and even requirements regarding the service of documents instituting international proceedings, must thus meet the Court's demands with regard to restrictions under Article 6(1) ECHR. The Court found in *Négrépontis-Giannisis* that the invocation of the (substantive) public policy exception against the recognition of an American adoption order was arbitrary and disproportionate and it therefore found a violation of the ECHR.

Article 1 of Protocol No. 1 ECHR only entails an obligation to recognize and enforce foreign judgments which are concerned with some sort of possession, even though the Court has also found a violation on the basis of this right in a case in which the applicant's status as an heir was concerned. The obligation under Article 1 of Protocol No. 1 ECHR—including the possibility to restrict this obligation—is furthermore similar to the obligation under Article 6(1) ECHR with regard to the recognition and enforcement of foreign judgments. There is clearly an overlap between these two obligations.

It has been shown that an obligation to recognize foreign family law judgments in which a status has been acquired or a family relationship has been established follows from Article 8 ECHR. This obligation is also not absolute, as is, of course, already indicated in the Article itself. However, in its case law in *Wagner* and *Négrépontis-Giannisis*, the Court found that there is a high threshold for the outright denial of recognition of international family law judgments establishing a family link where parties have a legitimate expectation that the judgment will be recognized and social reality demands recognition. However, this may be different in the situation where some of the effects of the foreign family law judgment have been recognized in the Contracting Party, as was found by the Court in *Harroudj*, which concerned the recognition of a *kafala* (adoption).

Regarding the outright denial of recognition of foreign family law judgments, traditional rules of private international law invoked by the (national courts of the) Contracting Parties against the recognition (and enforcement) may essentially be overruled by the Court. It follows from the Court's case law that traditional private international law requirements concerning recognition and enforcement of foreign family law judgments must comply with the requirements of Article 8 ECHR. If such a requirement leads to a denial of recognition, it will be assessed as an interference under Article 8(2) ECHR. In *Wagner*, for example, the requirement that a foreign adoption should be in accordance with the *lex fori* (a choice of law requirement) was set aside by the Court, while in *Négrépontis-Giannisis* the invocation of the substantive public policy exception by the Greek courts, which led to the denial of the recognition and enforcement of the foreign judgment, was deemed by the Court to be a violation of Articles 6 and 8 ECHR. However, in its admissibility decision in *Hussin*, the Court found in relation to a jurisdiction requirement that the ECHR could not be invoked against this decision, reiterating that it is not possible to complain before the Court about a situation to which the applicant herself has contributed.

It has been discussed in this research that the findings in *Wagner* and *Négrépontis-Giannisis* in particular have been hailed as ushering in a new methodology for private international law in this regard. I would not necessarily go that far, as it is possible to point to certain facts in both cases—facts relating to the legitimate expectations of the applicants that the foreign judgment would be recognized—which would make it possible for the Court to interpret its own findings in subsequent cases in a more narrow fashion. Moreover, the Court's findings in *Hussin* demonstrate that it would certainly go too far to write off all private international law rules against recognition and enforcement of foreign family judgments. Nevertheless, national courts should carefully consider such private international law requirements in light of the obligation to recognize and enforce foreign family law judgments following from Article 8 ECHR.

It should be pointed out that while there may be a development toward a more recognition-friendly framework for international foreign family law judgments, important grounds for refusal remain in place. It has, for example, been demonstrated that the rights of others, which in international family law judgments may particularly play an important role, trump the obligation to recognize and enforce. This follows, inter alia, from the Court's judgments in *Green and Farhat* and *Pini*. More generally, the obligation to recognize and enforce does not entail an obligation to recognize and enforce foreign judgments violating the ECHR.

As discussed in Chap. 8, the second aspect of the impact of the ECHR on the recognition and enforcement of foreign judgments is that the ECHR may also be an obstacle to recognition and enforcement. It is, in principle, well established that the recognition and enforcement of foreign judgments can (also) be denied on the basis of Article 6(1) ECHR. This would be the case if the proceedings abroad have been unfair, or if the defendant could not have been aware that proceedings were brought against him or her in another country.

However, the precise details of the role of Article 6(1) ECHR in this regard are somewhat unclear, as the Court has created some confusion in its case law. In *Pellegrini v. Italy* the Court held that Contracting Parties have the obligation with regard to foreign judgments originating from third countries to avail themselves as to whether the proceedings did not violate Article 6(1) ECHR. The Court thus insisted on full compliance with the requirements of Article 6(1) ECHR in *Pellegrini*.

Yet the Court has since appeared to suggest that foreign judgments emanating from third countries should only be denied recognition and enforcement if not doing so would lead to a 'flagrant denial of justice'. This would suggest that the standard of control with regard to Article 6(1) ECHR should be attenuated. In its later case law the Court has acknowledged the fact that it is unclear which standard should be used, but it has not provided further guidance on this aspect. One of the problems with the standard of a 'flagrant denial of justice' is that it is unclear what this exactly entails. The few cases in which this standard has been further discussed give the impression that the procedural shortcomings have to be quite serious in order to qualify as a 'flagrant denial of justice'. This would consequently suggest a lenient standard of control for foreign judgments emanating from third countries.

This is, in my opinion, an unattractive standard for the recognition and enforcement of foreign judgments. After all, by either recognizing or enforcing a foreign judgment a State gives effect to such a judgment within its territory, which it previously did not have. Once this judgment has been recognized and enforced by the receiving State, the effect of such a judgment is essentially equal to that of a domestic judgment. From that perspective, it would hardly seem fair to an injured party to use a different standard in relation to Article 6(1) ECHR.

The Court's judgment in *Pellegrini* does not answer the question of whether the standard of full compliance introduced in this case and the obligation to deny recognition and enforcement also applies to foreign judgments originating from other Contracting Parties. However, as it is clear that the procedural safeguards in the ECHR should already be protected in other Contracting Parties, it is, in my opinion, easy to argue that this should be the case. A possible complication with foreign judgments emanating from other Contracting Parties is that the local remedy rule may apply: in principle, complaints concerning an unfair procedure in the Contracting Party of origin of the judgment should be brought in that Contracting Party.

The jurisprudence of the national courts of the Contracting Parties under analysis demonstrates that the absence of fair proceedings abroad will, in principle, lead to the denial of recognition and enforcement of foreign judgments. The fairness of the proceedings abroad is, in fact, a requirement for the recognition and enforcement of foreign judgments. However, the exact standard of control with regard to Article 6(1) ECHR is difficult to tell from the available case law.

With regard to the Court's case law on the invocation of the substantive rights guaranteed in the ECHR against the recognition and enforcement of foreign judgments, a clear distinction should be made from the perspective of the Court between cases concerning the enforcement of a foreign judgment emanating from another Contracting Party and cases concerning foreign judgments originating from a third country. It follows from the Court's decision in *Lindberg* that it appears to be difficult to successfully invoke one of the substantive rights guaranteed in the ECHR against the recognition and enforcement of a foreign judgment originating from another Contracting Party before the Court in Strasbourg. In this case the Court essentially applied the local remedy rule: the necessity to first exhaust national procedures. As noted above, this would require an applicant to seek a remedy within the Contracting Party of the origin of the foreign judgment and then go to Strasbourg, instead of awaiting enforcement proceedings in another Contracting Party. However, it has been found that this does not necessarily mean that the national courts of Contracting Parties should always follow suit in relying on the local remedy argument.

The Court has dealt only once with the invocation of one of the substantive rights guaranteed in the ECHR against the recognition and enforcement of a foreign judgment originating from a third country. The Court examined the enforcement of the foreign judgment as a restriction to the applicant's right to property *ex* Article 1 of Protocol No. 1 ECHR and after balancing the interests of society as a whole in the enforcement against the applicant's interest in denying the enforcement, the Court held that there had not been a violation. Yet even though the Court in its assessment of the restriction did acknowledge the international dimension of the case, it is still of limited relevance for private international law in general, as it concerned a forfeiture order to help combat (international) drug trafficking, which is a very specific topic and gave rise to the wide margin of appreciation of the Contracting Party in this regard.

There is, similarly, little case law to be found in the national legal orders under analysis with regard to the recognition and enforcement of foreign judgments that possibly violate one of the substantive rights guaranteed in the ECHR, even though the principle of the refusal to recognize and enforce such foreign judgments has been recognized. Nevertheless, the substantive rights guaranteed in the ECHR appear not to have been invoked often in national jurisprudence, leaving many questions open in this regard.

9.5 Concluding Remarks

The rights guaranteed in the ECHR have an impact on all three main questions of private international law. Even though the Court's case law on this topic remains somewhat limited, it is clear that issues of private international law will largely be covered by the rights guaranteed in the ECHR. It follows that the result of the application of the rules of private international law of the Contracting Parties should be in conformity with the ECHR. It has been demonstrated in this book that in some areas this impact of the ECHR is still somewhat underestimated.

An important question throughout this research has been whether the application of the rights guaranteed in the ECHR to issues of private international law would leave room for specific private international law concerns. It has been argued, particularly by specialists of private international law, that if the scrutiny of the rights guaranteed in issues of private international law was too strict, there would be too little room left for the application of a foreign law or the recognition and enforcement of foreign judgments, particularly where these originated from third countries. In this book, however, it has been argued that the rights guaranteed in the ECHR concerned with issues of private international law by their nature leave room for such concerns. The rights guaranteed in the ECHR that are concerned with issues of private international law are, after all, not absolute rights.

It is interesting to note that there appears to be a tendency in the Court's case law concerning issues of private international law pointing to a less strict control of the rights guaranteed in the ECHR by the Court in such cases. In many issues of private international law the Court leaves a wide margin of appreciation to the Contracting Parties, for various reasons. Moreover, even in situations in which the Court had previously appeared to draw a strict line, such as, for example, with regard to Article 6(1) ECHR and the enforcement of foreign judgments emanating from third countries in *Pellegrini*, in later cases the Court has seemingly distanced itself from this line. One could therefore conclude that although the possible impact of the ECHR on private international law is enormous, the Court's approach appears to mitigate this impact somewhat.

What could further limit the impact of the ECHR on private international law is that the Court scrutinizes the procedural behavior of the parties very strictly in cases of private international law. One could, for example, cite the aforementioned local remedy argument with regard to the enforcement of foreign judgments originating from other Contracting Parties. Moreover, in multiple cases, such as, for example, *McDonald*, *Hussin*, and *Ammdjadi*, the Court held that no violation of the ECHR could be found because of its standard case law that applicants cannot complain about a situation to which they have themselves contributed. This may further limit the possibility to successfully invoke one of the rights guaranteed in the ECHR in issues of private international law. This may, in light of another trend of private international law—the increased role of party autonomy—even become a serious impediment, as it could be possible that the Court would set aside cases where the applicant could, for example, have prevented issues with a repugnant foreign law by entering into a choice of law agreement, as it essentially found in *Ammdjadi*. A similar observation could be made with regard to issues of jurisdiction in private international law. One can hardly imagine that the Court has introduced this line of reasoning in issues of private international law by design, but it is nevertheless an interesting observation.

A new area developed by the Court deviates a little from the aforementioned tendency to give leeway to the Contracting Parties in issues of private international law with regard to the ECHR. The Court has held that the ECHR essentially entails an obligation for Contracting Parties to recognize and enforce foreign judgments. The Court has found that particularly foreign family law judgments in which a status has been acquired should be recognized, notwithstanding traditional grounds of refusal in the private international law regimes of the Contracting Parties, such as the public policy exception. This is an area of private international law where the full impact of the ECHR has yet to fully permeate into the national legal orders of the Contracting Parties. However, even with this case law one could argue that the Court has already begun to limit this right, as it has done in its latest case on this topic in *Harroudj*, as it held that giving partial effect to a foreign judgment did not violate the obligation to recognize foreign judgments.

In this book national jurisprudence of a few selected legal orders has been examined, namely England, the Netherlands, and Switzerland. Even though no fully comparative research has been undertaken, it is interesting to observe some of the differences in how the rights guaranteed in the ECHR are treated in issues of private international law in the various Contracting Parties. Additional comparative research could result in further valuable insights into the impact of the ECHR on private international law.

In conclusion, one may thus state that while the exact impact of the ECHR in many areas of private international law is still unclear due to the limited number of cases in which the Court has dealt with such issues, it is hoped that this research has contributed in further explaining that private international law is not immune to the impact of the rights guaranteed in the ECHR. Quite to the contrary, it follows from this book that the rights guaranteed in the ECHR have already had a considerable impact on the three main issues of private international law. It is quite conceivable that some aspects of the private international law regimes of Contracting Parties have to be adapted somewhat in order for the Contracting Parties to fulfill their obligations under the ECHR.

In particular, the manner in which national courts assess the rights guaranteed in the ECHR in relation to a foreign applicable law or a foreign judgment should be reconsidered, as it appears to be prudent for courts to regard the rights guaranteed in the ECHR more as a starting point in the discussion, instead of relegating their role to a correcting device afterwards by means of the public policy exception. Placing the rights guaranteed in the ECHR at the forefront would equally be of use in other discussions, such as the impact of the ECHR on jurisdiction and the obligation to recognize and enforce foreign judgments.

Table of Cases

European Court of Human Rights

A. and Others v. the United Kingdom [GC], no. 3455/05, ECHR 2009.

AGOSI v. the United Kingdom, 24 October 1986, Series A no. 108.

Air Canada v. the United Kingdom, 5 May 1995, Series A no. 316-A.

Airey v. Ireland. 9 October 1979, Series A no. 32.

Aït-Mouhoub v. France, 28 October 1998, *Reports of Judgments and Decisions* 1998-VIII.

Al-Adsani v. the United Kingdom [GC], no. 35763/97, ECHR 2001-XI.

Al-Jedda v. the United Kingdom [GC], no. 27021/08, ECHR 2011.

Al-Sadoon and Mufdi v. the United Kingdom, no. 61498/08, ECHR 2010 (extracts).

Al-Skeini and Others v. the United Kingdom [GC], no. 55721/07, ECHR 2011.

Ammdjadi v. Germany (dec.), no. 51625/08, 9 March 2010.

Ashingdane v. the United Kingdom, 28 May 1985, Series A no. 93.

Assanidze v. Georgia [GC], no. 71503/01, ECHR 2004-II.

Ateş Mimarlik Mühendislik A.Ş v. Turkey, no. 33275/05, 25 September 2012.

Austria v. Italy, no. 788/60, Yearbook of the European Convention on Human Rights 1961.

Axen v. Germany, 8 December 1983, Series A no. 72.

Banković and Others v. Belgium and 16 Other Contracting States (dec.) [GC], no. 52207/99, ECHR 2001-XI.

Beer and Regan v. Germany [GC], no. 28934/95, 18 February 1999.

Ben El Mahi v. Denmark (dec.), no. 5853/06, *ECHR* 2006-XV.

Besseau v. France, no. 73893/01, 7 March 2006.

Bladet Tromsø and Stensaas v. Norway [GC], no. 21980/93, ECHR 1999-III.

Blagojević v. the Netherlands (dec.), no. 49032/07, 9 June 2009.

Bosphorus Hava Yolları Turizm ve Ticaret Anonim Şirketi v. Ireland [GC], no. 45036/98, ECHR 2005-VI.

Brualla Gómez de la Torre v. Spain, 19 December 1997, Reports of Judgments and Decisions 1997-VIII.

Buchholz v. Germany, 6 May 1981, Series A no. 42.

Burdov v. Russia, no. 59498/00, ECHR 2002-III.

L.R. Kiestra, *The Impact of the European Convention on Human Rights on Private International Law*, DOI 10.1007/978-94-6265-032-9

Burghartz v. Switzerland, judgment of 22 February 1994, Series A-280-B.
Calabro v. Italy, No. 59895/00, 21 March 2002.
Canea Catholic Church v. Greece, 16 December 1997, Reports of Judgments and Decisions 1997-VIII.
Cardot v. France, 19 March 1991, Series A no. 200.
Chapman v. the United Kingdom [GC], no. 27238/95, ECHR 2001-I.
Cruz Varas v. Sweden, 20 March 1991, Series A no. 201.
D.D. v. France (dec.), no. 3/02, 8 November 2005.
Daoudi v. *France*, no. 19576/08, 3 December 2009.
Darby v. Sweden, 23 October 1990, Series A-187.
De Geouffre de la Pradelle v. France, 16 December 1992, Series A no. 253-B.
Dinu v. Romania and France, no 6152/02, 4 November 2008.
Dombo Beheer B.V. v. the Netherlands, 27 October 1993, Series A no. 274.
Drozd and Janousek v. France and Spain, 26 June 1992, Series A no. 240.
Edificaciones March Gallego S.A. v. Spain, 19 February 1998, Reports of Judgments and Decisions 1998-I.
Einhorn v. France (dec.), no. 71555/01, ECHR 2001-XI.
Eriksson v. Sweden, 22 June 1989, Series A no. 156.
Ern Makina Sanayi ve Ticaret A.Ş v. Turkey, no. 70830/01, 3 May 2007.
Eskinazi and Chelouche v. Turkey (dec.), no. 14600/05, ECHR 2005-XIII (extracts).
Fayed v. the United Kingdom, 21 September 1994, Series A no. 294-B.
Fouklev v. Ukraine, no. 71186/01, 7 June 2005.
Freimanis and Lidums v. Latvia (dec.), no. 73443/01, 30 January 2003.
Galić v. the Netherlands, (dec.) no. 22617/07, 9 June 2009.
García Manibardo v. Spain, no. 38695/97, ECHR 2000-II.
Gaygusuz v. Austria, 16 September 1996, *Reports of Judgments and Decisions* 1996-IV.
Golder v. the United Kingdom, 21 February 1975, Series A no. 18.
Groppera Radio AG and Others v. Switzerland, 28 March 1990, ECHR Series A no. 173.
H. v. France, 24 October 1989, Series A no. 162-A.
Handyside v. the United Kingdom, judgment of 12 December 1976, ECHR Series A no. 24.
Harroudj v. France, no. 43631/09, 4 October 2012.
Hentrich v. France, 22 September 1994, Series A no. 296-A.
Hirsi Jamaa and Others v. Italy [GC], no. 27765/09, 23 February 2012.
Hirst v. the United Kingdom (no. 2) [GC], no. 74025/01, ECHR 2005-IX.
Hornsby v. Greece, 19 March 1997, *Reports of Judgments and Decisions* 1997-II.
Huc v. Romania and Germany (dec.), no. 7269/05, 1 December 2009.
Hussin v. Belgium (dec.), no. 70807/01, 6 May 2004.
Iglesias Gil and A.U.I. v. Spain, no. 56673/00, ECHR 2003-V.
Ignaccolo-Zenide v. Romania, no. 31679/96, ECHR 2000-I.
Ilaşcu and Others v. Moldova and Russia [GC], no. 48787/99, ECHR 2004-VII.

İlhan v. Turkey [GC], no. 22277/93, ECHR 2000-VII.
Ireland v. the United Kingdom, 18 January 1978, Series A no. 25.
Issa and Others v. Turkey (dec.), no. 31821/96, 30 May 2000.
Issa and Others v. Turkey, no. 31821/96, 16 November 2004.
J.A. Pye (Oxford) Ltd and J.A. Pye (Oxford) Land Ltd v. the United Kingdom [GC], no. 44302/02, ECHR 2007-III.
James and Others v. the United Kingdom, 21 February 1986, Series A no. 98.
Jasiūnienė v. Lithuania, no. 41510/98, 6 March 2003.
Johnston and Others v. Ireland, 18 December 1986, Series A no. 122.
Jovanovski v. The Former Yugoslav Republic of Macedonia, no. 31731/03, 7 January 2010.
K. v. Italy, no. 38805/97, ECHR 2004–VIII.
Karalyros and Huber v. Hungary and Greece, no. 75116/01, 6 April 2004.
Kart v. Turkey [GC], no. 8917/05, ECHR 2009 (extracts).
Keegan v. Ireland, 26 May 1994, Series A no. 290.
Kin Kin-Stib and Majkić v. Serbia, no. 12312/05, 20 April 2010.
König v. Germany, 28 June 1978, Series A no. 27.
Kopecký v. Slovakia [GC], no. 44912/98, ECHR 2004-IX.
Kreuz v. Poland, no. 28249/95, ECHR 2001-VI.
Krombach v. France, no. 29731/96, ECHR 2000-II.
Kroon and Others v. the Netherlands, 27 October 1994, Series A no. 297-C.
Kutić v. Croatia, no. 48778/99, ECHR 2002-II.
Lautsi v. Italy [GC], no. 30814/06, 18 March 2011.
Le Compte, Van Leuven and De Meyere v. Belgium, 23 June 1981, Series A no. 43.
Lindberg v. Sweden (dec.), no. 48198/99, 15 January 2004.
Lithgow and Others v. the United Kingdom, 8 July 1986, Series A no. 102.
Lizanets v. Ukraine, no. 6725/03, 31 May 2007.
Loizidou v. Turkey (preliminary objections), 23 March 1995, Series A-310.
Losonci Rose and Rose v. Switzerland, no. 664/06, 9 November 2010.
Maire v. Portugal, no. 48206/99, ECHR 2003-VII.
Mamatkulov and Askarov v. Turkey [GC], nos. 46827/99 and 46951/99, ECHR 2005-I.
Marckx v. Belgium, 13 June 1979, ECHR Series A no. 31.
Markovic and Others v. Italy [GC], no. 1398/03, ECHR 2006-XIV.
Mary Green and Ajad Farhat v. Malta (dec.), no. 38797/07, 6 July 2010.
Matrakas and Others v. Poland and Greece, no. 47268/06, 7 November 2013.
Maumousseau and Washington v. France, no. 39388/05, ECHR 2007-XIII.
McDonald v. France (dec.), no. 18648/04, 29 April 2008.
McVicar v. the United Kingdom, no. 46311/99, ECHR 2002-III.
Mentzen alias Mencena v. Latvia (dec.), no. 71074/01, 7 December 2004.
Michaud v. France, no. 12323/11, ECHR 2012.
Mikulić v. Croatia, no. 53176/99, ECHR 2002-I.
M.S.S. v. Belgium and Greece [GC], no. 30696/09, ECHR 2011.
Multiplex v. Croatia, no. 58112/00, 10 July 2003.

Muñoz Diaz v. Spain, no. 49151/07, 8 December 2009.
Muñoz Díaz v. Spain, no. 49151/07, ECHR 2009.
Négrépontis-Giannisis v. Greece, no. 56759/08, 3 May 2011.
Neulinger and Shuruk v. Switzerland [GC], no. 41615/07, ECHR 2010.
Nuutinen v. Finland, no. 32842/96, ECHR 2000-VIII.
OAO Neftyanaya Kompaniya Yukos v. Russia, no. 14902/04, 20 September 2011.
Oliveira v. the Netherlands, no. 33129/96, ECHR 2002-IV.
Öcalan v. Turkey (dec.), no. 46221/99, 14 December 2000.
Öcalan v. Turkey [GC], no. 46221/99, ECHR 2005-IV.
Osman v. the United Kingdom, 28 October 1998, Reports of Judgments and Decisions 1998-VIII.
P., C. and S. v. the United Kingdom, no. 56547/00, ECHR 2002-VI.
P.P. v. Poland, no. 8677/03, 8 January 2008.
Patrono, Cascini and Stefanelli v. Italy, no. 10180/04, 20 April 2006.
Pellegrini v. Italy, no. 30882/96, *ECHR* 2001-VIII.
Pfeifer and Plankl v. Austria, 25 February 1992, Series A no. 227.
Pini and Others v. Romania, nos. 78028/01 and 78030/01, ECHR 2004-V (extracts).
Pla and Puncernau v. Andorra, no. 69498/01, ECHR 2004-VIII.
Platform Ärtze für das Leben v. Austria, 21 June 1988, ECHR Series A no. 139.
Podkolzina v. Latvia, no. 46726/99, ECHR 2002-II.
Povse v. Austria (dec.), no. 3890/11, 18 June 2013.
Powell and Rayner v. the United Kingdom, judgment of 21 February 1990, Series A no. 172.
Prince Hans-Adam II of Liechtenstein v. Germany [GC], no. 42527/98, ECHR 2001-VIII.
Pravednaya v. Russia, no. 69529/01, 18 November 2004.
Qama v. Albania and Italy, no. 4604/09, 8 January 2013.
Rasmussen v. Denmark, 28 November 1984, Series A no. 87.
Ringeisen v. Austria, 16 July 1971, Series A no. 13.
Romańczyk v. France, no. 7618/05, 18 November 2010.
Saccoccia v. Austria (dec.), no. 69917/01, 5 July 2007.
Saccoccia v. Austria, no. 69917/01, 18 December 2008.
Saccoccia v. Austria, no. 69917/01, 18 December 2008.
Schalk and Kopf v. Austria, no. 30141/04, 24 June 2010.
Sidiropoulos and Others v. Greece, 10 July 1998, Reports of Judgments and Decisions 1998-IV.
Silver and Others v. the United Kingdom, 25 March 1983, Series A no. 61.
Slivenko v. Latvia [GC], no. 48321/99, ECHR 2003-X.
Soering v. the United Kingdom, 7 July 1989, Series A no. 161.
Sporrong and Lönnroth v. Sweden, 23 September 1982, Series A no. 52.
Steel and Morris v. the United Kingdom, no. 68416/01, ECHR 2005-II.
Stjerna v. Finland, 25 November 1994, Series A-299-B.
Stran Greek Refineries and Stratis Andreadis v. Greece, 9 December 1994, Series A no. 301-B.

Stubbings and Others v. the United Kingdom, 22 October 1996, Reports of Judgments and Decisions 1996-IV.
Sunday Times v. the United Kingdom, 26 April 1979, ECHR Series A no. 30.
Swedish Engine Drivers' Union, 6 February 1976, Series A no. 20.
Sylvester v. Austria (dec.), no. 54640/00, 9 October 2003.
Sylvester v. Austria (no. 2), no. 54640/00, 3 February 2005.
Tinnelly & Sons Ltd and Others and McElduff and Others v. the United Kingdom, 10 July 1998, *Reports of Judgments and Decisions* 1998-IV.
Tolstoy Miloslavsky v. the United Kingdom, 13 July 1995, Series A no. 316-B.
Ünal Tekeli v. Turkey, no. 29865/96, ECHR 2004-X (extracts).
Von Hannover v. Germany, no. 59320/00, ECHR 2004-VI.
Von Maltzan and Others v. Germany (dec.) [GC], nos. 71916/01, 71917/01 and 10260/02, ECHR 2005-V.
Vrbica v. Croatia, no. 32540/05, 1 April 2010.
W.K. v. Italy (dec.), no. 38805/97, 25 June 2002.
Wagner and J.W.M.L. v. Luxembourg, no. 76240/01, ECHR 2007-VII (extracts).
Waite and Kennedy v. Germany [GC], no. 26083/94, ECHR 1999-I.
Winterwerp v. the Netherlands, 24 October 1979, Series A no. 33.
Women On Waves and Others v. Portugal, no. 31276/05, 3 February 2009.
X and Y v. the Netherlands, 26 March 1985, ECHR Series A no. 91.
X. v. Switzerland (dec.), no. 8407/78, 6 May 1980, D.R. 179.
Zabawska v. Germany (dec.), no. 49935/99, 2 March 2006.
Zabawska v. Germany (dec.), no. 49935/99, 3 March 2006.
Zvoristeanu v. France (dec.), no. 47128/99, 7 November 2000.

European Commission of Human Rights

Batali v. Switzerland (dec.), no. 20765/92, 9 January 1995.
Decision of the European Commission of Human Rights, no. 6200/73, 13 May 1976, 2 Digest of Strasbourg Case law relating to the European Convention on Human Rights (Article 6) (Köln, Heymann 1984), p. 269.
G. and E. v. Norway (dec.), no. 9278/81 & 9415/81 (joined), DR 35.
Gauthier v. Belgium (dec.), no. 12603/86, 6 March 1989.
Gill and Malone v. the Netherlands and the United Kingdom (dec.), no. 24001/94, 11 April 1996.
H v. the United Kingdom (dec.), no. 10000/82, 4 July 1983, D.R. 33.
Kirchner v. Austria (dec.), 12883/87, 14 October 1991.
Lawless v. Ireland, no. 332/57, 2 Yearbook of European Commission on Human Rights (1960).
X and Y v. the United Kingdom (dec.), no. 7229/75, 15 December 1977.
X v. Luxembourg (dec.), no. 5288/71, 10 July 1973.
X v. Sweden (dec.), no. 7973, 28 February 1979.
X v. the Federal Republic of Germany (dec.), no. 1611/62, Yearbook of the European Convention on Human Rights (1965).
X. v. Belgium and the Netherlands (dec.), no. 6482/74, 10 July 1975, *DR* 6, p. 77.
X. v. Switzerland (dec.), no. 8407/78, 6 May 1980, D.R. 179.

European Court of Justice

ECJ 2 April 2009, Case C-394/07, *Gambazzi*, ECR 2009, I-2563.

ECJ 14 October 2008, Case C-353/06, *Grunkin and Paul*, ECR 2008, I-7639.

ECJ 2 May 2006, Case C-341/04, *Eurofood IFSC*, ECR 2006, I-3813.

ECJ 1 March 2005, Case C-281/02, *Owusu v. Jackson*, ECR 2005, I-1383.

ECJ 9 December 2003, Case C-116/02 *Erich Gasser GmbH v. MISAT Srl*, ECR 2003, I-14693.

ECJ 2 October 2003, Case C-148/02, *Garcia Avello*, ECR 2003, I-11613.

ECJ 10 July 2003, *Booker Aquaculture and Hydo Seafood*, Cases C-20/00 and C-64/00, ECR 2003, I-7411.

ECJ 11 May 2000, Case C-38/98, *Régie Nationale des Usines Renault SA v. Maxicar SpA*, ECR 2000, I-2973.

ECJ 28 March 2000, Case C-7/98, *Krombach v. Bamberski*, ECR 2000, I-1935.

ECJ 20 March 1997, Case C-323/95, *David Charles Hayes and Jeannette Karen Hayes v. Kronenberger GmbH.*, ECR 1997, I-1711.

ECJ 6 December 1994, Case C-406/92, *Tatry v. Maciej Rataj*, ECR 1994, I-5439.

ECJ 1 July 1993, Case C 20/92, *Hubbard v. Hamburger*, ECR 1993, I-3777.

ECJ 8 December 1987, Case C-144/86, *Gubisch Maschinenfabrik/Giulio Palumbo*, ECR 1987, I-4861.

CJEU 25 October 2012, Case C-133/11, *Folien Ficher and Fofitec* (not yet published).

International Court of Justice

ICJ, Netherlands v. Sweden (Case concerning the Application of the Convention of 1902 governing the Guardianship of Infants, Judgment of 28 November 1958) (*Boll* case), ICJ Rep. 55.

Permanent Court of International Justice

PCIJ, 7 September 1927, Series A No. 10, p. 18-19 (*Lotus*).

England

Al-Bassam v. Al-Bassam, [2004] EWCA Civ. 857.

Douglas & Others v. Hello Ltd. & Others [2005] EMLR 609, [2005] 4 All ER 128, [2005] 2 FCR 487, [2005] EMLR 28, [2005] 3 WLR 881, [2005] HRLR 27, [2005] EWCA Civ 595, [2006] QB 125.

Douglas & Others v. Hello Ltd. & Others [2007] UKHL 2.

Golubovich v. Golubovich 2010] EWCA Civ 810.

Government of the United States of America v. Montgomery (No.2) [2004] UKHL 37.

Hemain v. Hemain [1988] 2 FLR 388.

Joint Stock Company (Aeroflot—Russian Airlines) v. Berezovsky & Anor [2012] EWHC 3017 (Ch).

Kuwait Airways Corpn v. Iraqi Airways Co (Nos 4 and 5) [2002] 2 AC 883.

Lubbe v. Capre Plc, [2000] 1 WLR 1545.

Mark v. Mark [2004] EWCA Civ. 168, [2005] Fam. 267.

Mark v. Mark [2005] UKHL 42.
Maronier v. Larmer [2002] EWCA Civ. 774, [2003] Q.B. 620.
Merchant International Company v. Natsionalna Aktsionerna Kompaniya "Naftogaz Ukrayiny" [2012] EWCA Civ 196.
Merchant International Company v. Natsionalna Aktsionerna Kompaniya "Naftogaz Ukrayiny" [2011] EWHC 1820 (Comm).
Nasser v. United Bank of Kuwait [2001] EWCA Civ 556, [2002] 1 All E.R. 401 (CA).
NG v. KR, [2008] EWHC 1532 (Fam), [2008] EWHC 1532 (Fam), [2009] 1 FLR 1478, [2009] 1 FCR 35, [2008] Fam Law 1082.
Oppenheimer v. Cattermole [1976] AC 249.
OT Africa Line Ltd v. Hijazy (The Kribi) [2001] 1 Lloyd's Report 76.
R (Ullah) v. Special Adjudicator [2004] UKHL 26.
Re: X & Y (Foreign Surrogacy) [2008] EWHC 3030 (Fam).
Re J (a child) [2005] UKHL 40.
Re N (Recognition of Foreign Adoption Order [2009] EWHC 29 (Fam.), [2010] 1 FLR 1102.
Singh v. Entry Clearance Officer (New Delhi) [2004] EWCA Civ 1075, [2005] QB 608.
Spiladia Maritime Corp v. Cansulex Ltd, [1987] AC 460.
The Atlantic Star [1974] A.C. 436.
Williams & Humbert Ltd v. W&H Trade Marks (Jersey) Ltd [1986] A.C. 368.

France
Cass. 1re civ., 26 October 2011, *JDI* 2012, p. 176 (note Guillaumé).
Cass. 1re civ., 10 May 2006.
Cass.civ. 11 March 1997, *Rev.crit.dr.int.priv. 1997*, p. 585 (note H. Gaudemet-Tallon).
Cass.civ. 1 June 1994, *Rev.crit.dr.int.priv.* 1995, p. 103 (note J. Déprez).
Cass. 1re civ., 10 February 1993, *Rev.crit dr.int.priv.* 1993, 620 (note J. Foyer).
Cour de Paris 14 June 1994, *Rev. crit.dr.int.priv.* 1995, 308 (note Y. Lequette).

Germany
BverfG 30 November 1982, *IPrax* 1984, p. 88.
BverfG 31 May 1971, 31 BVerfGE 58; *NJW* 1971, p. 1508.

Italy
Italian Constitutional Court 26 February 1987, *Rev.crit.dr.int* 1987, p. 563 (note B. Ancel).

The Netherlands
HR 18 March 2011, *RvdW* 2011, 392.
HR 7 January 2011, *NJ* 2011, 134.
HR 12 December 2008, *RvdW* 2009, 41; *NIPR* 2009, 1.
HR 19 October 2007, *NIPR* 2007, 267.

HR 1 September 2006, *RvdW* 2006, 769; *JOL* 2006, 475; *JPF* 2006, 136 (note A.E. Oderkerk).
HR 3 December 2004, *NIPR* 2005, 3.
HR 29 November 2002, *NJ* 2003, 35.
HR 5 April 2002, *NJ* 2004, 170 (note Vlas).
HR 10 September 1999, *NJ* 2001, 41.
HR 15 April 1994, *NJ* 1994, 576, *NIPR* 1994, 210.
HR 30 March 1990, *NJ* 1991.
HR 26 October 1984, *NJ* 1985, 696.
Hof Amsterdam 10 May 2011, *RN* 2011, 82.
Hof Amsterdam 3 May 2011, *NIPR* 2011, 295.
Hof Amsterdam 28 April 2009, *JOR* 2009, 208.
Hof Amsterdam 17 July 2008, *NIPR* 2009, 31.
Hof Amsterdam 9 February 2006, *JPF* 2006, 71 (note A.E. Oderkerk), *NIPR* 2006, 98.
Hof Amsterdam 6 March 2003, *NIPR* 2005, 305.
Hof Arnhem 4 November 2003, *NIPR* 2004, 43.
Hof 's-Hertogenbosch 27 November 2008, *NIPR* 2009, 95.
Hof 's-Gravenhage 3 October 2007, *NIPR* 2008, 7.
Hof 's-Gravenhage 18 April 2007, *NIPR* 2007, 184.
Hof 's-Gravenhage, 21 December 2005, *EB* 2006, 32; *NJF* 2006, 154.
Rb. Alkmaar 16 January 2002, *NIPR* 2002, 170.
Rb. Amsterdam 17 March 2011, *LJN* BP8070.
Rb. Amsterdam 23 September 2009, *NIPR* 2010, 21.
Rb. Amsterdam, 31 October 2007, *NIPR* 2007, 308.
Rb. Amsterdam 23 November 2005, *NIPR* 2006, 14.
Rb. Haarlem 11 December 2012, *NIPR* 2013, 24.
Rb. Haarlem 22 July 2008, *NIPR* 2008, 275.
Rb. Haarlem 1 February 2005, *NIPR* 2005, 124.
Rb. 's-Gravenhage 21 March 2012, LJN BV 9748.
Rb. 's-Gravenhage 3 November 2008, *NIPR* 2010, 23.
Rb. 's-Gravenhage 12 January 2006, LJN AV 2498.
Rb. 's-Gravenhage 22 April 2004, *NIPR* 2005, 224.
Rb. Rotterdam 22 March 2001, *NIPR* 2001, 300.
Rb. Rotterdam 11 January 2001, *NIPR* 2001, 146.
Rb. Utrecht 31 October 2007, *NIPR* 2008, 33.
Rb. Utrecht 5 November 2003, *NIPR* 2004, 236.
Rb. Zwolle-Lelystad 20 July 2005, *NIPR* 2005, 327.
Ktg. Amsterdam, 5 January 1996, *NIPR* 1996, 145.

Switzerland
ATF 134 III 467 (25 June 2008).
ATF 132 III 661 (14 August 2006).
ATF 132 III 609 (14 July 2006).
ATF 132 I 134 (4 May 2006).

ATF 131 III 511 (31 May 2005).
ATF 131 III 153 (22 December 2004).
ATF 131 II 169 (7 February 2005).
ATF 128 I 63 (4 March 2002).
ATF 126 III 327 (4 July 2000).
ATF 126 III 249 (28 April 2000).
ATF 126 III 101 (6 October 1999).
ATF 125 I 257 (24 June 1999).
ATF 122 III 344 (3 September 1996).
ATF 116 II 625 (19 December 1990).
ATF 111 Ia 12 (13 March 1985).
ATF 103 Ia 199 (9 February 1977).
ATF 85 II 305 (17 October 1959).
Judgment of the *Tribunal fédéral*, 5A_171/2010, 19 April 2010 (unpublished).
Judgment of the *Tribunal fédéral*, 4A_305/2009, 5 October 2009 (unpublished).
Judgment of the *Tribunal fédéral*, 5A.4/2005, 24 May 2005 (unpublished).
Judgment of the *Tribunal fédéral*, 1P.390/2004/col, 28 October 2004 (unpublished).
Judgment of the *Tribunal fédéral*, 4P.48/2002, 4 June 2002 (unpublished).
Judgment of the *Tribunal fédéral*, 5P.250/2001, 17 April 2002 (unpublished).
Judgment of the *Tribunal fédéral*, 5 March 1991, *La Semaine judicidaire* 1991, p. 457.
Obergericht Zürich, BlZR 89 1990, no. 65, p. 139.
Obergericht Zürich, II. Zivilkammer, 1 May 1959, *Annuaire suisse de droit international* 1961, pp. 293–295.
Tribunal cantonal, Neuchâtel, IIe Cour civile, 26 July 2001.
Cour de justice GE, 14 November 1991, SJ 1992, p. 219.

United States

Kiobel, et al., v. Royal Dutch Petroleum, et al., 132 S.Ct. 472 (US 2011).
International Shoe v. Washington, 336 US 310.

Bibliography

Adede AO (1976) A fresh look at the meaning of the doctrine of denial of justice under international law. Can Yearb Int Law 14:73–95

Aemisegger H (2005) The federal judge vis-à-vis the jurisdiction of the ECHR. In: Pernice I, Stöbener P (eds) The future of the European judicial system in a comparative perspective. Nomos, Baden-Baden, pp 309–314

Akehurst M (1972–1973) Jurisdiction in international law. BYIL 46:145–257

Aldeeb S, Bonomi A (eds) (1999) Le droit musulman de la famille et des successions à l'épreuve des orders juridiques occidentaux. Schulthess, Zurich

Alkema EA (1988) The third-party applicability or "Drittwirkung" of the European convention on human rights. In: Matscher F, Petzold H (eds) Protecting human rights: the European dimension. studies in honour of Gérard J. Wiarda. Carl Heymanns Verlag KG, Köln, pp 33–45

Amerasinghe CF (2004) Local remedies in international law. Cambridge University Press, Cambridge

April S (1984) Blocking statutes as a response to the extra-territorial application of law. In: Olmstead CJ (ed) Extra-territorial application of law and responses thereto. ESC Publishing, Oxford

Arai-Takahashi Y (2002) The margin of appreciation doctrine and the principle of proportionality in the jurisprudence of the ECHR. Intersentia, Antwerp

Audit B (2008) Droit international privé. Economica, Paris

d'Avout L (2010) Droits fondamentaux et coordination des ordres juridiques en droit privé. In: Dubout E, Touzé S (eds) Les droits fondamentaux: charnières entre ordres et systems juridiques. Pedone, Paris, pp 165–198

Baratta R (2010) La reconnaissance internationale des situations juridiques personnelles et familiales. Recueil des Cours 348:253–499

Basedow J (2000) The effects of globalization on private international law. In: Basedow J, Kono T (eds) Legal aspects of globalization: conflict of laws, internet, capital markets and insolvency in a global economy. Kluwer International, The Hague, pp 1–10

Basedow J (2000) The communitarization of the conflict of laws under the treaty of Amsterdam. CML Rev 37:687–708

Basedow J, Kono T (eds) Legal aspects of globalization: conflict of laws, internet, capital markets and insolvency in a global economy. Kluwer International, The Hague

Beaumont P (2009) The jurisprudence of the European court of human rights and the European court of justice on The Hague convention on international child abduction. Recueil des Cours 335:9–103

Beaumont P (2009) Hague choice of court agreements convention 2005: background, negotiations, analysis and current status. J Private Int Law 5:125–159

Beaumont P, Johnston E (2010) Can exequatur be abolished in Brussels I whilst retaining a public policy defence? J Private Int Law 6:249–279

L.R. Kiestra, *The Impact of the European Convention on Human Rights on Private International Law*, DOI 10.1007/978-94-6265-032-9

Besson S (2008) The reception process in Ireland and the United Kingdom. In: Keller H, Stone Sweet A (eds) A Europe of rights: the impact of the ECHR on national legal systems. Oxford University Press, Oxford, pp 31–106

Bitter JW (1979) De Nederlandse Grondwet en de bescherming van grondrechten in het Nederlands internationaal privaatrecht [The Dutch constitution and the protection of fundamental rights in Dutch private international law]. Ars Aequi 23:440–447

Blackburn R, Polakiewicz J (2001) Fundamental rights in Europe: the European convention on human rights and its member states, 1950–2000. Oxford University Press, Oxford

Boele-Woelki K (2006) International privaatrecht [Private international law]. Ars Aequi 55:5503–5504

Bogdan M (2011) General course on private international law, Recueil des Cours 348. Martinus Nijhoff Publishers, Leiden

Bollée S (2007) L'extension du domaine de la méthode de reconnaissance unilatérale. Rev.crit.dr.int.priv. 96:307–355

Bomhoff JA (2004) Het negatief declaratoir in de EEX-Verordening. Strategie, misbruik van procesrecht en de doorwerking van grondrechten in het Europese IPR [The negative declaratory in the Brussels-I regulation. strategy, abuse of procedure and the impact of fundamental rights on European private international law]. NIPR 22:1–8

Bonomi A (1999) Mandatory rules in private international law: the quest for uniformity of decisions in a global environment. Yearb Private Int Law 1:215–247

Borrás A (2005) Le droit international privé communautaire: realités, problems et perspectives d'avenir. Recueil des cours 317:313–536

Bos TM (2008) Het faillissement van YUKOS en de beginselen van een behoorlijke procesorde [the insolveny of YUKOS and the principles of due process]. WPNR (Weekblad voor privaatrecht, notariaat en registratie) 139:41–43

Brand RA, Jablonski SR (2007) Forum non conveniens: history, global practice, and future under The Hague Convention on choice of court agreements. Oxford University Press, New York

Brems E (2003) The margin of appreciation doctrine of the European Court of Human Rights: accomodating diversity within Europe. In: Forsythe DP, McMahon PC (eds) Human rights and diversity: area studies revisited. Nebraska University Press, Lincoln, pp 81–110

Briggs A (2011) The rejection of abuse in international civil procedure. In: Feria R de la, Vogenauer S, Prohibition of abuse of law. Hart Publishing, Oxford, pp 261–277

Briggs A (2006) Decisions of British courts during 2005 involving questions of private international law. BYBIL 76:554–596

Briggs A (2005) The impact of recent judgments of the European Court on English procedural law and practice. Zeitschrift für Schweizerisches recht 124:231–262

Briggs A (2005) Decisions of British courts during 2004. Private international law. BYBIL 75:537–593

Briggs A (2003) Decisions of British courts during 2002. Private international law. BYBIL 73:453–496

Briggs A, Rees P (2009) Civil jurisdiction and judgments. Informa, London

Brownlie I (2008) Principles of public international law. Oxford University Press, Oxford

Bucher A (ed) (2011) Loi sur le droit international privé. Convention de Lugano, Helbing Lichtenhahn, Bâle

Bucher A (2010) La dimension sociale du droit international privé: cours général. Recueil des Cours 341, Martinus Nijhoff Publishers, Leiden

Bucher A (2010) Jurisprudence suisse en matière de droit international privé de la famille et des successions. RSDIE 20:189–245

Bucher A (2007) Jurisprudence suisse en matière de droit international privé 2007. RSDIE 17:315–321

Bucher A (2004) Le couple en droit international privé. Helbing & Lichtenhahn, Bâle

Bucher A (2002) Jurisprudence suisse en matière de droit international privé de la famille et des successions. RSDIE 12:267–316

Bucher A (2000) La famille en droit international privé. Recueil des cours 283:9–186
Bucher A (1993) L'ordre public et le but social des lois en droit international privé. Recueil des Cours 239:9–116
Cassese A (2005) International law. Oxford University Press, Oxford
Cassin R (1969) Amicorum discipulorumque liber I: Problèmes de protection internationale des droits de l'homme. Pédone, Paris
Cheshire GC et al (2010) Private international law. Oxford University Press, Oxford
Chong A (2012) Transnational public policy in civil and commercial matters. LQR 128:88–113
Christoffersen J (2009) Fair balance: proportionality, subsidiarity and primarity in the European convention on human rights. Nijhoff, Leiden
Clapham A (1993) The 'Drittwirkung' of the convention. In: MacDonald R St J et al (eds) The European system for the protection of human rights. Martinus Nijhoff, Dordrecht, pp 63–82
Clapham A (1993) Human rights in the private sphere. Clarendon Press, Oxford
Clarkson CMV, Hill J (2011) The conflict of laws. Oxford University Press, Oxford
Cliteur PB, Vonken APMJ (eds) (1993) Doorwerking van mensenrechten [The impact of human rights]. Wolters-Noordhoff, Groningen
Coester-Waltjen D (2006) Anerkennung im internationalen Personen-, Familien- und Erbrecht und das europaeische Kollisionsrecht. IPRax 26:392–400
Coester-Waltjen D (1998) Die Wirkungskraft der Grundrechte bei Fällen mit Auslandsbezug—familien- und erbrechtlicher Bereich [The impact of fundamental right in cross-border cases—the area of family and inheritance law]. In: Coester-Waltjen D (eds) Die Wirkungskraft der Grundrechte bei Fällen mit Auslandsbezug [The impact of fundamental rights in cross-border cases], C.F. Müller, Heidelberg, pp 9–32
Cohen D (1989) La Convention européenne des droits de l'homme et le droit international privé. Rev.crit.dr.int.priv. 78:451–483
Corbion L (2004) Le déni de justice en droit international privé. Presses universitaires d' Aix-Marseille, Aix-en-Provence
Cordero Moss G (2007) Between private and public international law: exorbitant jurisdiction as illustrated by the Yukos case. Rev Central East Eur Law 32:1–17
Costa J-P (2002) Le tribunal de la Rote et l'article 6 de la Convention européenne des droits de l'homme. Revue trimestrielle des droits de l'homme 13:470–476
Cuniberti G (2011) The discreet influence of abuse of law in international civil procedure. In: de la Feria R, Vogenauer S (eds) Prohibition of abuse of law. Hart Publishing, Oxford, pp 279–288
Cuniberti G (2008) The recognition of foreign judgments lacking reasons in Europe: access to justice, foreign court avoidance and efficiency. ICLQ 57:25–52
Cuniberti G, Rueda I (2011) Abolition of exequatur. Addressing the commission's concerns. RabelsZ 75:286–316
Daelman C (2011) The interaction between human rights and private international law. Tijdschrift@ipr.be 2011:70–73
Davis D, Straw J (2012) We must defy Strasbourg on prisoner votes. The Telegraph, 24 May. www.telegraph.co.uk/news/uknews/law-and-order/9287633/We-must-defy-Strasbourg-on-prisoner-votes.html. Accessed (date)
de Boer Th M (2010) Living apart together: the relationship between public and private international law. NILR 57:183–207
de Boer Th M (2010) Samenloop van verdragen en verordeningen op het terrein van het internationaal familierecht [concurrence of treaties and regulations in the area of international family law]. Familie en jeugdrecht 32:308–315
de Boer Th M (1996) Facultative choice of law. the procedural status of choice-of-law rules and foreign law. Recueil des Cours 257:223–427

de Boer Th M (2008) Unwelcome foreign law: public policy and other means to protect the fundamental values and public interests of the European community. In: Malatesta A et al (eds) The external dimension of ec private international law in family and succession matters. CEDAM, Padova, pp 295–330

de Groot G-R, Kuipers JJ (2008) The new provisions on private international law in the Lisbon treaty. Maastricht J Eur Comp Law 15:109–114

De Ly F (2011) Arbitration and the European convention on human rights. In: Lévy L, Derains Y (eds) Liber amicorum en l'honneur de Serge Lazareff. Pedone, Paris, pp 181–205

de Vareilles-Sommières P (1997) La compétence international de l'état en matière de droit privé: droit international public et droit international privé. LGDJ, Paris

de Visscher Ch (1935) Le déni de justice en droit international, Recueil des Cours 52: 363-442.

de Wet E (2008) The reception process in the Netherlands and Belgium. In: Keller H, Stone Sweet A (eds) A Europe of rights: the impact of the ECHR on national legal systems. Oxford University Press, Oxford, pp 229–309

de Wet E (2006) The emergence of international and regional value systems as a manifestation of the emerging international constitutional order. Leiden J Int Law 19:611–632

de Winter LI (1968) Excessive jurisdiction in private international law. ILCQ 17:706–720

Dicey AV, Morris JHC, Collins LA (2012) The conflict of laws. Sweet & Maxwell, London

Dickinson A (2010) Surveying the proposed Brussels I "bis" regulation: solid foundations but renovation needed. Yearb Private Int Law 12:247–309

Dickinson A (2007) Legal certainty and the brussels convention: too much of a good thing? In: de Vareilles-Sommières P (ed) Forum shopping in the European judicial area. Hart, Oxford, pp 115–123

Docquir B (1999) Le droit international privé à l'épreuve de la Convention européenne des droits de l'homme. Annales de Droit de Louvain 59:473–522

Dolinger J (2000) Evolution of principles for resolving conflicts in the field of contracts and torts. Recueil des Cours 283:187–512

Donnely J (2008) Human rights: both universal and relative (a reply to Michael Goodhart). Hum Rights Quart 30:194–204

Donnely J (2007) The relative universality of human rights. Hum Rights Quart 27:281–306

Donovan SF, Roberts A (2006) The emerging recognition of international civil jurisdiction. AJIL 100:142–163

Duintjer-Tebbens H (2006) From Jamaica with pain: enkele aantekeningen bij het arrest van 1 maart 2005 van het Hof van Justitie in de zaak Owusu [From Jamaica with pain: a few notes on the judgment of 1 March 2005 of the ECJ in the case Owusu. In: van der Grinten P, Heukels T (eds) Crossing borders: essays in European and private international law. Nationality law and Islamic law in honour of Frans van der Velden. Kluwer, Deventer, pp 95–103

Dutoit B (2005) Droit international privé Suiss. Helbing & Lichtenhahn Verlag, Bale

Eissen MA (1993) The principle of proportionality in the case-law of the European Court of Human Rights. In: MacDonald R St J et al (eds) The European system for the protection of human rights. Martinus Nijhoff, Dordrecht, pp 125–146

Engel C (1989) Ausstrahlungen der Europäischen Menschenrechtskonvention auf das Kollisionsrecht [Emanations of the European convention on human right on conflict of laws]. RabelsZ 53:3–51

Enneking LFH (2012) Multinational corporations, human rights violations and a 1789 US statute: a brief exploration of the case of Kiobel vs Shell. NIPR 30:396–400

Enneking LFH (2012) Foreign direct liability and beyond. Exploring the role of tort law in promoting international corporate social responsibility and accountability. Eleven International Publishing, The Hague

Erauw J (2006) Handboek Belgisch international privaatrecht [Handbook Belgian private international law]. Kluwer, Mechelen

Esplugues Mota CA (ed) (2011) Application of foreign law. Sellier, Munich

Fallon M (1995) Les conflits de lois et de juridictions dans une espace économique integré. Recueil des cours 253:8–282

Fawcett JJ (2007) The impact of article 6(1) ECHR on private international law. ILCQ 56:1–48

Fentiman R (2010) International commercial litigation. Oxford University Press, Oxford

Fentiman R (2006) Civil jurisdiction and third states: Owusu and After. CML Rev 43:705–734

Fentiman R (1998) Foreign law in English courts: pleading, proof and choice of law. Oxford University Press, Oxford

Fernández Arroyo DP (2004) Exorbitant and exlusive grounds of jurisdiction in European private international law: will they ever survive? In: Mansel H-P (ed) Festschrift für Erik Jayme, vol I. Sellier European Law Publishers, Munich, pp 169–186

Flauss J-F (2002) L'exequatur des jugements étrangers devant la Cour européenne des droits de l'homme. In : Bieber R (ed), Mélanges en l'honneur de Bernard Dutoit, Libraire Droz 2002, Genève, pp 69–87

Flauss J-F (2001) Chroniques: CEDH et droit du contentieux. L'Actualité juridique droit administratif 2001

Foblets MC, Rutten SWE (2006) De toelaatbaarheid van de verstoting: recente ontwikkelingen in het Nederlands, Frans en Belgisch internationaal privaatrecht [The admissibility of the repudiation: recent developments in Dutch, French and Belgian private international law]. In: van der Grinten P, Heukels T (eds) Crossing borders: essays in European and private international law. Nationality law and Islamic law in honour of Frans van der Velden. Kluwer, Deventer, pp 195–213

Focarelli C (2012) Denial of justice. In: Wolfrum R (ed) The Max Planck encyclopedia of public international law. Oxford University Press, Oxford. www.mpepil.com. Accessed Apr 2012

Francioni F (ed) (2007) Access to justice as a human right. Oxford University Press, Oxford

Franzina P (2011) Some remarks on the relevance of article 8 of the ECHR to the recognition of family status judicially created abroad. Diritti umani e diritto internazionale 5:609–616

Fulchiron H (2010) The French family judge encounters cultural pluralism. In: Foblets M-C (ed) Cultural diversity and the law: state responses from around the world. Bruylant, Brussels, pp 613–633

Fulchiron H (2002) Droits fondamentaux et règles de droit international privé: conflits de droits, conflits de logiques? In: Sudre F (ed) Le droit au respect de vie familiale au sens de la Convention européenne des droits de l'homme. Bruylant, Bruxelles, pp 353–386

Gannagé L (2008) A propos de l'absolutisme des droits fondamentaux. In: Ancel JP (ed) Vers des nouveaux equilibres entre ordre juridiques: liber amicorum Hélène Gaudemet-Tallon. Dalloz, Paris, pp 265–284

Gannagé L (2001) La hiérarchie des normes et les méthodes du droit international privé: étude de droit international privé de la famille. L.G.D.J, Paris

Gaudemet-Tallon H (2006) Le "droit au juge" à l'épreuve des règles de compétence judiciaire internationale (matière civile et commercial). In: Léger P (ed) Le droit à la mesure de l'homme. Pedone, Paris, pp 173–189

Gaudemet-Tallon H (2005) Le pluralisme en droit international privé: richesses et faiblesses. Recueil des cours 312:9–488

Gaudemet-Tallon H (2004) Nationalité, statut personnel et droits de l'homme. In: Mansel H-P (ed) Festschrift für Erik Jayme. Sellier, Munich, pp 205–221

Gaudemet-Tallon H (1991) Forum non conveniens: une menace pour la convention de Bruxelles (a propos de trois arrets anglais récents. Rev.crit.dr.int.priv 80:491–524

Gebauer M (2007) Lis Pendens, negative declaratory-judgments actions and the first-in-time principle. In: Gottschalk E et al (eds) Conflict of laws in a globalized world. Cambridge University Press, New York, pp 89–100

Geeroms S (2004) Foreign law in civil litigation: a comparative and functional analysis. Oxford University Press, Oxford

Gerards JH (2011) EVRM. Algemene beginselen [ECHR. General principles]. Sdu Uitgevers, Den Haag.

Gerards JH (2005) Judicial review in equal treatment cases. Nijhoff, Leiden
Gerards JH, Terlouw A (eds) (2011) Amici Curiae. Adviezen aan het Europees Hof voor de Rechten van de Mens [Amici Curiae. Advice to the European Court of Human Rights]. Wolf Legal Publishers, Nijmegen.
Girsberger D et al (eds) (2004) Zürcher Kommentar zum IPRG: Kommentar zum Bundesgesetz über dat Internationale Privatrecht (IPRG) vom 18. Dezember 1987. Schulthess, Zürich
Goldman B (1969) La protection internationale des droits de l'homme et l'ordre public international dans le fonctionnement de la règle de conflict de lois. Cassin R, Amicorum discipulorumque liber I: Problèmes de protection internationale des droits de l'homme. Pédone, Paris, pp 449–466
Gondek M (2009) The reach of human rights in a globalising world: extraterritorial application of human rights treaties. Intersentia, Antwerp
Goodhart M (2008) Neither relative nor universal: a response to Donnelly. Hum Rights Quart 30:183–193
Greer SC (2000) The margin of appreciation: interpretation and discretion under the European convention on human right. Council of Europe, Strasbourg
Grgic A (eds) (2007) The right to property under the European convention on human rights. Human rights handbooks no. 10. Council of Europe, Strasbourg
Grisel E (2002) Le recours au Tribunal fédéral en matière de reconnaissance et d'exécution des jugements étrangers. In: Bieber R (ed) Mélanges en l'honneur de Bernard Dutoit. Libraire Droz, Genève, pp 89–101
Guinchard E (2005) Procès équitable (Article 6 CESDH) et droit international privé. In: Nuyts A, Watté N (eds) International civil litigation in europe and relations with third states. Bruylant, Brussels, pp 199–245
Hammje P (1997) Droits fondamentaux et ordre public. Rev.crit.dr.int.priv. 86:1–31
Hartley TC (2008) The Brussels regulation and non-community states. In: Basedow J (ed) Japanese and European private international law in comparative perspective. Mohr Siebeck, Tübingen, pp 19–25
Hartley TC (2006) The modern approach to private international law. International litigation and transactions from a common-law perspective. Recueil des Cours 319:9–324
Hartley TC (2005) Choice-of-court agreements, lis pendens, human rights and the realities of international business: reflections on the gasser case. In: Jobard-Bachellier M-N, Mayer P (eds) Le droit international privé: esprit et méthodes. Mélanges en l'honneur de Paul Lagarde, Dalloz, Paris, pp 383–391
Hay P (1991) Flexibility versus predictability and uniformity in choice of Law. Reflections on current European and United States conflicts law. Recueil des Cours 226:282–412
Harris DJ et al (eds) (2009) Law of the European convention on human rights. Oxford University Press, Oxford
Hess B (2012) Staatenimmunität und ius cogens im geltenden Völkerrecht: der international Gerichtshof zeigt die Grenze auf [immunities of the State and ius cogens in current public international law: the ICJ illustrates the boundaries]. IPRax 32:201–206
Higgins R (1999) Allocating competence: Jurisdiction (1993). In: Reisman WM (ed) Jurisdiction in international law. Ashgate, Dartmouth
Higgins R (1984) The legal bases of jurisdiction. In: Olmstead CJ (ed) Extra-territorial application of law and responses thereto. ESC Publishing, Oxford
Hill J (2003) The exercise of jurisdiction in private international law. In: Capps P et al (eds) Asserting jurisdiction. International and European legal perspectives. Hart Publishing, Portland
Hins AW, Nieuwenhuis AJ (2010) Hoofdstukken grondrechten [Chapters fundamental rights]. Ars Aequi Libri, Nijmegen
Hofmann R (1994) Human rights and the ordre public clause of german private international law. Tel Aviv Univ Stud Law 12:145–155

Ibili F (2007) Gewogen rechtsmacht in het IPR. Over forum (non) conveniens en forum necessitatis [Weighed jurisdiction in private international law. On forum (non) conveniens and forum necessitatis]. Kluwer, Deventer

Janis MW et al (2008) European human rights law: text and materials. Oxford University Press, Oxford

Jayme E (2003) Menschenrechte und Theorie des Internationalen Privatrechts' (speech delivered on 24 January 1992). Jayme E, Internationales Privatrecht und Völkerrecht [Private International law and international law]. C.F. Müller Verlag, Heidelberg, pp 95–109

Jayme E (1995) Identité culturelle et intégration: le droit international privé postmoderne. Recueil des Cours 251

Jenks CW (1953) The conflict of law-making treaties. BYIL 30

Jessurun d'Oliveira HU (1975) Openbare orde en rechtsvergelijking [Public policy and comparative law]. In : Jessurun d'Oliveira HU et al (eds) 't Exempel dwinght. Opstellen aangeboden door vrienden en vereerders and prof. mr. I. Kisch ter gelegenheid van zijn 70ste verjaardag, Tjeenk Willink, Zwolle, pp 239–261

Joubert N (2007) La notion de liens suffisants avec l'ordre juridique (Inlandsbeziehung) en droit international privé. LexisNexis Litec, Paris

Juenger FK (1984) Judicial jurisdiction in the United States and in the European communities: a comparison. Mich Law Rev 82:1195–1212

Juenger FK (1984) La Convention de Bruxelles du 27 septembre 1968 et la courtoise international. Réflexions d'un Américain. Rev.crit dr.int.priv. 37

Juenger FK (1972) The German constitutional court and the conflict of laws. AJCL 20:290–298

Juratowitch B (2007) The European convention on human rights and English private international law. J Private Int Law 3:173–199

Kahn-Freund O (1976) General problems of private international law. A.W. Sijthoff, Leyden

Kamminga MT, Extraterritoriality. In: Wolfrum R (ed) The Max Planck encyclopedia of public international law, Oxford University Press, Oxford. www.mpepil.com, Accessed Apr 2012

Kamminga MT, Zia-Zarifi S (eds) (2000) Liability of multinational corporations under international law. Kluwer Law International, The Hague

Kegel G (1994) Introduction, international encyclopedia of comparative law, vol III. Mohr, Tübingen

Keller H, Stone Sweet A (eds) (2008) A Europe of rights: the impact of the ECHR on national legal systems. Oxford University Press, Oxford

Kerameus KD (1997) Enforcement in the international context. Recueil des Cours 264:179–410

Kessedjian C (1997) International jurisdiction and foreign judgments in civil and commercial matters, Preliminary document No 7 of April 1997 for the attention of the special commission of June 1997 on the question of jurisdiction, and recognition and enforcement of foreign judgments in civil and commercial matters. www.hcch.net/index_en.php?act=conventions.publications&dtid=35&cid=98, Accessed Nov 2012

Kiestra LR (2011) Article 1 ECHR and private international law. NIPR 29:2–7

Kiestra LR (2010) De betekenis van het EVRM voor de internationale gerechtelijke vaststelling van het vaderschap [The meaning of the ECHR for the international judicial determination of paternity]. NIPR 28:27–30

Kinsch P (2011) La non-conformité du jugement étranger à l'ordre public international mise au diaspon de la Convention européenne des droits de l'homme. Rev.crit.dr.int.priv. 100:818–819

Kinsch P (2011) Private international law topics before the European Court of Human Rights. selected judgments and decision (2010–2011). Yearb Private Int Law 13:39–41

Kinsch P (2011) Choice-of-law rules and the prohibition of discrimination under the ECHR. NIPR 29:19–24

Kinsch P (2010) Recognition in the forum of a status aquired abroad—private international law rules and European human rights law. In: Boele-Woelki K et al (eds) Convergences and divergences in private international law—Liber Amicorum Kurt Siehr. Eleven International Publishing, The Hague

Kinsch P (2007) Droits de l'homme, droits fondamentaux et droit international privé. Recueil des Cours 318:9–332. Martinus Nijhoff Publishers, Leiden

Kinsch P (2004) Sklavenbesitz, religiöse Ehehindernisse und entschädigungslose Enteignungen: zur Vorgeschichte der Frage nach der Einwerkung der Grund- und Mensenrechte auf die Anwendung auslädischen Rechts [Ownership of slaves, religious impediments to marriage, and uncompensated expropiation: the history oft he question of the impact of fundamental- and human rights on the application of foreign law]. In Mansel H-P et al (eds) Festschrif für Erik Jayme Band I, Sellier, Munich, pp 419–435

Kinsch P (2004) The impact of human rights on the application of foreign law and on the recognition of foreign judgments—a survey of the cases decided by the European human rights institutions. In: Einhorn T, Siehr K (eds) Intercontinental cooperation through private international law—essays in memory of Peter E. Nygh. T.M.C. Asser Press, The Hague

Kloth M (2010) Immunities and the right of access to court under article 6 of the European convention on human rights. Martinus Nijhoff Publishers, Leiden

Kokott J (1998) Grund- und Menschenrechte als Inhalt eines internationalen ordre public [Fundamental- and human rights as the content of an international public policy]. In: Coester-Waltjen D et al (eds) Die Wirkungskraft der Grundrechte bei Fällen mit Auslandsbezug. C.F. Müller, Heidelberg, pp 71–114

Kramer XE (2011) Abolition of Exequatur under the Brussels I regulation: effecting and protecting right in the European judicial area. NIPR 29:633–641

Kramer XE (2004) Europees procesrecht en fundamentele procedurele vereisten: de rol van artikel 6 EVRM ter invulling van de openbare orde toets onder het EEX [European procedural law and fundamental procedural demands: the role of article 6 ECHR in order to shape the public policy exception under the Brussels Convention]. NIPR 22:9–16

Kratochvíl J (2011) The inflation of the margin of appreciation by the European Court of Human Right. Neth Quart Hum Rights 29:324–357

Kruiniger P (2008) Marokkaanse verstotingsvormen in de Nederlandse rechtspraktijk: een juridische beschouwing over de Marokkaanse khul' en talaq in het kader van de erkenning in Nederland [Moroccan forms of repudiation in the Dutch legal practice: a legal examination on the Moroccan khul' and talaq in the context of the recognition in the Netherlands]. Celsus juridische uitgeverij, Tilburg

Kuipers JJ (2012) EU law and private international law: the interrelationship in contractual obligations. Martinus Nijhoff Publishers, Leiden

Lagarde P (2010) Reference to public order ("Ordre Public") in French private international law. In: Foblets M-C (ed) Cultural diversity and the law: state responses from around the world. Bruylant, Brussels, pp 521–546

Lagarde P (2004) Développements futures du droit international privé dans une Europe en voie d'unification: quelques conjectures. RabelsZ 68:225–243

Lagarde P (1994) Public policy, international encyclopedia of comparative law, vol III. Mohr, Tübingen

Lagarde P (1986) Le principe de proximité dans le droit international privé contemporain. Cours général de droit international privé, Recueil des Cours 196

Lambert H (2006) The position of aliens in relation to the European Convention on Human Rights. Council of Europe Publishing, Strasbourg

Lawson RA (2004) Life after Bankovic: On the extraterritorial application of the European convention on human rights. In: Coomans F, Kamminga MT (eds) Extraterritorial application of human rights treaties. Intersentia, Antwerp, pp 83–123

Lawson RA, Schermers HG (1999) Leading cases of the European Court of human rights. Ars Aequi Libri, Nijmegen

Leach P (2011) Taking a case to the European Court of Human Rights. Oxford University Press, Oxford

Lequette Y (2004) Le droit international privé et les droits fondamentaux. In: Cabrillac R et al (eds) Libertés et droit fondamentaux. Dalloz, Paris, pp 97–118

Lerebours-Pigeonnière P (1950) La déclaration universelle des droits de l'homme et le droit international privé français. In: Le droit privé français au milieu du XXe siècle, Études offertes à Georges Ripert, Pichon et Durand-Auzias, Paris, pp 255–270

Lévy L, Derains Y (eds) (2011) Liber amicorum en l'honneur de Serge Lazareff. Pedone, Paris

Lewan KM (1968) The significance of constitutional rights for private law: theory and practice in West Germany. ICLQ 17

Looschelders D (2001) Die Ausstrahlung der Grund- und Menschenrechte auf das Internationale Privatrecht [The impact of fundamental and human right on private international law]. RabelsZ 65:464–491

Loucaides L (2006) Determining the extra-territorial effect of the European convention: facts, jurisprudence and the Bankovic case. Eur Hum Rights Law Rev 11:391–407

Lowe AV, Staker C (2010) Jurisdiction. In: Evans MD (ed) International law. Oxford University Press, Oxford, pp 313–339

Lowenfeld AF (2004) Jurisdiction, enforcement, public policy and res judicata: The Krombach Case', In: Einhorn T, Siehr K (eds) Intercontinental cooperation through private international law—essays in memory of Peter E. Nygh. T.M.C. Asser Press, The Hague, pp 229–248

Lowenfeld AF (1997) Forum shopping, antisuit injunctions, negative declarations and related tools of international litigation. AJIL 91:314–324

Lowenfeld AF (1996) International litigation and the quest for reasonableness. Clarendon Press, Oxford

MacDonald R St J (1992) The margin of appreciation in the jurisprudence of the European Court of Human Rights. collected courses of the Academy of European law 1 Book 2:95–161. Kluwer Academic Publishers, Dordrecht

Magnus U, Mankowski P (eds) (2012) Brussels I regulation. Sellier European Law Publishers, Munich

Mahoney P (1999) Speculating on the future of the reformed European Court of Human Rights. Hum Rights Law J 20:1–4

Mak C (2008) Fundamental rights in European contract law. A comparison of the impact of fundamental rights on contractual relationships in Germany, the Netherlands, Italy and England. Kluwer Law International, Alphen aan den Rijn

Mancini F (1999) Short note on abuse of procedure in community law. In: Taruffo M (ed) Abuse of procedural rights: comparative standards of procedural fairness. Kluwer Law International, The Hague, pp 233–236

Mann FA (1984) The doctrine of international jurisdiction revisited after twenty years. Recueil des cours 186:9–116

Mann FA (1964) The doctrine of jurisdiction in international law. Recueil des cours 111:1–162

Mansel H-P (2006) Anerkennung als Grundprinzip des Europaeischen Rechtsraums. RabelsZ 70:651–731

Marchadier F (2007) Les objectifs généraux du droit international privé à l'épreuve de la convention européenne des droits de l'homme. Bruylant, Bruxelles

Matscher F (2004) Die indirekte Wirkung des Art. 6 EMRK bei der Anerkennung und Vollstreckung ausländischer Entscheidungen [The indirect effect of art. 6 ECHR with regard to the recognition of foreign judgments]. In: Bork R (ed) Recht und Risiko: Festschrift für Helmut Kollhosser zum 70. Geburtstag vol 2, VVW, Karlsruhe, pp 427–445

Matscher F (1993) Die Einwirkungen der EMRK auf das Internationale Privat- und zivilprozessuale Verfahrensrecht. In: Matscher F (ed) Europa im Aufbruch: Festschrift für Fritz Schwind zum 80. Geburtstag, Manzsche Verlags- und Universitätsbuchhandlung, Wien, pp 71–85

Matscher F (1985) IPR und IZVR vor den Organen der EMRK—Eine Skizze–. In: Barfuss W (ed) Festschrift für Karl H. Neumayer zum 65. Geburtstag, Nomos, Baden-Baden, pp 459–478

Matscher F (1978) Etude des règles de compétence judiciaire dans certaines conventions internationales. Recueil des Cours 161:127–228

Mayer P (1996) Droit au proces equitable et conflit de juridictions', les nouveaux développements du procès équitable au sens de la Convention, actes du colloque du 22 mars 1996 en la grande chambre de la cour de cassation, organisé par l'Institut des hautes études européennes. Bruylant, Bruxelles, pp 125–138

Mayer P (2005) Les méthodes de la reconnaissance en droit international privé. In: Jobard-Bachellier M-N, Mayer P (eds) Le droit international privé: esprit et méthodes. Mélanges en l'honneur de Paul Lagarde, Dalloz, Paris, pp 547–573

Mayer P (1991) La Convention européenne des droits de l'homme et l'application des normes étrangères. Rev.crit.dr.int.priv. 98:651–665

Mayer P (1979) Droit international privé et droit international public sous l'angle de la notion de compétence.Rev.crit.dr.int.priv. 68:1–29; 349–388; 537–583

McLachlan CC (2008) Lis pendens in international litigation. Recueil des Cours 336:203–553

McLachlan C (2004) International litigation and the reworking of the conflict of laws. LQR 120:580–616

McLachlan C (1993) The influence of international law on civil jurisdiction. Hague Yearb Int Law 6:125–144

Meessen KM (1984) International law limitations on state jurisdiction. In: Olmstead CJ (ed) Extra-territorial application of laws and responses thereto. ESC Publishing, Oxford, pp 38–44

Meeusen J (2007) Instrumentalisation of private international law in the European union: towards a European conflicts revolution? Eur J Migr Law 9:287–305

Mehdi R, Nielsen JS (eds) (2011) Embedding "Mahr" in the European legal system. DJØF Publishing, Copenhagen

Melcher M (2013) (Mutual) Recognition of registered relationships via EU private international law. J Private Int Law 9:149–170

Michaels R (2005–2006) Two paradigms of jurisdiction. Mich J Int Law 27:1003–1069

Milanović M (2011) Extraterritorial application of human rights treaties. Oxford University Press, Oxford

Milanović M (2008) From compromise to principle: clarifying the concept of state jurisdiction in human right treaties. Hum Rights Law Rev 8:411–448

Miller S (2009) Revisiting extraterritorial jurisdiction: a territorial jurisdiction for extraterritorial jurisdiction under the European convention. EJIL 20:1223–1246

Mills A (2012) Rediscovering the public dimension of private international law. NIPR 30:371–375

Mills A (2009) The confluence of public and private international law: justice, pluralism in the international constitutional ordering of private law. Cambridge University Press, Cambridge

Mills A (2008) The dimensions of public policy in private international law. J Private Int Law 4:201–236

Mowbray AR (2012) Cases, materials, and commentary on the European convention on human rights. Oxford University Press, Oxford

Mowbray AR (2004) The development of positive obligations under the European convention on human rights by the European Court of Human Rights. Hart Publishing, Portland

Mora PD (2010) The legality of civil jurisdiction over torture under the universal principle. German Yearb Int Law 52:367–403

Muir Watt H (2013) Fundamental rights and recognition in private international law. Eur J Hum Rights 1:411–435

Muir Watt H (2011) Private international law beyond the schism. Transnatl Leg Theory 2:347–428

Muir Watt H (2008) European federalism and the "new unilateralism". Tulane Law Rev 82:1983–1998

Nadelmann KH (1961) Jurisdictionally improper fora, In: Nadelmann KH et al XXth century comparative law and conflicts law. Legal essays in honor of Hessel E. Yntema. A.W. Sythoff, Leyden, pp 321–335

Najm M-C (2003) Principes directeurs du droit international privé et conflits de civilizations: relations entre systèmes laïques et systèmes religieux. Dalloz, Paris

Niboyet M-L, De Geouffre de la Pradelle G (2011) Droit international privé. L.G.D.J., Paris

Nigro R (2010) The notion of "jurisdiction" in article 1: future scenarios for the extra-territorial application of the European convention on human rights. Ital Yearb Int Law 20:11–30

Nollkaemper PA (2009) Kern van het international publiekrecht [The essence of public international law]. Boom Juridische uitgevers, Den Haag

Normand J (1999) Final report: the two approaches to the abuse of procedural rights. In: Taruffo M (ed) Abuse of procedural rights: comparative standards of procedural fairness. Kluwer Law International, The Hague, pp 237–248

Nuyts A (2007) Study on residual jurisdiction (Review of the member states' rules concerning the "Residual Jurisdiction" of their courts in civil and commercial matters pursuant to the Brussels I and II Regulations). General report, final version dated 3 Sept 2007, pp 64–66. http://ec.europa.eu/civiljustice/news/docs/study_residual_jurisdiction_en.pdf. Accessed Oct 2012

Nuyts A (2007) The enforcement of jurisdiction agreements further to gasser and the community principle of abuse of rights. In: De Vareilles-Sommières P (ed) Forum shopping in the European judicial area. Hart Publishing, Oxford, pp 55–73

Nuyts A (2005) Due process and fair trial: jurisdiction in the United States and in Europe compared', 2 CILE Studies. In: Brand RA, Walter M (eds) Private law, private international law and judicial cooperation in the EU-US relationship, Thomson/West, Eagan MN, pp 27–73

O'Boyle M (2004) The European convention on human rights and extraterritorial jurisdiction: a comment on "Life after Bankovic". In: Coomans F, Kamminga MT (eds) Extraterritorial application of human rights treaties. Intersentia, Antwerp, pp 125–139

O'Boyle M (1998) The margin of appreciation and derogation under article 15: ritual incantation or principle? Hum Rights Law J 19:23–29

Oderkerk AE (2001) The importance of context: selecting legal systems in comparative legal research. NILR 48:293–318

Olmstead CJ (ed) (1984) Extra-territorial application of laws and responses thereto. ESC Publishing, Oxford

Oprea A (2007) La Convention europeénne des droits de l'homme et l'application des normes étrangère en droit international privé. Revista de drept internaţional privat şi drept privat comparat 2007:307–340

Orakhelashvili A (2003) Restrictive interpretation of human rights treaties in the recent jurisprudence of the European Court of Human Rights. EJIL 14:529–568

Othenin-Girard S (1999) La reserve d'ordre public en droit international privé suisse. Schulthess, Zurich

Othenin-Girard S (1999) Quelques observations sur le for de nécessité en droit international privé. RSDIE 9:251–285

Oxman BH, Jurisdiction of states. In: Wolfrum R (ed) The Max Planck encyclopedia of public international law. Oxford University Press, Oxford. www.mpepil.com. Accessed Apr 2012

Pamboukis C (2008) La renaissance-métamorphose de la méthode de reconnaissance. Rev.crit.dr.int.priv. 97:513–560

Paulsson J (2005) Denial of justice in international law. Cambridge University Press, Cambridge

Pavoni R (2012) Human rights and the immunities of states and international organisations. In: Vidmar J, De Wet E (eds) Hierarchy in international law: the place of human rights. Oxford University Press, Oxford, pp 133–207

Petzold H (1993) The convention and the principle of subsidiarity. In: MacDonald R St J et al (eds) The European system for the protection of human rights. Martinus Nijhoff, Dordrecht, pp 41–62

Pillet A (1903) Principes de droit international privé, Paris.
Pocar F (2006) Notes on the Pellegrini Judgment of the European Court of Human Rights. In: Erauw J (eds) Liber Memorialis Petar Šarčević. Sellier Munich, pp 575–581
Pontier JA (2005) Europees conflictenrecht. Een complexe geschiedenis in vogelvlucht [European conflict of laws. A bird-eye's view of a complicated history]. Vossiuspers, Amsterdam
Pontier JA, Burg E (2004) EU principles on jurisdiction and recognition and enforcement of judgments in civil and commercial matters according to the case law of the European Court of Justice. T.M.C. Asser Press, The Hague
Reed L (2005) Mixed private and public international law solutions to international crises. Recueil des Cours 306:177–410
Reiss JW (2009) Protocol No. 14 ECHR and Russian non-ratification: the current state of affairs. Harvard Hum Rights J 2:293–318
Robertson AH (1977) Human rights in Europe. Manchester University Press, Manchester
Rodger BJ (2006) Forum non conveniens post Owusu. J Private Int Law 2:71–97
Rogerson P (2003) Kuwait Airways Corp v Iraqi Airways Corp: the territoriality principle in private international law—vice or virtue? Curr Legal Probl 56:265–287
Rosner N (2004) Cross-border recognition and enforcement of foreign money judgments in civil and commercial matters. Doctoral Series, dissertation Groningen
Rossolilo G (2010) Personal identity at a crossroads between private international law, international protection of human rights and EU law. Yearb Private Int Law 11:143–156
Rutten SWE (1998) Mensenrechten en het ipr: scheiden of trouwen? [Human rights and private international law: to divorce or to marry?]. NJCM-Bulletin 23:797–811
Ryssdal R (1996) The coming of age of the European Convention on Human Rights. Eur Hum Rights Law Rev 1:18–29
Sadat-Akhavi SA (2003) Methods of resolving conflicts between treaties. Martinus Nijhoff Publishers, Leiden
Schilling T (2011) Das Exequatur und die EMRK [The Exequatur and the ECHR]. IPRax 31:31–40
Schlosser PF (2010) The abolition of exequatur proceedings—including public policy review? IPRax 30:101–104
Schlosser P (2000) Jurisdiction and international judicial and administrative co-operation. Recueil des Cours 284:9–428
Schlosser P (1991) Jurisdiction in international litigation: the issue of human rights in relation to national law and to the Brussels convention. Rivista di diritto internazionale 74:5–34
Schmidt GE (2007) Forum necessitatis bij echtscheidingen. NIPR 25:116–121
Schutte CB (2004) The European fundamental right of property: Article 1 of protocol no. 1 to the European convention on human rights: its origins, its workings and its impact on national legal orders. Kluwer, Deventer
Shaw MN (2008) International law. Cambridge University Press, Cambridge
Shelton D (2006) Normative hierarchy in international law. AJIL 100:291–323
Siehr K (2005) General problems of private international law in modern codifications—de lege lata and -de lege europea ferenda. Yearb Private Int Law 7:17–61
Siehr K (2004) Article 78. In: Girsberger D et al (eds) Zürcher Kommentar zum IPRG: Kommentar zum Bundesgesetz über dat internationale Privatrecht (IPRG) vom 18. Dezember 1987, Schulthess, Zürich
Siehr K (2002) Das internationale Privatrecht der Schweiz [The private international law of Switzerland]. Schulthess, Zürich
Siehr K (1996) The impact of international conventions on national codifications of private international law. In Borras Rodriguez A et al (eds) E pluribus unum: liber amicorum Georges A. L. Droz. Martinus Nijhoff Publishers, The Hague, pp 405–413
Sinclair I (1984) The diplomatic response. In: Olmstead CJ (ed) Extra-territorial application of law and responses thereto. ESC Publishing, Oxford

Sindres D (2012) Vers la disparition de l'ordre public de proximité? JDI 139:887–901
Sinopoli L (2002) Droit au procès equitable et exequatur: Strasbourg sonne les cloches à Rome. Gazette du Palais 122:1157–1168
Smit H (1961) The terms jurisdiction and competence in comparative law. AJCL 10:164–169
Spielmann D (2011) La reconnaissance et l'exécution des decisions judiciaries étrangères et les exigencies de la convention des droits de l'homme. Un essai de synthèse. Revue trimestrielle des droits de l'homme 22:761–786
Stone P (2010) EU private international law. Elgar European Law, Cheltenham
Stone Sweet A, Keller H (2008) The reception of the ECHR in national legal orders. In: Keller H, Stone Sweet A (eds) A Europe of rights: the impact of the ECHR on national legal systems. Oxford University Press, Oxford
Strikwerda L (2012) Inleiding tot het Nederlandse Internationaal Privaatrecht [Introduction to Dutch private international law]. Kluwer, Deventer
Strikwerda L (2004) De invloed van het EVRM op het Europese IPR [The impact of the ECHR on European private international law]. In Corstens GJM et al (eds) Europeanisering van het Nederlands Recht [The Europeanization of Dutch Law]. Kluwer, Deventer, pp 252–260
Struycken AVM (2010) The Netherlands surrogacy, a new way to become mother? In: Boele-Woelki K et al (eds) Convergence and divergence in private international law—Liber Amicorum Kurt Siehr, Schulthess, Zürich
Struycken AVM (2009) Co-ordination and co-operation in respectful disagreement: general course on private international law. Recueil des Cours 311, Martinus Nijhoff Publishers, Leiden
Struycken AVM (1992) Les conséquences de l'intégration européenne sur les développement du droit international privé. Recueil des cours 232:256–383
Stürner M (2011) Extraterritorial application of the ECHR via private international law? A comment from the German perspective. NIPR 29:8–12
Thoma I (2011) The ECHR and the ordre public exception in private international law. NIPR 29:13–18
Thoma I (2007) Die Europäisierung und die Vergemeinschaftung des nationalen ordre public [The Europeanization and Communitarization of domestic public policy]. Mohr Siebeck, Tübingen
Thurnherr D (2008) The reception process in Austria and Switzerland. In: Keller H, Stone Sweet A (eds) A Europe of rights: the impact of the ECHR on national legal systems. Oxford University Press, Oxford, pp 311–391
van Alebeek R (2008) The immunity of states and their officials in international criminal law and international human rights law. Oxford University Press, Oxford
van Bochove L (2007) Het ontbreken van de openbareorde-exceptie in de nieuwe generatie Europese procesrechtelijke verordeningen in het licht van artikel 6 lid 1 EVRM [The lack of a public policy exception in the new generation of European procedural regulations]. NIPR 25:331–339
van den Eeckhout V (2008) Promoting human rights within the Union: the role of European private international law. Eur Law J 14:105–127
van der Wilt H (2012) On the hierarchy between extradition and human rights. In: Vidmar J, De Wet E (eds) Hierarchy in international law: the place of human rights. Oxford University Press, Oxford, pp 268–315
van Dijk D et al (1993) Grensoverschrijdend privaatrecht: een bundel opstellen over privaatrecht in internationaal verband [Cross-border private law: a collection of essays on private law in an international context], Kluwer, Deventer
van Dijk P et al (eds) (2006) Theory and practice of the European convention on human rights. Intersentia, Antwerp
van Hedel JHGE (2008) Het recht op eerbiediging van het familieleven ex artikel 8 EVRM en het conflictenrecht [The right to respect for family life ex article 8 ECHR and the conflict of laws]. NIPR 26:125–133

van Hoek AAH (2000) Artikel 12 EG-Verdrag en het (internationale) procesrecht; hernieuwde kritiek op de cautio judicatum solvi [Article 12 EC-Treaty and (international) procedural law; renewed criticism of the cautio judicatum solvi]. NIPR 18:251–258

van Hoek AAH (2003) Erkenning van vonnissen in het privaatrecht: een studie naar de grenzen van wederzijdse erkenning [Recognition of judgments in private law: a study on the limits of mutual recognition]. NIPR 21:337–350

van Hoek AAH, Luchtman M (2006) The European convention on human rights and transnational cooperation in criminal matters. In Hoek AAH van et al (eds) Multilevel governance in enforcement and adjudication, Intersentia, Antwerp, pp 25–91

van Hoek AAH et al (2011) Making choices in public and private international immunity law—Preadviezen. T.M.C. Asser Press, Den Haag

van Houtte H (2002) From a national to a European public policy. In: Nafziger JAR, Symeonides SC (eds) law and justice in a multistate world: essays in honor of Arthur T. von Mehren. Transnational Publishers, Ardsley

van Lith H (2009) International jurisdiction and commercial litigation. T.M.C. Asser Press, The Hague

van Loon JHA (1993) De wisselwerking tussen internationaal privaatrecht en rechten van de mens [The interaction between private international law and human rights]. In: Dijk D van et al (eds) Grensoverschrijdend privaatrecht: een bundel opstellen over privaatrecht in internationaal verband [Cross-border private law: a collection of essays on private law in an international context]. Kluwer, Deventer, pp 135–148

Vidmar J, de Wet E (eds) Hierarchy in international law: the place of human rights. Oxford University Press, Oxford

Vischer F (1977) Drafting national legislation on the conflict of laws: the Swiss experience. Law Contemp Probl 41:131–145

Vlas P (2010) On the development of private international law in the Netherlands: from Asser's days to the codification of Dutch private international law (1910–2010). NILR 57:167–182

Volken P (2004) Art. 27. In: Girsberger D et al (eds) (2004) Zürcher Kommentar zum IPRG: Kommentar zum Bundesgesetz über dat Internationale Privatrecht (IPRG) vom 18. Dezember 1987. Schulthess, Zürich

Voltz M (2002) Menschenrechte und ordre public im internationalen Privatrecht [Human rights and public policy in private international law]. Lang, Frankfurt am Main

von Hein J (2008) Something old and something borrowed, but nothing new? Rome II and the European choice-of-law. Tulane Law Rev 82:1663–1707

von Mehren AT (1980) Recognition and enforcement of foreign judgments—general theory and the role of jurisdictional requirements. Recueil des Cours 167:9–112

von Mehren AT (1998) The transmogrification of defendants into plaintiffs: herein of declaratory judgments, forum shopping, and lis pendens. In: Basedow J (ed) Festschrift für Ulrich Drobnig. Mohr Siebeck, Tübingen, pp 409–424

von Mehren AT, Trautman DT (1966) Jurisdiction to adjudicate: a suggested analysis. Harvard Law Rev 79:1121–1179

von Mehren AT (2007) Adjudicatory authority in private international law. A comparative study. Martinus Nijhoff Publishers, Leiden

von Savigny FC (1880) A treatise on the conflict of laws, and the limits of their operation in respect of place and time [translation provided by W. Guthrie]. Clark, Edinburgh

Vonken APMJ (1998) De multiculturele samenleving en de bemiddelende rol van het internationaal privaatrecht en de mensenrechten. Iets over tolerantie, culturele identiteit en rechtspluralisme [The multicultural society and the mediating role of private international law and human rights. Something on tolerance, cultural identity and legal pluralism]. In: Cliteur PB (ed) Sociale cohesie en het recht [Social cohesion and the law]. Lelystad, Koninklijke Vermande, pp 97–166

Vonken APMJ (1993) De reflexwerking van de mensenrechten op het ipr [the reflex of human rights on private international law]. In: Cliteur PB, Vonken APMJ (eds) Doorwerking van mensenrechten [The impact of human rights]. Wolters-Noordhoff, Groningen, pp 153–185

Voyiakis E (2002) Access to court v state immunity. ICLQ 52:297–332

Wai R (2002) Transnational liftoff and judicial touchdown: The regulatory function of private international law in an era of globalization. Columbia J Transnatl Law 40:209–274

Wautelet P (2004) What has international private law achieved in meeting the challenges posed by globalization? In: Slot PJ, Bulterman M (eds) Globalisation and jurisdiction. Kluwer International Law, The Hague, pp 55–77

Weick G (2003) Human rights and private international law. In MacEldowney J, Weick G (eds) Human rights in transition. Lang Frankfurt am Main, pp 193–200

White RCA, Ovey C (2010) The European convention on human rights. Oxford University Press, Oxford

Whitten R (1981) The constitutional limitations on state-court jurisdiction: a historical-interpretative reexamination of the full faith and credit and due process clauses. Creighton Law Rev 14:499–606

Wildhaber L (2007) The European Convention on Human Rights and international law. ICLQ 56:217–232

Xenos D (2012) The positive obligations of the state under the European Convention of Human Rights. Routledge, London

Zaher K (2010) Conflict de civilisation et droit international privé. Harmattan, Paris

MIX
Papier aus verantwortungsvollen Quellen
Paper from responsible sources
FSC® C105338

If you have any concerns about our products,
you can contact us on
ProductSafety@springernature.com

In case Publisher is established outside the EU,
the EU authorized representative is:
Springer Nature Customer Service Center GmbH
Europaplatz 3, 69115 Heidelberg, Germany

Printed by Libri Plureos GmbH
in Hamburg, Germany